New Ways in *Germanistik*

New Ways in *Germanistik*

Edited by
Richard Sheppard

BERG
New York / Oxford / Munich
Distributed exclusively in the US and Canada by
St. Martin's Press, New York

First published in 1990 by
Berg Publishers Limited
– Editorial Offices –
165 Taber Avenue, Providence R.I. 02906, USA
150 Cowley Road, Oxford, OX4 1JJ, UK
Westermühlstraße 26, 8000 München 5, FRG

© Richard Sheppard 1990

All rights reserved.
No part of this publication may be reproduced
in any form or by any means
without the permission of
Berg Publishers Limited

Library of Congress Cataloging-in-Publication Data
New ways in Germanistik / edited by Richard Sheppard.
  p. cm.
Includes bibliographical references.
ISBN 0-85496-288-3
1. German literature—History and criticism—Congresses.
2. Criticism—Congresses.   3. German philology—Study and
teaching–Congresses.   I. Sheppard, Richard.
PT105.N49   1989
830.9—dc20   89-35881
                                                              CIP

British Library Cataloguing in Publication Data
New Ways in Germanistik.
  1. German literature. Criticism
  I. Sheppard, Richard
  830.9
  ISBN 0-85496-288-3

Printed in Great Britain
by Billing & Sons Ltd.

For
Gunter Coenen
Director of the London Goethe-Institute
1981–1988
and
Brian Rowley
Professor of European Literature (German)
University of East Anglia
1968–1988

The editor
would like to thank the
Goethe-Institute for their
generous support for this
project

Contents

Note on Book Titles viii

Introduction 1

1. From 'Being-Itself' to 'Post-Modernism' – Four Decades of Literature and Literary Criticism in the Federal Republic of Germany
   Helmut Kreuzer 9

2. The Unacknowledged Legislator of the Text – Some Observations on Literary Criticism in the Federal Republic of Germany
   Hans J. Hahn 34

3. Towards a Systematic Outline of an Integrative Theory of Literary History
   Michael Titzmann 58

4. The Reception of Sociological Theory by West German Literary Scholarship, 1970–85
   Jörg Schönert 71

5. Hans Robert Jauss's *Rezeptionsästhetik* – Theory and Application
   Margot Zutshi 95

6. Feminist Approaches to Kafka's *The Castle*
   Elizabeth Boa 112

7. Women Writing About Women Writing and Ingeborg Bachmann's *Malina*
   Elizabeth Boa 128

8. The Politics of Literature in the GDR – A Post-Structuralist Approach
   Chris Weedon 145

Contents

9. Unholy Families – The Oedipal Psychopathology of Four Expressionist *Ich-Dramen*
Richard Sheppard ... 164

10. Deconstructing Classicism – Goethe's *Helena* and the Need to Rhyme
Anthony Phelan ... 192

11. The Poetry of August Stramm – A Suitable Case for Deconstruction
Richard Sheppard ... 211

12. The Potential and Limits of a Marxist Methodology for *Germanistik*
David Jenkinson ... 243

13. From Althusser to Brecht – Formalism, Materialism and *The Threepenny Opera*
Steve Giles ... 261

14. Upstairs–Downstairs – Some Reflections on German Literature in the Light of Bakhtin's Theory of Carnival
Richard Sheppard ... 278

Notes on Contributors ... 316

Index ... 318

Note on Book Titles

The following system has been used throughout the volume:

(1) Where there is a well-known English translation of a work (e.g. Kafka's *The Castle*) the English title has been used.

(2) Where there is a relatively unknown English translation of a work available then the German title has been used but attention is drawn in parentheses to the title of the English translation, e.g. Günter Wallraff, *Ganz unten* (1985; E.T. as *The Lowest of the Low*, 1988).

(3) Where no English edition exists, but it is helpful to have an English translation of the title, the English equivalent follows the German in parentheses, e.g. Thomas Murner, *Die Narrenbeschwerung* (*The Conjuration of Fools*) (1518).

Introduction

When, in David Lodge's *Small World* (1985), Professor Philip Swallow is confronted with the word 'theory', he replies, misattributing his source: 'That word brings out the Goering in me. When I hear it I reach for my revolver.'[1] When Lodge was writing that novel, such a response would not have been uncommon in British departments of literature, and the origins of its violence are not hard to determine. Until quite recently, whether its practitioners knew it or not, literary studies in this country (as elsewhere in the West) rested to a large extent upon a series of presuppositions which were rarely made explicit but which, ultimately, derived from the literary aspirations and reading habits of the nineteenth-century *Bildungsbürgertum* (educated middle class). In literature, members of this class had seen a means of resisting or escaping from the urban, industrialised world which it had been largely responsible for creating, and, concomitantly, of preserving and cultivating that dimension of spirituality which seemed to be absent from the banalities of everyday life and the forms of orthodox religion.

From such attitudes derived those (Platonic) theories of art expounded by such diverse writers as Matthew Arnold, the Symbolists and Post-Symbolists, Wassily Kandinsky, the New Critics in Britain and the USA, and the so-called 'text-immanent' critics in post-war Federal Germany. Fundamentally, all these theories rested on a profound belief in the power of close reading (or viewing) to educate (i.e. 'lead out' or develop, 'bilden') the inherently spiritual core of human nature. And they all involved such 'classical' (or, as we have nowadays learnt to say, 'logocentric') concepts as centredness, organic wholeness, autotelicity and correspondences (all collected in the master-concept of the symbol which binds together the material and spiritual realms). They also all presupposed the adequacy and reliability of language (assuming that the substantive noun ultimately derived its substantiality from its groundedness in a metaphysical substance); the objective meaningfulness of the concept

1. Penguin, Harmondsworth, 1985, p.24.

'aesthetic'; the ability of the artist to exercise exhaustive control over his creation; the authority of the trained sensibility and the feasibility of defining the great tradition or canon of European literature in terms of hierarchy of spiritual power, thus turning literary history into an aspect of *Geistesgeschichte* (the history of the Objective Spirit).

Building on Nietzsche's critique of such assumptions, Modernism, especially during its later, embryonically post-modernist phase (Dada, Surrealism and Russian Formalism in particular, cf. Jameson, 1984, p.56), began to subvert such assumptions in the first decades of this century. However, several major Modernists (e.g. Eliot, Pound and Hugo Ball) soon sensed the radically ambivalent nature of that whole phenomenon (cf. Richard Sheppard's essay in this volume on August Stramm) and shied back from the most drastic implications of their early experimentalism to seek refuge in the synthetic shelter provided by various forms of neo-classicism and politico-religious orthodoxy. The Second World War, offering the horrifying spectacle of perhaps the most self-consciously cultivated nation in Europe practising legitimised butchery on an unprecedented scale, made the general validity of the educative claims of classical aesthetics even harder to accept. And the near-simultaneous (because related) hegemony of Post-Modernism on the artistic scene and consumer capitalism as a total (not to say latently totalitarian, cf. Jameson, 1984, p.57) way of life, with the USA leading the way in both areas thanks to the help of such thinkers as Derrida and Lacan, themselves in reaction against the European humanist tradition, all but completed the process of subversion.

Just as post-modernist (anti-)ontology replaced 'depth models' (involving the centred referent) with a 'conception of practices, discourses and textual play' (involving the de-centred textual assemblage) (Jameson, 1984, p.63), so too, consumer culture, notwithstanding the rhetorical appeals which its leading proponents habitually make to traditional virtues and the unique 'bourgeois ego or monad' (p.66), rests on the assumption that human beings are not Subjects endowed with *Geist*/a soul/a spiritual centre/a self/a transcendental signified, but, like nets, simply collections of holes held together with string. Consumables pass through these holes with ease, their shape and size being dependent upon the discursive location of the subject and the role (s)he plays there; and the shape of the net is, in consequence, deemed to be infinitely changeable. Which in turn means that the *logos* which, in the Christian–humanist tradition, united God, man and language, disappears; that metaphors of depth, together with feelings of anxiety and alienation, are discounted as meaningless; and that the ideal reader evaporates

Introduction

because there is, by definition, nothing within him or her to cultivate and educate. As Jameson put it, 'the alienation of the subject is displaced by the fragmentation of the subject'; 'the liberation ... from the older *anomie* of the centred subject may also mean, not merely a liberation from anxiety, but a liberation from every other kind of feeling as well, since there is no longer a self present to do the feeling' (1984, pp.63 and 64). Given which, the whole complex of logocentric assumptions and concepts crumbles, to use a metaphor from Hofmannsthal's entirely germane *Ein Brief* (*Chandos Letter*) of 1902, in the mouth like mouldy fungi; seem, in the present age, to be just so many fig-leaves with which the last adepts of the great tradition are vainly seeking to cover their conceptual nakedness in a world which is, in any case, no longer particularly interested in looking.

Thus, Swallow's impulse to react like a cultural Nazi to Morris Zapp's theoretical pisazz derives from the fact that he is badly on the defensive. He refuses to think about 'theory' (i.e. any theory which does not conform to his own assumptions) because to do so would be to expose the shaky foundations of his own conceptual world and thus run the painful risk of being convicted on the charge that his work is intellectually unjustifiable. That kind of loss of faith is, of course, exactly what the New Brutalists are waiting for. The sooner liberal ideas of culture lose their credibility in the very places where they have been institutionalised, the sooner libraries, museums and art galleries can be sold off unopposed or diverted from their founding educational ideals, and the sooner subsidies to institutions like theatres and orchestras can be stopped. The sooner teachers lose their conviction that there is a hidden potential within human nature which needs 'leading out' ('educating'), the sooner schools and universities can become entirely geared to training external skills.[2]

On the positive side, however, the dual onslaught by consumer culture and Post-Modernism has wonderfully concentrated the minds of those people teaching the humanities. Those who have chosen not to become grey ghosts ineffectually haunting their departments and bemoaning the loss of past splendours have had to address themselves to certain fundamental questions and either work out new answers or at least learn to state the old ones with more precision and conviction. Why teach literature? Why study

---

2. Cf. Anthony Burgess, 'Government and the Death of the Soul', *The Daily Telegraph Student Extra*, Spring 1989, pp.1, 3 and 4; Peter Abbs, 'Training Spells the End of Education', *The Independent*, 22 January 1989; Peter Abbs, 'The Poisoning of the Socratic Ideal', *The Guardian*, 23 January 1989.

literature? What is literature? What, if anything, makes it special? Is the literary canon simply a class- or gender-determined historical product, or does it involve values which truly are more abiding? How *can* texts be read? What are the advantages of one approach over any other? If the classical concepts cease to be self-evident and the validity of so much post-modernist theory is accepted, what are literary scholars left with? A plurality of approaches in a state of armed truce (cf. Helmut Kreuzer's essay below)? A new orthodoxy which requires belief in the impossibility of saying anything meaningful about a literary text? Or one huge mess of conflict and confusion? And, at a deeper level (assuming that the metaphor of depth does not of itself beg the entire question): What is language? How does it work? What are its limitations? What is human nature? How does a culture produce symbolic forms? What is reality? How can the study of literature help people to understand and relate to that reality? The avalanche of questions which tumbled from the mouth of Nietzsche's madman in *Die fröhliche Wissenschaft* (*The Gay Science*) (1881–1882) and which tormented so many major artists of the modernist epoch are now plaguing the critics who canonised their work. If the God who legitimised logocentric attitudes and values is dead, then is everything permitted (as it is on the wilder shores of Deconstruction)? And do the questions posed by critics derive from the fact that their minds are still, quite unnecessarily, darkened by the shadow of that dead God, weighed down, to continue the madman's metaphor, by his decomposing corpse when they could be out there where the action is, wind-surfing happily across the shiny surface of a culture which has committed itself to the primacy of the signifier over the signified; which thrives on the concept of surface-as-reality (cf. Jameson, 1984, pp.60–2); and which deems the fundamental problems to have been definitively solved?

The essays which comprise this volume all derive from the above complex of questions, but they were not produced by one, cohesive group of people, like the Research Group behind the multi-volume *Poetik und Hermeneutik* series, a selection from which, edited by Richard E. Amacher and Victor Lange, appeared in English in 1979 as *New Perspectives in German Literary Criticism* (Princeton U.P.). Nor do they preach one, accepted, post-modernist orthodoxy (like that which informed the *Tel Quel* group in its early days). Some are avowedly and consistently post-modernist in their approach; others begin from a post-modernist position but arrive, in the end, at greater or lesser reservations about the (anti-)ontology of absence which informs that approach; at least one involves a downright

Introduction

hostility to post-modernist aesthetics in behalf of a Marxist neo-humanism. While readily conceding that a simple style, like so-called simple faith, often conceals a knot of unresolved problems, the Editor has tried to avoid the more technical terminology of post-modernist analysis. If he has not always been successful, it is because new ways involve new and difficult thoughts, and because such thoughts can rarely be formulated with the colloquial ease and elegance of accustomed, well-tried ones.

Historically, most of the essays developed out of papers given at a conference on literary theory and German literary studies which was held, with the generous support of the London Goethe-Institute, in spring 1988 at the University of East Anglia. They range from the rigorously scientific (Titzmann), through the essayistic in the most positive sense of that word (Phelan), to the programmatic (Jenkinson); from the highly abstract (Schönert and Titzmann) to the more text-oriented (Giles and Boa); from the historical survey (Kreuzer and Hahn) to the very particular (Phelan and Sheppard); and from the introductory (Weedon and Zutshi) to the bravura piece for state-of-the-art specialists (Schönert). But in all cases, the basic motivating question is the same: why study German literature in an age when literature is no longer the cultural datum-line for most people and national identity seems to be being eroded by a cosmopolitan, multi-national culture? At one level, the answers are very diverse. But at another, that diversity converges on one specific, albeit unstated, answer: because German literary texts were generated by a culture which, of all Western European cultures, has had one of the strangest histories and undergone some of the most extreme historical experiences imaginable; and because the effects of that history are still with us. Or, to put it another way: even if it is nowadays difficult to justify literary studies in terms of Humboldtian-Arnoldian self-cultivation (*Bildung*), then, as the essays below imply, it certainly *can* be justified as an aspect of a more broadly-based critical discipline which, for want of a more vernacular term, I will call cultural semiotics.

As Michael Titzmann's analysis powerfully argues, every culture consists in a complex of sign-systems. Those which we subsume under the label 'literature' are among the densest of these, and once decoded, they offer insights into the problematic confronting the culture out of and within which they were generated. They also raise the question of the extent to which that problematic is an accurate or a fantasy presentation of the subject's relationship to his or her real conditions of existence (Althusser, 1977, pp.67–8). Literary texts may not be photographic representations of an objectively given

–5–

Introduction

external reality, or epiphanic symbols of a higher realm of Platonic essences, but, using the conceptual means provided by such sources as linguistics, politics, sociology, feminism, anthropology, social and intellectual history, their latently critical significance can be exposed – as several of the essays below variously attempt to do. But if one can approach the sign-systems of a past or alien culture with such a purpose in mind, then, provided that one is willing to make an imaginative leap via comparison and contrast, it is also possible to approach one's own culture in a similar way. Or, to put it more concretely: for non-native Germanists, the literary sign-systems generated by German culture are worthy of serious study partly for the insights they can give into the structure of that culture and partly because they form a distorting mirror in which we can see the problems of our own culture posed and resolved in a more drastic way. And for native Germanists, the same sign-systems are worthy of serious study because the problems to which they point are still with them, albeit buried under the reassuringly bright surfaces of internationalist pop.

And if that is so, then it can be said that post-modern methodologies have a critical relevance to the extent that they encourage and enable us, if we are willing to become outsiders to a certain extent, to look for semiotic saturation where convention pretends that none exists and to discover the epistemic significance of objects which are so familiar, so naturalised, that we no longer think of them as signs. Because the new methodologies encourage us not to abstract objects/texts from the cultural system which generated them, but to regard them as signs, they impel us to ask questions about the implied relationships between signifiers and officially sanctioned signifieds; between officially sanctioned signifieds and repressed (i.e. latently deconstructive) signifieds; and between the signs as wholes and the reality which lies beyond them. The new methodologies may not develop one's power of aesthetic enjoyment or ability to pass finely-wrought judgements on choice, abstracted *objets d'art*, but by freeing and developing the semiotic imagination, they permit the study of literature to remain a critical discipline without necessarily implying that an unbridgeable gap exists between literary and non-literary texts.

References

Althusser, L. (1977) *For Marx* (1965), New Left Books, London
Jameson, F. (1984) 'Postmodernism, or The Cultural Logic of Late Capitalism', *New Left Review*, no.146, 53–92

–1–

From 'Being-Itself' to 'Post-Modernism' – Four Decades of Literature and Literary Criticism in the Federal Republic of Germany

HELMUT KREUZER

Those who find periodisation annoying will enjoy a wry smile at the expense of German literary scholars because of the arbitrary divisions by means of which they carve up German literature into the literature of the 1950s, the 1960s, the 1970s and even the 1980s – a period which, though just passed, has already spawned at least two book titles![1] But as history is never so neat and tidy an affair, it is possible, depending upon one's criteria, to date the beginning of German literature of the 1950s either as early as the currency reform of 1948 (which drastically changed the economic context in which literature was produced) or as late as 1952–3, when Paul Celan and Ingeborg Bachmann were coming into prominence. It is just as hard to determine the beginning of the 1960s and, depending on the groupings and genres that one selects, one could, while conceding that that decade reached its apogee with the student protest movement of 1968 and the literature which it generated, opt either for the inception of *Gruppe 61*, or the Oberhausen Film Festival of 1962, or

---

A longer version of this article was first published as 'Vom "Sein" zur "Postmoderne"': Streiflichter auf vier Dekaden der Literatur und Literaturwissenschaft im westlichen Deutschland', in P.M. Lützeler, H. Lehnert and G.S. Williams (eds), *Zeitgenossenschaft: Zur deutschsprachigen Literatur im 20. Jahrhundert* (Athenäum, Frankfurt/Main, 1987), pp.296–323. This English version, which has been translated and adapted by Richard Sheppard, is printed here by kind permission of the Athenäum Verlag.

1. P.K. Kurz, *Zwischen Widerstand und Wohlstand: Zur Literatur der frühen 80er Jahre* (Josef Knecht, Frankfurt/Main, 1986); Arthur Williams, Stuart Parkes and Roland Smith (eds), *Literature on the Threshold: The German Novel in the 1980s* (Berg, Oxford, 1990).

the impact of documentary drama from 1963 onwards, or the publication of Wolf Biermann's *Drahtharfe* in 1965. The 1970s came into being no less haltingly, their ideological complexion having been significantly altered by the change in political climate whose most obvious manifestation was the anti-radicalism decree of 1972, and their literary symptomatology being such texts as Karin Struck's *Klassenliebe* (1973), Peter Schneider's *Lenz* (1973) and Verena Stefan's feminist novel *Häutungen* (1975).

To periodise literature by decades does not, of course, either preclude one from subsuming much longer periods under a historical or philosophical label or prevent one from acknowledging that certain phenomena remain consistent across such chronological divides. Nevertheless, it is not hard to find authors whose literary careers reflect periodic shifts. Having begun with a book on Clemens Brentano's poetics (1955–61) and progressed, via volumes of protest poetry, to the co-editorship of *Kursbuch* no.15, which, in 1968, proclaimed the 'Death of Literature', Hans-Magnus Enzensberger was, by the 1980s, editing the 'Other Library' of World Literature and, in a playful collection of poetry entitled *Wasserzeichen der Poesie* which appeared in that series printed in a variety of colours, offering his readers the chance of 'enjoying art and poetry in 164 ludic modes'. Or to use different examples: Enzensberger's *Museum of Modern Poetry* of 1960 had been followed, in 1970, by the politically committed, documentary and collectivist play entitled *Verhör in Habana*. In 1972, however, he published *Der kurze Sommer der Anarchie*, his more individualistically biographical collage dealing with Durruti, an anarchist leader in the Spanish Civil War, while the thirty-three strophes of his verse epic *Der Untergang der Titanic* (1978) were, given the apocalyptic mood and subject-matter, more akin to a range of texts from the 1980s. The same applies to Tankred Dorst. Having begun in the 1950s with texts for the puppet theatre, he enjoyed his first successes around 1960 with absurdist plays, and achieved fame in 1968 with the Stuttgart première of his revolutionary drama *Toller*.[2] *Sand*, dealing with the political murder of the playwright August von Kotzebue in 1819, followed in 1970; *Eiszeit*, a typically 1970s title for a text dealing with the ageing Knut Hamsun, appeared in 1973; and in 1981 he published the fantastic, mythological play *Merlin oder Das wüste Land* in which 'History' refutes 'Utopia' and from whose apocalyptic ending the Devil emerges supreme.

2. For a documentation and analysis of the reception of this controversial play throughout Europe 1968–1984, see R. Sheppard, *Tankred Dorst's* Toller: *A Case Study in Reception* (Lochee Press, New Alyth, 1989).

From 'Being-Itself' to 'Post-Modernism'

Although the religious and mythological themes in the literature of the 1980s occasionally provoke comparison with the post-1945 decade throughout which such avowedly Christian writers as Stefan Andres, Werner Bergengruen, Albrecht Goes, Elisabeth Langgässer, Gertrud von Le Fort, Luise Rinser, Reinhold Schneider and Rudolf Alexander Schröder played an important role,[3] such comparisons do not get us very far, given the differences in sociohistorical context. When, in the aftermath of Nazism and war, post-war writers expressed a longing for religious solace and certainty, or a desire to examine their consciences and confess their guilt, their motives differed significantly from those writers of the 1980s who were experiencing the pressures of political theologies of liberation, latter-day fundamentalism, the Christian Peace Movement, various kinds of a-political neo-mysticism and a conservative ecclesiastical establishment for whom religious disquiet and spiritual radicalism were as unwelcome as socio-political revolution. Where the writers of the late 1940s lived in the shadow of their immediate past, their descendants in the 1980s lived in the shadow of a hypothetical future. There was, of course, during the first post-war decade, an existentialist counter-current flowing from such French sources as Sartre and Anouilh which, in its avowed atheism, seemed guilty, from a Christian perspective, of 'nihilism'. By the second post-war decade, however, this particular constellation of forces had come to seem like a historical chapter which was now closed.

Accordingly, when the literary theory of the 1940s, using concepts developed by the various avant-garde movements from Symbolism to Surrealism, set out to establish a new literary canon, it rejected, in the name of pure literary values, not only the left- and right-wing modes of literary realism which had established themselves between the wars, but also the confessional writing of the post-war years. Thus, Hugo Friedrich's *Die Struktur der modernen Lyrik* (1956), the standard post-war treatise on poetry, which had sold 161,000 copies by 1985, excluded from discussion both the political and the con-

---

3. In this connection, one must also mention such Christian periodicals as *Hochland, Die neue Ordnung, Eckart* etc., with the *Frankfurter Hefte* on the left wing, as well as numerous translations of non-German Christian writers (such as Julien Green, whose works enjoyed a revival in the 1980s) and non-confessional, but religious writers such as Ernst Wiechert. Moreover, Max Bense confirmed the religious character of this literary decade when, in 1950, he described the 'current temptation of German writers' as 'theological emigration' and asked 'who would actually *not* like to be a Christian writer?' (M. Bense, *Ptolemäer und Mauretanier oder Die theologische Emigration der deutschen Literatur*, Haffmans, Zurich, 1984, p.14).

fessional poetry of the twentieth century[4] – partly for ideological reasons and partly because of its popular nature. Although Friedrich also ridiculed attempts to see significant differences between, say, the poetry of 1945 and 1955 where none in fact existed (p.7), such distinctions are, in my view, both real and demonstrable. One has only to list such central examples from the mid-1940s as the *Westzone* volumes from Werner Bergengruen's *Dies Irae* (1945) to Rudolf Hagelstange's *Venezianisches Credo* (1946), Albrecht Haushofer's *Moabiter Sonette* (1946) or Reinhold Schneider's *Die neuen Türme* (1946) to see that all were examples of an ethico-religious mode of poetry which dealt with experiences from the Third Reich or the War; and, using a consciously traditional form, all addressed the expectations of an educated, middle-class readership. By the mid-1950s, however, the Vienna Group was already in existence and we were being confronted with Eugen Gomringer's *Constellations* (1953) and Helmut Heissenbüttel's *Combinations* (1954) – i.e. literary texts which, conceived as analogies of abstract art, were aimed at those on the inside of the avant-garde literary scene. Between 1945 and 1950, the best-known anthologies had titles like *De Profundis* and *Ergriffenes Dasein*; in 1956, however, *Transit*, Walter Höllerer's completely novel anthology of avant-garde poetry, appeared. This volume not only claimed to represent the 'poetry of the mid-twentieth century', it was also, in retrospect, the precursor of *movens* (1960), in which the new, experimental poetry was presented with a new-found self-confidence.

The chronological model is also helpful when one tries to identify changes in critical approaches to literature. If one considers the first post-war decade, one continually finds critics discussing works of literature in terms of 'man and his world', Being and Nothingness, the plenitude and emptiness of existence. Similarly, the Heideggerian 'Question of Being' is posed in relation, say, to the 'world without transcendence' of Thomas Mann's novels,[5] the late poetry of Rilke and such diverse authors as Kafka and Raabe, Hofmannsthal and Grillparzer, Trakl and Stifter. A prime example of this kind of approach was Benno von Wiese's *Die deutsche Tragödie von Lessing bis Hebbel* (*German Tragedy from Lessing to Hebbel*) (1948; 8th edn, 1973), the first half of which bore the title 'Tragedy and Theodicy' and the second 'Tragedy and Nihilism'. The two halves were

4. H. Friedrich, *Die Struktur der modernen Lyrik* (Rowohlt, Reinbek b. Hamburg, 1956), p.8; cf. H. Kreuzer, *Veränderungen des Literaturbegriffs* (Vandenhoeck und Ruprecht, Göttingen, 1975), p.47.
5. The reference is to H.E. Holthusen, *Die Welt ohne Transzendenz* (Heinrich Ellermann, Hamburg, 1949; 3rd edn, 1954).

divided by a chapter on Kleist called 'The Fundamental Dissociation of Ego and World' in which one may read such statements as: 'This is the poesy of Being-Itself: terrible and holy at one and the same time' (Wiese, 1973, p.646). The preferred method involved in such 'existentialist literary criticism' was known as 'text-immanent interpretation', which von Wiese, despite the fact that he was dealing with a historical process, characterised as a mode of 'elucidatory interpretation which always focuses on the individual work of literature' (1973, p.v). That such an approach – 'interpretation' – could serve other ends became evident in the second post-war decade when the 'Question of Form' came more to the fore. One can easily see this, using Büchner as the acid test, by looking at the changing titles of the essays in Wolfgang Martens's collection *Georg Büchner* (1965), the fifty-third volume of the *Wege der Forschung* series. Karl Viëtor's essay 'The Tragedy of Heroic Pessimism' was published in 1934 and Robert Mülher's essay 'Georg Büchner and the Mythology of Nihilism' in 1951, but 1958 saw the appearance of Helmut Krapp's more formalist book on dialogue in Büchner's dramas, the introduction to which was published in Martens's volume under the title 'Büchner's Aesthetics'.[6]

Works which became well-known and influential in the 1950s and which, in retrospect, can be seen as significant precursors of a more formalist approach to literature, were already appearing in the 1940s. Thus, they testify to the chronological parallel between existentialist and formalist criticism, even if practitioners of these two approaches vied with each other at the time for intellectual predominance. In 1948, Ernst Robert Curtius's thematological approach enabled him to identify some of the recurrent *topoi* of Western literature[7] and the first volume of Paul Böckmann's *Form-Geschichte der deutschen Literatur* appeared in 1949. Influences from abroad had been permeating German literary criticism for several years: Erich Auerbach's *Mimesis* had been published in 1946 (7th edn, 1982); *Grundbegriffe der Poetik* by the Swiss Germanist Emil Staiger appeared in the same year (8th edn, 1968) and Wolfgang Kayser's *Kleine deutsche Versschule* and *Das sprachliche Kuntswerk* in 1946 (17th

---

6. H. Krapp, 'Zu Büchners ästhetischer Konzeption' in W. Martens (ed.), *Georg Büchner* (Wissenschaftliche Buchgesellschaft, Darmstadt, 1965), pp.386–405. For a discussion of the socialist Büchner of the 1970s, see G.P. Knapp, *Georg Büchner*, 2nd edn (Metzler, Stuttgart, 1984).

7. E.R. Curtius, *Europäische Literatur und lateinisches Mittelalter* (Francke, Berne, 1948; 10th edn, 1984; E.T. as *European Literature and the Latin Middle Ages*, Routledge and Kegan Paul, London, 1953). For a later version of the same approach, see M. Bäumer (ed.), *Toposforschung* (Wissenschaftliche Buchgesellschaft, Darmstadt, 1973).

edn, 1975) and 1948 (19th edn, 1983) respectively. The title of the latter book (which, like Kayser's earlier one, had been written in Lisbon) not only gained its author the Göttingen Chair in 1950, but was, in its aesthetic formalism and fixation on the 'work of literature as such', symptomatic of the second post-war decade as a whole. More than a few books produced in the 1950s could be described both as 'existentialist' and as 'formalist', and it is significant that von Wiese was able, in his tome on German tragic drama, to take Staiger's above-mentioned work on generic theory, which had defined tragedy in existentialist terms as a 'boundary situation' in which 'human existence fundamentally ceases' (Staiger, 1947, p.200), as its starting-point (Wiese, 1973, p.655).

Although Fritz Martini's *Das Wagnis der Sprache* (1954; 7th edn, 1984) – a much-published work containing readings of 'German narrative prose from Nietzsche to Benn' – shared, at one level, von Wiese's desire to cling to the text-immanent method of 'interpretation', it was also symptomatic of a change that was taking place in academic literary criticism. Thus, although its introduction makes simultaneous use of existentialist and formalist vocabularies, its emphasis is firmly on the 'linguistic event' and the 'new style' which is generated from the encounter between the various authors and 'Being-Itself'. Moreover, for Martini, the interpretation of individual works was not an end in itself, but a means of 'going beyond the individual and the historical' and of discussing 'typical forms of narration, of linguistic expression and formal synthesis in prose fiction'. Individual works were thus said to be important to the extent that they served a 'general and historical theory of prose fiction'. For Martini, as for so many others who came after him, a concern for 'linguistic expression and formal synthesis' went hand in hand with a 'historical theory' whose aim was the legitimisation of Modernism (in the sense in which that term was used in the 1950s) and the defence of 'radical experimentation in the fields of literature and thought' in the teeth of such conservative critics as Hans Sedlmayer and Hermann Pongs, who, in works like *Der Verlust der Mitte* (1948; 9th edn, 1976) and *Im Umbruch der Zeit* (1950; 3rd edn, 1958), had propagated a 'theory of loss – whether of the mid-point or of some primal innocence' (Martini, 1954, pp.1–6).[8]

8. Wolfgang Kayser documented his move towards Modernism in his much-cited book *Das Groteske: Seine Gestaltung in Malerei und Dichtung* (Gerhard Stalling, Oldenburg, 1957; E.T. as *The Grotesque in Art and Literature*, Indiana U.P., Bloomington, 1963). That Staiger refused to move in the same direction and continued to judge (and condemn) modernist literature of the 1950s and 1960s by classical criteria led to the 'Zurich literary controversy' of winter 1966/7 and, as with

Martini succeeded in establishing a new 'canon of modernist classics' which included Rilke, Thomas Mann, Hofmannsthal, Heym, Kafka, Döblin, Broch and Benn. Thereafter, a younger generation of critics began to produce a series of characteristic and highly successful works which took the 'Question of Form' still further and which, because they were couched in terms accessible to students, became long-running best-sellers: Eberhard Lämmert's *Bauformen des Erzählens* (1955; 8th edn, 1983), Volker Klotz's *Geschlossene und offene Form im Drama* (1960; 11th edn, 1985) and Franz Stanzel's *Theorie des Erzählens* (1955; 3rd edn, 1985) and *Typische Formen des Romans* (1964; 10th edn, 1981), the latter of which sold 14,000 copies within a year of its publication.

Käte Hamburger and Max Bense taught alongside Martini in Stuttgart in the second half of the 1950s. Hamburger had begun work on her novel theory of narrative and genre while in exile in Sweden and her ideas issued in the monumental *Logik der Dichtung* (1957),[9] the source of long-running controversies. Bense had been bringing out his *aesthetica* since 1954, and, on the basis of those publications – produced, significantly enough, in the context of a Technical University – he developed his *Theorie der Texte* (1962) and an avowedly 'modern aesthetic' in which overtly scientific modes of procedure were privileged over 'speculative and metaphysical' ones like 'interpretation'. As this 'modern aesthetic' was said to be based on 'concepts, ideas and results deriving from Mathematics, Physics, Communication Science and Information Theory', Bense could claim to have developed an 'exact, *technological aesthetic*' which made use of Peirce's theory of signs and Norbert Wiener's cybernetic theory (Bense, 1965, pp.313–32). Whatever their merits, Bense's ideas, by providing a theoretical basis for concrete poetry, abstract painting and experimental 'computer art', gained considerable international currency.

With that, West German literary theory had reached the juncture at which it could open itself out to and exert its own influence upon international critical theory. In 1958, the Benn-scholars Edgar and Marlene Lohner brought out their translation of Warren and Wellek's *Theory of Literature* (1949). As a much-published paperback, this book opened up unfamiliar, foreign vistas to students, making it

---

Sedlmayer and Pongs before him but unlike his Swiss opponent Walter Muschg, this refusal pushed him into an increasingly peripheral position (see the documentation in *Sprache im technischen Zeitalter*, no.2 (1967), pp.83–206).

9. The second edition (1968) became the basis of several translations and a paperback edition.

possible for them to see the German critical tradition in relation to North American New Criticism and Russian Formalism, and introducing them to the ideas of such theoreticians as Jan Mukařovský and Roman Jakobson. In the late 1950s and throughout the 1960s, the Prague and Parisian variants of Structuralism, the various attempts to establish a linguistically-based poetics and taxonomy of 'textual types', the world-wide interest in semiotics and the above-mentioned synthesis of aesthetics and Information Theory all helped to undermine traditional, hermeneutical approaches to literature, to make such approaches seem old-fashioned and methodologically questionable, and to establish the theoretical piece as the most important critical genre of the 1960s.

But in the very decade when formal questions were ousting older critical attitudes, a sociologically oriented counter-movement was developing. Indeed, by the end of the 1960s, the 'Question of Society' had come to dominate the discussion of literature not only in the public domain, but also, in the wake of the student protest movement, in university seminar rooms as well (see Jörg Schönert's essay below, pp.71–94).[10] As a result, textual analysis found itself forced to compete with Reception Theory. Although Wolfgang Iser's version could easily be assimilated to more formalist approaches, thus assuring its popularity in the USA, Hans Robert Jauss's version went far beyond Iser's text-centred approach in its claim that an investigation of the minds of the so-called 'receivers' of literature, with particular reference to their 'horizons of expectation', now constituted one of the central tasks of any literary scholar who wanted to rewrite literary history creatively (see Margot Zutshi's essay below, pp.95–111). Even if Jauss, making extensive use of the ideas of Hans-Georg Gadamer, remained within the hermeneutic fold, it was only a short step from his position to a complete revamping of literary criticism – to the supplanting of textual analysis as an end in itself by empirical, psychologically oriented investigation of reader response, for which a text was, in the first place, a channel of communication within a complex process of production, distribution, reception and text-processing (Siegfried J. Schmidt, Norbert Groeben).[11]

Historical studies profited from the dominance of sociology to a

10. It is significant that in J. Kolbe (ed.), *Ansichten einer künftigen Germanistik* (Hanser, Munich, 1969), Beda Allemann and Hans-Wolf Jäger (who later taught at the University of Bremen) made parallel cases for a 'structuralist approach' and a 'socio-critical approach' to the study of German literature.
11. *SPIEL* [*Siegener Periodicum zur Internationalen Empirischen Literaturwissenschaft*] (1982 et seq.) is a contemporary periodical that promotes this kind of approach.

greater extent, even, than empiricism.[12] Jost Hermand, a member of the historically oriented group of critics who had studied under Friedrich Sengle in Marburg, settled accounts with the methodological attitudes of the preceding decades and propagated the new doctrine of 'synthetic interpretation' (1968; 4th edn, 1973) with his eyes firmly fixed upon the more general, *epoch*-specific qualities of literature. Everywhere one looked in the late 1960s or early 1970s, literature was being examined in its 'social context'[13] and, incidentally, the ground prepared for those multi-volume social histories of literature which appeared under major imprints in the 1970s and 1980s. The study of the social presuppositions of literary forms and functions led to the notion of literary history as a history of the media[14] and alongside anthologies of the writings of Structuralists and Formalists, there appeared an ever-growing number of collections of essays dealing with such topics as pulp literature, literary sociology, dialectical-materialist literary history, non-fictional writing, film, radio, television, and the history, theory and critique of knowledge as such. The elitist concept of literature which had prevailed in the later 1950s, with its predilection for the abstract and

12. The following paragraphs are based partly on my essay in *Veränderungen des Literaturbegriffs* (note 4) entitled 'Zum Literaturbegriff der sechziger Jahre in der Bundesrepublik Deutschland' (pp.64–75). Later examples of the tendencies described there are: P. Stein (ed.), *Theorie der politischen Dichtung: Neunzehn Aufsätze* (Nymphenburger, Munich, 1973); P.-U. Hohendahl, *Literaturkritik und Öffentlichkeit* (Piper, Munich, 1974); F. Trommler, *Sozialistische Literatur in Deutschland: Ein historischer Überblick* (Kröner, Stuttgart, 1976); H. Denkler and K. Prümm (eds), *Die deutsche Literatur im Dritten Reich: Themen, Traditionen, Wirkungen* (Reclam, Stuttgart, 1976); R. Schenda, *Volk ohne Buch: Studien zur Sozialgeschichte der populären Lesestoffe 1770–1910* (DTV, Munich, 1977); W. Hinderer (ed.), *Geschichte der politischen Lyrik in Deutschland* (Reclam, Stuttgart, 1978). Bernd Neumann's *Identität und Rollenzwang: Zur Theorie der Autobiographie* (Athenäum, Frankfurt/Main, 1970); Georg Bollenbeck's *Zur Theorie und Geschichte der frühen Arbeiterlebenserinnerungen* (Scriptor, Königstein/Ts., 1976) and Helmut Scheuer's *Biographie: Studien zur Funktion und zum Wandel einer literarischen Gattung vom 18. Jahrhundert bis zur Gegenwart* (Metzler, Stuttgart, 1979) are all the products of a general sociological concern, but fuse it with typical topics of the 1970s which have the individual as their central point of focus.
13. Peter Bürger's *Theorie der Avantgarde* (Suhrkamp, Frankfurt/Main, 1974), a sociologically oriented work, was still very important for this type of discourse but also anticipated the mood of the later 1970s in its tendency to resignation. In the 1970s critics began to view genres as 'socio-literary institutions'; cf. W. Voßkamp, 'Gattungen als literarisch-soziale Institutionen' in W. Hinck (ed.), *Textsortenlehre – Gattungsgeschichte* (Quelle and Meyer, Heidelberg, 1977), pp.27–44.
14. See, for example, Helmut Schanze's 'Überlegungen zu einer Theorie der medialen Möglichkeiten', *LiLi*, no.6 (1972), pp.27–44 and *Medienkunde für Literaturwissenschaftler* (Fink, Munich, 1974) and his essay in H. Kreuzer (ed.), *Literaturwissenschaft – Medienwissenschaft* (Quelle und Meyer, Heidelberg, 1977).

the esoterically obscure, was supplanted by the concept of 'social relevance'; the representatives of the New Left rejected notions of artistic quality as their touchstones and replaced them by emancipatory and utopian ones; the business of literary interpretation was changed into the occasion for the exposure and critique of ideological stances; and political literature – especially that which had heralded the uprisings of the sixteenth, eighteenth and nineteenth centuries or been produced between the two World Wars – was rediscovered. A preoccupation with the 'Question of Society' was by no means the prerogative of left-wingers or the youngest generation of scholars of the late 1960s/early 1970s. The relatively conservative group around Sengle and Wolfgang Frühwald in Munich set up the International Archive for the Social History of Literature and documented the explosion of research in that area by means of a series of bibliographies; and in 1969, the first international symposium on exile literature was held – albeit in Stockholm. By the same token, scholars began to regard GDR and proletarian literature as objects of serious study, and such questions as the relationship between present-day writing and the 'classical heritage' or the Brecht-Lukács debate were discussed from political, rather than purely literary-historical perspectives.

The fact that students and lecturers of the 1968 generation were appointed to vacant or newly established chairs of German in the 1970s did not prevent the sociological approach from losing ground during that decade, retaining its contemporaneity and force only in the area of feminist criticism. Here, the literary critique of ideology was adapted into a critique of patriarchy in all its historical and present-day forms; the quest for a socialist culture was supplanted by the debate about a 'feminine aesthetic'; and the revision of bourgeois literary history which had begun in the 1960s was continued in the form of 'women's literary history'.[15] Furthermore, the most characteristic scholarly works of the later 1970s dealt neither with the collective nor with the literature of the masses, but with the individual and his or her opportunities for self-determination and self-realisation so that the earlier heresy of 'privatism' ceased to be unacceptable.

Just as, among writers, New Subjectivity became the watch-word, so, inside and outside of the women's movement, autobiographical

15. See the bibliography at the end of H. Gnüg and R. Möhrmann (eds), *Frauen Literatur Geschichte: Schreibende Frauen vom Mittelalter bis zur Gegenwart* (Metzler, Stuttgart, 1985); also R. Möhrmann, 'Feministische Ansätze in der Germanistik' in M. Heuser (ed.), *Frauen – Sprache – Literatur* (Schöningh, Paderborn, 1982), pp.91–115.

and biographical texts became very popular objects of study. Correspondingly, 'emotional involvement' (*Betroffenheit*) became a major driving force for authors and critics alike and 'authenticity' the most up-to-date criterion for making a positive judgement. Feminist studies synthesised the sociological concerns of the 1960s with the New Subjectivity of the 1970s, and the rediscovery of psychoanalysis played such an important role during that decade that Klaus Theweleit's two-volume *Männerphantasien* (1977–8; E.T. as *Male Fantasies*, 1987) must surely count as its most successful doctoral dissertation. One also notices a lowering of the barriers between writers and academics: established *literati*[16] turned their attention, to the accompaniment of scholarly applause, to historical subjects from the field of German literature; established Germanists published novels, poems, biographies and autobiographies[17] which were aimed at a literary audience and began to write with increasing frequency for the literary columns of major national newspapers. Indeed, one even finds novels being written about university departments of German: the semi-fictional, retrospective accounts of the student movement of 1968 which were being published in the 1970s were succeeded, in the 1980s, by novels dealing with the professional and personal problems of younger academics.[18]

Conversely, rigid professional terminology, methodological debates and theoretical precision began, in comparison, to seem more out of place, so that Feyerabend's 'anything goes' could well be adopted as the methodological slogan of the later 1970s. Although various successful critical anthologies which were published in the 1980s dealt with the Fantastic, Time, Style, the Consciousness of Progress and Decadence, Dream or Nature in literature and other areas of culture and the arts,[19] they eschewed any strict methodo-

---

16. E.g. Dieter Kühn's successful *Ich, Wolkenstein: Eine Biographie* (Insel, Frankfurt/Main, 1977) and *Der Parzival von Wolfram von Eschenbach* (Insel, Frankfurt/Main, 1986) or Ingeborg Drewitz's books on Bettina von Arnim of 1970 and 1984.
17. E.g. Hans Mayer's and Benno von Wiese's autobiographies. For a discussion of the *literati* among contemporary Germanists, see Kreuzer (1981), p.106 (n97).
18. E.g. Martin Walser's *Brandung* (Suhrkamp, Frankfurt/Main, 1985); Michael Zeller's *Follens Erbe: Eine deutsche Geschichte* (Oberon, Bad Homburg, 1986) and Brigitte Kronauer's *Berittener Bogenschütze* (Klett-Cotta, Stuttgart, 1986). The attention of English-speaking readers is drawn to B. Keith-Smith, 'The German Academic Novel of the 1980s, or the Tale of Four Hetero-Academic Novels', in Williams, Parkes and Smith (eds), *Literature on the Threshold*.
19. See C.W. Thomsen and J.M. Fischer (eds), *Phantastik in Literatur und Kunst* (Wissenschaftliche Buchgesellschaft, Darmstadt, 1980; 2nd edn, 1985); C.W. Thomsen and H. Holländer (eds), *Augenblick und Zeitpunkt: Studien zur Zeitstruktur und Zeitmetaphorik in Kunst und Wissenschaft* (Wissenschaftliche Buchgesellschaft,

logical approach. Instead, they evinced a renewed concern with the relationships between literature and the other arts and between other disciplines and the media, with particular reference to significant themes, images, thought-forms and life styles. The transition period between the 1970s and 1980s seems to have been marked by methodological pluralism and eclecticism: hence those anthologies of the early 1980s which, dealing with individual texts, took as their starting-point just such a pluralism – described in one instance as a 'many-hued collage of methodological sub-discourses' precisely because of the lack of one single, unifying principle.[20]

Given such a situation, it is clear why people should be nowadays returning to 'positivistic' ways of working. Indeed, all kinds of editions are in the process of appearing or being planned – from neglected, lost or repressed 'Texts of Early Modernism' (Jörg Drews, Hartmut Geerken, Klaus Ramm), 'Forgotten Modernist Writers' (Karl Riha, Franz-Josef Weber) and 'Modern Classics in the Third Reich' (Hans Dieter Schäfer), to competing editions of Goethe and whole libraries of professionally edited classic texts in which large amounts of effort on the part of numerous Germanists have been invested. But although the traditional canon of literary texts has re-established itself in schools, one hears a growing chorus of complaints about 'the decay of literate culture' and the increasing meaninglessness of printed works of literature in comparison with aural and visual forms and the technological media through which they are transmitted (a field of study, incidentally, in which more and more scholars are getting involved).

In 1985, the International Germanists' Congress, meeting for the very first time on German soil, took place in Göttingen under the rubric 'Controversies' – a somewhat misleading title, as it turned out, given that its participants tended to *study* controversies rather than *engage in* controversies over matters of opinion and approach.

Darmstadt, 1984); H.U. Gumbrecht and K.L. Pfeiffer (eds), *Stil: Geschichten und Funktionen eines kulturwissenschaftlichen Diskurselements* (Suhrkamp, Frankfurt/Main, 1986); G. Grossklaus and E. Oldemeyer (eds), *Natur als Gegenwelt: Beiträge zur Kulturgeschichte der Natur* (von Loeper, Karlsruhe, 1983); W. Drost (ed.), *Fortschrittsglaube und Dekadenzbewusstsein im Europa des 19. Jahrhunderts: Literatur – Kunst – Kulturgeschichte* (Carl Winter, Heidelberg, 1986); T. Wagner-Simon and G. Benedetti (eds), *Traum und Träumen: Traumanalysen in Wissenschaft, Religion und Kunst* (Vandenhoeck and Ruprecht, Göttingen, 1984).

20. See N. Groeben (ed.), *Rezeption und Interpretation: Ein interdisziplinärer Versuch am Beispiel der 'Hasenkatastrophe' von Robert Musil* (Gunter Narr, Tübingen, 1981); D.E. Wellbery (ed.), *Positionen der Literaturwissenschaft: Acht Modellanalysen am Beispiel von Kleists 'Das Erdbeben in Chili'* (C.H. Beck, Munich, 1985). The phrase quoted is to be found on p.7 of the latter volume.

Although various approaches to literature (operating in various subject areas) formed independent segments of the Congress, the differences separating the speakers played no significant role. Despite the gloomy situation in which the Congress took place, with the precarious situation of younger scholars, the high unemployment rate among trained teachers and the record level of unemployed arts graduates forming three of its most disturbing features from the professional point of view, the whole event felt more like a harmonious academic festival. Indeed, one commentator summed it up as follows:

> The time for fundamental controversies in the field of German literary scholarship seems to be over for the time being. Whether that is because the controversies of the 1970s have been set aside or more or less satisfactorily resolved, I would not care to say. Whatever the truth of the matter, it transpires that the overall topic to which the Göttingen Congress was asked to address itself . . . has been set too late. (Bohnen, 1986, p.177)

Or should the speaker have said 'too soon', given the emotionally charged controversies which have marked the intellectual life of the Federal Republic in the mid-1980s? One only has to think of the anti-semitism controversy provoked in 1986 by Rainer W. Fassbinder's *Der Müll, die Stadt und der Tod* (1980; 2nd edn, 1984), or the latter-day debates about Germany's identity, or the controversy among historians about how to assess the Nazis' policy of systematically planned and organised genocide (compared, for example, with the persecution of the Kulaks in the Soviet Union),[21] or the debates between Jürgen Habermas and the neo-conservatives or the proponents of Post-Modernism.

At the same time, it has to be conceded that the literature of the 1980s, like the literary theory of the same decade, involves tendencies which cannot be summed up in one single, overarching concept, are continuations of older modes of writing and criticism, and coexist within the new pluralism of today. Foreign writers in the Federal Republic, particularly those of Italian and Turkish extraction, have been developing a distinctive, polyglot literature which was recognised and encouraged by literary scholars (like the group around Harald Weinrich in Munich)[22] at precisely that juncture

---

21. For an extensive discussion of the so-called *Historikerstreit*, see Richard J. Evans, 'The New Nationalism and the Old History: Perspectives on the West German *Historikerstreit*', *Journal of Modern History*, vol.59 (1987), pp.761–97.
22. See the issue of *LiLi* (no.56, 1984) devoted to 'Gastarbeiterliteratur'.

when xenophobic feelings towards Turks and political refugees from
the Third World, sparked off by mass unemployment, were becoming a real political factor. Exile literature published in translation in
the Federal Republic, like Isabel Allende's novels *Das Geisterhaus*
(1984) and *Von Liebe und Schatten* (1986) and texts by German
authors, like F.C. Delius's novel *Adenauerplatz* (1984) or Günter
Wallraff's documentary reportage *Ganz unten* (1985; E.T. as *Lowest of
the Low*, 1988), probably the most widely-read new publication of the
1980s, can be seen as an aspect of the same set of problems. As in the
case of women's literature, the social-critical commitment of the
1960s has fused with the New Subjectivity of the 1970s to produce a
literature which deals authentically with the situation of individual
immigrant workers. Similarly, *the* television event of the 1980s,
Edgar Reitz's serial *Heimat*, had its roots in the regionalist literature
of the 1970s, long since regarded by literary scholars as a significant
contribution to the cultural scene. Indeed, the same regionalism
assured the recognition, by academics and general readers alike, of
such non-professional, provincial writers of the older generation as
Maria Beig and Anna Wimschneider, and paved the way in the
Federal Republic for the reception of German literature that had
been produced in German-speaking enclaves abroad.[23]

Despite what has been said above about the pluralism and eclecticism of the 1980s, it is quite clear that some trends have been more
spectacularly apparent than others – as even a cursory glance at the
foremost philosophical authorities of the last ten years will confirm.
Where the first post-war generation had fallen under the spell of
Catholic or existentialist thinkers like Romano Guardini or Karl
Jaspers, the second post-war generation preferred Karl Popper's
critical rationalism, and the generation after that operated under the
aegis of the critical theory of the Frankfurt School, Marxism or
Systems Theory. In the 1970s and 1980s, however, it was the titles of
French works and names like Foucault, Lacan, Derrida and, more
recently, Lyotard and Baudrillard which featured most prominently
in the footnotes and indexes of those critical works whose authors
prided themselves on being up-to-date theoretically. 'Discourse' has
ousted 'dialectics' as the buzz-word, and a whole gamut of concepts
with the prefix 'Post-' has become current: irrespective of their
specific originations and connotations, terms such as Post-Industrialism, Post-History, Post-Structuralism, Post-Modernism etc. are
nowadays being interrelated to an ever-increasing extent.

---

23. See A. Ritter (ed.), *Deutschsprachige Literatur im Ausland* (*LiLi*-Beiheft no.13)
(Vandenhoeck and Ruprecht, Göttingen, 1985).

This complex of ideas reached German Studies in the Federal Republic by way of Freiburg and, more particularly, the work of the group around Friedrich A. Kittler, their best-known exponent. But the general intrusiveness of the 'Question of (Post-)Modernism' cannot be adequately explained in terms of the professional activity of the Freiburg group and similar groups elsewhere. Rather, it seems to me that the post-structuralist demand for the 'abolition of the subject' (especially the writing subject) and the 'elimination of the human [*Geist*] from the humanities [*Geisteswissenschaften*]' (Kittler, 1980, pp.7–9)[24] has stirred people's imaginations across a whole range of disciplines so that publicists, sociologists and philosophers have been able to add their contributions as well to an increasingly raucous debate. New intellectual periodicals with mind-blowing titles and misleading subtitles have sprouted all over the place (like, for example, *Tumult: Zeitschrift für Verkehrswissenschaft*); the key words of the new critical trend have lost any specialist connotations; and a new enthusiasm for 'primal scenes',[25] the 'holy',[26] 'death' (up to and including imaginary 'self-immolation'),[27] the idea of the '(loss of the) body'[28] and the 'disappearance of the senses'[29] has inspired

24. For a discussion of the 'most up-to-date types of French hermeneutics and theory of texts', see M. Frank, *Das Sagbare und das Unsagbare: Studien zu neueren französischen Hermeneutik und Texttheorie* (Suhrkamp, Frankfurt/Main, 1980). The embarrassment felt by a Post-Structuralist when he has to appear in public in his capacity as a human being is nicely demonstrated by the opening of Winfried Kudszus's Freiburg lecture (in Kittler, 1980, pp.175–87): 'While I would like to begin my lecture, I am confronted by a fundamental objection which almost prevents me from saying another word. One has to consider from what perspective it might be possible for me to speak at all without succumbing to the fiction that I am standing here as a kind of speaker who might be able to express himself in this or that fashion. And when I say "I", I am setting out from premises which, on closer inspection, prove to be questionable or even nonsensical. At first sight, I have to admit, things look fairly straightforward: "I" am at present in Freiburg.'
25. F.A. Kittler and H. Turk (eds), *Urszenen: Literaturwissenschaft als Diskursanalyse und Diskurskritik* (Suhrkamp, Frankfurt/Main, 1977).
26. D. Kamper and C. Wulf (eds), *Das Heilige: Seine Spur in der Moderne*, 2 vols. (Athenäum, Frankfurt/Main, 1986).
27. See J. Baudrillard, *Der symbolische Tausch und der Tod* (Matthes and Seitz, Munich, 1982) together with the appendix by Gerd Bergfleth. On the theme of self-immolation, see H. Hesse (ed.), *Der Tod der Moderne: Diskussion* (Claudia Gehrke, Tübingen, 1983), pp.129–36.
28. E.g. J. Jung (ed.), *Mein Körper* (Salzburg, Residenz-Verlag, 1985); G. Mattenklott, *Der übersinnliche Leib* (Rowohlt, Reinbek b. Hamburg, 1982); H. Schipperges, *Kosmos Anthropos: Entwürfe zu einer Philosophie des Leibes* (Klett-Cotta, Stuttgart, 1982); D. Kamper, 'Körperlichkeit – Die Überholung des Körpers, mündlich und schriftlich' in J. Hörisch and H. Winkels (eds), *Das schnelle Altern der neuesten Literatur: Essays zu deutschsprachigen Texten zwischen 1968–1984* (Claassen, Düsseldorf, 1985), pp.131–40.

interdisciplinary colloquia, doctoral candidates and dilettantes alike.

Although such writings have filled a gap in the profession of criticism, they have failed to bring about the methodological predominance of Post-Structuralism, largely because of certain temptations to which post-modernist adepts are particularly prone: wilfully obscure metaphorical language, an apodictic tone of voice, the substitution of anecdote for hard argumentation and the eclectic use of disciplines and methodologies (Structuralism, psychoanalysis, linguistics and semiotics) even by writers who are not qualified in all of them (cf. David Jenkinson's remarks on p.253 below). Whoever succumbs to such temptations ends up by parodying him- or herself and provoking a polemical or satirical response which marks the end of pluralist co-existence (cf. Laermann, 1986). The historian is bound to regard the list of things which are said to have become impossible – 'realism, representation, meaning, signification, subjectivity, history, authorship etc.' (Huyssen, 1986, p.32)[30] – with scepticism and may even be seduced into agreeing with the expressed opinion of one practised panellist:

> At the moment, we must, if we really want to be state-of-the-art critics, speak of the Death of Modernism. But that's been the case for only two-and-a-half years. Two-and-a-half years ago we weren't discussing that question at all ... and in another two-and-a-half years we shan't discuss that question any more. But that means that theoretical considerations are being governed by the categorical imperative of continual change.[31]

One can incline to this diagnosis because it fits in with the chronological framework that I have used so far and, accordingly, hazard the question 'whether the concept of Post-Modernism, while doing justice to real shifts across a range of the arts, marks only a change in ideological temper throughout the industrialised West, so

---

29. D. Kamper and C. Wulf, *Das Schwinden der Sinne* (Suhrkamp, Frankfurt/Main, 1983).
30. Cf. Lehmann (1986), p.251: 'In the context of Post-Modernism, people have been talking for some time now of a "mythogenic cast of mind" ... Like Structuralism, psychoanalytical hermeneutics and linguistic theory, the philosophical deconstruction of such categories as subject, meaning, presence, intention and expression had, inevitably, to shatter the claim of history to be the primary or even the exclusive point of reference for aesthetic discourse. After a period when theoreticians oriented themselves almost exclusively according to the historical paradigm, these new perspectives and disciplines encourage them to take increased notice of *anthropological* paradigm.'
31. See Horst Folkers's remarks in *Der Tod der Moderne* (note 27), pp.149–50.

From 'Being-Itself' to 'Post-Modernism'

that it is, from this perspective, simply an alteration in our view of Modernism' (Lehmann, 1986, pp.252–3). Andreas Huyssen is, however, in no doubt that it is more than a question of 'shifts' and that a profound process of aesthetic transformation is under way:

> Thus, the Post-Modernism of the 1980s operates in an area of tension between tradition and innovation, conservation and renewal, mass culture and high art. But in no case is the second component of these binary pairs automatically privileged over the first – with the result that the old dichotomies – progress v. reaction, left v. right, rationalism v. irrationalism, future v. past, Modernism v. Realism, abstraction v. representationalism, avant-garde v. *kitsch* – become inoperative. (Huyssen, 1986, p.41)

So let us begin, using a few key concepts and examples, by registering some of those 'real shifts' in literature which are sporadically attributed to Post-Modernism. Towards the end of the 1970s, the New Subjectivity became, in part, a 'new irrationalism' (Kreuzer, 1981, pp.93–7) which, without any qualms, played off Nietzsche and Heidegger against Idealist, positivist or materialist traditions of thought, favoured mysticism and religious concerns, and even pointed to the 'return of the Devil'.[32] Myth[33] became respectable again right across the critical board, even among leftwingers; Hans Blumenberg acquired the status of philosophical guru;[34] and the former Brechtian, Heiner Müller (who, without giving up his position as a GDR writer, worked in the West alongside Robert Wilson, considered by many drama critics to be the master of theatrical Post-Modernism), became the touchstone for *literati*. Plays staged by top directors became even further removed from the literary word, and playwrights like Kroetz and Achternbusch (who were familiar with the practicalities of the theatre) directed their plays themselves.

Furthermore, a 'new mode of narration' began to discard the

---

32. See W. Falk, *Des Teufels Wiederkehr: Alarmierende Zeichen der Zeit in der neuesten Dichtung* (Burg-Verlag, Sachsenheim-Hohenhaslach, 1983). The issue of *Der Spiegel* which appeared on 22 December 1986 used the same title for its major article.
33. See A. von Bormann, 'Mythos und Subjekt-Utopie: Bemerkungen zur gegenwärtigen Mythos-Diskussion', *L'80*, no.34 (June 1985), pp.29–45; K.H. Bohrer (ed.), *Mythos und Moderne: Begriff und Bild einer Rekonstruktion* (Suhrkamp, Frankfurt/Main, 1983); M. Frank, *Der kommende Gott: Vorlesungen über die neue Mythologie* (Suhrkamp, Frankfurt/Main, 1982); and especially, K. Hübner, *Die Wahrheit des Mythos* (C.H. Beck, Munich, 1985).
34. The titles of such books by Blumenberg as *Arbeit am Mythos* (1979) or *Schiffbruch mit Zuschauer: Eine Daseinsmetapher* (1979) have an almost proverbial status in some circles.

contemporary tenet that narrative is actually no longer possible. This new mode supplies information like any well-researched reference work; it involves a plethora of literary references (thereby serving the current theoretical concern with 'inter-textuality'); it obeys the 'laws of giving pleasure' (Hage, 1986, p.6) by entertaining and gripping its readers; it loves the fictional crime that transcends both rationality and conscience,[35] it generates best-sellers and is prepared to fulfil an escapist function – and despite all that, it is enjoyed and even fêted by the critics! In the international context, Umberto Eco's *The Name of the Rose* (1980; G.T. 1982) was the prime example of this new mode, and in Germany, the nearest equivalent is Patrick Süskind's *Das Parfum* (1985; E.T. as *Perfume*, 1986). Dealing with an eighteenth-century perfume-maker who is also a mass-murderer for the sake of his art, Süskind's novel has been awarded the seal of critical post-modernist approval for demonstrating its contemporaneity by displacing its murderous genius 'into the age of d'Alembert, Holbach, Voltaire and Rousseau as though he [Grenouille, the novel's central character] were the dark side of the Enlightenment. Accordingly, the perfume which permeates all his passions and desires is nothing other than what Günther Anders called the "spectralisation of the world" and Jean Baudrillard its "simulation".'[36]

Baudrillard's concept of 'simulation' has found its way directly into the title of Bodo Morshäuser's *Berliner Simulation* (1983). Together with Bodo Kirchhoff (who wrote his doctorate on Lacan) and Rainald Goetz, Morshäuser belongs to a group of authors who write for the Suhrkamp Verlag and who are regarded as the mouthpiece of the 'post-punk intelligentsia':

> Pushers and pigs, trendies and undercover agents: whoever knows the names, names the roles. Simulation in Berlin, the theatre of the great city, the representation of urban apocalypse. Sounds good, but what's the director called? *Capital? Power?* In the 1970s, the author would have hired the former at the outset and the latter a bit later on. But we're in the mid-1980s now and Bodo Morshäuser can't think of anyone to blame for the 'Berlin Simulation'.[37]

35. According to Hage (1986), pp.15–17, 1985 was a boom year for literary detective novels.
36. Wolfram Schütte in the *Frankfurter Rundschau* of 5 April 1985. Another novel, rich in literary references, that deals with the shadow side of the eighteenth century is Peter Sloterdijk's *Der Zauberbaum: Die Entstehung der Psychoanalyse im Jahr 1785* (Suhrkamp, Frankfurt/Main, 1985).
37. Rainer Bieling in *Zitty* (West Berlin) of 13 October 1983, quoted in V. Hage and A. Fink (eds), *Deutsche Literatur 1983: Ein Jahresüberblick* (Reclam, Stuttgart, 1984), pp.198–9.

As a final and not unimportant instance, I offer you those examples of literary apocalypse which, merged with the image of the Deluge or a vision of nuclear Doomsday, are proliferating to such an extent across the various genres that scholars are beginning to write histories of the subject![38] Even former GDR authors like Sarah Kirsch and Günter Kunert have cast themselves in the role of 'chronicler[s] of the last days',[39] and Christa Wolf, the winner of the Büchner Prize in 1980 and widely considered in the West to be the outstanding contemporary woman writer, has, in her novel *Kassandra* (1983; E.T. as *Cassandra*, 1984), succeeded in fusing under one title the concern with myth, feminist issues and apocalypse which has so exercised German literature over the past ten years.

Although the phenomena that I have been discussing above are features of the literary map of the 1980s (which, in the view of many people, is overshadowed by documentary literature like that produced by Franz Alt and Wallraff), I see no inherent reason to label them 'post-modernist'. If, by Modernism, one is designating post-realistic, avant-garde tendencies, or, with particular reference to German cultural history, the series of '-isms' which runs from Nietzsche to Dada, then it could well be objected that those modern '-isms' had already been superseded after the First World War by the New Realism practised by that generation of political and confessional writers whose most typical representatives were Brecht and Jünger. But if one uses the word 'modern' as a historically fluid concept which designates what is novel, contemporary and pregnant with future promise, then the term 'post-modern' becomes totally devoid of sense.

As, however, this term has established a bridgehead in contemporary thinking, more than a few literary critics and scholars have felt obliged to distinguish between 'modernist' and 'post-modernist' and to fill the conceptual husk of Post-Modernism with some con-

---

38. See G.E. Grimm, W. Faulstich and P. Kuon (eds), *Apokalypse: Weltuntergangsvisionen in der Literatur des 20. Jahrhunderts* (Suhrkamp, Frankfurt/Main, 1986); K. Vondung, 'Apokalyptische Erwartung... zwischen 1910 und 1930', in T. Koebner, R.-P. Janz and F. Trommler (eds), *Mit uns zieht die neue Zeit: Der Mythos Jugend zwischen Jahrhundertwende und Drittem Reich* (Suhrkamp, Frankfurt/Main, 1985), pp.519–45.
39. See the *Stuttgarter Zeitung* of 8 November 1983. As examples of 'novels of catastrophe' one may cite: A.A. Guha's *Ende: Tagebuch aus dem Dritten Weltkrieg* (Fischer, Frankfurt/Main, 1983); Matthias Horx's *Glückliche Reise: Roman zwischen den Zeiten* (Rotbuch, Berlin, 1983) and Udo Rabsch's *Julius oder Der schwarze Sommer* (Claudia Gehrke, Tübingen, 1983). For discussions of such texts, see G. Stadelmaier, 'End ohne Enden oder: Wie man Weltuntergänge überlebt. Es retten sich, wie sie können – die Schriftsteller' in *Apokalypse* (note 38), pp.358–68, and K. Modick in *Die Zeit* of 2 January 1987.

crete content.⁴⁰ The results of such attempts do not, however, add up, since those who have made them sometimes use, as their examples of Post-Modernity, only authors who have been writing for less than a decade,⁴¹ sometimes, in addition, authors who have been writing for several decades or who even belong to the nineteenth century, and sometimes authors who have, until now, been classified according to quite different historical categories. Consequently, we are going to arrive at some kind of consensus only when the meaning of the term Modernism has been fixed or replaced by something less equivocal. As things stand, however, the debate surrounding the concept of Modernism is not just a matter for historians of art and literature: it is also a controversy which has implications for the history of ideas, the philosophy of history and political thought in general. Modernism – for some participants in the debate an outmoded project and for others, notably Habermas, a project that has still to be realised – is, when understood in a positive way, viewed mainly in terms of the central idea of the Enlightenment: the notion of the autonomous subject. But when it is understood in a negative way, that same concept tends to be reduced to instrumental reason as that is manifested in modern economics, science and technology. Creative writers, too, notably Günter Grass, locate the core of the debate in such problems and oppositions rather than in any purely aesthetic concerns, asking themselves: 'Why the Enlightenment? Why its state of misery? . . . Because the Enlightenment, as a process which has already been going on for three centuries, has to put a question-mark over itself if it does not want to fade away or turn into a decorative flourish of Post-Modernism.'⁴²

In Grass's usage, the term Modernism covers three centuries (rather than the period immediately prior to the 1980s or the period stretching from Arno Holz to Dada and Mallarmé to Musil); and for other writers still, it can even expand to cover the whole of the 'modern' epoch which is said to date from the discovery of the New World. We are in the midst of a *querelle* in which the *anciens* are proclaiming the persistence of the modern age, and the *modernes*, like the Catholic philosopher Romano Guardini over three decades ago

40. There are several examples of this in *Kontroversen*, vol.10 (see References). English-speaking readers are referred to the essays on the Post-Modernism debate of Fredric Jameson, Dan Latimer and Terry Eagleton which were published in the *New Left Review*, nos.146, 148 and 152 (1984/5).
41. H. Schlaffer, 'Der Aufzug der neuen Romantiker', *FAZ*, 19 May 1979.
42. See Günter Grass's introduction to *Der Traum der Vernunft: Vom Elend der Aufklärung*, edited by the West Berlin Akademie der Künste, Erste Folge (Luchterhand, Darmstadt and Neuwied, 1985), p.8.

in his *Ende der Neuzeit* (1950), its end. Where the *anciens* propagate a historical teleology, most of the *modernes* argue for the rejection of the idea of history as a linear progression, for a kind of neo-medievalism which is governed by notions of myth, return, and Being rather than becoming.[43]

In the process, one sees such apparently paradoxical alliances being forged that the catch-phrase of the 'New Impenetrability [*Unübersichtlichkeit*]' (Habermas, 1985) is by no means inappropriate. Where, on the one hand, avowedly pro-bourgeois philosophers (like the liberal, Odo Marquard, and the American conservative, Hilton Kramer) ally themselves with the left-wing Habermas and the party of Enlightenment and Modernity, anti-utopians, on the other, see themselves as the subversive opponents of 'the system':

> Political order comes to an end . . . as soon as people stop believing that Utopia has been realised and give up hoping in the future possibility of Utopia. I believe that we are currently in a situation where the broad mass of the people are not prepared to tolerate this kind of blackmail any longer and accept neither of the two alternatives. Nor, however, do they find themselves in a state of melancholy apathy but in one of radical indifference *vis-à-vis* the whole notion of political order . . . The Anti-Utopia of the a-political, of radical indifference, has arrived.[44]

I cite this passage not as a diagnosis of our age, but as an example of an ideology which is being positively received or even praised by German intellectuals because of its post-modernist cachet.[45] Typical intellectual veterans of 1968 experience the 'Anti-Utopia of the a-political' not, of course, as the triumph of subversiveness, but as the hopeless consequence of their political autobiographies. They no

---

43. Cf. formulations like the following by Wolfgang Schirmer: 'If one looks at our age from the point of view of the philosophy of culture, the modernist epoch proves to be a period of transition between two great eras – the Middle Ages and a future which is still unknown' (quoted in B. Schmidt, *Postmoderne – Strategien des Vergessens*, Luchterhand, Darmstadt and Neuwied, 1986, p.50).
44. Cf. Baudrillard's discussion contributions, quoted in *Der Tod der Moderne* (note 27), pp. 103–4.
45. In an article entitled 'Warum uns die Bundestagswahl nicht interessiert', Michael Rutschky (cf. note 49), a German writer who actually heard Baudrillard's 'subversive' pronouncement, published the following statement in *Die Zeit* of 2 January 1987 concerning the kind of politics which follows from Post-Modernism for the 'avant-garde cadres who read the literary supplements of newspapers': 'Whoever, in a hundred years' time, wanted to understand the nature of the "turning-point" which conservative politicians were talking about in the 1980s could do no better than search in the broad area of culture . . . : Peter Handke and Botho Strauss, the critiques of rationality and the Enlightenment; the return of the sacred and a yearning for religious experience; the

longer see apocalypse as an element in some history of salvation or as a revolutionary stage along the road to a secular Utopia, but as the synonym for a catastrophe which, although situated in the future, is already present in our consciousness.

A questionnaire circulated by *Die Zeit* at the end of 1986 which asked the question 'Is there any future for hope?' discovered that the lament most inimical to hope is currently being intoned by literary intellectuals. They, having formerly deferred to the 'Blochian obligation to rejoice at progress',[46] are now spreading a gloomy *fin-de-siècle* mood on the assumption, as before, that they, as the possessors of true consciousness, must now remedy that false consciousness enshrined in the 'principle of hope' in which they once believed. Karl Markus Michel placed his ultimate hopes only in despair, describing it as 'the following wind which will possibly carry us further than the self-righteous faith in progress which nowadays lacks a church'. And Peter Schneider turned the question round, asking:

> How can the future be saved from our hopes? We are surrounded, besieged and besotted by hopes which, written in capital letters for all to see, have long since been dashed ... That someone will not give up his hopes or let his hopes be taken from him no longer seems to me to be such a positive thing.

Such sentiments are not the result of realistic insight, but an expression of disappointed illusions – as is particularly evident from Schneider's response to the questionnaire, in which he listed all those countries which have failed to realise the expectations invested in them by the German literary intelligentsia of his generation: Cuba, China, Vietnam, Greece, Spain, Portugal and Nicaragua.[47]

Beneath the surface of an apparently stable, neo-conservative society there is no shortage of co-existing and conflicting fears, insecurities and directionlessness on the one hand and, on the other, of either soberly rational or avowedly religious commitment to plans for saving the planet Earth. The resonant power of 'Post-ism' in the 1980s almost certainly derives from our subconscious awareness of

---

rediscovery of the body and the Will to Power (a word which has, incidentally, been assimilated into German!); even the return of the idea of the German Nation. It is people like us who have given substance to that "turning-point". Within the cultural life of the Federal Republic, the left wing has given birth to something like a right wing.'

46. See Heidrun Hesse's introduction to *Der Tod der Moderne* (note 27).
47. See *Die Zeit* of 26 December 1986 where Michel's and Schneider's responses (*inter alia*) were quoted.

standing at the end of an era – an end that was actually initiated by the dropping of the atomic bomb on Hiroshima. The limitation of that 'Post-ism' consists, however, in the fact that playful irresponsibility, anarchist quietism ('Nothing can be done') and 'the gay gospel of a new freedom – the freedom from the future and prescriptive self-realisation'[48] – are offered as panaceas in this time of 'waiting' and 'change'.[49]

In reality, the long-overdue process of transformation requires a 'powerful development of human inventiveness'[50] if we are to change the principle governing the shaping of human history from one of exploitation to one of conservation and cultivation. Early history provides us with an example of just such a change when, at a much lower technological level, societies based on hunting became societies based on agriculture. What part literature and literary theory can and will play in that process of change will depend on their ability to help us revise our image of human nature and history, and that is closely bound up with the way in which they respond to the 'Question of Modernism'. When all is said and done, the importance of that question seems to me to lie in its capacity for making us define our attitudes to certain central questions regarding our cultural, economic and political future – questions which have little to do with the ephemeral restrictions and styles imposed by contemporary post-modernist authors and theoreticians. As the attitudes that we will be forced to define will, inevitably, have meta-sociological implications involving human nature as such, the place of man in Nature and the history of Nature,[51] the 'Question of Modernism' is, as a historical question, closely connected with the reassertion of the 'Question of Being', albeit in an unfamiliar form.

48. See Heidrun Hesse's introduction to *Der Tod der Moderne* (note 27).
49. I am, of course, quoting the titles of two best-selling works of non-fiction published in Germany in 1983: Michael Rutschky's *Wartezeit* and Fritjof Capra's *The Turning Point* (1st edn, 1982; G.T. as *Wendezeit*). Capra, a sub-atomic physicist by profession, is one of the most influential propagators of 'Holism'.
50. See G. Ropohl, 'Technik als Gegennatur', in Grossklaus and Oldemeyer, *Natur als Gegenwelt* (note 19), pp.97–8 and the 1986 introduction to the paperback edition of H. Kreuzer (ed.), *Literarische und naturwissenschaftliche Intelligenz* (DTV, Munich, 1987; 1st edn, 1969).
51. Cf. H. and G. Böhme, *Das Andere der Vernunft* (Suhrkamp, Frankfurt/Main, 1985). English-speaking readers are referred to Carolyn Merchant, *The Death of Nature* (Wildwood House, London, 1982).

Helmut Kreuzer

Postscript for English-speaking Readers

Perhaps it is necessary to add for the sake of English-speaking readers that there are distinct Spanish, British and American traditions for using the word 'post-modern' as a historical term. Spanish historians of literature use it to refer to those developments in the first half of this century which superseded the Modernism of the turn of the century; Toynbee used it to refer to the fourth, post-1875 phase of Western history (that of global Imperialism), the first three being the Dark Ages, the Middle Ages and the Modern Age; and prominent North American critics began to apply the term in the late 1950s and 1960s to post-war American literature – first with negative and then with positive connotations. The North American usage of the term spread into other arts and disciplines, reaching the Federal Republic in the 1970s (cf. several articles on this development in vol.22 of *Amerikastudien*, published in 1977). In the 1980s, Germans began to apply the term to German phenomena.

References

Bense, M. (1965) 'Zusammenfassende Grundlegung moderner Ästhetik' in H. Kreuzer and R. Gunzenhäuser (eds), *Mathematik und Dichtung: Versuche zur Frage einer exakten Literaturwissenschaft*, Nymphenburger, Munich, pp.313–32

Bohnen, K. (1986) 'Nachbemerkung' in A. Schöne et al. (eds), *Kontroversen, alte und neue: Akten des VII. Internationalen Germanistenkongresses Göttingen*, 11 vols., Max Niemeyer, Tübingen, vol.10, pp.176–7

Habermas, J. (1985) *Die neue Unübersichtlichkeit*, Suhrkamp, Frankfurt/Main

Hage, V. (1986) 'Zur deutschen Literatur 1985' in V. Hage and A. Fink (eds), *Deutsche Literatur 1985: Jahresüberblick*, Reclam, Stuttgart, pp.7–47

Huyssen, A. (1986) 'Postmoderne – eine amerikanische Internationale?' in A. Huyssen and K.R. Scherpe (eds), *Postmoderne: Zeichen eines kulturellen Wandels*, Rowohlt, Reinbek b. Hamburg, pp.13–44

Kittler, F.A. (ed.) (1980) *Austreibung des Geistes aus den Geisteswissenschaften*, Schöningh, Paderborn

Kreuzer, H. (1981) 'Neue Subjektivität: Zur Literatur der 70er Jahre in der Bundesrepublik Deutschland' in M. Durzak (ed.), *Deutsche Gegenwartsliteratur: Ausgangspositionen und aktuelle Entwicklungen*, Reclam, Stuttgart, pp.75–106

Laermann, K. (1986) 'Lacancan und Derridada: Über die Frankolatrie in den Kulturwissenschaften', *Kursbuch*, no.84, 34–43

Lehmann, H.-T. (1986) 'Mythos und Postmoderne – Botho Strauss, Heiner Müller' in *Kontroversen*, vol.10, pp.249–55

Martini, F. (1954) *Das Wagnis der Sprache*, Klett-Cotta, Stuttgart

Staiger, E. (1947) *Grundbegriffe der Poetik*, Atlantis, Zurich

Wiese, B. von (1973) *Die deutsche Tragödie von Lessing bis Hebbel*, 8th edn, Hoffman and Campe, Hamburg

–2–

The Unacknowledged Legislator of the Text – Some Observations on Literary Criticism in the Federal Republic of Germany

HANS J. HAHN

In contrast to its success in the fields of economics, technology, literature and film, recent West German literary criticism has, Reception Theory excepted, failed to make a major impact on the wider international scene. In general, post-war German literary criticism avoided the *Kahlschlag* philosophy of a 'showdown between the intellect and its opponents' (Berg, 1981, p.600) and paid homage instead to speculative philosophy and strong irrational or even anti-rational sentiments. To this day, German students of literature tend to focus on aesthetics rather than stylistics, an attitude which has recently led to the observation that literary criticism in West Germany tends towards ideological rather than textual criticism and that, in Germany, a distinction must, in marked contrast to the French and Anglo-American schools, be drawn between both disciplines (Hinck, 1983, p.16). When analysing the various trends in West German literary criticism, we shall, however, attempt to adhere to the Anglo-American view and deal with both disciplines together.

Literary Criticism During the Post-War Era (1945–1965): A Return to Traditional Formalism?

At those few universities unscathed by the Second World War, academic critics began by readopting the old, elitist attitudes and attempted to salvage an already discredited literary tradition, oblivious of post-war Germany's new literary voices. Thus, Germanists like Emil Staiger and Wolfgang Kayser and journalists like Friedrich Sieburg, Max Rychner and Günter Blöcker, with Ernst Robert Curtius as their spiritual mentor, reaffirmed traditional values while claiming to be totally preoccupied with matters of style and language. Returning to the literary traditions of the 1920s and 1930s, such critics were isolated from the international scene so that the New Criticism remained virtually undiscovered. Heinz Otto Burger, for example, asked to review methodological problems at the first post-war conference of Germanists (1950), followed a rigorously 'werkimmanent' line; suggested that philology and literary history should no longer be considered part of 'Dichtungswissenschaft'; and maintained that he had introduced this methodology as early as 1942 in *Gedicht und Gedanke*, apparently oblivious of the fact that he had then also attempted to trace 'Germany's mission as evinced by the confessional stance of its poets' (Burger, 1941, pp.305–39). While professing a methodology that was allegedly free from ideological and 'geistesgeschichtlich' adulteration, critics of this persuasion were also opposed to *all* forms of empiricism or positivism since they seemed, even more than Dilthey's historicism, to prevent a return to a subjective and irrational approach. In their attempt to 'understand what moves us' (Staiger, 1955, pp.10–11), this group of critics ignored the historical complexities of reception and literary influence and reintroduced philosophical complexities which, by now, lacked a scholarly foundation.

This insistence on 'werkimmanente Interpretation' has, somewhat unfortunately, been described as formalism. Although the term is correct to the extent that its users emphasised the 'auratic' nature of literature – i.e. its independence of historical and social influences – it is misleading inasmuch as it is ultimately based on subjective value-judgements and criteria, even while it seems to justify its judgements with reference to the Age of Goethe or some vaguely defined and often elitist 'higher sensibility'. Thus, referring to Benedetto Croce's *Aesthetics*, Wolfgang Kayser, the other leading figure of post-war *Germanistik*, reduced all literary expression to subjective-emotional considerations, stressing the complete coincidence of form and content without any reference to the external world (Kayser, 1961, p.15).

An examination of Staiger's Zurich lecture on modern literature (1966) demonstrates the shortcomings of such subjectivism. He condemned the nihilistic tendencies in modern literature; deplored its concern with the ugly, the vulgar and the inhuman; and rejected the choice of Auschwitz as subject-matter for a literary text, diagnosing it as a sympton of cultural degeneration. Staiger thus demystified the basis of his own subjective value-judgements, revealing himself as a moral critic who was firmly embedded in the ethos of the nineteenth-century bourgeoisie. Similar considerations apply to Curtius, Sieburg, Rychner, Blöcker and Hans Egon Holthusen – who acted as the collective mouthpiece of the Adenauer era, concealing their elitist and autocratic assumptions within a framework of subjective value-judgements. The influence of Heidegger on Staiger is particularly evident, notably the former's view of the ontological nature of language as the essence of human existence, man's means of comprehending truth (Heidegger, 1950, p.7). For Heidegger, the relationship between the artist and his work is unique and total: both are divorced from the outside world, and all extrinsic subject-matter (such as history, society, literary reception and production) becomes, in consequence, marginal to the critic's exclusive concentration on the transcendental character of the work in and for itself.

Although the literary critic will always be committed to close textual analysis, the role of these older critics was problematic to the extent that they maintained a silence about the ideological position of so many Germanists during the Nazi period. By shying away from the 'fall from Grace' of *Germanistik* (Schonauer, 1981, p.407), they inadvertently discredited close reading and fostered an interest in ideologies amongst representatives of the next generation. It is thus not surprising that a new group of literary critics grew up who were passionately opposed to the Staiger–Kayser school and its dependence upon Heidegger's ontology and Existentialism. Consequently, their preoccupation with neo-Marxist methodologies was, in part at least, the result of these early forms of subjectivism.

Literary Criticism during the the 1960s: A Cultural Revolution?

In the 1960s, a new school of literary critics found inspiration in the philosophical writings of Adorno, Horkheimer and other representatives of the Frankfurt School, whilst others turned to the writings of Lukács and Benjamin. Although Adorno and Horkheimer had returned to Germany in the 1950s to re-open the Frankfurt Institute for Social Research, their impact was felt only towards the end of the Adenauer era, as a response to discussions about alienation and man's existential situation. In the ensuing debates, the attitudes of Adorno and Horkheimer were still predominantly negative. Arguing from an anti-fascist stance, they predicted the advent of a new phase of barbarism and cultural regression which would be brought about by the transformation of enlightened ideas into irrational nature myths, and they related this transformation to the advance of capitalism with its enormous degree of professional and technological specialisation (Wilson, 1986, pp.287–302). Critics opposed to the 'negative dialectics' which characterised this school of thought maintained that its proponents were hostile towards social progress because they understood technology exclusively as a means of domination on the grounds that the opportunity for radical social change had been missed. Within such a framework, therefore, art and literature could be defined only in negative terms, 'in relationship to that which is not' (Adorno, 1970, p.347), and the arts became divorced from a 'culture industry', with the individual losing his or her freedom and with it, the prerequisites for enlightenment (Adorno, 1967, p.69).

Whilst the main body of this critical theory had a profound influence on such progressive critics of the 1960s as Hans Magnus Enzensberger, Hans Robert Jauss and Günther Anders, they, too, inevitably began to dissociate themselves from the negative attitude towards the culture industry on the grounds that such hostility emphasised the enigmatic and hermetic nature of art. In particular, elements from within the student movement turned against Adorno, whose aesthetics were criticised as 'one-dimensional', restricted exclusively to an auratic art and oblivious of any other social functions. Riding on the new wave of Pop Art, these elements found inspiration in works by Herbert Marcuse like *Eros and Civilisation* (which had been translated into German as early as 1957, but made little impact until the late 1960s). Marcuse's ideas made possible a general understanding of art and culture in relation to real-life conditions by reconciling the economic base with its ideological superstructure:

> The rationality of domination has separated the Reason of science and the Reason of art, or, it has falsified the Reason of art by integrating art into the universe of domination . . . Here is the original link . . . between science, art, and philosophy. It is the consciousness of the discrepancy between the real and the possible, between the apparent and the authentic truth, and the effort to comprehend and to master this discrepancy. (Marcuse, 1964, pp.228–9)

During the latter phase of the student movement, as the ideological balance turned against Adorno, Walter Benjamin came back into the limelight. His later work, produced during the 1930s, encouraged a phase of self-reflection, culminating in a brief period during which *Germanistik* attempted to break the mould of sacred tradition (Mosler, 1977, pp.204 and 245). Recognising that 'the bourgeois apparatus of production and publication can assimilate and spread an astonishing number of revolutionary themes without seriously questioning its own position', Benjamin demanded from the intellectual, even in his role as a producer, solidarity with the proletariat (Benjamin, 1977, vol.II, 2, p.692). Moreover, his essay 'The Work of Art in the Age of its Technical Reproducibility' (1936) explored the consequences of modern techniques of reproduction for such literary concepts as 'genius' and 'creativity', and suggested that art had lost its auratic peculiarity: 'For the first time in world history the technical reproducibility of the work of art has emancipated it from its parasitical dependency upon ritual' (Benjamin, 1977, vol.I, 2, p.481). Like Brecht, Benjamin rejected the enigmatic aura of aesthetic totality and broke out into the sphere of politics – or rather, true to his own dialectics, he politicised art and endowed politics with an aesthetic function: 'This is the situation of the aestheticisation of politics which Fascism goes in for. Communism responds to that by the politicisation of art' (Benjamin, 1977, vol.I, 2, p.508).

While the philosophical differences between the schools of thought which formed around the work of Adorno and Benjamin were important to the extent that they gave rise to variations within a broadly defined, neo-Marxist aesthetic, all the adherents of these schools of thought shared a desire to emancipate literature from its bourgeois confines and to re-sensitise it to the social and economic reality of its environment (see Jörg Schönert's essay below, pp.71–94). While such a change in theoretical emphasis did not involve the rejection of textual analysis, literature was conceived of both as a socio-historical product and as something which can help the reader to comprehend otherwise incomprehensible social relations (cf. Schonauer, 1981, p.419). The socio-literary studies of Lucien Goldmann and Georg Lukács were regarded as models for such an approach, and their main followers in Germany were Jauss, Hans Norbert Fügen, Levin L. Schücking and Leo Löwenthal (see Löwenthal, 1964; Goldmann, 1966 and 1967; Fügen, 1970 and 1971; Jauss, 1970). In a similar spirit, Enzensberger's *Kursbuch* published its first issue in 1965, transgressing the conventions of the literary review by including transcript, reportage, documentation and non-polemical discourse. And at the height of the student revolt in 1968, its most sensational issue went so far as to announce the death of literary criticism – a judgement whose ambivalence was understood by only a few people at the time. Following in the philosophical tradition of Adorno, Enzensberger reaffirmed the loss of literature's role in life, declaring that it had ceased to be relevant for society: 'Culture is the only terrain in which the bourgeoisie still dominates without a challenge' (1968, p.193). He did, however, suggest an escape route for the poet: since literature had lost its function and, with it, any useful criteria for making value-judgements, a revolutionary role on its part was pure illusion. Nevertheless, this very situation of impotence could enable it to return to its earlier auratic function, outside the socio-political domain and within the realm of pure subjectivity.

Walter Böhlich's 'Autodafé' (1969) continued Enzensberger's argument. Examining previous declarations of the death of bourgeois literature and literary criticism, and relating this complex to the theme of the Death of God, he wondered why we still 'build new churches to the dead God' and why 'a dead aesthetic continues to assist in the annihilation of what is living' (Böhlich, 1969, 'Kursbogen'). At this point, Böhlich turned to Benjamin. Recognising the dependence of literature on modern means of communication, he understood both as functions of capitalism and argued that both writers and critics will have to recognise the impossibility of their own intellectual dominance: 'Can we not have a type of criticism which begins not from the notion of the timeless nature, but from its relative and temporal nature and no longer attempts to see literature in terms of what it is said to be but in terms of the purposes it serves and the ends to which it is used?' (Böhlich, 1969, 'Kursbogen').

Many similar statements on the futility of literature followed, all concerned with the bourgeois bias of the discipline and its indebtedness to a nineteenth-century heritage of nationalism, educational privilege, and an irrational mythology. Although, in 1969, Eberhard Lämmert pleaded for an end to traditional German Studies and its integration into such disciplines as Comparative Literature so as to overcome its nationalist and bourgeois origins (1969, p.85), the inertia and self-interest endemic among the discipline's practitioners prevented any such dissolution. However, the question of whether the survival of German Studies is meaningful in a world where literature has become an element of an expanding leisure industry continues to occupy critical minds today. Thus, the opening speaker at the 1982 Germanists' Conference in Göttingen asserted that if *Germanistik* could not define its social function, its continued existence was in doubt; and a recent article in *Die Zeit* bemoaned the total paralysis of German literary criticism on the ground that it had remained embedded in hermeneutic theory and had thus failed to participate in public debate in the media or to comment on contemporary works (Dyck, 1985, pp.41–2).

Where today's criticism may sound over-pessimistic, too self-centred in its sophisticated scepticism, the voices of the late 1960s were optimistic, putting their trust in the cultural revolution which had begun its march through the universities. Students of German occupied their institutions, hoping to achieve a collective act of liberation that would lead them out of the cage of bourgeois intellectualism and end the tradition of *Germanistik* as a 'Luxuswissenschaft' ('luxury subject'). Resolutions were passed which threatened the abolition of German literary studies and opposed the trend towards making universities into 'knowledge factories'; and the student revolutionaries demanded an awareness of the inherent violence of capitalism together with the emancipation of public language from established rules. Moreover, the cultural revolution threatened to overthrow the 'Großkritiker' and to replace them by a new school of left-wing critics (like Enzensberger, Hamm, Pehlke and the brothers Peter and Michael Schneider) for whom *Germanistik* had become profoundly suspect. In their view, the critic had become little more than a 'pseudo-producer' who had developed the division of labour to such an extent that he had brought about his own abolition (Schneider, 1965, pp.98–123). Furthermore, his much vaunted 'objectivity' was said to be a pretentious and disguised form of elitism and his escape into timelessness, together with his categorical claim to be the upholder of good taste, little more than a hankering after a privileged education. Blöcker's demand for creativity was derided, as was Holthusen's belief in originality, Jens's flirtation with a daemonic world-view and Hohoff's particular sensitivity in matters of taste (Hamm, 1968, pp.20–39).

And yet, literary reviews were, for a considerable time, hardly affected by the critical aesthetics of this revolutionary phase, thus confirming the view – so often expressed in left-wing circles of the 1960s and 1970s – that literary criticism had ceased to influence public taste and literary production. Within *Germanistik* itself, however, the search began for materialist theories of literature, continuing the tradition begun by Benjamin and developed above all in the periodical *Argument*. Wolfgang Fritz Haug, for example, took over the term 'Warenästhetik' ('Commodity Aesthetics') from Marx's *Critique of Political Economy* in order to highlight the 'exchange nature' of all commodities. In Haug's view, the transformation of our world of ideas into one of commodities had to lead to a transformation of our perception; the concept of the aesthetic had been reduced to that of sense-perception; and the relationship between perception and illusion had led to the dominance of the latter over the former since it was now perceived as part of an overall system of trade (Haug, 1983, p.10). The detailed examination of the above relationship became Haug's main concern: he attempted to expose the various forms of capitalist barter evident in literature and concluded with a comprehensive condemnation of capitalism and the aesthetics deriving from it. He thus had to reject the main tenets of Frankfurt-based Critical Theory because of its indebtedness to hermeneutic methods which he accused of merely perpetuating new paraphrases of themselves. Haug's later work attempted to distance itself from a too narrow interpretation of Marx's economic philosophy which, in his view, restricted the scope of human action, and later editions of the *Kritik der Warenästhetik* attempted to correct such 'economic overstatement' (1983, p.185) and keep his system more open-ended.

Within the wider context of student unrest, a new form of criticism evolved, concerned less with the artistic product and more with its reception by the reading public. Reception Theory began to establish itself in the early 1970s, with Jauss as one of its main representatives, closely followed by Iser, Lämmert and Schücking. The 'paradigm shift in literary criticism' which Jauss proclaimed (1969, pp.44–56) and which is discussed more fully in Margot Zutshi's article below was influenced partly by French Structuralism and partly by Foucault's theory of discursive change. This rejected the claim of any given text to absolute validity and concentrated on the fundamental shifts occurring between epochs (Foucault, 1977, pp.39–43, 61–2 and 68–86). Reception Theory in Germany was, however, primarily indebted to German Hermeneutics – in particular to the notion of the 'hermeneutic difference between the original and today's understanding of the work' (Jauss, 1970, p.183) – even if it took issue with Adorno's view of art's objective truth and claimed that the work was determined by its 'historically proven capacity to pleasurably extend the cultural horizons of its various publics' (Johnson, 1987, p.60).

By means of Reception Theory, Jauss hoped to bridge the divide between history and aesthetics which was such a prominent feature of Adorno's work and, in contrast to Adorno and mainstream literary criticism, opposed the concentration on the canonical texts, the Arnoldian touchstones of literature. Such an approach, Jauss argued, separated literature from the socio-historical reality of its age and consigned it to a privileged place that was out of reach, situated in the 'sphere of a higher intellectual world' (Jauss, 1970, p.166 and pp.147–9). Instead, Jauss investigated such issues as the original reader's knowledge of the work; his frame of mind and experience of life; his socio-historical environment; the tension between the literary work and other literary products of the time; the tension between contemporary expectations and the expectations of today's reader; and the work's relationship to the general body of literature. Within a broader context, Jauss's reception theory is related to Communication Studies, based on Roman Ingarden's epistemological approach, and Hermeneutics. This links him with Structuralism and, in the widest possible sense, with such Marxist literary critics as Benjamin, Goldmann and certain theorists of the Frankfurt School. Without abandoning the sociological approach, Jauss's methodology freed the literary critic from the confines of neo-Marxist ideology, and his emphasis on historical context, at a time when a renewed interest in history was in the air, also permitted a return to a more conventional, text-centred literary criticism. This latter feature was the result of Jauss's indebtedness to the phenomenological tradition established by Husserl and Heidegger and, in particular, to Hans-Georg Gadamer's *Wahrheit und Methode* (1965).

According to Gadamer's Hermeneutics, any attempt to understand a work will depend on the questions being posed in any given cultural environment. At the same time, the reader has to try to see the work in the context of its own dialogue with history, mindful of the restrictions which our limited perspective imposes upon us.[1] Following on from Gadamer, Jauss employed the term 'horizon of expectations' to describe the reader's attitude towards the text, insisting that there is no difference in priority between the horizon of expectations of the original author and reader and subsequent ones, including that of the present-day critic. Since we can never go beyond our own horizon of expectations, we can never gain an *a priori* understanding of the work itself. Consequently, the work cannot make any claim to universality, just as the critic cannot make final and objective value-judgements. With reference to Adorno, Jauss attempted to demonstrate the dialectics of Hermeneutics by arguing that the recipient experiences the work of art as something alien, but rediscovers himself as a result of the process of aesthetic reception and assimilation (Jauss, 1977, p.59).

Critics of Jauss and the Constance School of Reception Theory

1. Hermeneutics has, in general, played a major part in all forms of literary criticism. It also formed the basis for the New Criticism of Richards, Empson and Wellek and has, at least implicitly, played a major part in discussions on the totality of art and its fragmentation in the post-Hegelian epoch, especially in connection with aspects of neo-Marxism (cf. Strelka, 1978, pp.14–17 and Jay, 1984, pp.18, 472–80).

attacked the exaggerated position assigned to the public which had occurred at the expense of other literary and historical criteria. In particular, the later, post-modernist critics have taken issue with Jauss's methodology on a number of grounds. Christian Enzensberger, for instance, rejected the communicative validity of literature on the grounds that it can ultimately reproduce only the reader's own illusions, but cannot lead towards man's social or cultural emancipation (1981, pp.18–19 and 106). Karl Heinz Bohrer deplored the hermeneutical identification of hero and reader which, in his view, detracts from a direct involvement with the historical dimension of the work by escaping into Aristotelian timelessness (1981, pp.33–4). Johannes Klein was critical of the hermeneutic disposition on the grounds that it can lead to a certain passivity, and that a terminology based on 'understanding' and 'effectiveness' will always emphasise the receptive attitude at the expense of spontaneity and active cognition (1974, pp.223–4). Other criticism returned to the arguments of the 1960s, warning that literature could end up as nothing more than communication and literary criticism as nothing more than a series of sociological case studies. Finally, it was also suggested that the extremely complicated methodological approach might be inappropriate to literary studies and could lead to a highly subjective interpretation of a given text (Strelka, 1978, p.22).[2]

Literary Criticism during the Neo-Conservative Phase

Since the mid-1970s, discussions about an intellectual, political and cultural *Tendenzwende* in Germany have, at least in some quarters, led to the proclamation of an 'Anti-Enlightenment' (Habermas, 1977, pp.54–72). The term *Tendenzwende* came rapidly to signify a counter-ideology opposed to the excesses of the student revolution, but it also gained support, albeit for different reasons, from leading representatives of the 1960s who, disaffected because of the failures of their own 'cultural revolution', succumbed to cultural pessimism. Having turned their backs on the emancipatory and rational tradition of an enlightened Modernism with its commitment to a

---

2. For an assessment of Reception Theory in the GDR see Weimann (1973), pp.5–33. Whilst welcoming the turning away both from 'formalism' and from the general critique of Socialist Realism as developed by Lukács and his school, Weimann criticises Jauss's one-sided preoccupation with literary reception at the cost of literary production. Jauss's concept of 'horizon of expectations' is therefore rejected, since it falls short of the social and economic content within which a text should be seen.

normative, traditional humanism, they became alienated from their former objectives. Terry Eagleton defined the post-modernist sense of alienation as a 'grisly parody of socialist utopia': 'By raising alienation to the second power, alienating us even from our own alienation, it persuades us to recognize that utopia not as some remote *telos* but, amazingly, as nothing less than the present self, replete as it is in its own brute positivity and scarred through with not the slightest trace of lack' (1985, p.61).

Such a definition of an alienation from alienation would certainly encompass the German scene. Rejecting the modernist belief in the epistemological function of art, the German Post-Modernists isolated art both from other spheres and from any tenable theory of truth or meaning. Within the German version of the post-modernist debate, the focus was on the emergence of a new subjectivism which rejected socio-literary or critically reflective forms of literary criticism and considered socio-historical factors as accidental and irrelevant. Given the strong German tradition of irrationalism and the contemporary desire for new mythologies, it is perhaps not surprising that the discussion in Germany today is preoccupied with dichotomies such as progress/regression, reason/myth, left/right, history/loss of history, intellect/senses etc. (Huyssen and Scherpe, 1986, p.9). A new and peculiar 'twilight of existentialist disorientation' has taken hold of many intellectuals, and French and American influence has not only caused the replacement of dialectics and Hermeneutics by discourse, but has also established a general 'Postism' (Kreuzer, 1987, p.309). In order to provide the roughest of sketches of this latest phase in German literary criticism, we shall focus on four major aspects.

Post-Modernism versus Modernism

The controversies between these two warring factions are reminiscent of the eighteenth-century Battle of the Books. The Modernists, with Habermas as their leading representative, see themselves as champions of the Enlightenment which, in their view, ought to govern all human activity. Thus, the different artistic modes are said to be repositories of endangered meanings, manifestations of the consciousness of an epoch which is in turn an aspect of the humanist tradition, rooted in antiquity. Consequently, art, too, must play its part in the general process of human emancipation; become liberated from its self-imposed 'hibernation'; and be allowed to interact with the 'cognitive' and the 'practical moral' aspects of human experience (Habermas, 1979, p.43). The various avant-garde movements are said to be of particular importance for modernity: because the avant-garde is said to see itself 'as invading unknown territory, exposing itself to the dangers of sudden, of shocking encounters, conquering an as yet unoccupied future' (Habermas, 1981, p.4), it can successfully re-integrate art into life.

Representatives of Post-Modernity refute the Modernists' holistic view. Peter Bürger, a leading Post-Modernist, accused Habermas of not recognising the structural and social differences between the three spheres of art, morality and science: 'While autonomous art carries with it the idea of its self-transcendence, this cannot be said to be true of science in the same way' (1981, p.20). By 'smoothing out the *ruptures* in the development of culture', Modernism is said to overlook contradictions in our cultural development and to ignore the ever-increasing signs of a general crisis of orientation (cf. Schmidt, 1986, p.66). Instead of focusing on the Enlightenment as a high-point of European culture, Bürger views the end of the eighteenth century simply as an important starting-point 'when autonomous art constituted itself' in an attempt 'to counter the advance of empirical scientific processes in its dealings with nature' (1981, p.20). Moreover, Bürger sees the same phenomenon as the direct response to a 'loss of authority of religious world views' and the 'fragmentation of human activities'; and this, in turn, leads opponents of 'autonomous art' to insist on the internal logic of art and to reject the Enlightenment's 'aesthetic impact' (1981, p.21). Bürger is also critical of Habermas's definition of art as 'post-auratic' and favours instead the return to a ritually induced aura which distances art from everyday life and cultivates art as a beautiful illusion and substitute for religion. On these grounds, Bürger rejects the avant-gardes and turns instead to late nineteenth-century aestheticism, where 'the process toward ever more radical autonomy reaches its high point' (p.21).

Simultaneously with his attack on Modernism from Max Weber via Lukács to the Frankfurt School, Bürger mapped out the key stages in the development of autonomous art. The aesthetic theory of the *Geniezeit*, with its hostility towards technological and scientific progress and such rationalist concepts as the rules of drama, brought about, in his view, a new barbarism in its attempt to overcome the alienation of man from Nature. With reference to Benjamin's concept of 'aura' and Adorno's notion of *Kunstreligion*, Bürger drew on the similarity between art and religion inasmuch as both afford protection from the consequences of the modernist process of rationalisation (P. Bürger, 1983b, p.29). Despite some general reservations about the concept of Post-Modernism, Bürger recognised certain changes in aesthetic sensibility among the cultured middle class such as: 'a positive attitude towards the architecture of the *Fin de Siècle* and, correspondingly, a much more critical assessment of modern architecture; a derigidification of the dichotomy between high and low art which for Adorno, were still irreconcilably opposed to each other; . . . [and] a return to the traditional novel even amongst representatives of the experimental form' (1983a, pp.177–8). It would appear that Bürger wishes to reaffirm the traditional German distrust of rationalism in its Franco-Latin version in favour of German irrationalism and a 'culture of the heart', thus distancing German literature and culture from its Western European neighbours once again.

A New Interest in Myth

The renewed interest in myth is noticeable in most intellectual disciplines associated with Post-Modernism. Hans Blumenberg, for example, sees a cyclical return to mythology during periods 'in which there are rapid changes of speed in the constraints on their systems' (1979, p.41). Others view myth as symptomatic of a general crisis of orientation (Kurz, 1987, p.21). Representatives of this school believe that myths can bring about the integration of our feelings with our everyday environment, generate a 'new naïvety' and replace traditional views of the linear development of history ('Geschichte') by a return to more subjective stories ('Geschichten'). By being seen in relation to the mythical horrors of the past, the apparent horrors and anxieties of the present are said to lose their immediacy and become relative (C. Bürger, 1983, p.495).

Iser sets ups parallels between literature and myth. Both of these, it is claimed, generate 'the illusion of a perception which endows the unavailable with a certain *gestalt*' (1986, p.177), and both appear to come to terms with the 'ungraspable' in order to build up a relationship between our innermost sensations and the perceived world outside. Indeed, literature is viewed as 'a continuation of myths, whose main function consisted in allaying primeval terror through its images' (p.177). The enthusiastic response to Tolkien in Germany and the success of Michael Ende demonstrate how the combination of fairy-tale motifs, individualised stories and aspects of ecclesiastical tradition can lead to a whole school of fantasy literature. As Heine noted in his critique of the Romantic movement, traditional symbols, spiritual ideas and parables combine in an attempt to create a vision of infinity (Heine, 1972, p.14). Indeed, a renewed interest in the Romantic movement went hand in hand with the new preoccupation with myth. At first, this was limited to the earlier Romantic period with a re-examination of its 'New Mythology' as developed by Novalis, Schlegel, Schelling and Baader, but, more recently, interest has focused on the later Schelling, Brentano, von Arnim and Jacob Grimm. Important contributors to this trend include Manfred Frank, Karl Heinz Bohrer, Peter Bürger and Gerhart von Graevenitz. Frank and Bürger see myth in a dialectical relationship to the *Logos* and its manifestations since the Enlightenment. To quote Frank: '[The *Logos*] is born out of mythology and is, at the same time, death and the introversion of myth' (1983, p.17). This attitude enables us to make connections between Frank's ideas and Ernst Cassirer's categorisation of myth as one of the 'symbolic forms' since he, too, defines myth as a conceptual form. Nevertheless, Cassirer draws a fundamental distinction between myth and consciousness (or *Logos*) by maintaining that the real mythical consciousness does not distinguish between subject and object, but is, instead, appropriated by its subject-matter (1964, p.94). With the boundaries between subject and object removed, connections can also be made between Cassirer's concept of myth and post-structuralist theories of linguistics, since here, too, language is divorced from the speaker – its proper function as a medium for discussion having been lost and the traditional distinctions between narrative, mythical and scientific discourse having been suspended. As a result, the distinction between author and reader becomes irrelevant; the work becomes depersonalised; and the notion of individuality dissolves.

Bohrer's view of the literary importance of myth is even more radical. Unlike Frank, who acknowledges a social need for solidarity in myths and an established relationship to traditional forms, Bohrer, seeking to liberate myth from all social and political confines, reduces it entirely to the free play of the imagination. Following on from his earlier work on Schlegel, he argues that myth, once equated with imagination, will have to turn against reason; that art will gain complete autonomy; and that myth and imagination will become synonymous. Using a somewhat simplified example, the difference between Frank's position and Bohrer's is apparent in their divergent attitudes to Walter Benjamin. Whereas Frank comes close to Benjamin's view of considering myths in literature as objects for intellectual analysis (1983, p.18 and 1982, Chapters 1 and 2), Bohrer emphasises the anagogical character of myth which helps it to escape from the rationalism of the Enlightenment (1983, pp.63–4).

Von Graevenitz tried to break out of such traditional modes of thought. Because, for him, myth reveals its reality 'outside reason'

(1987, p.vii), he tried to focus on mythical thought in the post-Classical age and emphasises the mediating influence of the patristic tradition. Using Foucault's theory of comparison, he 'compares mythic topoi' in order to discover 'archeological isomorphisms', and adopting elements from reception theory and Structuralism, he built up his own mythographic method. *Germanistik* itself becomes central for von Graevenitz's epistemology of myths: 'The academic history of mythology had by necessity to lead into the history of methodology as practised by German literary scholars and into their professional self-understanding' (1987, p.292).

The renewed interest in the mythological mode tries to appropriate life and art neither in conceptual, nor in other logical or rational forms. It should instead be seen as an attempt to rediscover a mythical totality believed to be lost, where the distinctive borders between subject and object are removed. Wunberg's study *Wiedererkennen*, though outside the bounds of Post-Modernism, may illustrate this approach since it focuses on aesthetic perception within a consumer society. Modernity is seen here as coinciding with the European Industrial Revolution and as producing an 'information surplus' to which the individual reacts with oblivion (1983, p.21). The aesthetic perception of the subject is defined as *anagnorisis*; it operates within the polarities of oblivion and recognition and is thought to redefine the borders between aesthetic object and subject in such a manner as to bring about a new totality claim, a claim which had been perceived as under threat since the end of Hegelian philosophy. Representatives of the mythological school are at one with Post-Structuralists in their opposition to modernist logocentrism and instead seek to bridge the division in the self between the conscious and the unconscious.

The Dissolution of the Subject and the Disinterested Character of Art

Bohrer's most recent book applies a deconstructionist methodology to the subject within the later Romantic movement (cf. Anthony Phelan's comments on p.194 below). By using the term 'aesthetic' as an alternative to 'subjective', Bohrer assumes the post-modernist view that art lies outside any given socio-economic context, occupying a separate ontological site. According to Bohrer, 'aesthetic subjectivity' began in about 1810 and manifested itself in diaries and fictionalised letters. In contrast to the traditional notion of the autonomous subject, rooted within the Enlightenment, Bohrer posits a new 'aesthetic subjectivity' which exists outside of the tradition of rationality and history, and which, based on imaginative-aesthetic categories, is believed to be more condition than essence. Bohrer defines 'aesthetic subjectivity' as follows: 'Its experience of itself always transcends consciousness, either in its dependence on the monumentalism of an experience of the here and now which cannot be transferred or attached to the cultural text, or in its transcendence of the isolated Self into the trans-subjective sphere of nature (death, love)' (1987, p.12). In the twentieth century, Bohrer maintains that this 'aesthetic subjectivity' emerged in the works of Kafka, Rilke, Musil and others; found itself in opposition to the 'closed-off subjectivism' ('verschlossener Subjektivismus') of modernity; and offered in exchange a 'programme of the bared heart', a reference to Baudelaire's 'Mon coeur mis à nu'. The reference suggests that the emerging 'subject', being ontologically separate from any given life-world, can afford to expose itself and is no longer bound by social considerations. A key notion in Bohrer's investigations of 'aesthetic subjectivity' is authenticity – a concept which is closely related to Kierkegaard's search for the truth of his inner existence, as reflected in his diaries. Within the aesthetic condition, this quality becomes suspended or even sublimated and, once subsumed into the radical self-interests of its own subjectivity, is no longer connected to philosophical or historical categories.

Although based on some rather different premises, and responding far more exactly to the 1960s and the alleged crisis in literature, a parallel can be drawn between Bohrer and Christian Enzensberger, with the latter denying the very existence of authenticity and operating instead with the concepts of 'play' and 'disinterestedness' which are said to liberate art from any 'real' purpose in life. Arguing from a typically post-revolutionary position and accepting the ineffectiveness of literature in the socio-political domain, Enzensberger has withdrawn from the public into the private, subjective sphere, with personal experience as the starting-point for literary production and reception. He discusses literature within the dichotomy of sense and interest, arguing that the preponderance of the latter over the former has led literary criticism into an impasse which is marked by a deficit of meaning (1981, pp.61–2). Broadly speaking, interest is defined as self-interest: it has a materialist base, whereas sense is defined as a utopian dissolution of interest into disinterested beauty. The implied reference to a Kantian 'disinterestedness' (p.162) is symptomatic of Enzensberger's attempt to return to a pre-Marxist position, even if, as Hohendahl has demonstrated, large sections of Enzensberger's aesthetics owe a great deal to the Frankfurt School in general and Marcuse in particular (Hohendahl, 1980, pp.181–4). Enzensberger refers specifically to the early Frankfurt School,

Adorno in particular, where he discovers evidence of a definition of art based on countervailing interest, art opposed to the post-auratic 'interest claim' which he also finds in the work of the British Marxist Christopher Caudwell. Although Enzensberger applauds Caudwell's assertion that art derives from man's primary social activities – i.e. a common system of material production – he maintains that both Caudwell and Adorno failed to recognise their own class interests, misunderstood the illusory function of *all* art (not just the bourgeois form) and consistently saw art as a weapon in the class struggle (1981, pp.284–5).

From a Marxist point of view, Enzensberger's attitude is reactionary in that he accepts that literature no longer serves social interests and so might once more become a refuge for the privileged. Because the reader or spectator identifies with the fictitious hero, he or she severs all connections with the real world. Similarly, although art may be able to regain access to life, it can do so only after it has divested itself of the political and social dimensions – a process by means of which Enzensberger attempts to leave behind the political agitation of the 1960s without dissociating himself completely from the aesthetic considerations of the Frankfurt School and the 'German tradition'.

A Feminist Aesthetics

Whilst the origins of a feminist aesthetics in West Germany fall chronologically in the neo-conservative period, their relation with feminism in general makes any categorisation somewhat difficult, given the controversial and highly complex nature of the subject. Nevertheless, its themes and styles of argument justify its discussion within the general framework of Post-Modernism. The 1968 feminist movement had been declining since the early 1970s, and by the mid-1970s a 'New Feminism' was establishing itself. In 1976, several incidents combined to put this new movement on the map: the feminist journal *Courage* was founded, followed by *Emma* a year later; the first 'Summer School for Women' was held in West Berlin; and the influential journals *Ästhetik und Kommunikation*, *Kursbuch* and *Alternative* featured articles on feminist aesthetics.[3]

3. For further information on feminist aesthetics, see *New German Critique*, no.27 (1984) and no.31 (1985). These issues are devoted to feminist aesthetics with articles by Biddy Martin, Helen Fehervary, Jessica Benjamin, Carol Poore, Michael Schneider, Sigrid Weigel and Miriam Hansen. A recent series of German publications, edited by Renate Berger and Sigrid Weigel, and entitled *Frau und Literatur* has appeared in the Verlag Argumente, West Berlin. Judging by my own

The Unacknowledged Legislator of the Text

A topography of feminist aesthetics illustrates the German movement's close links with modern feminism worldwide and with the Ecology Movement and other cultural fringe groups in particular. Such connections also suggest that traditional academic institutions played a less active role in its inception. The proponents of a feminist aesthetic today are to be found primarily in such industrial cities of North Germany as Hamburg, Berlin, Cologne, Bielefeld, Düsseldorf and Dortmund, as well as Frankfurt and Munich. The 'mandarin' tradition of German universities with its conservative, professorially dominated character and penchant for abstract theorising has been reluctant to accept both the inter-disciplinary and the more concrete nature of women's studies programmes (Altbach, 1984, p.464).

Looking at feminist aesthetics as an outsider, one is immediately struck by its discursive style and deconstructionist approach – theory being associated with masculine rigour, competitive ambition and the fraudulent claim to objectivity made by male science. Gisela Ecker includes inwardness, 'illumination in the here and now', the use of the continuous present, the muted, multiple or absent *telos*, a fascination with process and a horizontal world amongst the important features of women's writings and pleads for 'the integration of ... "kitchen table discourse" into writing (even academic), the various forms of abstention from competition, the gesture of undoing hierarchies in all art forms' (1985, p.17). Indeed, the standard (male) intellectual approach is contrasted with post-structuralist 'writing the body', a style which is open to instinctual drives and desires emerging from the unconscious; which applies 'body metaphors of fluidity'; and which often advocates 'a narcissistic return to symbiotic wholeness' (Ecker, 1985, p.18). Silvia Bovenschen advocates the communication of 'specifically feminine modes of perception' by returning to individual examples of female creativity which, rather than pursuing a universal female vision, evince 'women's manner of looking at things' (1985, pp.31 and 37). What is being attempted here is a deconstructionist re-evaluation of traditional (male) values, 'the attempt to revitalise that "Other" which was excluded from culture along with the female sex' (Weigel, 1985, p.76). Indeed, the project of balancing out a one-sidedly cerebral approach can, it is argued, lead to new feminine values including 'continuity, the unconscious, the rhythmic, the archaic', to the

---

inter-library loan search, much of this information has yet to be absorbed by British academics. The Arbeitsstelle für feministische Literaturwissenschaft at the Literaturwissenschaftliche Seminar of the University of Hamburg, directed by Sigrid Weigel, Inge Stephan and Marianne Schüller, can provide further information.

demand for a new creativity based on 'female fantasies', and to 'pictures of that which is not, sketches that make future-music, engender future-desires' (Altbach, 1984, p.461). According to this aesthetic, a general feminisation of art would lead to a new creativity and overcome the present cultural crisis which manifests itself in the various proclamations of the death of art (Bovenschen, 1985, p.50).

In line with other post-modern schools of thought, the debate about feminist aesthetics centres on myth and a new concept of subjectivity – in this case the 'myth of non-alienated expression of gender and sexual identity' and a subjectivity which 'is a compound of what is expressed through the symbolic order and of what reaches back into pre-Oedipal and pre-verbal experience, with the unconscious emerging through gaps and fissures of what is expressed in language' (Ecker, 1985, pp.19–20). The new feminist aesthetics in West Germany has been profoundly influenced by French post-structuralist philosophers such as Barthes, Lacan, Derrida and, to a slightly lesser extent, Foucault, and also by the French post-structuralist feminists Julia Kristeva and Hélène Cixous. Indeed, Ecker stresses the importance of Derrida, Kristeva and Cixous in the deconstruction of Western phallocentric thinking, whilst Sigrid Weigel recognises some pitfalls in the psychological approaches of Cixous and Luce Irigaray, since they define the feminine system, in opposition to male principles, from too biological an angle.

To an outsider, the biological approach of a feminist aesthetics is its most problematic aspect since the development of an essentially female counter-culture would have not only to overthrow post-Aristotelian Western civilisation – in itself an unrealistic undertaking – but also to replace a phallocentric system with a uterocentric one. Thus, it would implicitly negate its claim to be abolishing a system of domination and aggression. Marxist feminists have seen this problem and have rejected the notion of a universal femininity. In West Germany, the alienation of feminists from the left seems stronger than in other countries: this is presumably the consequence of conflicts between the women's movement and a male-dominated Socialist German Student Federation (SDS) in the late 1960s. Also unacceptable to the school of feminine aesthetics is the Bloomsbury notion of *androgyny*, since it 'only prescribes a gender dichotomy in a much deeper and more significant way because it eternalises that dichotomy in terms of *social* gender roles' (Weigel, 1985, p.77).

Furthermore, despite accepting that there are certain similarities to colonised cultures, West German feminists seem to reject any suggestion that their situation and emancipatory problems are comparable with those of a sub-culture (Kreuzer, 1987, p.306). Nevertheless, there does seem to be considerable overlap between the programme of a feminist aesthetics, feminist novels by such writers as Karin Struck, Verena Stefan and Christa Wolf, and the Greens' programme. In all three cases, the values propagated by matriarchal art are intended to demonstrate 'nature's unity with human beings as opposed to nature's exploitation and utilisation by men . . . It shows the erotic to be the strongest creative force as opposed to devaluing and suppressing it as the ascetic patriarchal religions and moral systems have done' (Göttner-Abendroth, 1985, p.93).

Such sentiments reveal a certain common ancestry (like the hippy flower power movement) and a common tradition – indicating once more the proximity of feminine aesthetics and other post-modern movements to the 'Cultural Revolution' of the 1960s. And yet, in common with other branches of the post-modern movement, representatives of a feminist aesthetics have sought to overcome the cultural pessimism of the late 1960s. In rejecting the traditional Hegelian notion of a culture based on the synthesis of classical antiquity and Christianity, attempting to find a new function for art, and opening up the borders between art and other life-forms, the feminist aestheticians employ a relatively utopian, but new and vigorous attitude to literature and literary criticism. It is too early for us to assess the success of such post-modern approaches. It may well be that Post-Modernism has exhausted the potential of the Frankfurt School and that their own approaches, in common with those of other contemporary critics, simply signal the end of the post-Hegelian school of aesthetics. The development of literature in the 1970s and 1980s suggests that the proclaimed death of literature, morality and philosophy has been yet another overstatement, repeating the Hegelian diagnosis of the end of the period of art.

The new directions discussed above are somewhat reminiscent of the literary critical trends in Britain between the wars. There, too, we witnessed a change of emphasis from the search for the 'Just City' in the 1930s to the 1950s pose of the 'Wise Fool' who is 'seriously unserious' and who can only produce artificial paradigms of reality, set in an anagogical order. Both then and now, the resulting balance between play and reality is paradoxical and difficult to maintain; and just as the 1930s gave way to the 1950s, which were, in turn, overtaken by the 1960s, so the post-modernist position too, will one day, surely, be replaced by a new stance which once more declares literature as a criticism of life.

References

Adorno, T. (1967) 'Résumé über Kulturindustrie' in *Ohne Leitbild*, Suhrkamp, Frankfurt/Main, pp.60–71

Adorno, T. (1970) 'Aesthetische Theorie' in G. Adorno and R. Tiedemann (eds), *Gesammelte Schriften*, 19 vols., Suhrkamp, Frankfurt/Main, vol.7, pp.7–387

Altbach E. (1984) 'The New German Women's Movement' in *Signs: Journal of Women in Culture and Society*, 9, no.31, 454–69

Benjamin, W. (1977), *Gesammelte Schriften*, 12 vols., Suhrkamp, Frankfurt/Main, vols.I, 2 and II, 2

Berg, J. (1981) 'Literatur in der Bundesrepublik: Literatur in der Restaurationsphase' in J. Berg et al. (eds), *Sozialgeschichte der deutschen Literatur von 1918 bis zur Gegenwart*, Fischer, Frankfurt/Main, pp.565–645

Blumenberg, H. (1979) *Arbeit am Mythos*, Suhrkamp, Frankfurt/Main

Böhlich, W. (1969) 'Autodafé', *Kursbuch*, no.15, 'Kursbogen'

Bohrer, K.H. (1981) 'Die Antizipation beim literarischen Werturteil. Über die analytische Illusion', in *Plötzlichkeit: Zum Augenblick des ästhetischen Scheins*, Suhrkamp, Frankfurt/Main, pp.29–43

Bohrer, K.H. (1987) *Der romantische Brief: Die Entstehung ästhetischer Subjektivität*, Hanser, Munich

Bovenschen, S. (1985) 'Is there a Feminine Aesthetics?' in Ecker, pp.23–51

Bürger, C. (1983) 'Arbeit an der Geschichte' in K.H. Bohrer (ed.), *Mythos und Moderne*, Suhrkamp, Frankfurt/Main, pp.493–507

Bürger, P. (1981) 'The Significance of the Avant-garde for Contemporary Aesthetics: A Reply to Jürgen Habermas', *New German Critique*, no.22, 19–22

Bürger, P. (1983a) 'Das Altern der Moderne' in L. von Friedeburg and J. Habermas (eds), *Adorno Konferenz*, Suhrkamp, Frankfurt/Main, pp.177–80

Bürger, P. (1983b) 'Institution Literatur und Modernisierungsprozeß' in *Zum Funktionswandel der Literatur*, Suhrkamp, Frankfurt/Main, pp.9–33

Burger, H. (1941) 'Die deutsche Sendung im Bekenntnis der Dichter' in *Von deutscher Art in Sprache und Dichtung*, 5 vols., Kohlhammer, Stuttgart and Berlin, vol.5, pp.305–39

Cassirer, E. (1964) *Philosophie der symbolischen Formen, Zweiter Teil, Das mythische Denken*, Wissenschaftliche Buchgesellschaft, Darmstadt

Dyck, J. (1985) 'Stumm und ohne Hoffnung: Totale Paralyse der Germanistik', *Die Zeit*, 14 June 1985

Eagleton, T. (1985) 'Capitalism, Modernism and Postmodernism', *New Left Review*, no.152, 60–73

Ecker, G. (1985) *Feminist Aesthetics*, The Women's Press, London

Enzensberger, C. (1981) *Literatur und Interesse*, revised edn, Hanser, Munich

Enzensberger, H.M. (1968) 'Gemeinplätze, die neueste Literatur betreffend', *Kursbuch*, no.15, 187–97

Foucault, M. (1977) *Language, Counter-Memory, Practice: Selected Essays and Interviews*, ed. D. Bouchard, Cornell U.P., Ithaca and New York
Frank, M. (1982) *Der kommende Gott: Vorlesungen über die neue Mythologie*, Suhrkamp, Frankfurt/Main
Frank, M. (1983) 'Die Dichtung als "Neue Mythologie"' in K.H. Bohrer (ed.), *Mythos und Moderne*, Suhrkamp, Frankfurt/Main, pp.15–41
Fügen, N. (1970) *Die Hauptrichtungen der Literatursoziologie*, Bouvier, Bonn
Fügen, N. (1971) *Wege der Literatursoziologie*, Luchterhand, Neuwied and Berlin
Gadamer, H.-G. (1965) *Wahrheit und Methode: Grundzüge einer philosophischen Hermeneutik*, 2nd edn, Niemeyer, Tübingen
Goldmann, L. (1966) *Dialektische Untersuchungen*, Luchterhand, Neuwied and Berlin
Goldmann, L. (1967) *Weltflucht und Politik: Dialektische Studien zu Pascal und Racine*, Luchterhand, Neuwied and Berlin
Göttner-Abendroth, H. (1985) 'Nine Principles of a Matriarchal Aesthetic' in Ecker, pp.81–95
Graevenitz, G. von (1987) *Mythos: Zur Geschichte einer Denkgewohnheit*, Metzler, Stuttgart
Grossman, A. and Lennox, S. (1987) 'The Shadow of the Past', *The Women's Review of Books*, 4, no.12, 15
Habermas, J. (1977) 'Stumpf gewordene Waffen aus dem Arsenal der Gegenaufklärung: An Prof. Kurt Sontheimer' in F. Duve, H. Böll and K. Staeck (eds), *Briefe zur Verteidigung der Republik*, Rowohlt, Reinbek b. Hamburg, pp.54–72
Habermas, J. (1979) 'Consciousness Raising or Redemptive Criticism: The Contemporaneity of Walter Benjamin', *New German Critique*, no.17, 30–59
Habermas, J. (1980) 'Die Moderne – ein unvollendetes Projekt', *Die Zeit*, 19 September 1980
Habermas, J. (1981) 'Modernity versus Postmodernity', *New German Critique*, no.22, 3–15
Hamm, P. (1968) 'Der Großkritiker: Literaturkritik als Anachronismus' in *Kritik/von wem/für wen/wie? Eine Selbstdarstellung der Kritiker*, ed. P. Hamm, Hanser, Munich, pp.20–39
Haug, W.F. (1983) *Kritik der Warenästhetik*, Suhrkamp, Frankfurt/Main
Heidegger, M. (1950) 'Der Ursprung des Kunstwerkes' in *Holzwege*, Vittorio Klostermann, Frankfurt/Main, pp.7–68
Heine, H. (1972) 'Die Romantische Schule' in *Säkularausgabe*, 27 vols., Akademie-Verlag, Berlin-GDR, vol.8, pp.7–118
Hinck, W. (1983) *Germanistik als Literaturkritik*, Suhrkamp, Frankfurt/Main
Hohendahl, P.-U. (1980) 'Literatur und Interesse: Eine politische Ästhetik von Christian Enzensberger' in R. Grimm and J. Hermand (eds), *Basis: Jahrbuch für deutsche Gegenwartsliteratur*, 10, 178–93
Huyssen, A. and Scherpe, K.-H. (eds) (1986) *Postmoderne: Zeichen eines*

kulturellen Wandels, Rowohlt, Reinbek b. Hamburg

Iser, W. (1969) 'Überlegungen zu einem literarischen Studienmodell' in J. Kolbe (ed.), *Ansichten einer künftigen Germanistik*, Hanser, Munich, pp.193–208

Iser, W. (1986) 'Changing Functions of Literature' in J.P. Stern (ed.), *London German Studies*, vol.3, Institute of Germanic Studies, London, pp.162–80

Jauss, H. (1969) 'Paradigmawechsel in der Literaturwissenschaft', *Linguistische Berichte*, 3, 44–55

Jauss, H. (1970) 'Literaturgeschichte als Provokation der Literaturwissenschaft' in *Literatur als Provokation*, Suhrkamp, Frankfurt/Main, pp.144–207 (E.T. as 'Literary History as a Challenge to Literary Theory' in *Toward an Aesthetic of Reception*, Minnesota U.P., Minneapolis, 1982, pp.3–45)

Jauss, H. (1977), *Aesthetische Erfahrung und literarische Hermeneutik*, vol.I, Fink, Munich, 1977

Jay, M. (1984) *Marxism and Totality: The Adventures of a Concept from Lukács to Habermas*, Polity Press, Cambridge

Johnson, P. (1987) 'An Aesthetics of Negativity/An Aesthetics of Reception: Jauss's Dispute with Adorno', *New German Critique*, no.42, 51–70

Kayser, W. (1961) *Das sprachliche Kunstwerk*, 7th edn, Francke, Berne and Munich

Klein, J. (1974) 'Die Arbeit der kritischen Literaturwissenschaft als einer literatursoziologisch orientierten Disziplin', *Neuere Sprachen*, 73, 217–25

Kreuzer, H. (1987) 'Vom "Sein" zur "Postmoderne": Streiflichter auf vier Dekaden der Literatur und Literaturwissenschaft im westlichen Deutschland' in P.M. Lützeler, H. Lehnert and G.S. Williams (eds), *Zeitgenossenschaft: Zur deutschsprachigen Literatur im 20 Jahrhundert*, Athenäum, Frankfurt/Main, pp.296–324 (E.T. in an abbreviated form constitutes the first essay in this volume)

Kurz, P.K. (1987) *Apokalyptische Zeit: Zur Literatur der mittleren 80er Jahre*, Knecht, Frankfurt/Main

Lämmert, E. (1969) 'Das Ende der Germanistik und ihre Zukunft' in J. Kolbe (ed.), *Ansichten einer künftigen Germanistik*, Hanser, Munich, pp.79–105

Löwenthal, L. (1964) *Literatur und Gesellschaft*, Luchterhand, Neuwied and Berlin

Marcuse, H. (1964) *One-Dimensional Man: Studies in the Ideology of Advanced Industrial Society*, Routledge and Kegan Paul, London

Mosler, P. (1977) *Was wir wollten, was wir wurden: Studentenrevolte – zehn Jahre danach*, Rowohlt, Reinbek b. Hamburg

Schmidt, B. (1986) *Postmoderne – Strategie des Vergessens*, Luchterhand, Darmstadt and Neuwied

Schneider, P. (1965) 'Die Mängel der gegenwärtigen Literaturkritik', *Neue deutsche Hefte*, no.7, 98–123

Schonauer, F. (1981) 'Literaturkritik in der BRD' in M. Durzak (ed.),

Deutsche Gegenwartsliteratur: Ausgangspositionen und aktuelle Entwicklungen, Reclam, Stuttgart, pp.404–24

Staiger, E. (1955) *Die Kunst der Interpretation*, Atlantis, Zurich

Strelka, J. (1978) *Methodologie der Literaturwissenschaft*, Niemeyer, Tübingen

Wallach Bologh, R. (1987) 'Max Weber on Erotic Love: A Feminist Inquiry' in S. Lash and S. Whimster (eds), *Max Weber, Rationality and Modernity*, Allen and Unwin, London, pp.242–59

Weigel, S. (1985) 'Double Focus: On the History of Women's Writing' in Ecker, pp.59–81

Weimann, R. (1973) '"Rezeptionsästhetik" und die Krise der Literaturgeschichte', *Weimarer Beiträge*, 19, no.8, 5–33

Wilson, H. (1986) 'Critical Theory's Critique of Social Science: Episodes in a Changing Problematic from Adorno to Habermas, Part 2', *History of European Ideas*, 7, 287–302

Wolf, C. (1985) 'A Letter about Unequivocal and Ambiguous Meaning, Definiteness and Indefiniteness; about Ancient Conditions and New View-Scopes; about Objectivity' in Ecker pp.95–108

Wunberg, G. (1983) *Wiedererkennen: Literatur und ästhetische Wahrnehmung in der Moderne*, Gunter Narr, Tübingen

–3–

Towards a Systematic Outline of an Integrative Theory of Literary History

MICHAEL TITZMANN

Introduction

In the following pages I wish to establish a terminological and methodological framework within which to discuss the history of literature and which must fulfil the following three conditions. First, it must include as many as possible of the theoretical and terminological distinctions that are needed for an adequate account of literary history, and it should be so constructed as to be open to any other distinctions that may be subsequently emerge. Second, it must enable the methodological and terminological problems involved in literary historiography to be situated, as far as possible, within a systematic science of literature. It must therefore establish which problems in literary studies are logically prior to the process of writing literary history. And third, it must be open-ended and flexible enough to integrate all those problem areas and modes of investigation currently held to be relevant to literary history, no matter which of the currently competing methodologies have generated them. I shall therefore call the literary history which I am proposing an *integrative literary history*.

My argument is grounded in two kinds of presupposition. Theoretically, I shall assume that literary science, like any other branch of science (see Stegmüller, 1969) must satisfy the elementary rules of logic and scientific investigation. Thus, the concepts used by literary science must be defined or at least be capable of definition, and its propositions must be free from contradiction. Moreover, the claims made by literary science must be capable of direct or indirect empirical verification – direct in the sense that the basic assertions

Translated and adapted from the German by Steve Giles and Richard Sheppard.

involved in an argument must be directly confirmable by means of textual data, and indirect in the sense that those assertions which cannot be directly confirmed are deduced logically from those which can be. Terminologically, I shall presuppose the acceptability of two elementary sets of concepts. First, a series of formal, abstract concepts: element – relation – structure – system – function. Because these concepts are trans-disciplinary, they are also available to mathematicians, (social) historians, psychologists, sociologists, ethnologists, biologists and historians of science. Second, a series of concepts – sign, sign-system etc. – which derive from semiotics in general and linguistics in particular. These presuppositions permit various approaches, of course, and mine is semiotic and structuralist.

The Nature of Literary Historiography

The feasibility of writing literary history depends on two crucial preconditions: the existence of a set of texts and their chronological distribution. Hence the importance on the one hand of those concepts deriving from semiotics, since it is through them that we acquire our understanding of the signification of texts at any given time, and on the other, of editorial philology which, where necessary, reconstructs the definitive form of texts and dates them. Although a chronologically ordered set of texts constitutes the *events* which form the empirical basis of literary historiography, that discipline involves more than the mere listing of texts diachronically inasmuch as any given literary history is actually an abstraction based on a set of interpreted texts – i.e. a system which has been (re)constructed using that set of sub-systems which interpretative acts have created out of textual events.

If we are to (re)construct literary history, we first have to analyse or interpret texts; and in order to do this, we need a theory of interpretation (see Titzmann, 1977, for an attempt to show what such a theory might look like). All literary interpretation is grounded in a theory of interpretation which is either unconscious and implicit or conscious and explicit. As science has to make its presuppositions and procedures explicit in order to make them accessible to rational examination and verification, a science of literature is inconceivable without a rational theory of interpretation which can, at least in principle, be made explicit. Such a theory would consist of a set of (defined) descriptive terms (concepts) and a set of interpretative rules. We need a set of descriptive terms to be able to distinguish and label regularly occurring and significant textual structures. Such an inventory has its origins in various theories: linguistic theories, which deal with syntax, semantics, pragmatics and natural language; or poetological theories, which deal with the structural possibilities of texts, metrical and rhetorical structures, speech acts and linguistic situations (see Wünsch, 1989), narrative structures (see Titzmann, 1980, p.15), and genres (see Hempfer, 1973). Although, in the absence of such an inventory, we will have to refer to relevant structures in *ad hoc* terms, the second component of a theory of interpretation must, as an absolute requirement, be given more precise definition. That is to say, we require a set of interpretative rules to establish which operations are valid when we produce a model of the text which, using terms derived from mathematical logic, sets out to map its most relevant features and their interrelationships. These rules must provide us with an apparatus which, when interpretative disagreements arise, enables us to decide which interpretation is scientifically acceptable and to what extent that is so.

It is, however, vital to make a fundamental distinction between those interpretations of texts which are produced by literary science and the reception of texts by contemporary or later readers (see Titzmann, 1977, and especially Wünsch, 1989). By this I mean that one cannot replace the interpretation of any given text by an account of the history of its reception for the simple reason that we can obtain information about the reception *of* texts only *from* other texts – i.e. by means of interpretation. It is, of course, true that any given interpretation is itself an act of reception. But because the reception of texts by non-professional readers is not bound by scientifically acceptable norms and rules, I will assume for the purposes of this essay that only those acts of reception which attempt to comply with such norms and rules can count as textual analysis or interpretation. This is not to say that the history of any given text's reception does not provide the literary historian with important raw data. Nevertheless, the history of literature is much more than the history of its reception, so that reception has to be seen as an important, but ultimately subordinate aspect of literary history.

The Hermeneutic Problem

An interpretation is historically adequate only if, within the scientific framework so far established, it reconstructs the reading which a text had for an optimal or ideal reader in the culture and period by and for which it was originally produced. Such a reader would be endowed with all the intellectual and cultural presuppositions required to understand the texts which were available in the period in question. Interpretation can, of course, make use of a hermeneutic apparatus unavailable to the original readers – but only if those readers could, in principle, have perceived and paraphrased the structures brought into relief by that apparatus in terms of their own intellectual and linguistic system. The evidence that an ideal reader could have met this requirement can, of course, be provided only *after* the putative intellectual system has been reconstructed. Thus, an interpretation which complied with the norms and rules of a scientifically acceptable theory of interpretation, but for which the above evidence could not be provided, needs to be distinguished from a historically adequate interpretation. In fact, the interpretation of any given text will almost inevitably be incomplete, simply because a complete interpretation would have to elucidate all the meanings of the textual structures it has revealed. Although such an interpretation is theoretically utopian, an incomplete interpretation can, nevertheless, be both adequate and scientifically accurate.

Although, during the process of interpretation, texts – the raw material of literary historiography – can be analysed as complex semantic systems, they are never isolated systems. Rather, they stand in a diversity of relationships to a complex environment consisting of various other interrelated systems. Any theory of interpretation must take account of this situation by formulating interpretative rules which specify what data from what contexts may be used, under what conditions, and in what ways. Only those data may be used which were elements of contemporary cultural knowledge and whose structural relevance to the text can be demonstrated. At the same time, although an interpreter's acquaintance with contemporary cultural knowledge may enable him or her to deduce conclusions from a text that could not have been deduced otherwise, any interpretative conclusion reached on the basis of textual data alone is always valid, provided that the rules of science are observed, and cannot be falsified by the incorporation of cultural knowledge. This principle is binding in two respects. First, if we did not accept its validity, it would be impossible for a text to be creative, innovative or original, since, in order to be so, it must either contradict or seek to extend established knowledge. And second, the reconstruction of cultural knowledge would also be impossible. In the case of the present day, we can infer the cultural knowledge of groups and individuals not only from their verbal utterances but also from their observable non-verbal behaviour. Where the past is concerned, however, we can infer such knowledge only from their semiotic products – above all from their linguistic texts. Since, to a very great extent, we obtain cultural knowledge by interpreting texts, our familiarity with this knowledge, logically speaking, cannot be presupposed in every scientifically correct interpretative conclusion. In other words, although the interpretation of a text can *tend* towards completeness if it incorporates contemporary cultural knowledge, it can be scientifically correct and/or historically adequate even without reference to such knowledge.

Textual Meaning and Cultural Knowledge

We are now in a position to be more specific about what we understand by textual meaning. The meaning of a text is the set of all those propositions which can be deduced from the text – with or without reference to contemporary cultural knowledge – plus all those propositions which can be logically derived from them. I use the term 'propositions' here advisedly, in order to distinguish them from the sentences which constitute them, since the same proposition can follow from various sentences in the same text or in different texts (see Bellert, 1970 and 1973; Titzmann, 1977 and 1981). Moreover, propositions can be explicit or implicit. Explicit propositions have a semantic equivalent in a series of signs on the text's surface, whereas implicit propositions have no such equivalent and thus represent tacit presuppositions or implications of the set of linguistic signs which constitute the text.

The concept of cultural knowledge is fundamental not only to a theory of interpretation, but also to an integrative literary history such as I am proposing here, and it consists in the set of all those propositions which the members of any given cultural system hold to be true. Furthermore, as we have no direct access to the minds of members of past cultures, their knowledge must be reconstructed from the texts which their culture produced. I should add that I am using the term 'knowledge' in the broad sense established by recent work in the sociology of knowledge (see Berger and Luckmann, 1971, and Jörg Schönert's essay below pp.71–94), the history of science (see Kuhn, 1963), and the history of knowledge (see Foucault, 1984). In other words, the concept of knowledge includes all those statements which members of a culture explicitly or implicitly believe to be true. Similarly, every proposition which forms part of a system of cultural knowledge can be termed an epistemological element, and the epistemic system of any given culture consists in the systematically ordered set of all such elements. While general knowledge is the set of those epistemological elements which most members of a culture hold to be true, group-specific knowledge involves only those epistemological elements which are held in common by the members of one or more groups. These groups can be constituted using a wide variety of social criteria: age, sex, social status, education, profession, religion, political affiliation and other ideological positions. Because group-specific knowledge can be relevant to the process of literary interpretation, our theory of interpretation must identify the conditions which apply here too.

We must first of all distinguish between conscious and non-conscious knowledge – and by the latter term I mean knowledge which is so self-evident that it does not usually impinge upon the consciousness of individuals. This form of knowledge can, however, become conscious if, for example, it is confronted with a different epistemic system peculiar to an alien group or culture. And knowledge can be described as conscious if it materialises as an explicit proposition (or set of propositions) in a sufficiently large number of texts. If, however, such knowledge normally occurs only as an implicit proposition and is to be found as an explicit proposition in only a few texts, then we may say that it is potentially conscious as far as that culture is concerned. But if a proposition is implicit in a large number of texts and never materialises in them explicitly, then it is impossible to decide whether it is a conscious or potentially conscious epistemological element. Furthermore, cultural knowledge includes both pre-theoretical everyday knowledge (which may be partly implicit) and theoretical knowledge peculiar to theologies, philosophies and sciences. Anything about which a culture can make an assertion can be the subject of propositional knowledge. Consequently, cultural knowledge includes knowledge about events and individuals; regularities and systems; values and norms; actual behaviour; texts and sign-systems; problems, together with their solutions and problem-solving strategies; and both indigenous and alien knowledge.

The transmission and inhibition of knowledge in any given culture are regulated more or less systematically by social structures and institutions and are two of the central elements in any process of socialisation (see Jörg Schönert's essay below, pp.81–5). Indeed, cultural knowledge underpins the production, distribution and reception of texts, for it is via such knowledge that texts are correlated with other structures of the socio-cultural system. Generally speaking, the affective and emotional structures of the subjects of any given culture are also elements in the epistemic system – at least to the extent that they involve cognitive and evaluative elements. Members of a culture learn (and then know) which emotions their culture distinguishes and denotes linguistically; they also know which emotions are permissible, expected or forbidden in which type of situation and in relation to which class of person.

Cultural knowledge is not, however, given: we have to infer it, primarily from a culture's texts, and this has four important consequences. First, interpretation is necessary in the reconstruction of cultural knowledge. Second, as not every proposition in a text amounts to an epistemological element, we require, in addition to general rules of scientific interpretation, supplementary rules for the reconstruction of any given epistemic system which would enable us to select, from the sum total of propositions, those which are genuinely epistemological elements for the cultural group in question. Third, because we are concerned not with the assumptions made by individual subjects, but with those made by groups or cultures, we need to identify a statistically representative corpus of texts that has been selected from the total number of texts available to us. Since all texts are not of equal cultural status, that corpus must be both qualitatively and quantitatively representative. In other words, it must include those texts which contemporaries perceived as being prototypical and exemplary. And fourth, because we are trying to reconstruct what a culture believed during a specific era, we will need to establish a system of periodisation in terms of epochs. These will have been abstracted from various complexes of texts, and their fundamental characteristics and structures will have been seen to remain constant over a period of time.

Texts and Literary Texts

So far we have spoken only of texts in general, rather than so-called literary texts. But because poetological theories deal with textual structures that are not specific to literature; and because hermeneutic theories formulate interpretative rules that can be used outside the field of literature, we will need to refer to both kinds of text in order to reconstruct literary history. Nevertheless, because we are primarily concerned here with the history of literary texts, we must establish what we understand by that concept. Moreover, given that the debate in the 1970s about the criteria of 'literariness' got nowhere, we shall adopt a pragmatic concept of literature, based on the perceptions of contemporaries and the cultural knowledge which these imply. Thus, on this basis, we can say that literature is the set of all those texts which a particular culture considers to be literary or which manifest the same structures as such texts, while noting at the same time that the sum total of texts produced by any given culture is not neatly divisible into two simple categories labelled, respectively, 'literature' and 'non-literature'. Quite obviously, further valid sub-categorisations can also be made – e.g. 'textual type', 'genre' and 'discourse' (see Hempfer, 1973; Titzmann, 1988).

Culture as Epistemic System

We are now in a position to make some important general assertions. To begin with, the intellectual structure of any given epoch consists in an ordered set of basic epistemological premises and can thus be reconstructed as a hierarchical set of propositions which forms the precondition for all other propositions. This intellectual structure includes categories and rules of thought, rules of formulation and basic postulates about the structure of reality. It thus regulates the production of knowledge in any given culture. At the same time, elements of that intellectual structure can also be elements of cultural knowledge – as is the case with logic and the theory of science. Because any given culture's implicit concept of reality involves ontological assumptions – basic postulates about the structure of reality – it inevitably determines what that culture holds to be (im)possible. Thus, the notion of a concept of reality is absolutely fundamental to literary science (see Wünsch, 1989). To give one example only: when a literary text is deemed 'fantastic', it involves phenomena which contradict the basic assumptions of the prevailing concept of reality, whereas it is deemed 'mimetic' if nothing within it contradicts those assumptions. On this principle, nineteenth-century 'Realism' is so designated *not* because its fictional worlds 'copy' the real world – something which is impossible anyway – but because nothing in those fictional worlds contradicts the prevailing concept of reality. In other words, nineteenth-century 'Realism' is 'realistic' because it devises worlds which are both possible *and* conceivable. Whatever appears as 'reality' to any given culture is always a cultural construct – a product of the interaction between its epistemic system and reality – and, moreover, whether or not individuals perceive or respond to data which contradict this construct will depend upon the strength of the epistemic system rather than on 'reality' as such.

Although a culture's epistemic system regulates and limits the ways in which individual subjects think and produce texts, such constraints do not preclude deviation, innovation, originality or creativity. Any new literary or non-literary text may attempt to transform the epistemic system – in terms of either the knowledge which the latter admits or its epistemological premises. But the text in question will achieve this aim only if its deviation from the norm is both perceived and accepted; and this will occur only to the extent that it fulfils the epistemic system's needs. Indeed, whether and to what degree such deviation is contemplated and ultimately accepted is itself functionally dependent on the state of the prevailing epistemic system. Thus, in the literary system of the seventeenth century, originality was ruled out *a priori*, whereas, ever since the *Sturm und Drang* movement of the late eighteenth century, originality has been regarded as an essential prerequisite.

The sum total of those texts, theories, cognitive sets and discourses which are relevant to the thinking of one or more of the cultural groups in any given historical period constitutes that period's intellectual synchrony. This includes not only texts produced within the period itself, but also texts from other periods and cultures that are debated within that period because they are still relevant to it. Thus, the intellectual synchrony of the Age of Goethe includes not only classical literature, but also various classical theories such as those of the four humours or the four elements. Conversely, Aristotelian physics was no longer part of the intellectual synchrony of the Age of Goethe because it had been replaced during the eighteenth century by the discourse of modern physics. Given the above discussion, it follows that the process of reception is not something isolated and autonomous. Rather, the data provided by reception history are indices of structures of knowledge, thinking and feeling, and involve all the various (inter-textual) ways in which texts refer to other texts, genres, discourses and epistemic systems. By now it will, I hope, be plain that I understand the concept of culture in a broad, ethnological sense (see Panoff and Perrin, 1973) – as the sum total of rule-governed or deviant human practices specific to a spatio-temporally bounded social system, together with the structures which underpin those practices or are generated by them. Thus, the epistemic system and forms of speech in which that system is manifested (and from which it can be reconstructed) form one component of a culture, so understood. The other comprises the social system in the narrower sense – i.e. social structuring in groups, strata and institutions, together with the set of socially coded practices and individual modes of behaviour.

Literature as a Cultural Sub-System

In its entirety, a culture consists of a set of sub-systems, which can themselves be subdivided further if necessary. Each of these sub-systems can have its own history in the sense that the temporal boundaries of cultural sub-systems may not coincide with those of social, economic and political systems. One such cultural sub-system is formed by what is designated 'literature'. One can, of course, write histories of literary sub-systems in isolation from their cultural and social context, and although that kind of literary historiography can provide accurate descriptions of literary structures and transformations within the literary sub-system, an integrative literary history of the kind that I am proposing can deal with its object more adequately. It is better able to account for the historical status of individual texts; describe their impact within the total historical process; correlate the literary sub-system with other sub-systems and analyse change in the literary sub-system.

Nevertheless, although literature is one aspect of a larger epistemic and social system, even an integrative literary history must begin by artificially isolating the literary sub-system from its broader context. The literary sub-system of any given epoch (which may include such further, heterogeneous sub-systems as textual types defined by formal or ideological characteristics) consists of basic propositions and cultural knowledge in the sense described above. These basic propositions can be derived either from individual texts or from the representative corpus as a whole; and they denote regularities in the literary sub-system such as generic conventions, values, norms, and the ideological and anthropological assumptions underlying any given text or set of texts. For example, one could without difficulty formulate a set of propositions to describe the educational trajectories followed by literary heroes in the Age of Goethe since these conform to a limited set of rules constitutive of this particular literary/anthropological sub-system. Furthermore, these trajectories (together with the propositions describing their shape) are closely bound up with other cultural modes of discourse (e.g. politics or theology) and the epistemic system as a whole.

The individuals and institutions which mediate or control the production, distribution and reception of literature are not part of the literary sub-system but of its extrinsic institutional context. Moreover, their nature and modes of operation are, on the whole, not immediately given to us but have to be inferred from other texts. Like the epistemic system as a whole, the literary sub-system is relatively autonomous in the sense that, although it has permanently to process extrinsic data, its own structures determine which data it processes and how. At first sight, it is true, literature seems to have various direct relationships to non-literary 'realities', whether these are cultural (involving intellectual or social history) or natural. But whenever a 'reality' is posited and 'literature' is produced or received, an epistemic system is already operating as an invisible but determining context. And if it is true that such an epistemic system determines whether or how 'reality' is perceived and interpreted, then it necessarily follows that literature never directly reflects reality as such but simply offers transcriptions of culturally determined ways of thinking about reality. It is not so much the French Revolution or the First World War which have a transformative impact on the literary sub-system, but rather the way in which such events are processed by existing cultural knowledge, which has itself been conditioned and regulated by the prevailing epistemic system. Reality is directly relevant to intellectual history but not to literary history; and although literature may contribute to the prevailing epistemic system by thematising 'realities' unarticulated by other modes of cultural discourse, it does so only within the conditions set by that epistemic system. Because the function of literature in any given epoch depends on and can be inferred from the specific relationships between the structures of the literary sub-system and those of the prevailing epistemic system, that function can be determined only when both the literary sub-system and the prevailing epistemic system have been reconstructed.

Change takes place in any given literary (sub-)system whenever a number of its fundamental constitutive propositions are transformed, and such changes can occur in the work of a single author, within a genre, or across the literary sub-system as a whole. As the theoretical problems raised here are the same in all three cases, I shall restrict myself to using the last one as an example. A change in the literary sub-system can occur if a text is innovative in structural terms, provided that these new structures are perceived and accepted – i.e. taken over by other texts. Whether or not deviant literary structures are positively received, so that such change can occur, is, of course, a function of either the literary sub-system or the epistemic system as a whole since, logically speaking, a change can occur only if it meets the needs of the cultural (sub-)system. The relative importance of the propositions undergoing transformation will determine whether such change can be described as *immanent*, leading merely to a new condition of the same sub-system, or *transcendent*, leading to a qualitatively new sub-system or epoch.

Either way, change is, in my view, a process dependent on systemic rationality in that it represents an attempt to solve problems which have developed within the system. Because the literary sub-system and its relations to its epistemic environment will determine what is perceived as a problem and what counts as a solution, any solution may lead to new problems. Thus, systemic rationality means that any given system can be said to behave rationally when it operates in terms of its own premises, even though these premises may be objectively erroneous.

References

Bellert, I. (1970) 'On a Condition of the Coherence of Texts', *Semiotika*, 2, 335–63

Bellert, I. (1973) 'On various Solutions of the Problem of Presupposition' in J.S. Petöfi and H. Rieser (eds), *Studies in Text Grammars*, Reidel, Dordrecht, pp.79–95

Berger, P. and Luckmann, T. (1971) *The Social Construction of Reality*, Penguin University Books, Harmondsworth

Broich, U. and Pfister, M. (eds) (1985) *Intertextualität: Formen, Funktionen, anglistische Fallstudien*, Niemeyer, Tübingen

Foucault, M. (1984) *The Foucault Reader*, ed. Paul Rabinow, Penguin, Harmondsworth

Hempfer, K. (1973) *Gattungstheorie*, Fink, Munich

Kuhn T. (1970) *The Structure of Scientific Revolutions*, Chicago U.P.

Lotman, J. (1972) *Die Struktur literarischer Texte*, Fink, Munich

Panoff, M. and Perrin, M. (1973) *Dictionnaire de l'Ethnologie*, Payot, Paris

Petöfi, J. (1979) *Text vs Sentence: Basic Questions of Text Linguistics*, 2 vols., Buske, Hamburg

Pfister, M. (1977) *Das Drama: Theorie und Analyse*, Fink, Munich

Renner, K. (1983) *Der Findling: Eine Erzählung von H. von Kleist und ein Film von G. Moorse. Prinzipien einer adäquaten Wiedergabe narrativer Strukturen*, Fink, Munich

Stegmüller, W. (1968–73) *Probleme und Resultate der Wissenschaftstheorie und analytischen Philosophie*, 4 vols., Springer, Berlin, Heidelberg and New York

Titzmann, M. (1977) *Strukturale Textanalyse: Theorie und Praxis der Interpretation*, Fink, Munich

Titzmann, M. (1980) 'Struktur, Strukturalismus' in K. Kanzog and A. Masser (eds), *Reallexikon der deutschen Literaturgeschichte*, 4 vols., de Gruyter, Berlin and New York, vol.4, pp.256–78

Titzmann, M. (1981a) 'Zum Verfahren der strukturalen Textanalyse – am Beispiel eines diskursiven Textes', *Analyse & Kritik: Zeitschrift für Sozialwissenschaften*, 3, 64–92

Titzmann, M. (1981b) 'Zur Beziehung von "Inhaltsanalyse" und "strukturaler Textanalyse"' in G. Bentele (ed.), *Semiotik und Massenmedien*, Ölschläger, Munich, pp.218–34

Titzmann, M. (1983) 'Probleme des Epochenbegriffs in der Literaturgeschichtsschreibung' in K. Richter and J. Schönert (eds), *Klassik und Moderne*, Metzler, Stuttgart, pp.98–131

Titzmann, M. (1989a) 'Theoretisch-methodologische Probleme einer Semiotik der Bild-Text-Relationen' in R. Brednich, F. Büttner, W. Harms and G. Jäger (eds), *Text und Bild, Bild und Text*, Niemeyer, Tübingen (forthcoming)

Titzmann, M. (1989b) 'Kulturelles Wissen – Diskurs – Denksystem: Zu einigen Grundbegriffen der Literaturgeschichtsschreibung', *Zeitschrift für französische Sprache und Literatur*, no.1, 1988, 47–61

Wünsch, M. (1989) *Die fantastische Literatur der frühen Moderne (1890–1930)*, (*Habilitationsschrift*, Munich, 1984), Fink, Munich

−4−

The Reception of Sociological Theory by West German Literary Scholarship, 1970–85

JÖRG SCHÖNERT

The Sociological Reorientation of Literary Studies

In the heyday of those critical pundits who inspired my generation's post-graduate theses, it was customary, when reading for a higher degree, not just to attend lectures in the philosophy department, but, because literary history was seen as an aspect of the history of ideas, to study philosophy as such. Nevertheless, as readers of this volume will by now be aware, the West German academic landscape changed during the 1960s in many ways. Whoever, like myself, began to study German literature in the early 1960s and wanted to be in touch with the intellectual innovators in his or her university, attended lectures given by sociologists and political scientists. And within the discipline of philosophy, it was, above all, theoreticians of science like Popper, Sneed and Stegmüller who stimulated academic interest across traditional subject boundaries. Indeed, for many students of the humanities at that time, the social sciences began to take over from philosophy as their touchstone; and for the vast majority of those who hoped to become teachers in secondary schools, the study of philosophy as a subsidiary subject was gradually supplanted first by educational theory and later by sociology and political science.

In 1962, there appeared the first edition of Jürgen Habermas's higher doctoral thesis *Strukturwandel der Öffentlichkeit: Untersuchungen zu einer Kategorie der bürgerlichen Gesellschaft*. Between 1962 and 1974, when the Luchterhand paperback came out, that book went through

German original written with the kind assistance of Lutz Danneberg (Hamburg), Friederike Meyer and Claus-Michael Ort (Munich); translated into English by Richard Sheppard.

six editions, so that, by the end of the 1960s, it was virtually impossible for a student to write an essay on the literary history of the late eighteenth century without using such fashionable concepts as 'repräsentative' versus 'bürgerliche Öffentlichkeit' ('typical' versus 'educated, upper middle-class reading public') and 'kulturräsonierendes und kulturkonsumierendes Publikum' ('cultural elites' as opposed to the 'broadly-based reading public who consumed the work produced and transmitted by the elites'). Furthermore, whoever considered themselves real, state-of-the-art professionals, knew how to build quotations into their essays from such texts as Reinhart Koselleck's *Kritik und Krise: Zur Pathogenese der bürgerlichen Welt* (1959) or Max Horkheimer's and Theodor W. Adorno's *Dialektik der Aufklärung* (1947) (E.T. as *Dialectic of Enlightenment,* 1973), not to mention socio-philosophical works by Walter Benjamin or socio-historical works by Werner Conze, Hans-Ulrich Wehler, Jürgen Kocka and Reinhart Koselleck.

Sociology, too, became one of the inspirational sources for a new mode of literary criticism[1] which set itself the task of discarding older, text-immanent methodologies. The proponents of 'new-style *Germanistik*' wanted to transform pre-theoretical 'literary criticism' into a theoretically based 'science of literature' and so, at the 1966 Germanists' conference in Munich, having rejected the notion of a literature which existed outside of social categories, they presented the history of the subject and its political involvement as a topic for discussion and entered the lists on behalf of 'literature and society'. Moreover, in the wake of the Grand Coalition's new policy towards the GDR, Germanists actually began to recognise and accept the kind of literary criticism which was being practised in East German universities, and which, being Marxist, normally had its institutional base within social science departments. At first, it should be added, West German critics of this persuasion could set only the concept of 'literary life' (with all its metaphorical implications of a natural and biological order)[2] against the more developed, albeit

1. On the early history of the discipline, see G. Hübinger, 'Literaturgeschichte als gesellschaftswissenschaftliche Disziplin: Ihre Begründung durch Georg Gottfried Gervinus', *Geschichte und Gesellschaft*, vol.11 (1983), pp.5–25.
2. For a discussion of this concept, see H. Kreuzer, 'Trivialliteratur als Forschungsproblem' (1965), *DVjs*, vol.41 (1967), pp.173–91; reprinted in H. Kreuzer, *Veränderungen des Literaturbegriffs* (Vandenhoeck and Ruprecht, Göttingen, 1975), pp.7–26 (especially pp.24–5). Other relevant titles include E. Becker and M. Dehn, *Literarisches Leben: Eine Bibliographie* (Verlag für Buchmarktforschung, Hamburg, 1968) and R. Wittmann, 'Die bibliographische Situation für die Erforschung des Literarischen Lebens im 19. Jahrhundert (1830–1880)' in *Buchmarkt und Lektüre im 18. und 19. Jahrhundert* (Niemeyer, Tübingen, 1983), pp.232–52.

dogmatically socialist, notion of a harmonious 'literary society' and the history of the social, economic and political preconditions of literature.

Although it is very tempting to give this essay a polemical bias in the light of the educational and professional experience of my generation of literary scholars, I shall resist that temptation and venture a somewhat drier account of the various sociological approaches to literature which have developed in West Germany over the last fifteen to twenty years and which are encapsulated in the list of references at the end of this article.[3] In doing that, I shall take as my basic assumption the widely accepted, albeit very general proposition that literature is both socially determined and a social determinant (see David Jenkinson's essay below, pp.243–60). This binary opposition should not, of course, be regarded as something static, but as something dynamic, for it is a reciprocal relationship and needs to be understood both in terms of the various modes of literary communication and in terms of the overall process of social change.

In a rigorously sociological discussion of literature's potential for affecting individuals and society as a whole, one would have to guard against a form of shorthand which is endemic among literary scholars. It is not the texts themselves which have an effect, but the *reading* of those texts – or, to put it another way, the active reception of those texts. Conversely, sociological elements find their way into texts only via the experiences of their authors and their authors' more or less conscious reactions to those experiences. On the other hand, if, when reading literary texts, we read certain socially determined complexes and collectively formed evaluations into their semantic structures and libidinal economies without asking how, in any given case, those elements have got there or how we have managed to recognise and abstract them, such a procedure is legitimate only because both the production and the reception of texts are determined by a patterned set of physiological and psychological processes and by internalised social norms.

To analyse such complex interrelationships, one would need to establish a theoretical framework like that implied in Siegfried J. Schmidt's concept of an empirical science of literature. Furthermore,

---

3. For a good survey of the subject, see J.-D. Müller, 'Literaturgeschichte/Literaturgeschichtsschreibung' in D. Harth and P. Gebhardt (eds), *Erkenntnis der Literatur: Theorien, Konzepte, Methoden der Literaturwissenschaft* (Metzler, Stuttgart, 1982), pp.195–227 and J. Schönert, 'The Social History of Literature: On the Present State of Distress in the Social History of German Literature', *Poetics*, vol.14 (1985), pp.303–19.

one would also need to develop a theory of the literary imagination and literary reception and learn to understand the ways in which authors, middle-men and readers are socialised.[4] To put it more precisely: if one compares authors from a given period with one another on the grounds that they are voicing an experiential complex which is typical of the period, then one has already made the assumption that one's chosen authors are, to a great extent, responding to that complex according to certain structural regularities and rules of literary production (cf. Michael Titzmann's remarks above, pp.62–4). Similarly, the fact that we, as readers of any given text, are able to read that text in comparable ways and ascribe a clear 'meaning' to it derives from the fact that we receive texts according to certain regularities and rules as well. Even literary specialists are subject to such socialisation, and when they, as a result of either haphazard or systematic reading, produce interpretations that are widely accepted, they are rewarded by the acclaim of those sections of the general public to which those interpretations make sense.

But in this paper, I wish, given Michael Titzmann's detailed discussion of them above, to bracket out such fundamental considerations about the relationships between social process and literary reception, base and superstructure, social process, discursive modes and symbolic systems,[5] and simply remark that they are foregrounded to a greater or lesser extent in all the various types of sociologically oriented literary scholarship to be discussed below, and ought, therefore, to be variously taken into account in any given case.

Social History, Sociology and the Interpretation of Texts

Accordingly, let me confine myself to the headings under which I have grouped the various texts in the bibliography at the end of this article; and if English-speaking readers are chagrined to find only German names and titles on that by no means exhaustive list, then that is because I am going to deal with matters which are, in the first

4. In this area, research is still in its infancy. See, for example, Norbert Groeben's work on the psychology of literature and, on the problems involved in literary comprehension, D. Meusch and R. Viehoff, 'Empirical Research in Understanding Literary Discourse' in A. Bokay, T. Olivi and J.S. Petöfi, *Research in Discourse Comprehension* (forthcoming).
5. On the theoretical status of analyses of social process in those areas of the social sciences concerned with culture, see O. Schwemmer, *Handlung und Struktur: Zur Wissenschaftstheorie der Kulturwissenschaften* (Suhrkamp, Frankfurt/Main, 1987).

place, highly relevant to the study of literature in Germany, albeit not the exclusive province of Germanists.

In the case of sociologically or socio-historically oriented modes of interpretation (Section 1 of my bibliography), the writers seem, to put it very simply, to be concerned to derive experiences from literary texts which can then be assimilated to their own conceptions of society and social processes. This kind of reading has its own traditions and categories for systematising the various types of relationship between text and society. It is, for example, interested in ideological perspectives – and here one thinks of Georg Lukács's concern to establish the class-specific ideological stances in any given text (something which Pierre Bourdieu, in recent years, has done in a more sophisticated way) –, in social motifs, social problems and literature as a ludic means of processing extra-literary problems.[6] Although, in the late 1960s, it was the ideas of Lukács above all from which the practitioners of 'ideological criticism' derived their inspiration, one could, where it was a case of sophisticated literary scholars from that early period seeking connections between sociological experience and the aesthetic structure of the work of art, sense the more or less explicit traces of Adorno's sociology of art, with its philosophical assumptions about the 'essence of art'.[7]

More recent studies of the sociology of texts[8] have stopped looking for the sociological determinants of aesthetic forms and content and turned their attention – as, for instance, in the case of Hans N. Fügen's attempt to establish a sociological interpretation of novels (1982) – towards sociologically determined processes which are said to be 'inscribed' in texts. That is to say: texts and genres are understood as models of specific social processes; and on the basis of patterns of social interaction, the interrelationships of fictional characters are stylised into 'scenes', 'constellations' and 'configurations'.[9] Although theoreticians like Fügen do, of course, acknowledge the difference between reality and fiction by stressing the model status of literary texts,[10] Fügen's approach represented a new way of

---

6. See K. Eibl, *Kritisch-rationale Literaturwissenschaft: Grundlagen zur erklärenden Literaturgeschichte* (Fink, Munich, 1976).
7. Cf. Scharfschwerdt (1977), pp.151–4 and 157–9; Voßkamp (1978), pp.15–18.
8. Cf. the programmatic account to be found in P. Zima, *Textsoziologie* (Metzler, Stuttgart, 1980).
9. See also B. Jendricke, 'Sozialgeschichte der Literatur: Neuere Konzepte der Literaturgeschichte und Literaturtheorie' in von Heydebrand, Pfau and Schönert (1988), pp.27–88 (especially pp.49–54).
10. In this respect, Fügen's approach is less impressive than Hans-Ulrich Mohr's more comprehensive one (1983 and 1985).

organising questions about the content of literary works in that he used categories derived from the sociological analysis of behaviour to describe the behaviour of fictional characters. Furthermore, as Wilhelm Voßkamp's concept of the 'sociology of novels' (1978) indicated,[11] the various literary genres, rooted as they are in various social processes, are particularly suitable for readings organised around such sociological criteria as stance, role and norm. Unlike Fügen, however, Voßkamp's hypothesis did not posit homologies between social events and fictional modes of behaviour, but, using Niklas Luhmann's Systems Theory as its basis, derived specific ways in which 'meaning' is generated from transcriptions of literary visions of how things might be. When, according to Voßkamp, various elements of human experience are selected and interrelated according to the rules which govern a particular genre, hypothetical visions of meaning are created which interact with the subjective needs of author and reader alike. By this means, the relationship between literature and society is defined in terms of the functional history of genres. Correspondingly, critical interest is directed either towards the abstract structures inherent in the various genres (in which, of course, functions have been institutionalised) or towards the prototypical texts (like *Wilhelm Meister* in the case of the *Bildungsroman*) which have been instrumental in shaping them.

The practitioners of the above approach are often accused of ignoring the event which is constituted by the individual text in their eagerness to fit that event neatly into an overall pattern. But, conversely, the same critics are just as vulnerable to that accusation when, using a set of assumptions derived from sociology and social history, they describe an individual text as a particular instance of the way in which more general, extra-literary problems and experiences – uncovered by historiographical reconstruction – are worked through. Indeed, this kind of approach is inherently prone to regard literary texts as 'source material' which confirms or modifies established historical accounts. This is true even when the literary historian points out that historical events and experiences are inscribed in literary texts in a way which differs from what happens in the normal source texts used by historians, and that texts which have been shaped according to the rules of aesthetics need to be read in a different manner from, say, official documents or memoirs (cf. Frühwald, 1986).[12] From which it follows that we would have

11. Cf. Jendricke, 'Sozialgeschichte der Literatur', pp.54–8.
12. See also W. Frühwald, 'Die Ehre der Geringen: Ein Versuch zur Sozialgeschichte literarischer Texte im 19. Jahrhundert', *Geschichte und Gesellschaft*, vol.9 (1983), pp.69–86.

achieved a very great deal if we could manage to describe literary forms and structures in a way which made them appropriate source material for social historians.

A reading of literary texts that is determined by sociological considerations fulfils certain needs on the part of the reader, or, to use Siegfried J. Schmidt's terminology, it involves a certain way of 'processing' literature that is legitimised by certain social expectations. One can start either from the assumption that problems and experiences can be given shape in literary texts which, in terms of the actual history of social problems or the historical reconstruction of those problems, appear unimportant, or from the assumption that literature does not simply reflect socio-economic progress but also addresses its cost. And in either case, it becomes possible to uncover memories, embedded in literary texts, which exist in competition with the hegemonic memory of the past and the prevailing discursive modes. Moreover, whenever social historians are particularly interested in texts which have had a profound effect on the course of history, or themselves display the marks of such an effect, the socio-historical reading of literary texts will rediscover, to use Luhmann's terminology, the complexity of those very historical processes which have been simplified by the hegemonic memory of that history. This is why, in the last decade, the questions of a 'textually embedded social history' and 'literature as a repository of socio-historical problems and processes' have provoked a response at precisely that juncture when professional historians were having difficulty over their sources and concerning themselves with 'everyday history' (e.g. Jürgen Kuczynski's four-volume *Geschichte des Alltags des deutschen Volks*, 1982-3), history written from below and the history of mentalities and discursive modes (see especially the work of Michel Foucault, but also Luhmann's book *Liebe als Passion* (1982) (E.T. as *Love as Passion*, 1986)).

At all events, it is at this precise point that the real methodological problems begin. Although it is possible, by comparing texts with one another, to say in any given case that they represent reactions to social change, it is quite another matter to be able to infer from them the nature and chronology of that change. And over and above that, one still has to determine with some care which processes in the areas of economics, politics, science, culture and the family can be brought into especially close proximity with the process of writing and reading literature. Most of these methodological problems are never even considered by the proponents of 'textually embedded social history' but dealt with by means of implicit decisions taken tacitly by the scholar who is doing the interpreting.

The fact that such an interest in the perspectival interpretation of texts could, stimulated by trans-disciplinary study, make such headway among Germanists in recent years, derived from two factors. First, from those scholars' need to legitimise their profession (something which was achieved in this instance by turning the study of literature into a joint venture with historiography) and second, from the move away from the text-immanentist assumption that it is the task of the critic to interpret texts exhaustively by arriving at a total view of any given text which can subsume and unify all its possible readings.

The Sociology of Texts

However, even before people began to be interested in 'textually embedded social history', questions about the 'social history of the text' had already extended the range of literary studies quite considerably. Although much of the initial interest in the reception and sociological influence of literature was, of course, directed at bestsellers and pulp literature,[13] it is possible to ask sensible questions about popular and unpopular texts alike – but, as Michael Titzmann's essay above argues, only in the context of an overarching history of the status and function of literature. The foundations for such extended explorations had been laid by Communication Theory, according to which the production, distribution and reception of literature were three aspects of one process. Furthermore, the Constance School of criticism around Wolfgang Iser and Hans Robert Jauss claimed that it had devised an advanced theory of the text and textual interpretation to which it gave the name 'Rezeptionsästhetik' (Reception Theory). In retrospect, this theory seems more anthropological than sociological because it restricted the process of literary communication to the relationship between the reader and the work and derived its arguments from the structure of the texts rather than the sociological situation and activity of the readers (see Margot Zutshi's essay below, pp.95–111).

In contrast, a more strictly defined sociology of literature directed its attention towards all activities which are related to literature, to the sociology of 'literary life' and the commercial side of literature (see Section 2 of my bibliography). Regarding the literary text as a

---

13. Cf. Gunter Grimm, *Rezeptionsgeschichte: Grundlegung einer Theorie* (Fink, Munich, 1977), pp.117–22 and Günther Fetzer and Jörg Schönert, 'Zur Trivialliteraturforschung 1964–1976', *Internationales Archiv für Sozialgeschichte der deutschen Literatur*, vol.2 (1977), pp.1–39.

'black box', the questions and methodology peculiar to this approach concerned only those processes which lead to or derive from texts (cf. Voßkamp, 1978, pp.2–18). The work of Fügen and Alphons Silbermann, for example, sought to delineate a 'sociology of textual environments' by using empirical techniques of statistical analysis as well as more consciously sociological procedures, and, by so doing, these critics showed that they were in tune with recent developments in the social sciences. Finally, when Werner Faulstich declared in 1986 that the earlier sociological approaches to the whole business of literature were as antiquated as the notion of a flat earth (1986, p.125), he meant that the complex strands of the interrelationships between literary activity and social reality could be properly understood only in terms of the sophisticated concepts developed by Systems Theory on the basis of the work done by Talcott Parsons and Luhmann. Nevertheless, in contrast to Voßkamp or the systems-theoretical model developed by the Munich Group for Research into the Social History of Literature (see von Heydebrand, Pfau and Schönert, 1988), Faulstich delimited the applicability of Systems Theory across the whole literature-related field without attempting to develop a homogeneous and methodologically sound way of connecting the structures and functions of that field with the structures and functions of the texts themselves.

In my view, literary scholarship that is grounded theoretically in the sociology of communication ought not, as usually occurs in the sociology of literature, to isolate either the relationship between the author and the text, or the relationship between the text and the processes by which it is produced and distributed, or the relationship between the reader and the text. Rather, it should aim to synthesise a semiotic theory of texts with a theoretical understanding of those processes which constitute the textual environment. Hans Ulrich Gumbrecht (Section 3 of my bibliography) began to do this when, in 1975, he came up with a hypothesis which stressed elements from the theory of communicative actions.[14] Likewise, Siegfried J. Schmidt situated his theoretical observations on the nature of texts within a comprehensive theory of the way in which literary texts are communicated as a particular mode of social activity, and, in his project for an empirical science of literature, came to radical conclusions.[15] Because Schmidt claimed that texts are given their special status as literature by virtue of their dependence on social conventions and processes, the object of the discipline

---

14. Cf. Jendricke, 'Sozialgeschichte der Literatur', pp.73–5.
15. Ibid., pp.75–84.

proposed by Schmidt was to be those activities which led to the composition, distribution, reception and processing of literary texts. Indeed, such texts were said to be worthy of scholarly study only to the extent that they were the products of concrete acts of communication ('Kommunikate') whose nature could be established empirically. Because, according to Schmidt, the object of literary scholarship had to be the complexes formed by texts, contexts and agents, the written or printed text was given the functional status of a 'communicative base' – with the result that the traditional interpretations produced by literary scholars became nothing more than *Kommunikate* of a particular type.

The first publications in which Schmidt set out the above ideas still involved elements derived from the sociology of communication, Reception Theory and the theory of texts; and these were synthesised with borrowings from Systems Theory. Later attempts by Schmidt's Siegen Group to develop these ideas severed connections with traditional sociological Systems Theory (which had manifested itself in Schmidt's work more in the deployment of concepts than in the establishment of a theoretical basis) and focused instead on the connection with 'autotelic poetic systems'[16] – a development which I will discuss below in the context of Luhmann's writings on aesthetics. The theoretical underpinnings of this later development were formed by the work of the neuro-biologist Humberto Maturana and the epistemological paradigm known as 'Constructivism' that had been developed in the USA (see the volume entitled *Der Diskurs des radikalen Konstruktivismus* (1987) which Schmidt edited for Suhrkamp).[17]

The extent to which Schmidt's notion of an empirical science of literature is useful for literary historians still remains to be seen. That well-ensconced literary mandarins were unwilling, without a struggle, to sacrifice their favourite pastime of 'textual interpretation' to the constructivist demands and to see their public pronouncements on the meaning of texts as just another way in which the 'literary system' reproduces itself, is not surprising – especially since, in the culture of West Germany, there is a growing need to help people develop a sense of existential meaning with the aid of

16. Among the numerous recent publications by Siegfried J. Schmidt, see 'Empirische Literaturwissenschaft in der Kritik', *SPIEL*, vol.3 (1984), pp.291–332; 'On Writing Histories of Literature: Some Remarks from a Constructivist Point of View', *Poetics*, vol.14 (1985), pp.279–301; 'Text – Rezeption – Interpretation' in E. Ibsch and D. Schram (eds), *Rezeptionsforschung zwischen Hermeneutik und Empirik* (Rodopi, Amsterdam, 1987). pp.23–46.
17. See S.J. Schmidt (ed.), *Der Diskurs des radikalen Konstruktivismus* (Suhrkamp, Frankfurt/Main, 1987).

literature. Be that as it may, Schmidt's earlier onslaughts on 'subjective impressionism' ('Gesinnungsinterpretation') ought wonderfully to concentrate the minds of the critical establishment upon the need to agree on the rules by means of which literary interpretation can be self-consistent, communicable and relevant to people's needs. It remains to be seen whether it is possible to evade the constructivist critique, conducted at the level of the theory of science, by taking refuge in a decon structive approach to texts which has been relieved of the burden of theory.

The Appropriation of Elements from and the Transformation of Sociological Theory

Sociologists may well heave a huge sigh of relief at the sight of Germanists giving up the attempt to ground the practice of literary criticism in the social sciences, since Germanists, along with other people who work in the humanities, have, in the last two decades, often simply plundered those disciplines, tearing, in the process, individual concepts out of their rightful, systemic contexts in order to use them as more or less handy metaphors. Such transdisciplinary pillaging needs to involve the methodical assimilation of concepts appropriate to the specific object of investigation (i.e. literature); and anyone embarking upon such a course would need to be aware that, apart from the sociology of symbolic forms and the sociology of knowledge, most types of sociological theory were evolved for the analysis of real sociological contexts and not for the analysis of semiotic structures. Although such key concepts as structure, function and system can be used in both areas, this very flexibility has helped foster the arbitrariness and confusion of categories which resulted from the near simultaneous acceptance of linguistic and literary-critical Structuralism into the repertoire of concepts current among Germanists. I do not want to go any deeper into this somewhat murky area and will restrict myself to a discussion of the concept of 'institution' (see Section 4 of my bibliography) which, borrowed from sociological Systems Theory, has had a very good innings among literary critics. Indeed, Gottlieb Gaiser's programmatic article (1982) was one of the first texts to identify the sociological provenance of this category – which cannot, of course, be neatly slotted into any reductionist discussion of heterogeneous sociological theory.[18]

18. On the problem of adapting sociological theories, see F. Meyer and C.-M. Ort,

Nevertheless, as a minimal definition, one can say that institutions give objective expression to behavioural complexes in the service of certain needs or on behalf of certain interest groups, formalise reciprocal expectations; and, in so doing, legitimise certain roles and relationships. To evolve a genuinely sociological approach, it would be necessary to work out the precise nature of the processes of institutionalisation (e.g. the creation, establishment and maintenance of conventions, rules and patterns) and the various ways in which institutions are formed in the area of literary communication. Where corresponding forms of material and bureaucratic organisation (Peter Bürger's concept of 'apparatuses') can be discerned in such related areas as book production and distribution, journalistic and scholarly reflection upon texts, and the various means by which writers etc. help themselves, it is not hard to translate these sociological perspectives and procedures into terms appropriate to the field of literature. And it is, of course, self-evident that the concept of 'institution' involves the awareness that institutions develop and change and can, as such, be viewed in a historical perspective. But can the concept of 'institution' be applied to the semiotic systems constituted by the texts themselves? Gaiser (1982) did not go beyond literature-related activities, but Voßkamp, by relating complex, problematic experiences in real life to various patterns according to which literary problems are formulated and resolved (1978, p.32), explicitly developed his idea of 'genres as socio-literary institutions' for application to both social systems and symbolic forms. As the embodiments of the symbolising processes of selection and combination, literary schemata function, according to Voßkamp, as the means by which collective experiences are synthesised and hence stabilised. Although Voßkamp's hypothesis has proved to be a useful heuristic model for reconstructing the history of literary genres, one would need to enlarge it by showing how, alongside literary genres, other models of the various processes of institutionalisation might be included within the whole symbolic system formed by literary texts.

In my view, Peter Bürger's literary-historical concept of the 'institution of literature' (which, theoretically developed, saw the light of day in 1977) provides a salutary example of how a sociological concept can be appropriated in a partial, because metaphorical, way.[19] Bürger is interested in the social function of literature within

---

'Konzept eines struktural-funktionalen Theoriemodells für eine Sozialgeschichte der Literatur' in von Heydebrand, Pfau and Schönert (1988), pp.85–117 (especially pp.86–7).

19. See also Jendricke, 'Sozialgeschichte der Literatur', pp.58–65.

historical circumstances, themselves involved in a continual process of change, and defines that 'institution' in terms of its dominant function in any given set of historically determined social circumstances. Thus, for example, he sees the concept of aesthetic autonomy that was developed in the late eighteenth century as the product of the literary interests and social behaviour of the rising bourgeoisie. One might begin by pointing out that it is impossible to undertake any very differentiated historical analysis of the sociological function of literature if one works at the highly abstract level of 'autonomous art' (whose social function is deemed to consist in its very lack of function). Indeed, if Rainer Wild (1982) had set out from such a premise (see Section 8 of my bibliography), he would have been unable to differentiate between the various ways in which art can function or to relate those modes of operation to their various contexts. Most pertinently, however, my objection to Bürger's generalised extension of the concept of 'institution' relates to the way in which he reduces all the operational contexts of literary communication to one common denominator – with the result that their analytical relevance evaporates and the competing or subsidiary functions assumed by literature at any given time are simply repressed in favour of its alleged 'dominant function'.

Bürger's subsequent writings on the 'institution of literature' developed the same idea historically in order to explain the 'functional changes' which literature has undergone (1983, pp.9–32). Nevertheless, he failed to broaden the theoretical basis of the concept (even if he did arrive at a more precise description of the 'material apparatuses' through which the 'institution of art' is mediated). Indeed, Ulrich Meyer's sociologically based critique of the concept of 'institution' (in Bürger, 1983, pp.41–8) shows just how slippery that concept is, given that it can be applied to sociological sub-systems as well as aesthetic norms. However, Meyer weakened his case theoretically by identifying, with reference to the socio-philosophical ideas of Antonio Gramsci, Bürger's concept of the 'institution of art' as one of the means by which social hegemony is enforced.

Similarly, in a book which involved one of the most recent, not to say one of the most ambitious applications of the concept of the 'institution of literature' to an analysis of 'literary culture in the age of Liberalism', Peter-Uwe Hohendahl wrestled with its interactionist, materialist and normative usage (1985, pp.26–51) in an attempt to reconcile 'sociological theory and the theory of literature' (pp.36–7). Hohendahl, correctly in my view, identified three important junctures in this whole process: first, the various types of relationship that are possible between social and aesthetic norms (cf. Anz, 1984); second, the analytical separation of the ways in which institutions are created from the apparatuses which shape this process; and third, the sub-division of the global concept of 'institution' into various secondary institutions. To my way of thinking, a terminologically consistent use of the concept of 'system' could open up far richer ways of looking at texts. Hohendahl's thinking stayed within the bounds of literature-related activities (as instanced by the fact that that part of his argument where he shows how patterns of reading mediate between readers and institutions (pp.51–4) is consigned to an excursus), and Bürger had to synthesise his macroscopic descriptions of the way in which literature has changed its function with microscopic analyses of texts by means of the well-worn concept of ideology.

At the Aachen Germanists' Congress of 1982, Hans-Ulrich Mohr, a specialist in English literature, showed how it might be possible to describe the collective and individual functions of aesthetic experience in a way which was both theoretically sophisticated and pertinent to the analysis of particular texts. The consistency of Mohr's theoretical model derived not least from the fact that he did not relate the semiotic systems constituted by fictional texts directly to social events. Rather, he began instead by correlating those systems with the dominant (or competing) conceptual models of the organization of society in particular and of the world in general from which the corresponding sets of values, norms and roles had been derived. According to Mohr (1983), these 'cultural patterns' are worked through and reconstructed in literary texts in such a way that in the process of reading, the various modes of identity which dominate a particular epoch or group can be modified or compensated for. Thus, according to Mohr, the functions of literature can be reconstructed on the one hand in terms of the processes by which fictional texts are created, shaped and received, and on the other, in terms of the patterns of social interaction and the sociological models according to which reality is constructed. In other words, Mohr is attempting to perform the classic alchemist's trick of integrating (symbolic) concepts derived from the sociology of knowledge with the theory of social processes.

Thus, Mohr's approach differs from the usual means by which a direct link is forged between theories of sociological process and literary-critical theories of the text in that he relates the socialisation of the typical reader to those signals within any given text which enable him or her to orient him- or herself psychologically, epistemologically and sociologically. To put things very simply: this interconnection can be described as the correlation of social processes with mentalities and textual types (or discursive modes). Nevertheless, it is worth asking whether it might not be more fruitful in the first instance to play down the empirical analysis of literary functions (which need to be related to changes in the attitudes and behaviour of the reader) and to develop an approach to texts which is based on the sociology of knowledge (cf. Michael Titzmann's contribution to this volume). Such an approach could, by means of a 'sociology of discourse', be developed into a global, albeit utopian, theory of semiotic systems which would allow us to relate literary texts to social processes – especially to the extent that these have an effect upon our cognitive structures, value-systems and affective dispositions.

The Sociology of Culture and Sociological Theories of Literature

One can assume that literary constructions of reality (cf. the work of Max Scheler, Alfred Schütz, Peter Berger and Thomas Luckmann) are in competition with other and, moreover, that these constructions will generate a variety of sociological repercussions without it being necessary to investigate how, in any given case, this comes about. What we call 'knowledge' (cf. Michael Titzmann's remarks above, p.62) consists of elements taken from the constructions of reality proposed by science, religion, myths, the arts etc. and, in literary texts, such elements are fused with specific value-systems and affective structures which have themselves been borrowed from other constructions or reality. To account for such reciprocal borrowings and the overall complexion which such borrowings take on in any given case, one hopes that the sociology of knowledge would investigate social factors – like the vested interest of groups for example. To use a somewhat loose formulation, the history of collective wisdom, value-systems and affective structures would then emerge as the factor which mediates between the structures of textual systems and those complexes of collective attitudes which govern social processes. As matters stand, scholars of German literature are fond of using either the term 'mentality' (a concept derived from the French school concerned with the history of mentalities) or the term 'habitus' (a concept derived from Bourdieu's sociology of culture) as ways of talking about this middle ground.

Nevertheless, in 1986, Thomas Luckmann, a specialist in the sociology of knowledge (Section 5 of my bibliography), focused on the category of 'institution' in order to discuss problems that had arisen from positing an analogy between 'communicative genres' and 'social institutions'. In doing this, he was dealing with an aspect of the basic problem which I have touched upon several times in this paper already: how do social processes correlate with the symbolic systems constituted by works of literature? Luckmann insisted that a fundamental distinction had to be made: whereas institutions solved social problems, communicative genres, working through speech and writing, solved, in the first place, only problems of communication and comprehension. That would mean, for example, that although the *Bildungsroman* provided an exemplary model of how it is possible to narrate the life-story of one individual, the question of whether such narratives were at all relevant to the problems encountered by its readers (cf. Mohr 1983 and 1985) or had the power to provoke behavioural changes would, to a very great extent, have to remain a matter of unverifiable speculation.

Over the last few years, a theoretically ambitious sociology of culture has been gaining influence among professional West German social scientists, and the twenty-seventh special issue of the *Kölner Zeitschrift für Soziologie und Sozialpsychologie*, entitled 'Culture and Society', affords a good insight into current thinking in this area. In 1979, using theoretical insights derived from psychoanalysis as well, Wolfgang Lipp's essay 'Cultural Types, Cultural Symbols and the World of Social Processes' (see bibliography, Section 6) had focused on the abstract problems involved in the analysis of societies and social processes in relation to symbolic forms. Although Lipp's analysis of the way in which socially relevant and culturally powerful symbols are produced could well be applied, in a suitably modified form, to the field of literature, Lipp was, even after surveying the whole range of theory from Marx to Parsons, only able to come to the conclusion that the problems have merely been identified – not disentangled or solved (p.472).

As far as we can tell from their first applications to the field of literature, Pierre Bourdieu's ideas have, when compared with the attempts of West German sociologists of culture to establish a theoretical foundation for their subject, three main advantages for literary scholars. They were worked out expressly in relation to literature; they combine theoretical principles with the results of empirical research; and they have as their central theme the sociophilosophical problem of power. Bourdieu views culture and the arts as an arena where the struggle for social power is fought out and divides up the 'social sphere' into several smaller areas, one of which is labelled 'literature'. According to Bourdieu, social battle-lines are established by means of the distribution of economic, social and cultural resources and decked out with the insignia of the combatants' 'lifestyles' and 'habituses'. Thus, literary texts are said to signify the various embattled power-structures. It is possible that Bourdieu's sociology of culture has, in recent years, provoked renewed interest among literary scholars (Section 6 of my bibliography) precisely because his way of thinking and writing eschews sociological jargon and because his theoretical frame of reference appears to synthesise Systems Theory (with its stress on the functional nature of structure), a theory of symbolic interaction, the history of mentalities and such aspects of Marxist theory as the notion of 'class-society'.

The project of reconstructing 'discursive modes' along the lines laid down by Michel Foucault has, in recent years, aroused even greater interest (Section 7 of my bibliography). This is probably due in the first place to the fact that Foucault's general approach provides a relatively straightforward way of situating literary texts in non-literary contexts where they are free to display previously unsuspected levels of significance. Now, although Foucault postulated a connection between the semiotic system constituted by any given discourse and the social processes which produce it, he concealed the precise nature of that connection behind the almost metaphysical assumption that all types of discourse are determined by the power of the social. The fact that, in German intellectual circles, Foucault's concept of discourse can be overlaid with a further, utopian discourse of communication *à la* Habermas (his so-called 'ethics of discourse'), and that Lacanian concepts can be superimposed on all that as well has so confused the issues that one yearns for a miracle to occur which would bring some terminological uniformity into the whole situation (cf. Fohrmann and Müller, 1988). I will not attempt here to arrive at an operational definition of the concept of 'discourse' but confine myself instead to asking the literary-critical proponents of that concept to give me a theoretically watertight and convincing explanation of how social structures can be 'reflected' in the structures of any given discursive mode. It would also be interesting to know whether these 'discursive modes' are simply the consequences of various social processes or whether they can themselves determine or alter the shape of those processes.

In asking such questions, I am not denying the heuristic value of the concept of discourse – provided, of course, that it is understood as an abstraction which enables one to analyse, contextualise and discern some pattern in a large body of texts. Nevertheless – and here I am in agreement with Claus-Michael Ort (see Section 8 of my bibliography) – the genealogy of discursive modes must be linked with their sociology. At the risk of overlaying one imprecise and global category with another of like kind, it seems to me that it would be possible to simplify many problems of literary history by relating discursive modes to *mentalities* (see Section 7 of my bibliography). For example, our understanding of the discourse peculiar to the educated middle classes at the end of the eighteenth century could be extended by looking at those literature-related practices which characterised the public activity of such sub-groups as ministers of religion, aristocrats, the urban bourgeoisie, academics and civil servants, and which were shaped not by class interests, but by a community of thought-forms, values and affective disposition. In saying that, I intend to imply that a literary history which was based on the history of mentalities should concern itself with more than just the discursive modes peculiar to social elites, and that in all instances, texts should be read not simply as the manifestations of knowledge and elaborated feelings, but also as the manifestations of what is 'unknown' and repressed. In such a way, a history of literature which concerns itself with mentalities can impose limitations on the scarcely realisable demand for a comprehensive social history of literature.

The Social Theory of Literature and the Social History of Literature

The notion of a social history of literature (Section 8 of my bibliography) has become somewhat dusty in recent years, and if one wanted to resurrect it again on a properly systematic basis, one would need to develop a sociological explanation for both the synchronic connection between literature and society and the correlation between social and literary change.[20] A certain amount of material on these questions is to be found in the publications of former members of the Munich Research Group (see the publications produced by von Heydebrand, Ort and myself which are listed in my bibliography). Although we aimed to appropriate and adapt Parsons's Systems Theory for the study of literature, and, in the process, arrive at some degree of terminological rigour, we did not manage to solve that fundamental problem – touched upon so

---

20. On fundamental questions of epistemological theory, see G. Rusch, *Erkenntnis, Wissenschaft, Geschichte: Von einem konstruktivistischen Standpunkt* (Suhrkamp, Frankfurt/Main, 1987).

often in the preceding pages – of how it is possible to combine an understanding of the social processes out of which literature is generated with the practical business of interpreting the texts themselves. Nevertheless, I will say this: we did at least *try* to evolve a coherent methodological framework in which the heuristic presuppositions of textual analysis could be defined in such a way as to prevent literary historians, when attempting to reconstruct the interactions between the sub-systems of any given society, from offering over-simplified accounts of the relationship between social and textual structures. In doing this, we based our work on two premises: first, that literature must be seen in the first instance as an area in which acts of social communication take place, the interrelationships between which can be systematically described; and second, that the social sub-system constituted by literature changes in relation to changes elsewhere in the social system. Thus, we viewed literary texts both as the results of and a means for directing social activity: within the system of symbolic forms, such texts are embedded in contexts which can be described by means of a reformulated concept of discourse.

To put it more precisely, such questions, posed on the basis of a social theory of literature, focused on the way in which experience is processed by means of literary texts. Moreover, the messages embedded in literary texts were viewed as just one of a range of competing and complementary social agencies through which a sense of meaning is generated. Thus, this kind of social history of literature aimed to reflect changes both in the structure of sociocultural processes and in the symbolic cultural system which is partially constituted by literature. Being a perspectival construct within the general context formed by literary theory and history, the social theory of literature and the social history of literature were bound up with the particular research interests of its proponents and the particular social roles which those people had decided to play – by which I mean that other interests and roles were by no means precluded.

Niklas Luhmann – A Sociological Aesthetic?

Nevertheless, the organisational needs of manageable 'scientific communities' are served better by global theory than by the pluralism of competing partial theories, and the Bielefeld sociologist Niklas Luhmann (Section 9 of my bibliography) who, with his outline of a general theory of social systems (1984), reached the top of the contemporary tree as far as the construction of global theories was concerned, seems set to meet those needs. Several years ago, Luhmann, whose complex books provided the means of stilling many a literary critic's hunger for theory once and for all, entered the fold of literary criticism himself. He was, for example, invited on several occasions to participate in the annual Spring Colloquium in Dubrovnik, and his essay 'The Work of Art and the Self-Reproduction of Art' (1987), dealing with theoretical and historical questions of aesthetics without making strict distinctions between the various arts, was written for the 1985 Dubrovnik Colloquium on Style.[21] The starting-point of Luhmann's account of the historical processes which govern the last two hundred years is the fairly straightforward proposition that, at the end of the eighteenth century, a relatively autonomous social system termed 'art' (or 'literature') was established. Luhmann describes this system as a 'self-reproducing, autotelic' system of functions. He also numbers it among the autonomous systems of differentiation which characterise present-day society and which, in his view, produce 'the elements of which they consist by means of elements of which they consist' (p.620). Social systems are constituted by communication, and as far as literature is concerned it follows that the persistence of literary systems is assured by ever new modes of literary communication. So how does Luhmann arive at his concept of the work of art? He regards the work of art as a 'compact means of communication or programme which generates countless messages about the work of art' and adds: 'Only in this way does it become social reality' (p.627). So far, so good: we are dealing with a social theory of art which has been abbreviated to the point of becoming an aphorism. But in the further course of his highly abstract argument, Luhmann stops referring to processes of communication and concentrates on their general substitute, the work of art, which he then implicitly re-ontologises to the extent that he no longer addresses himself to the problem of how it might function as a communicative programme. In Luhmann's thinking, the form and style of a work of art become significant modes of self-referentiality (form) and syn-referentiality (style), by which, in the first place, the reader is to understand a kind of inter-textuality: 'the style of a work of art makes it possible for one to see what it owes to other works of art and what it means for other works of art that are still to be produced' (p.632). More-

---

21. See also N. Luhmann, 'Das Medium der Kunst', *DELFIN*, vol.4, no.7 (1986), pp.6–15; 'Schwierigkeiten mit dem Aufhören' in D. Baecker and G. Stanitzek (eds), *Interviews: Archimedes und wir* (Merve, Berlin, 1987), pp.74–98.

over, 'style' is said to be the means of creating the link between 'aesthetic system and social environment' (p.646).

By bracketing out the subject who produces and experiences works of art and makes inter-textual connections, Luhmann's Systems Theory marches with the conceptual world of Post-Structuralism. I do, of course, concede that his account of the historical processes which constitute and develop the 'social system of art' is most illuminating. Nevertheless, the abstractions by means of which he shifts attention away from the processes by which the work of art is 'humanly produced and experienced' (p.622) and towards the work of art in its 'stylistic dialogue' (p.644) with other works of art bring, at first sight, the debate back to that very (hermetic) conception of art which German literary scholarship, newly attuned to the social sciences, had left behind in the 1960s! So one needs to press the question of whether it is Luhmann's ambition to replace the philosophically oriented aesthetics of Modernism by a sociologically oriented aesthetics deriving from Post-Modernism. Or, alternatively, is one to understand Luhmann's assimilation of the terminology of aesthetics to the conceptual structure of Systems Theory as a process of retrenchment which allows 'aesthetic values' still to be affirmed 'in a situation from which there is no exit' (p.661)? Luhmann's essays on aesthetic theory deserve more systematic investigation. Even if it transpires that he is simply putting the old wine of Idealist aesthetics into the new wine-skins of Systems Theory, the variety of concepts offered by such sociologically revisionist literary criticism would provide a deal of space for methodological experimentation, comparative criticism and further theoretical work.

References

1. Sociologically and Socio-historically Oriented Modes of Interpretation

Frühwald, W. (1986) 'Sozialgeschichte und Literaturgeschichte' in W. Schieder and V. Sellin (eds), *Sozialgeschichte in Deutschland*, Vandenhoeck and Ruprecht, Göttingen, pp.110–33

Fügen, H. (1982) 'Zur Wissenschaftlichkeit und Systematik der soziologischen Roman-Interpretation', *Internationales Archiv für Sozialgeschichte der Literatur*, 7, 1–20

Voßkamp, W. (1978) 'Methoden und Probleme der Romansoziologie: Über

Möglichkeiten einer Romansoziologie als Gattungssoziologie', *Internationales Archiv für Sozialgeschichte der Literatur*, 3, 1–37

2. The Sociology of Literature as the Sociology of Literature-related Activities

Albrecht, R. (1980) 'Aspekte der gegenwärtigen Literatursoziologie in der Bundesrepublik Deutschland', *Diskussion Deutsch*, 11, 54, 434–43

Faulstich, W. (1986) 'Systemtheorie des Literaturbetriebs: Ansätze/ Ergänzungen', *LiLi*, 16, 62 and 63, 125–33 and 164–9

Scharfschwerdt, J. (1977) *Grundprobleme der Literatursoziologie: Ein wissenschaftsgeschichtlicher Überlick*, Kohlhammer, Stuttgart

(See also the special number of *Poetics*, 12 (1983) devoted to the sociology of literature.)

3. Literature as a Socially-governed Process of Communication: An Empirically-based Science of Literature

Gumbrecht, H.-U. (1975) 'Konsequenzen der Rezeptionsästhetik oder Literaturwissenschaft als Kommunikationssoziologie', *Poetica*, 7, 388–413

Schmidt, S.J. (1981–2) *Grundriß der empirischen Literaturwissenschaft*, 2 vols., Vieweg, Brunswick and Wiesbaden (E.T. as *Foundations of the Empirical Study of Literature*, Buske, Hamburg, 1982)

4. Literary-critical Adaptations of Sociological Concepts

Anz, T. (1984) 'Vorschläge zur Grundlegung einer Soziologie literarischer Normen', *Internationales Archiv für Sozialgeschichte der Literatur*, 9, 128–44

Bürger, C. (1977) *Der Ursprung der bürgerlichen Institution Kunst: Literatursoziologische Untersuchungen zum klassischen Goethe*, Suhrkamp, Frankfurt/Main

Bürger, P. (1977) 'Institution Kunst als literatursoziologische Kategorie: Skizze einer Theorie des historischen Wandels der gesellschaftlichen Funktion der Literatur', *Romanistische Zeitschrift für Literaturgeschichte*, 1, 50–76

Bürger, P. (ed.) (1983) *Zum Funktionswandel der Literatur*, Suhrkamp, Frankfurt/Main

Gaiser, G. (1982) 'Institution und Institutionalisierungsprozesse im System der Literatur', *Sprachkunst*, 13, 269–81

Hohendahl, P.V. (1985) *Literarische Kultur im Zeitalter des Liberalismus*, Beck, Munich, pp.26–54

Mohr, H.-U. (1983) 'Literaturgeschichte als systemtheoretisch und rollentheoretisch orientierte Rekonstruktion der Funktion ästhetischer Erfahrung', *Mitteilungen des deutschen Germanistenverbandes*, 30, 18–28

Mohr, H.-U. (1985) 'Ästhetische Erfahrung und sozialgeschichtlicher Prozeß: Systemtheoretisch und rollentheoretisch orientierte Überlegungen zu einer Funktionsgeschichte der Literatur', *SPIEL*, 4, 2, 297–350 (E.T. as 'Aesthetic Experience and Functional History: Literary History as Reconstruction of the Function of Aesthetic Experience in terms of Role Theory and Social Systems Theory', *Poetics*, 14 (1985), 525–49)

5. The Sociology of Knowledge and Literary Scholarship

Luckmann, T. (1986) 'Grundformen der gesellschaftlichen Vermittlung des Wissens: Kommunikative Gattungen', *Kölner Zeitschrift für Soziologie und Sozialpsychologie*, Special Issue 27, 191–211

6. The Sociology of Culture

Fischer, L. and Jarchow, K. (1987) 'Die soziale Logik der Felder und das Feld der Literatur: Einleitende Anmerkungen zum kultur- und literaturtheoretischen Ansatz Pierre Bourdieus', *Sprache im technischen Zeitalter*, 102, 164–72
Lipp, W. (1979) 'Kulturtypen, kulturelle Symbole, Handlungswelt', *Kölner Zeitschrift für Soziologie und Sozialpsychologie*, 31, 450–84
Müller, H.-P. (1986) 'Kultur, Geschmack und Distinktion: Grundzüge der Kultursoziologie Pierre Bourdieus', *Kölner Zeitschrift für Soziologie und Sozialpsychologie*, Special Issue 27, 162–90

7. The History of Discursive Modes and Mentalities

Fohrmann, J. and Müller, H. (1988) *Diskurstheorien und Literaturwissenschaft*, Suhrkamp, Frankfurt/Main
Raulff, U. et al. (eds) (1987) *Mentalitäten-Geschichte: Zur historischen Rekonstruktion geistiger Prozesse*, Wagenbach, Berlin
(See also the special number of of *kultuRRevolution*, 11 (1986) devoted to 'The Power of Discursive Modes', especially 4–7 and 60–71.)

8. The Social History of Literature

Heydebrand, R. von, Pfau, D. and Schönert, J. (eds) (1988) *Zur theoretischen Grundlegung einer Sozialgeschichte der Literatur: Ein struktural-funktionaler Entwurf*, Niemeyer, Tübingen
Ort, C.-M. (1986) 'Literarischer Wandel und sozialer Wandel: Theoretische Anmerkungen zum Verhältnis von Wissenssoziologie und Diskursgeschichte' in M. Titzmann (ed.) (1990), *Modelle des literarischen Strukturwandels*, Niemeyer, Tübingen
Plumpe, G. (1985) 'Systemtheorie und Literaturgeschichte. Mit Anmerkungen zum deutschen Realismus im 19. Jahrhundert' in H.U.

Gumbrecht and U. Link-Heer (eds), *Epochenschwellen und Epochenstrukturen im Diskurs der Literatur- und Sprachhistorie*, Suhrkamp, Frankfurt/Main, pp.251–64

Schönert, J. (1983) 'Neuere theoretische Konzepte in der Literaturgeschichtsschreibung: Positionen, Verfahren und Probleme in der Bundesrepublik und DDR' in T. Cramer (ed.), *Literatur und Sprache im historischen Prozeß: Vorträge des deutschen Germanistentages Aachen 1982*, 2 vols., Niemeyer, Tübingen, vol.1, pp.91–120

Wild, R. (1982) *Literatur im Prozeß der Zivilisation: Entwurf einer theoretischen Grundlegung der Literaturwissenschaft*, Metzler, Stuttgart

(See also the special number of *Geschichte und Gesellschaft*, 9, 1 (1983) devoted to literature and social history and the special number of *Poetics*, 14, 3/4 (1983), edited by Siegfried J. Schmidt and entitled *On Writing Histories of Literature*.)

9. Luhmann among the Literary Critics

Luhmann, N. (1985) 'Das Problem der Epochenbildung und die Evolutionstheorie' in H.U. Gumbrecht and U. Link-Heer (eds), *Epochenschwellen und Epochenstrukturen im Diskurs der Literatur- und Sprachhistorie*, Suhrkamp, Frankfurt/Main, pp.11–33

Luhmann, N. (1987a) 'Das Kunstwerk und die Selbstreproduktion der Kunst' in H.U. Gumbrecht and K. Pfeiffer (eds), *Stil: Geschichte und Funktionen eines kulturwissenschaftlichen Diskurselementes*, Suhrkamp, Frankfurt/Main, pp.620–72

Luhmann, N. (1987b) 'Paradigmawechsel in der Systemtheorie – Ein Paradigma für den Fortschritt?' in R. Herzog and R. Koselleck (eds), *Epochenschwellen und Epochenbewußtsein*, Fink, Munich, pp.305–22

–5–

Hans Robert Jauss's Rezeptionsästhetik – Theory and Application

MARGOT ZUTSHI

Introduction

Critics have been almost unanimous in their assessment of the importance of Hans Robert Jauss's essay of 1970, 'Literary History as a Challenge to Literary Theory', the revised and expanded version of his inaugural lecture at the University of Constance in 1967,[1] and the following are just three of their comments: 'The most significant document of German literary theory in the last few decades' (Holub, 1984, p.69), 'the origin of modern Reception Theory' (Schmidt, 1979, p.158), 'the most fruitful and provocative contribution to the debate in recent years' (Vaget, 1979, p.399). In his essay, which is structured like a manifesto, Jauss put forward a radical programme for the renewal of literary studies, his starting-point being 'the insight that the historical essence of a work of art lies not only in its representational or expressive function but also in its influence' (1982, p.15).

Jauss's concluding statements provide part of the explanation why his essay has had such an extraordinary impact on literary studies in West Germany, especially *Germanistik*. Here, he maintains that literature has a moral and social function and that it plays a part 'in the emancipation of mankind from its natural, religious and social bonds' (p.45). Thus, as outlined by him, a new literary history, based on the reception of literary works, would be able to discover how literature fulfils its 'socially formative' role and, as a result, 'the gap between literature and history, between aesthetic

---

1. Jauss, 1970. I shall be quoting from and referring in the text to the English translation by Timothy Bahti (1982). The title of the original lecture, 'What is and for What Purpose does one study Literary History?', alludes to Schiller's inaugural address as a historian at Jena in 1789 (see Holub, 1984, pp.53–7).

and historical knowledge' would finally be bridged (p.45). The key words here are 'emancipation' and 'history, echoing as they do the insistent demands made at the time for literary study to become 'socially relevant' as well as the innumerable calls for a return to a historical approach. Taken overall, Jauss's version of Reception Theory, which focuses attention on the reader at the expense of author and text, did in fact seem to offer solutions to a variety of major problems and, consequently, to provide a way out of the 'crisis in *Germanistik*'.[2] Wolfgang Iser's reader-response criticism, on the other hand, which is usually bracketed with Jauss's early theory under the heading of *Rezeptionsästhetik*, made less of an impact initially – and this may have a lot to do with the fact that Iser concentrated almost exclusively on the novel, which meant that his aims seemed far more limited.[3] Moreover, with his concept of the 'implied reader' and his emphasis on individual texts, Iser ultimately remained within the traditions of the New Criticism and its practice of close reading (cf. Jörg Schönert's remarks above, p.78). His role in helping to bring about the much-discussed – and still disputed – 'paradigm shift' in West German literary scholarship thus tends to be regarded as less central than that played by Jauss (cf. Holub, 1984, pp.1–12 and Jauss, 1969).

In this essay, I wish to outline Jauss's thesis and examine some of the ways in which his ideas have been applied to literary texts or, to put it more accurately, to studies in the history of literature. For it will be seen that in the attempt to reconstruct and analyse a work's reception at a particular time or over a certain period, the text itself moves to the periphery of the inquiry. Our understanding of it may be increased by what the critic finds out about its reception, but his or her activity has very little to do with 'interpretation' in the usual sense of that term. In my account of Jauss's thesis, I shall ignore the wide-ranging theoretical debate which his ideas have set in motion (in which major East German and, more recently, American scholars have also taken part), as well as Jauss's own subsequent corrections and amendments.[4] But the main objections to his proposals, which concern above all the notion of the 'horizon of expectations' ('Er-

2. See Jürgen Kolbe (ed.), *Ansichten einer künftigen Germanistik* (Hanser, Munich, 1969), especially the essays in Section I.
3. Iser gave the first outline of his theory in a lecture entitled 'Die Appellstruktur der Texte' at the University of Constance in 1970 (Warning, 1975, pp.228–52; E.T. as 'Indeterminacy and the Reader's Response' in J. Hillis Miller (ed.), *Aspects of Narrative: Selected Papers from the English Institute* (Columbia U.P., New York and London, 1971), pp.1–45).
4. For a detailed summary of early critical comment on Jauss's theory, see Grimm (1975), pp.26–55.

wartungshorizont') and his concept of the reader, will be briefly discussed after my summary. When I come to consider some of the practical implications of Jauss's theory, further points will be raised, since each of the two essays I shall be considering – one on the early reception of Thomas Mann's *Buddenbrooks* (Vaget, 1979) and the other on the influence or impact ('Wirkung') of Goethe's *Werther* (Jäger, 1974) – exemplifies some of the problems involved, either directly or indirectly.[5]

'Literary History as a Challenge to Literary Theory'

Jauss begins his essay by characterising the 'steady decline' (p.3) of literary history during the last 150 years, after its great achievements in the nineteenth century. He claims that what passes for literary history nowadays orders its material according to genres, general tendencies, and other criteria; lists works under such headings in chronological order; and intersperses all that with the occasional *excursus* on a particular writer's work and biography. Alternatively, we get an account of the 'life and work' of great authors as they succeed one another in time, with the 'lesser' ones either left out or placed somewhere in between. Such a description of literature which merely follows the established canon is, Jauss argues, not history at all but 'pseudo-history' (p.21).

The reason for the current state of affairs is said to be the absence of a guiding principle which could provide a link between past and present, as did the idea of a national literature in the nineteenth century, for example. Jauss shows how the Russian Formalists on the one hand, and Marxist literary theory on the other tried to solve this fundamental problem. But in his view, both attempts were doomed to failure because of the one-sidedness of their respective positions. Where the Formalists confined their analysis of literary change to aesthetic and linguistic factors and ignored 'the general process of history' (p.18), the Marxists were unable to move beyond an orthodox theory of reflection ('Widerspiegelung').[6] Accordingly, Jauss himself, in seven theses or propositions, addresses the question of a new literary history, and in the first one demands 'the grounding of the traditional aesthetics of production and representation in an aesthetics of reception and influence' (p.20). Reception gains such

---

5. The terms 'Wirkung' and 'Rezeption' and their current use by theorists are discussed in Wünsch (1984), pp.894–6.
6. Holub is one of several scholars who regard Jauss's view of Marxist literary criticism as too one-sided (1984, p.131).

central importance in Jauss's thinking because for him, it is the continuing dialogue between text and reader which constitutes literary history, being a process which involves 'the receptive reader, the reflective critic, and the author in his continuing productivity' (p.21).

At the centre of Jauss's theory, however, we find the concept of a changing and dynamic 'horizon of expectations' – and this forms the subject of his three following propositions. As will be seen, the key term covers not only the literary experience of the reader, but also his 'experience of life' (p.24). Jauss believes that it is possible to describe the reception and impact of a literary work at the time of its publication objectively because readers share a set of expectations which can, in their turn, be empirically ascertained. These expectations include the contemporary ideas about genre, knowledge of the formal and thematic aspects of already familiar works, and an awareness of the difference between poetic and practical language: 'The new text evokes for the reader (listener) the horizon of expectations and rules familiar from earlier texts, which are then varied, corrected, altered, or even just reproduced' (p.23).

Furthermore, if it challenges the literary expectations of its first readers, a new work may bring about a 'change of horizon' ('Horizontwandel') and this would be an objective criterion of its aesthetic value. On the other hand, the more a work merely fulfils its reader's expectations, the nearer it comes to being 'culinary' art (p.26). Here, Jauss is reformulating the ideas of the Russian Formalists (who equated artistic innovation with literary value), but, by bringing in the afore-mentioned 'wider horizon of experience of life' (p.24), he hopes to overcome the limitations of their approach. Jauss then goes on to suggest what is to be gained by reconstructing the horizon of expectations against which a particular work has been created and perceived. This procedure may enable us to find out how the original reader understood the work and so make apparent the 'hermeneutic difference' (p.28) between past and present understanding; and it may also make us conscious of the intervening history of the work's reception which mediates between these two positions. In addition, such reconstruction would prevent us from judging the work in accordance with anomalous criteria derived from works belonging to a different literary epoch.

The three final propositions look more closely at what a history of literature based on Reception Theory would involve and might achieve. One novel feature would be the combination of diachronic and synchronic methods of analysis, as used in linguistics. To describe its diachronic dimension, Jauss adapts the evolutionary model of the Russian Formalists (who saw the process of literary change in terms of a 'ceaseless struggle between the new and the old' (p.34) which takes place entirely within the 'literary series'). However, Jauss sees this process in more complex terms – as one in which the passive reception by readers and critics is translated into the author's active reception and production: 'The next work can solve formal and moral problems left behind by the last work, and present new problems in turn' (p.32).[7] In Jauss's view, a synchronic investigation would mean describing and classifying all the literature published in a particular year. As with linguistics and the study of grammar, such a cross-section would reveal the system inherent in the literature produced during that period of time: its genres, stylistic types, rhetorical figures, etc. on the one hand, and its literary themes, archetypes, symbols and metaphors on the other. Further cross-sections, before and after, would have to be treated in a similar manner for the purpose of comparison, to see which forms and ideas had changed or persisted.

Such an account of literary development would, according to Jauss, be completed by investigating one further aspect of the whole process, the effect that literary works may have on society, via their aesthetic form: 'The social function of literature manifests itself in its genuine possibility only where the literary experience of the reader enters into the horizon of expectations of his lived praxis, preforms our understanding of the world, and thereby also has an effect on his social behavior' (p.39). To maintain, as some sociologies of literature do (see Jörg Schönert's article above, especially pp.76–7), that literature has only ever *reflected* social processes, does not therefore adequately describe the relationship between literary history and history in general. Indeed, Jauss argues that a new literary form can have 'the greatest conceivable impact on a moral question' (p.42), and illustrates this point by citing the case of *Madame Bovary* for which Flaubert was prosecuted after its publication in 1857 in the *Revue de Paris*. The novel's stylistic innovations – its use of an impersonal narrator and the *style indirect libre* – represented a challenge to its first readers in that it compelled them 'to perceive things differently' (p.43), thus undermining their certainties on the question of adultery, an issue of public morality.

In the course of the critical debate which followed the publication of Jauss's essay in 1970 and which continued for at least a decade, every conceivable aspect of his theory came under attack, and some

---

7. The English translation here says the opposite of the German original (cf. the first paragraph of Section X in Jauss, 1970, p.189).

issues were discussed again and again, often at great length. Two of the main targets were his concept of an objectively ascertainable 'horizon of expectations' and his undifferentiated notion of the reader. Here, the immediate objections were that it is impossible to describe or portray the past objectively,[8] and that the central concept of the 'horizon of expectations' is far too vague. The uncertainty surrounding the precise meaning of this term (and also those of the compounds which Jauss constructed with its help) also extended to his idea of the reader, on whom the possibility of reconstructing the various horizons of expectation depends almost entirely (Jauss, 1982, p.22). Indeed, it is clear that although Jauss talks of readers in general, he in fact assumes a very high degree of 'literary competence' (Culler, 1981, pp.50–1), i.e. an ideal reader who is able to respond adequately to the different elements and strategies of the text as though he or she were a literary critic or writer (Wünsch, 1984, p.905). Furthermore, Jauss's exclusion of any pyschological perspective is said to result in a limited and one-dimensional view of the reading experience. Indeed, according to Schmidt: 'he adheres to a concept of audience that fails to differentiate according to social standing, education, sex, reading preferences – to name but a few of the many variables' (1979, pp.158–9).[9]

Jauss's idea of artistic innovation as the chief criterion of literary value, an idea which he took over more or less unaltered from the Russian Formalists, also came under heavy attack. In regarding novelty or aesthetic distance as a universal norm, he actually contradicted what he had said elsewhere in his essay, where he accused some critics of judging literary works in accordance with criteria which are alien to them (Jauss, 1982, p.29). By suggesting that only those works which can bring about a change of horizon have literary value, Jauss also laid himself open to criticism from another quarter inasmuch as he seemed to be restating the art/non-art dichotomy of German literary criticism, which was in fact beginning to be widely questioned at the time (see Schulte-Sasse, 1976). It is arguable, for example, that underlying his discussion of *Madame Bovary* – a novel which he contrasts with Feydeau's *Fanny*, a contemporary best-seller

---

8. Jauss himself has repeatedly stated that in reconstructing the past, objectivity is impossible. See for example his essay 'History of Art and Pragmatic History' in *Toward an Aesthetic of Reception*, pp.46–75 (especially pp.53–4). Michael Titzmann's essay in this volume investigates, however, the extent to which and the terms on which such an undertaking might be possible.
9. Moreover, Stückrath, in discussing Jauss's own application of his theory, argues that he is above all interested in the author as reader (1979, pp.119–23).

on the same subject of adultery – is the assumption of a fundamental difference between 'real' literature ('Dichtung') on the one hand and popular or mass literature ('Trivialliteratur') on the other (Jauss, 1982, pp.27–8). An equally contentious issue was the assertion, made in his final proposition, that literature can, by means of its formal and aesthetic characteristics, bring about a change in the reader's consciousness and thereby influence society in a concrete way. The reaction to this idea was almost unanimous scepticism, especially as far as the role of artistic form is concerned, and it was repeatedly pointed out that there is no way in which the influence of literature and art on society can actually be proved, as Jauss seemed to claim (see Vaget, 1979, p.406; Wünsch, 1984, p.905).

The debate surrounding Jauss's Reception Theory also revealed that critics quite often disagreed fundamentally on how to interpret different aspects of his theory. This was mainly because Jauss failed fully to integrate the many diverse ideas which his essay brought together – from philosophy, aesthetics, literary theory, sociology, etc. to Communication Theory and semiotics. This meant, for example, that contradictions remained between his stated intentions or programme, and certain assumptions which underlay his analyses of particular problems (Stückrath, 1979, pp.118–19). On the central question of a new literary history based on reception, there seemed, however, to be general agreement from the beginning. It was dismissed as impracticable for a variety of reasons, but mainly on the grounds that the amount of effort required for such a task would far outweigh the possible gains (Grimm, 1975, pp.50–1). Other objections were even more fundamental in that critics either refused to accept that a work's reception was any more important for literary history than the process of its creation, or insisted that the two were of at least equal significance.[10] So the critical discussion, to which Jauss himself contributed several essays,[11] did not lead to the expansion and development of his theory as a whole as he initially hoped (Jauss, 1975, p.381). As we have seen, critics either confined themselves to clarifying individual issues, as often happens where such broad-based and all-embracing theories are concerned,[12] or

10. See for example Jürgen Söring, *Literaturgeschichte und Theorie* (Kohlhammer, Stuttgart, Berlin, Cologne and Mainz, 1976), pp.101–5, and the chapter 'Marxist Reception Theory: The East-West Debate', in Holub (1984), pp.121–34.
11. The most important of these are: 'Der Leser als Instanz einer neuen Geschichte der Literatur', *Poetica*, vol.7 (1975), pp.325–44; 'Zur Fortsetzung des Dialogs zwischen "bürgerlicher" und "materialistischer" Rezeptionsästhetik' (Warning, 1975, pp.343–52); and the postscript to Jauss (1975), pp.380–400.
12. Cf. Käte Hamburger's controversial genre theory of 1957, *Die Logik der Dichtung* (2nd edn, Ernst Klett, Stuttgart, 1968) which, even though her overall thesis was

investigated the various sources and antecedents of Reception Theory in general (cf. Günther, 1971). Jauss himself eventually moved away from his early theoretical position and, in his later writings in this area, has concentrated mainly on the analysis of the aesthetic experience.[13]

Applications

To test the usefulness of Jauss's theory for literary study and to illustrate some of its shortcomings, Hans Rudolf Vaget applied the crucial concept of the 'horizon of expectations' to a major literary work, Thomas Mann's *Buddenbrooks*, limiting his analysis to the novel's original reception as documented in about forty articles and reviews, all dating from the years immediately following the novel's publication in 1901. This meant first of all that the reader's 'lived praxis' (Jauss, 1982, p.39), an essential dimension of Jauss's concept, was excluded from the inquiry – necessarily so, according to Vaget, since it would be impossible to reconstruct this aspect of the horizon of expectations. It also meant that the reactions being studied were those of people professionally engaged with literature, who were therefore not representative of the reading public in general. The latter's views could be discovered only from contemporary letters or diaries; and although these do exist, Vaget argued that the extensive research necessary for such a task would not be justified. The narrowness of Vaget's sample had its advantages, however, in that it made it relatively easy for him to abstract the literary expectations of the early *Buddenbrooks* readers from the documents available; and the fact that Mann was unknown at the time explains why these expectations were confined mainly to questions of genre and thematic aspects.[14]

As far as genre is concerned, the initial response to the novel was mixed: there was praise for its realism, authenticity, and accuracy of description – characteristics which were obviously perceived as

---

generally dismissed, led to a wide-ranging debate on such issues as point of view in fiction, 'literary' versus 'non-literary' language, etc.

13. In a recent essay, Jauss gives an outline of the development of his ideas over the last two decades: 'The Identity of the Poetic Text in the Changing Horizon of Understanding' in M. Valdés and O. Miller (eds), *Identity of the Literary Text* (Toronto U.P., 1985), pp.146–74. The section: 'My own work: a retrospective and prospective glance' (pp.159–72) is of particular relevance.

14. The novel itself then came to play a decisive role in forming the horizon of expectations for Thomas Mann's subsequent works, and these in turn must have brought about further changes of horizon.

'norm-fulfilling' and normative. But its great length and the narrative strategies employed, especially the extensive use of the *leitmotif*, gave rise to scepticism and negative comments, indicating that these formal innovations represented a challenge to the conventions of the social novel. Mann's treatment of the already familiar theme of decadence provoked similarly critical reactions because, for the first time, decadence was being diagnosed in the mercantile upper middle class which, in a well-known and popular earlier example of the genre, Gustav Freytag's *Soll und Haben* (1855; E.T. as *Debit and Credit*, 1857), had been portrayed as an entirely solid pillar of society.

Vaget also pointed out that there were bound to be other, perhaps now forgotten aspects of the novel which the study of its early reception could bring to light. But instead of pursuing this topic, he focused on the methodological problems involved in working with Jauss's concept. Having quite deliberately treated the reactions to *Buddenbrooks* 'as if they were situated in a social and ideological no-man's-land' (1979, p.406), Vaget argued that it would then be necessary to show in what way they were determined by historical and social factors – i.e. to recreate the reader's 'wider horizon of experience of life' (Jauss, 1982, p.24). But despite the intention, expressed in his last proposition, of bridging the gap between literary history and sociological research, Jauss had given no indication as to how this might be achieved. Thus, Vaget concluded that 'the real *Buddenbrooks* reader of 1901, like the reader who was involved in later stages of the novel's reception, remains a phantom' and, moreover, that it would be 'mere speculation' to draw conclusions about the novel's 'socially formative effects' from the extremely limited evidence available (1979, p.405).

By virtue of his attempt to reconstruct the contemporary horizon of expectations for Mann's first novel, Vaget believed that he had demonstrated that, even in the case of a relatively recent work, such a reconstruction was impossible, and his concluding comments echoed the widely-held view that Jauss's programme as a whole was not viable. But like other critics, Vaget located the importance of Jauss's Reception Theory in its invigorating effect on literary criticism in general, and particularly in the role it had played in bringing about the long-overdue questioning and redefinition of traditional concepts used in the study of literature (Vaget, 1979, p.407). Vaget's analysis of the first critical reactions to *Buddenbrooks* does, however, throw some light on the way in which changes in the literary expectations of readers come about. Indeed, Vaget's findings seem to confirm the theories of the Russian Formalists concerning the evolutionary process of literary change, including their idea that artistic innovation is a major determining factor. This is perhaps not surprising, given some of Jauss's basic assumptions and his closeness to Russian Formalism – indeed, despite his intention of connecting the 'literary series' with the 'non-literary series', his overall emphasis remains on the former (1982, p.18). At the same time, it is arguable that an investigation like Vaget's achieves little more than traditional literary scholarship might aim for. Although it can help us establish the individual work 'in its historical context, and interpret it by its own age's aesthetic canons', so that we may recognise 'its uniqueness and individuality' (Gardner, 1963, p.20), such an approach, dwelling on the contemporary reader and his or her understanding of the text, inevitably brings the author and the work's genesis back into view, very much against Jauss's express intention. The same approach also raises the question of the status of early reception documents in relation to subsequent ones: if the initial reactions to a particular work can, via the criterion of artistic innovation, tell us something about its aesthetic value, does this not mean that contemporary voices should carry even more authority than later ones (cf. Stückrath, 1979, pp.122–8)? These and a number of other related issues (e.g. that of the 'adequacy' or 'inadequacy' of different interpretations) remain unresolved in Jauss's theory even though he is certainly not unaware of such problems – as various statements throughout his text and elsewhere in his writings demonstrate.

In an essay on the reception of Goethe's *Werther* which bears the apposite subtitle 'An Exemplary Case for Reception Theory', Georg Jäger tried to solve some of the problems left unanswered in Jauss's theory. In order to do this he adopted a quite different theoretical framework which he derived mainly from Prague Structuralism, in particular the work of Jan Mukařovský whose writings, like those of the Russian Formalists, first became known in West Germany in the late 1960s (see Günther, 1971; Holub, 1984, pp.29–36). Mukařovský's ideas enabled Jäger to change or re-define Jauss's central categories for his own project – in which he examined the different contemporary reactions to Goethe's first novel both in their socio-historical context and in relation to the work's aesthetic structure. Thus, the sociological dimension of reception, implicit in Jauss's theory but ignored by him in practice, assumed central importance in Jäger's investigation.

With the help of a communication model which also drew attention to 'extrinsic' material factors like book production and distribution, Jäger aimed to ground Reception Theory in a sociology of literature. Jäger's theoretical framework (which it is impossible to describe here, even in outline) was based on the premise that the literary text is the material artefact and that it becomes an aesthetic object only in the reader's consciousness, as the individual concretisations and interpretations to which it gives rise. These can, Jäger argued, be assigned to particular social groups and classified accordingly. Thus, the idea of the unchanging artefact on the one hand and its various historical concretisations on the other, replaced Jauss's less specific notion of the horizon of expectations which all readers are supposed to have in common. As we shall see, Jäger also distinguished between the implied or intended reader, a structural aspect of the text itself, and the reader as an empirical and sociological entity (1974, pp.389–93).

Jäger took issue with traditional literary history and its interpretation of the phenomenon known as 'Werther fever',[15] arguing that the contemporary reactions to Goethe's novel cannot be adequately explained without taking into account certain social and historical factors hitherto ignored – like, for example, the rise of a secular reading public, who brought their experience of devotional literature ('Erbauungsliteratur') to their reading of fiction. In his analysis, Jäger concentrated on two closely related types of 'non-aesthetic' concretisation: the devotional and the didactic, in neither of which 'the aesthetic norm' (Mukařovský, 1970) predominated. He also mentioned a third, 'non-aesthetic' type of concretisation, the romantic or sentimental one ('trivialempfindsam'), in which the book was read simply as a triangular love story.[16] The 'aesthetic' norm was, according to Jäger, prevalent only in reviews in those learned journals where new writing was introduced to the educated public (i.e. to the culturally dominant group), and here the novel was at first unanimously praised and no danger from it foreseen: '*Werther* did not become a problem . . . until its success took it beyond the social group which had experience with reading fiction' (1974, p.395).

Of the two main and, on the whole, simultaneous reading patterns peculiar to the early reception of *Werther*, it was the devotional concretisation which, as Jäger convincingly shows, gave rise to 'Werther fever'. Devotional literature, which predominated over all

15. See the introduction to and the various documents printed in the Wagenbach edition (Goethe, 1982); also the chapter 'Kultivierung des Eigenmenschlichen' in L. Balet and E. Gerhard, *Die Verbürgerlichung der deutschen Kunst, Literatur und Musik im 18. Jahrhundert* (Ullstein, Frankfurt/Main, Berlin and Vienna, 1973), pp.180–232.
16. This kind of response was characteristic of the 'second *Werther* period', i.e. the novel's reception from the late 1780s onwards, and can be linked to the spread of the lending libraries during the preceding years (Jäger, 1974, p.394).

other reading matter until the mid-nineteenth century, was designed to bring about identification by having a strong effect on the reader's emotions; and this in turn meant that absence of distance was regarded as a criterion of value, the sign of a good book (Jäger, 1974, p.402). The same effect was aimed for in the novel – which had begun to replace religious writing but had retained some of its characteristics. Thus, because *Werther* was not intended for readers whose sole experience with literature had been this type of writing, it was inevitable that they should have misunderstood the novel and, for example, interpreted the protagonist's suicide as a kind of martydom: 'The hero appears as a holy figure demanding to be emulated. The novel turns into legend' (Jäger, 1974, p.403). Other factors contributed to such a response, especially an intense concentration on very few books which meant that these tended to be read again and again, and were sometimes known by heart.

The same lack of distance characterised the didactic concretisation, but here, the assumption that a book contains moral and social instruction, that it teaches virtue, determined the reading pattern. Thus, Werther's behaviour and reflections tended to be criticised and evaluated in relation to concrete problems. Similarly, his thoughts and feelings became the subject of a public debate in which social and political aspects predominated and which caused the novel to be widely condemned because it seemed to propagate views diametrically opposed to the rational ideals of the Enlightenment (Jäger, 1974, pp.404–6). As with the devotional concretisation, there was a failure to distinguish fiction from real life – a kind of response which, however, corresponded to the role which the novel itself assigned to the reader, both thematically and through its very form.

Right at the beginning, in the preface, the Editor of Werther's letters speaks directly to the readers and, on behalf of the hero, appeals for their sympathy and compassion while at the same time encouraging them to project their own problems into the work. This kind of intimate relationship with literature is also apparent throughout the rest of the novel, where particular authors or works (Klopstock, Homer, Ossian, *The Vicar of Wakefield*) play an important role for the characters. Such literary interests create a bond between them and help them to express their feelings for one another: life is experienced through literature. Jäger saw in the epistolary novel the formal equivalent of this idea of the text/reader relationship, emphasising that especially in Goethe's innovatory treatment of the genre, distance was eliminated altogether: 'The reader, who sees and lives with Werther, is forced into identification'

(1974, p.407). The novel's one-sided perspective, complete absence of the usual didactic elements, its realism and radical subjectivity all helped to generate the types of concretisation described by Jäger and, in addition, led to the protagonist's point of view being identified with that of the author. It was mainly in response to the widespread criticism from his contemporaries, Jäger argued, that Goethe subsequently made substantial changes to both structure and content, all of them designed to increase distance and make identification with Werther more difficult. Thus, in the 'classical' version of 1787, the Editor's report is used to strengthen the work's 'outer' perspective, with the result that Werther's attitudes now appear as pathological. Conversely, the newly inserted story of the young peasant (who murders his rival out of love) has the function of illustrating 'the consequences of Werther's way of thinking' (Jäger, 1974, p.409). By means of these and other changes designed to steer the reader's response, Goethe 'brought the work more into line with the social and political views of his critics' (Jäger, 1974, p.409).[17]

By examining certain textual aspects of Goethe's *Werther* in relation to the work's early reception, Jäger demonstrated that that relationship, although very complex, was by no means arbitrary. In fact, given the close correspondence between the role assigned to the reader within the novel and the reactions of Goethe's contemporaries, it seems quite inaccurate to speak of 'misunderstandings' as critics have invariably done (including Jäger himself). One would be equally justified in saying that those early readers responded correctly because they did so in accordance with the work's express intention (see Müller-Salget, 1981, p.542). But to look at the problem from today's point of view: they failed to read the novel 'as literature', a process which would have involved an appreciation of its carefully worked-out composition, or an understanding of it in generic terms (i.e. as a particular kind of epistolary novel which was written in such a way as to maximise the illusion of spontaneity, authenticity and truth).

The apparent failure on the part of the contemporary public to consider the work's literary and aesthetic qualities alo helps to explain why no 'change of horizon' took place, resulting instead in 'belated attempts at self-censorhip' on the part of Goethe (Müller-Salget, 1981, p.543). Jäger's analysis of the various *Werther* concretisations shows that the majority of its early readers did not

---

17. H. Link discusses the reception of *Werther* as an example of 'Rückkoppelung' (i.e. feedback from public to author) in *Rezeptionsforschung: Eine Einführung in Methoden und Probleme* (Kohlhammer, Stuttgart, Berlin, Cologne and Mainz, 1976), pp.52–63.

distinguish between real life and what they were reading about in books; nor did they apparently differentiate at all between fiction and certain other types of writing. Conversely, the kind of reception based on 'literary competence' (which Jauss's theory assumes to be the norm) was extremely rare, being confined to a very small minority indeed. Thus, Jäger's investigation illustrates the contention that during the period in question, conflicting attitudes regarding the role and function of literature existed side by side, and that these were, on the whole, very different from our own. His study also suggests that a similar variety of reading patterns, both simultaneous and successive and extending along lines of social stratification, may be discovered in other, albeit less spectacular cases of literary reception – indeed, wherever a work has gained a wider audience.

In contrast to Vaget, who examined what the initial reviewers and critics had to say about *Buddenbrooks* and so concentrated entirely on 'competent' readers, Jäger almost completely ignored this type of concretisation. Rather, he was concerned to find a more convincing answer than had hitherto been given to the question as to *why* people reacted to *Werther* in the way they did; and this meant identifying the different groups of readers involved and asking what particular experiences and expectations they had brought to their reading of the novel. Although the literary text is not irrelevant to such an investigation, it is no longer studied for its own sake, whether as an autonomous 'work of verbal art' ('Wortkunstwerk'), or from some other point of view, for example that of the author's intention. Consequently, its aesthetic structure is of interest mainly to the extent that it helps explain reception, though here it is of crucial importance. Similarly, the question of meaning, usually at the centre of literary analysis, hardly arises in this context, and the same applies to several other issues, such as the problem of literary value, or the adequacy and admissibility of particular approach. Indeed, instead of asking 'What does this text mean?', a study like Jäger's tries to establish under what social, historical and cultural conditions a given literary work has generated different kinds of meaning.

For the early reception of *Werther*, this approach also involved providing statistical information on such matters as book production, the spread of literacy, the rise of lending libraries, etc. (Jäger, 1974, pp.399–401). Jäger also took into account a wide variety of reception documents, many of them written by people who felt that they had to protect others (especially the young and women) from the negative effects of reading Goethe's novel. In accordance with his clearly defined objectives, Jäger drew his own conclusions from all this material, but without making any wider claims as to the work's lasting influence on the society of its time, as Jauss had done in connection with *Madame Bovary*. Like any socio-historical interpretation, Jäger's conclusions could of course be questioned, whether on account of the methodology employed, or because of the limited selection of reception documents used – which inevitably excluded the majority of readers (Wünsch, 1984, p.912).[18] But notwithstanding such possible objections, Jäger may, within the limits he set himself, be said to have achieved one of the aims of Jauss's Reception Theory, which was to bridge 'the gap between literature and history, between aesthetic and historical knowledge' (Jauss, 1982, p.45).

Conclusion

Less than two decades after the publication of the revised version of Jauss's lecture, it can be argued that, having played a decisive role as a catalyst, the essay is now of merely historical interest for literary studies. Indeed, the attempts by Vaget and Jäger to put Jauss's theory into practice have, each in its own way, demonstrated this. By confining itself to the kind of recipient who corresponds to an abstract or 'ideal' reader, Vaget's investigation revealed how close Jauss's ideas remain to traditional forms of literary criticism (Wünsch, 1984, p.906). Conversely, Jäger's socio-historical study, which described and classified different types of concretisation without evaluating them, showed that only by abandoning or fundamentally changing Jauss's central categories can some of his declared aims be achieved. Both Vaget's and Jäger's essays illustrate not only that Jauss's theory is of limited practical use as it stands, but also that it is not capable of being developed any further. The two quite different approaches which Jauss tried to combine – text-oriented on the one hand and historical and sociological on the other – point in opposite directions, and nearly all subsequent research into literary reception has followed either the one or the other of these. The same basic division is observable in the theoretical debate as well, with hermeneutical and empirical standpoints confronting each other as alternatives (see Ibsch and Schram, 1987).

Nevertheless, the new interest in the reader led to a great deal of

---

18. In his essay 'Trends in Literary Reception: Die neuen Leiden der Wertherwirkung', John Neubauer examines some of the problems involved in trying to create a 'social profile' from 'a collection of random responses' (*German Quarterly*, vol.52 (1979), pp.69–79, especially p.74).

practical research into reception, both historical and empirical, with investigation into 'real' readers and their past or present responses to a particular literary text emerging as a means of overcoming Jauss's unsatisfactory central concepts (Wünsch, 1984, pp.907–12). Such an emphasis had even wider implications, in that it raised the question as to what the majority of ordinary people were actually reading.[19] Thus, in the 1970s, scholars began to investigate a great variety of non-canonical forms, and, alongside reception studies, popular or mass literature ('Trivialliteratur') became a major focus of literary theory and research (see Rucktäschel and Zimmermann, 1976). These developments in turn brought about a broadening of the narrow definition of literature as 'poetry' ('Dichtung'), and also contributed to the revision of the established literary canon which was taking place during the same period (Holub, 1984, pp.8–10). Reception Theory and research in general – whatever the particular definition of 'the reader' – powerfully recalled literary scholarship to the question of historical context, and, together with other theoretical developments, profoundly undermined the notion of the timelessness of literature, resulting in the relativisation of the classical canon.

References

Culler, J. (1981) *The Pursuit of Signs: Semiotics, Literature, Deconstruction*, Routledge and Kegan Paul, London

Gardner, H. (1963) *The Business of Criticism*, Oxford U.P.

Goethe, J.W. (1982) *Die Leiden des jungen Werther*, neu herausgegeben mit Dokumenten und Materialien, Wertheriana und Wertheriaden von Hans Christoph Buch, Wagenbach, Berlin

Grimm, G. (1975) 'Einführung in die Rezeptionsforschung' in *Literatur und Leser: Theorien und Modelle zur Rezeption literarischer Werke*, Reclam, Stuttgart, pp.11–84

Günther, H. (1971) 'Grundbegriffe der Rezeptions– und Wirkungsanalyse im tschechischen Strukturalismus', *Poetica*, 4, 224–43

Holub, R. (1984) *Reception Theory: A Critical Introduction*, Methuen, London and New York

---

19. The most influential early text on this subject was Helmut Kreuzer's essay 'Trivialliteratur als Forschungsproblem: Zur Kritik des deutschen Trivialromans seit der Aufklärung', *DVjs*, vol.41 (1967), pp.173–91.

Ibsch, E. and Schram, D. (eds) (1987) *Rezeptionsforschung zwischen Hermeneutik und Empirik*, Rodopi, Amsterdam

Jäger, G. (1974) 'Die Wertherwirkung: Ein rezeptionsästhetischer Modellfall' in W. Müller-Seidel (ed.), *Historizität in Sprach- und Literaturwissenschaft: Vorträge und Berichte der Stuttgarter Germanistentagung 1972*, Fink, Munich, pp.384–409

Jauss, H. (1969) 'Paradigmawechsel in der Literaturwissenschaft', *Linguistische Berichte*, 3, 44–56

Jauss, H. (1970) 'Literaturgeschichte als Provokation der Literaturwissenschaft' in *Literaturgeschichte als Provokation*, Suhrkamp, Frankfurt/Main, pp.144–207. (E.T. as 'Literary History as a Challenge to Literary Theory' in *Toward an Aesthetic of Reception*, Minnesota U.P., Minneapolis, 1982, pp.3–45)

Jauss, H. (1975) 'Racines und Goethes Iphigenie – Mit einem Nachwort über die Partialität der rezeptionsästhetischen Methode' in Warning, 1975, pp.353–400

Mukařovský, J. (1970) *Aesthetic Function, Norm and Value as Social Facts* (1936), Ann Arbor, Michigan

Müller-Salget, K. (1981) 'Zur Struktur von Goethes "Werther"', *Zeitschrift für deutsche Philologie*, 100, 527–44

Rucktäschel, A. and Zimmermann, H. (eds) (1976) *Trivialliteratur*, Fink, Munich

Schmidt, H. (1979) '"Text-Adequate Concretisations" and Real Readers: Reception Theory and its Applications', *New German Critique*, 17, 157–69

Schulte-Sasse, J. (1976) *Literarische Wertung*, 2nd edn, Metzler, Stuttgart

Stückrath, J. (1979) *Historische Rezeptionsforschung: Ein kritischer Versuch zu ihrer Geschichte und Theorie*, Metzler, Stuttgart

Vaget, H. (1979) 'Rezeptionsästhetik: Schwierigkeiten mit dem Erwartungshorizont am Beispiel der *Buddenbrooks*', *Monatshefte*, 71, 399–409

Warning, R. (ed.) (1975) *Rezeptionsästhetik: Theorie und Praxis*, Fink, Munich

Wünsch, M. (1984) 'Wirkung und Rezeption' in W. Kohlschmidt and W. Mohr (eds), *Reallexikon der deutschen Literaturgeschichte*, 4 vols., 2nd edn (1958–84), vol.4, de Gruyter, Berlin and New York, pp.894–919

–6–

Feminist Approaches to Kafka's *The Castle*

ELIZABETH BOA

In Kafka's (1970, p.13) sketch *Bachelor's Ill Luck* (1911), gender norms appear as oppressive ideas in the bachelor's ('Junggeselle') head which, at the end, he despairingly strikes. 'Jung' ('young') but not 'gesellig' ('sociable'), he is oppressed by the thought of becoming an 'alter Junggeselle' ('old bachelor'), a counterpart of the 'alte Jungfer' ('old maid') woman becomes at twenty-five. The various comforts the old bachelor will *not* have add up to aspects of an imagined woman who would be a companion after the man's working day. She would cook, whereas the bachelor must carry home his supper; she would preside over a private household, whereas the bachelor lives in lodgings; where the sick bachelor will lie alone for weeks, a nurse-wife would tend a husband. Wives generally become mothers, but this man cannot imagine fatherhood: the imagined husband would be allowed to keep repeating that he has no children – information a bachelor cannot properly offer. Moreover, the bachelor's bed is in the corner, the position of beds occupied by one person only, or he lies in the corner of the bed, the position of fear not desire. Thus, the sexual woman is absent, whether as object of pre-marital pleasures which the bachelor is not enjoying or as imagined wife in bed, and her absence leaves a gap dividing the imagined companion/cook/nurse from an unimaginable mother.

In *The Castle* (1922), the sexual woman has come out of hiding, but woman remains divided. The many female figures are not rounded characters but fragmented facets of 'imagined femininity' (Bovenschen, 1979) and K. fails to integrate the facets, a feat which might allow him to become integrated into village society. In what follows, I shall first place the fragmentation of woman in a historical landscape of sexual ideology and then try to approach *The Castle* by different theoretical paths, for there are now many feminisms (cf.

Weedon, 1987). 'Images criticism' measures stereotypes against what women are supposedly really like and is associated with a liberal humanism which claims for women the same autonomy men supposedly enjoy. Radical feminism, in contrast, sees the liberal programme as merely trying to make women like men and posits instead a fundamental antagonism between the sexes, but tends to biologistic arguments which make change difficult to envisage. Accordingly, the structuralist anthropology of Lévi-Strauss and Lacanian psychoanalysis have been of interest to feminists as analyses of patriarchy which purport to avoid biologism and so might be appropriated to the feminist cause. In a final section I shall, however, draw on Marxist feminism to argue that, although Structuralism and psychoanalysis can be illuminating, they misleadingly elevate features of particular societies – which could be changed – to the status of necessary truths. I hope that the interplay of theory and literary text will be mutually illuminating: the theories highlight aspects of the novel; the novel, however, resists reduction and highlights the limits of the theories.

Bourgeois Ideology: The Fragmented Woman

The masculinity which Kafka's bachelor fails to achieve, even in his imagination, requires the femininity prescribed by a bourgeois patriarchy rooted in the late eighteenth century, when enlightened stress on common humanity and Rococo celebration of pleasure in both sexes gave way to a rhetoric of sexual difference. Rousseau's strictures (1964, pp.446–55) were blatantly oppressive: women must be indoctrinated to serve men's needs at all times; where man is only sometimes male, woman is exclusively sexual, at least until the menopause. Nevertheless, she must conceal sexual desire and, by feigned reluctance, entrap a man in marriage to whom she must then be faithful to assure paternal certainty. The German Idealists screened oppression by an appeal to natural difference between the sexes. Fichte (1971, pp.304–43) saw woman as the passive vessel of the substance of life which active man vitalises: women feel no desire, only life-long love for one man, and should accept the double morality. Hegel (1972, pp.151–68) placed women in the family, the first stage of ethical life, but reserved civil society and the state, the sphere of universal humanity, for men.

Idealism unleashed a virulent discourse of binary oppositions between passivity and activity, Nature and Spirit, female being *an sich* ('in itself') and human becoming *für sich* ('for itself'). Man was seen as the human norm, and woman, although less divided, as less human, closer to animals or, in a Romantic variation, to angels. Since bourgeois man demanded control of the maternal body yet access to the object of desire, female desire was defined as non-existent or passive. Fichte equated activating spirit with active penis: woman lacked both. Thus, the woman whom Kafka's bachelor cannot imagine impregnating is a spectral remnant of bourgeois femininity, and his failure is not surprising, given the monstrous proportions the stereotype-mother had assumed. Krafft-Ebing (1972, p.13), for example, magisterially proclaimed that woman's weak sexual urge disappeared entirely with the first pregnancy. Kafka's imagination was dominated by a monster father, but the monster mother lurks there too: Georg Bendemann does not just abrogate his father's role, he pollutes his mother's memory in lifting his fiancée's skirt.

By the late nineteenth century, four tendencies had become marked. First, universal humanity, the screen masking male interests, gave way to an overt cult of masculinity with nationalist and racist overtones. Second, the feminist challenge unleashed hysterical assertions of what men and women might properly be and do, thus sexualising all social practices. Third, Idealist a-sexual femininity – always an unstable concept, as witness the literary preoccupation with adulterous transgression – was reaffirmed ever more obsessively at a time when rapid urban growth and mass prostitution brought equally obsessive interest in the whore, so dividing woman into twin stereotypes: the Wife/Mother who feels no sexual desire and the Whore who is nothing but sexual desire. Consequently, the intercourse necessary to bring the former into being became a shameful act and the crucial proof of masculinity was tainted with guilt as a pollution of innocence or demeaning commercial exploitation. Finally, the social roles lost their natural aura, producing the distinction between biological sex and social gender – though the terms 'weiblich' ('female') and 'männlich' ('male') were used in both senses. Such conceptual blurring fuelled anxiety that society was becoming decadent and feminised: the cult of masculinity made men of sensitivity fear for their sexual identity and, as Foucault (1981, p.101) argued, gave birth to the type of the modern homosexual as a transgression defining normality. Conversely, the very basis of civilisation was seen as threatened by the 'Mann-Weib' ('man-woman'), a term which implied both that emancipated women were lesbians and that lesbians were monstrous. The types reflected a fear that sexual difference, so defined as to establish masculinity as the human norm and source of legitimate power, might collapse.

Weininger and Freud belong in this latter context. As a self-hating Jewish homosexual, Weininger (1980) projected his sense of lack on the feminised Jewish race and on women. He dissolved man and woman into male and female qualities: the female, associated with an impersonal, sub-human sexual drive, is always the negative of the male, associated with mind from which human individuality springs. Logically, biological males or females could have a majority of traits with the opposing label, since, according to the theory, individuals are always a mix. Nevertheless, Weininger simply asserted that all women are inferior to men. But his comment that woman is man's guilt become flesh (1980, p.402) is suggestive: contradictory male desires project the motherly vessel of propagation or the whorish vessel of impersonal desire. Thus, Weininger assuaged yet fed fears of collapsing sexual difference by allowing for deviations from pure masculinity while asserting its supreme value, even as his female types became foils defining masculinity. Contemporary conservatives, including many women, continued to elevate motherhood, while radicals preferred the *hetaera*, Bachofen's (1948) mythical, decommercialised whore. Thus, Karl Kraus (1958, p.14) affirmed Wedekind's Lulu as a 'Vollweib' ('full-female'), using Weininger's technical term, but attacked sexual equality which would require men to seek government permission to menstruate (1986, p.50). In sum, practices or feelings ascribed to women were felt to feminise men, and women's entry into male preserves to pollute or to turn women into surrogate men.

Freud distinguished more clearly than Weininger between sex and gender: while we are born sexual, gender is constructed. But the Oedipal story confirmed Fichte's deduction of activating spirit from active penis, and universal humanity remained a male preserve: civilisation was the product of male sublimation. Thus, the radical uncoupling of sex and gender led to the reaffirmation of patriarchy and to the stigmatisation of all deviance from the weighty demands of masculinity or from an infantile femininity. Nietzsche's model of the psyche, otherwise close to Freud's, centred power rather than pleasure in relations between the sexes, and his a-social vision of absolute freedom is an ancestor of that existentialist transcendence which caused Simone de Beauvoir (1983) to hate her female body. Nietzsche's *Übermensch* springs as absolute individual from a *tabula rasa* of all social identity excepting only gender: the *Übermensch* is actually *Übermann*, and woman is either his plaything or the mother of superboys (Nietzsche, 1980, pp.84–6). Thus, Nietzschean and Freudian sublimation share with Idealism the same structure of higher and lower evaluations: as a subject, man is alienated or enslaved by convention or instinct, but he can recognise his oneness with Spirit, assert his existential freedom, or transmute instinct into civilisation. Nevertheless, no matter how the higher realm is defined, woman has no entry; and whether the lower realm is Nature, will or instinct, she is the castrated second sex, the passive object of active male desire.

A Kaleidoscope of Images

For practitioners of 'images criticism', *The Castle* seems a rich hunting ground. In the foreground of the narrative is woman as prey of the sexual drive: the Castle officials personify the active principle and women are the whorish, passive receptacles. Then there is the innocent heroine of romance: knight errant K. arrives in the realm of a sinister castle to save the heroine, Frieda, from the clutches of Count Westwest and his henchmen. And Frieda oscillates disconcertingly between whore and heroine. In bourgeois ideology, romantic love is the prelude to marriage, yet marriage is the death of romance and whores cannot be wives. Therefore, motherly Gardena must safeguard Frieda's passage into the haven of marriage which will extinguish her disturbing sexuality and her romantic aura – the contradictory effluvia which young women are required to emit in order to capture a husband. Thus, Gardena is also a dragon guarding the heroine and the domestic sphere, to be outwitted or placated. The domestic sphere is not private: Gardena's inn is a place of public concourse with far from private bedrooms for sexual intercourse. Mother-guardians of nubile maidens were once young Madonna-mothers, like the final apotheosis of Schlegel's Lucinde: Frau Brunswick retains a mystic aura as she suckles a baby Frieda and she is the love-object of a heroic boy-child, Hans. But degraded by village life and the unethereal tasks of motherhood, she will fade away as Gardena, the wife of an older Hans, swells into being. Indeed, massive Gardena and puny Hans are like the couple in misogynist jokes. In general, wives are either silly young geese or the older power behind husbands (common justifications for women's exclusion from the public domain). Thus, home-maker Frieda is a drag on K.'s pursuit of higher ideals like justice, truth and freedom, and Mizzi of the kittenish name and round but ageing face makes paper boats but runs the Village Superintendent's office. Spinsters who have rejected female destiny come in two types. Amalia, whose defiance leaves her with dull loveless eyes, remains locked in daughterhood; and Gisa, the New Woman of liberal feminism, is a martinet schoolmarm at work, but at home satisfies her opulent body and frustrated maternal instinct with her cat. Finally, Olga, the sister and companion-at-arms, has no weapon but her sexuality, and no aim like land-surveying: her efforts subserve those of her brother and K. In sum, men are only sometimes male, but women are always wives, sisters, daughters, whores or mothers.

Clearly, then, sexual ideology has shaped the women's features and there are signs of conventional anti-feminism: compared with other New Women (like Gregor Samsa's sister or Fräulein Bürstner), a shift from ambivalence to denigration is discernible in Gisa. This complaint, like much 'images criticism', springs, however, from a libertarian feminism which urges women's equal claims to the freedoms men supposedly enjoy. The radical feminist, in contrast, might see Gisa as merely seeking power like a man, and to the Socialist, she and her male colleague might embody authoritarian education in a class society oppressive to men as well as women. The socialist feminist will, however, note Gisa's extra grotesquerie and reflect on the difficulty of combining motherhood and a career in both liberal *and* socialist societies: the meaning of images shifts depending on the reader's politics. These problems concern the aesthetics of reception and the issue of what women are actually like – on which feminists differ – and there are further textual reasons which make 'images criticism' inadequate. Since the women in *The Castle* are not presented as 'true to life', to complain that they are not is to miss the point. The travesty of romance denaturalises the characters, uncovering stereotypes which are starkly exhibited, not blended to produce the illusion of rounded character. Moreover, the women are heavily focalised through a male character. K. sees Frieda through ideological spectacles now as Romantic heroine, now as domestic burden; now as sex object, now as loving heart; now as wife exclusively devoted to her husband, now as mother exclusively devoted to the Assistants/children; now as prize wrested from the Other Man, now as slut who runs off with the Other Man; now as the highest aim in life, now as a drag on his higher aims. As much as the images he sees, K.'s way of seeing is an object to be studied, and we are thrown back behind his eyes into the Imaginary which conditions their operation.

But *The Castle* is also a conversation piece: the images speak, being more than just figments of K.'s imagination, and femininity invades the imagination of women too. How does this happen? If character is estranged, so is the socialising institution of the family: biological fathers have shrunk to midget proportions, and family functions are detached from both blood relations and temporal development. Thus, Gardena functions as mother to Frieda, and Frieda as mother to the Assistants and wife to one of them; there is a baby Frieda and an adult Frieda, a son Hans and a husband Hans; Amalia feeds senile parents as a mother does babies; and even the schoolmarm's cat/baby Mietze echoes Mizzi the wife/secretary. Furthermore, father–son conflict has lost all personal quality and pervades the whole novel as K. woos yet defies the Castle. Although he claims legitimate power as a patrimony – asserting that the Castle must recognise its rightful land-surveyor who will measure and define relations in the Village – he also, as an emancipated bourgeois man, wants to seize power and replace an arbitrary, crumbling system with a new, rational order. Indeed, the relationship between K. and Klamm is not a quarrel between persons, but conveys the contradictory structure of modern patriarchy. K. shares a patrilinear initial letter with Klamm: as Klamm is to K., so K. is to the Assistants. Klamm penetrates the bedrooms and imaginations of Frieda and Gardena as much as he does K's. In liberal society, men are subjected to authoritarian order yet must simultaneously be free-booting agents of free enterprise, and this contradiction produces contradictory roles for women which do not correspond to their personal capacities but which they must play to assure their security. And these roles invade the imagination, producing neurotic attachment to cats in those who do not conform!

The village women are more impressive than the men: Gardena literally outweighs her husband; Olga and Amalia are gutsier than their weedy brother; and Gisa is more dominant than her male colleague. All this could, of course, be K.'s focus: if a woman is powerful or rebellious, then she assumes more aura in male chauvinist eyes than a man would. But K.'s focus cannot account for Amalia's punishment. Although Amalia has rebelled, not against her father but against Castle Law, the daughter's rebellion breaks the father, but not the Law, which exacts a terrible punishment. Yet there is no evident mediation between Castle Law and Village executors, no official order, so why do the villagers punish a girl's defiance of one official so harshly while treating upstart K.'s pretensions with relatively benign indifference? In the eyes of the villagers, it would seem, Amalia's transgression poses the greater threat: K.'s mentality, which exaggerates the significance of women's conformity or otherwise to feminine norms, so pervades the whole village that the Imaginary produces highly concrete effects. That is to say, femininity is an idea shaped by and shaping power relations: whatever the qualities of individuals, women are, as a whole, more subjected than men. Thus, *The Castle* strikingly raises the central feminist question: what is the source of women's oppression? If it is mental – an ideology which real people cannot simply follow because it is contradictory – then what is its basis? Or is the ideology basic, as Idealist theories claim? Answers to this question differentiate between competing theories, some of which I want now to consider.

A Radical Reading: Compulsory Heterosexuality

Despite the image of the Castle rising above the Village, there is no simple flow of power from above. Amalia's punishment and the parallels between Klamm and K. suggest that the Castle is a metaphor for the local workings of power within the Village, with sexuality as a crucial transmission point. This accords with Foucault (1981, p.97) and, before him, Nietzsche: power in modern society is not hierarchically ordered, and its endlessly complex workings infuse myriad social transactions so that the bureaucratic confusion of the Castle is a metaphor for the confusion of Village affairs. But the Castle officials are all male, there is a major domination, a systematic relation more basic than class hierarchy, and a *droit de seigneur* places women at the mercy of men from the onset of puberty. Count Westwest is a ludicrous echo of Almaviva, Don Juan or the Marquis de Sade, and although the material power and aura of aristocratic patriarchy have gone, the sexual structure underlying it survives in drab Sortini's sordid grabbings. Sexuality is the foundation of patriarchy, male sexuality is rapacious and the sex act a violent invasion. Accordingly, when K. first sees Frieda, she is an enigma associated with the Castle, the symbol of power. The eye peers through a peep-hole at Klamm, and the penis demands entry: to penetrate Frieda is to penetrate the Castle.

But the act destroys the enigma, and the victory is pyrrhic: the slave cannot recognise the master. This is a battle in the imagination since post-coital Frieda is not the victim of some *Ur*-assertion of physical force; nor does dominance make modern man a tribal patriarch. Rather, the act is a symbolic display of the masculinity necessary to win status in a competitive culture and a compensation for the lack of social power. It confirms masculinity in the eyes of others and, crucially, of the self, so that men shrivel who do not dominate in such a way. Male dominance is achieved not so much by force as by the illusion of romantic love – symbolised in Gardena's girlhood memories of Klamm. Thus, it is not a paradox that the officials are all male, even though the most impressive villagers are female. Women are conditioned into subjection through the cult of love – in man's life a thing apart, we are told, but woman's whole existence – and then maintain their own systematic oppression in marriage as the only path to economic security. Gardena's massive body is the sign of maternal strength, but she upholds an institution which subjects all that power to rule by puny men. Marriage makes her heart-sick and sick in body because her sexual and emotional needs are starved as she performs that massive social labour of women which male-centred economic theory ignores.

Amalia sees through the illusion, however, to the underlying rapacity, and recognises the crux of patriarchy in compulsory heterosexuality – which, to her, is the universal degradation of women by men (Rich, 1987). Thus, Amalia's transgression denies the basis of patriarchy, whereas K. merely displays a structural contradiction which can find an interim solution through the victory either of the Father or of the rebellious Son. But the Son will become a Father, and K.'s treatment of the Assistants does not augur well for an overthrow of patriarchy. Although Bürgel outlines a reconciliation of Father and Son, in this utopia the Castle remains male. Moreover, K.'s softer attitude to Frieda, the domestic woman, and his affair with Pepi, the whore, confirm the major stereotypes with a minor softening of tone: a gentle paternalism responding to Frieda's ideal femininity; a loosening of moral rigour so that radical man can enjoy free love with a mistress rather than commerce with prostitutes. Unlike Josef K., who slinks off once a week to Elsa, K. shacks up with Pepi! There is no such resolution for Amalia: she remains branded by the law of compulsory heterosexuality. She is, however, not a lesbian, but pure negation, and like Bürgel's utopia, this too signals a limit in Kafka's vision. In contrast, the relationship between K. and Barnabas has homoerotic undertones. But on recognising that the way to the Castle does not lie through Barnabas, K. represses any love for the slim angel: heterosexual masculinity is the sign of power.

The Castle offers an anatomy of modern patriarchy, but K.'s subjective sufferings predominate as the narrative and K. move on, leaving Frieda, the Barnabas family and Amalia behind; and the only utopian opening is not the overthrow of patriarchy but its confirmation. Thus, *The Castle* is not a radical feminist text, but highlights problems in radical feminism inasmuch as the figures with radical potential are Gardena, the matriarch, and rebellious Amalia. But how is a radical separatist such as Amalia to establish matriarchy? Even if conception could be mechanised, what is a separatist mother to do with a boy-child? For if men are essentially rapacious, then the son must be cast off at puberty, psychologically an impossible strategy. But if sexuality is socially constructed, then women cannot just stand apart, leaving male-dominated culture and socio-economic oppression uncontested. Amalia has mothering skills and perhaps instincts, given that she nurses her parents, but no social power. Gisa's motherliness is more dubious: she uses her cat's paw as a weapon against K., but leaves the job of bathing the cat/baby in a baby-bath to motherly Frieda, a common practice of professional women who have some social power. Gisa also has sexual power over Schwarzer who, despite his Castle connections, creeps to listen at her door in the same way that K. creeps to Klamm's door. Her power is signalled by the bizarrely circling pupils of her eyes – a sharper version of Amalia's dull loveless gaze – which bore into Schwarzer but resist mutual penetration, indicating that the power would shrivel were she to allow Schwarzer entry. Likewise, as a mother, she would dwindle and pine like Frau Brunswick, losing her power over K. which comes from her professional status. Thus, the disparate nature of women's domestic, sexual or professional power leaves scant hope for united sisterhood as envisaged by radical feminism.

Structuralism: The Exchange of Women

Radical feminism revalues the natural types of bourgeois ideology: Fichte's activating male principle becomes mere rapacity, and the passive vessel of propagation becomes the agent of mother-power. But because the sexual types are based in unchanging biology, patriarchy could be overthrown only by an equally monolithic matriarchy. Structuralism, in contrast, purports to explain patriarchy without recourse to biology. According to Lévi-Strauss (1967, pp.549–70), two cultural universals define humanity: the incest prohibition and language. Indeed, relations between the sexes are a language, but men and women do not speak in dialogue: men speak with men and women are the spoken, the sign. Woman as sign surmounts a contradiction in male perception between the same woman, seen as *object* who arouses sexual instincts of appropriation, and as *subject* of another's desire. Thus, what makes woman a subject is being desired by another man, and through exchange, she becomes a means of alliance with the other, whether she is given or received. In like manner, K. sees Frieda now as *object* of his own desire, now as a *subject* of Klamm's desire, so turning her into a sign through which he might communicate with Klamm: to receive Frieda from Klamm would integrate him into the Village and establish his competence as speaker of a language.

Lévi-Strauss (1967, p.569) quaintly admits, however, that woman is not only a sign: in a world of men she is, after all, a person, and even K. eventually recognises that he has treated Frieda purely as a sign. But woman as producer of signs is limited to one partner because her language subsists within the overarching matrimonial dialogue of men, and when Frieda sinks out of K.'s life, she enters into a duo with Jeremias where her loving care is a value-in-use: safely married, she is consumed rather than exchanged. In contrast, Amalia has gone out of circulation, and her potential value-in-use withers. Indeed, in this novel of endless conversations, she is remarkably silent: having rejected the duologue, her utterance is difficult to understand, as Olga comments. Unlike Lévi-Strauss, however, *The Castle* shows the reduction of woman to sign or value, whether in exchange or use, to be an oppressive denial of subjecthood which Amalia combats in the most assertive claim to autonomy in the whole novel. A technical critique of Lévi-Strauss, notably the claimed trans-historical universality of the structures, is not possible here (Leach, 1970, pp.18–20), but his affinities with German Idealism are worth noting. The notion of the duo transcended in men's universal language echoes Hegel's dialectic; the effusions on woman's emotional richness and mystery recall Hegel's more egregious moments; and the concept of the deep-structure is gendered as the exchange of women, because woman, as in the work of Fichte and in the Idealist tradition as a whole, is conceived as the passive object of active male desire. Conversely, a woman who is not or has not been desired would not be a subject, but an undefined monster. Lévi-Strauss has invented anthropological proofs for the ideological baggage he set out with.

Lacan: The Phallic Castle

Lévi-Strauss (1967, p.570) writes of two myths which, he claims, express the pleasure denied social man of living for oneself, 'entre soi': the myth of a paradise where women will not be exchanged, and the myth of a Golden Age before the confusion of languages made words into a thing for everyone. For Lacan, too, the notion of an absolute self from whom the Word issues is a myth, because language precedes the subject, being the social medium through which subjectivity and gender are constituted. But whereas Lévi-

Strauss claims that men speak while women are spoken, Lacan argues more consequentially that both sexes are spoken. Nevertheless, patriarchy remains universal because the symbolic order of language is phallocentric. Two Lacanian concepts are of interest here: the mirror stage and the phallus as empty prime signifier in the differential system of language. The mirror stage, a crucial moment in the emergence of subjectivity through recognition of inner and outer world, gives rise to a radical ex-centricity of the self. Before all social determination, the ego is set in a fictional direction as the infant assumes its specular image or double in the mirror as its ego-ideal because it seems to offer bodily control. Thus, the double is both a fantasy of absolute subjecthood and the first heteronomous image of many, and although the specular I will be deflected into the social I, Lacan argues that it remains in the Imaginary as a fortress or castle whose function is to defend the ego against the Other, even though it is itself Other:

> The formation of the I is symbolized in dreams by a fortress, or a stadium – its inner arena and enclosure, surrounded by marshes and rubbish-tips, dividing it into two opposed fields of contest where the subject flounders in quest of the lofty, remote inner castle whose form (sometimes juxtaposed in the same scenario) symbolizes the id in a quite startling way. Similarly on the mental plane, we find realized the structures of fortified works, the metaphor of which arises spontaneously, as if issuing from the symptoms themselves, to designate the mechanisms of obsessional neurosis – inversion, isolation, reduplication, cancellation and displacement. (Lacan, 1980, p.5)

Analogously, as K. flounders in quest of the lofty, remote inner castle, he seeks an illusory autonomy, that pleasure denied social man of living *entre soi*, in narcissistic union with the self. Barnabas in his first angelic appearance and the charmingly infantile Assistants are emissaries of the Other as mirror-image of the self. But they fail to assuage K.'s deep isolation because later alienations block his vision – with the result that he does not recognise these joyous, infantile, other selves, now become obstacles to patriarchal ambition. Frieda is, however, both drawn to the emissaries of a pre-Oedipal mother–child union, and yet oppressed by their endless needs and consuming demand for love as they conflict with the rights of K., the father.

The Freudian id gives birth to the super-ego. Likewise, Lacan's specular image is the ex-centric basis for future identifications as the subject is en-gendered in language, then subjected to the alienations of social existence, beginning with those generated in the patriarchal family through the Oedipus complex. Analogously, while the core of the Castle may be the imaginary self, it is cocooned in a vast confusion of papery onion layers, each in itself flimsy, but suffocating in their bulk. Male scribes inscribe the paperwork of identity, and the Castle's highest point is a veiled phallus, a round tower 'mercifully covered partially with ivy' (Kafka, 1983, p.18). Superimposed on the inner castle of the pre-linguistic self are the patriarchs like Klamm (reminiscent of the Czech word for illusion), whose *nom/non* is echoed in the castrated diminutive, K. But according to Lacan, we are all castrated, Self and Other, male and female, and the phallus is an empty sign of lack or absence. Thus, Klamm is not an actual father who could grant or deny K.'s wishes, but the *absence* of what could satisfy – that is the empty signifier.

Lacan distinguishes three psychic elements in his account of the advent of the phallus: needs requiring satisfaction, the demand for love, and desire. Since, in the mother–child relationship, the Other is seen as able to provide, but also to withhold, satisfactions, the child poses an unconditional demand beyond any single need, the demand for love. Any satisfaction is then translated ambiguously into a proof of love but also a fobbing-off of the unconditional demand, while an unsatisfied need is felt as the denial or absence of love and is then conceived as lying *beyond* the demand for love. This is the genesis of desire uncoupled from love. Thus, K. is gripped by unassuageable desire. Satisfaction of specific needs – permission to stay, shelter, a job – leads only to a sense of rejection of the unconditional demand: he is being fobbed off. When Frieda offers unconditional love, K.'s desire stretches out beyond her, and even the Castle itself lacks what would answer desire so that its officials are as frightened of K. as he is of them. They desire what K. cannot give: he cannot be the phallus which the castrated Castle lacks. Its tower, half-veiled by ivy, seems drawn by a child's hand, and when visible, it loses its value as prime signifier, becoming the insane self-display of some wretched inmate, a penis not a phallus. When K. first arrives, he looks up into 'apparent emptiness' (Kafka, 1983, p.7). That is the truth: the phallus is an empty signifier under which the signified constantly shifts. The Castle is nothing, and the meanings it takes on are constituted by the needs and desires of K. and the villagers. But specific meanings can never be *the* meaning which constantly recedes before unassuageable desire, for *the* meaning is deeply contradictory in that K. desires recognition from and yet unity with the Other, to be separate and yet to merge. Thus, he seeks to merge with Klamm through Frieda or to merge with Frieda against Klamm as Oedipal obstacle, while also claiming to define himself in the narcissistic illusion of the mirror phase, a condition of absolute isolation. On this reading, the women in *The Castle* become spectral emanations of an unconscious drama without resolution.

Up to the mirror phase, the emergent psyche is ungendered. But the supposedly empty prime signifier is gendered as the phallus. Why?

> The phallus is the privileged signifier of that mark in which the role of the logos is joined with the advent of desire.
>
> It can be said that this signifier is chosen because it is the most tangible element in the real sexual copulation, and also the most symbolic in the literal (typographical) sense of the term, since it is equivalent there to the (logical) copula. It might also be said that, by virtue of its turgidity, it is the image of the vital flow as it is transmitted in generation. (Lacan, 1980, p.287)

And further on: the future of the phallic signifier 'depends on the law introduced by the father into this sequence', the sequence being the differential path taken by the sexes (p.289). Thus, despite the claim that the phallus is not the penis, Lacan here has recourse to empirical fathers and to anatomical difference, and, like Freud's circularity in explaining the origins of patriarchy, the argument is viciously circular: the signifier from which sexual difference will flow is chosen because of the sexual difference it is to explain. Thereafter, Lacan's deductions are banal and flattering to men: they elevate the male member, linked by a bad pun to the logical copula; men's greater repression fuels culture; women are more sexual but can put up with lack of pleasure and are necessarily seen as either virgins or whores. That Lacan's story maps well with aspects of Kafka's text does not prove its universal validity, but merely that both men inhabited a similar culture. It does not map, however, with Amalia. According to Lacanian theory, there is no speech outside the phallocentric symbolic order, at most, perhaps, the rhythms of a feminine semiotic (Kristeva, 1986, pp.93–8). But although Amalia says little, her action speaks volumes, and the sense of what she does say is plain to a sister-reader of the text, if not to her sister in the text: she is trapped not by language but by social practices which actions could change.

The Castle as Ideological Reflection of Village Practice

Although structuralist and psychoanalytic theory throw into relief the patriarchal relations explored by *The Castle*, the novel resists reduction to these master-plots and highlights gaps in the theories. Gisa has not been reduced to a token of exchange in the Village economy since, in modern society, women are not simply commodities in a marriage market, and Amalia's resistance is inexplicable by structuralist or Lacanian theory because patriarchy is not a seamless monolith. Lévi-Strauss and Lacan perpetuate the error Marx noted in the *Theses on Feuerbach*: although Feuerbach explains God as the alienated projection of the human essence, he does not see that the abstract individual whom he analyses belongs to a particular form of society. Similarly, Structuralism and neo-Freudianism are ideological reflections of a particular form of society, projected as universals.

The Castle, too, is a projection, outlined on high by a thin layer of snow, and its power is mental, being, if you like, a sign divided into signifier and constantly shifting signified. But does the Castle as Idea or phallic signifier determine the social practice of the Village, as Idealism, Structuralism and Lacanian psychoanalysis would claim, or do material practices in the Village shape the Castle? Recent Marxist feminist debate on this issue threatens to become scholastic. The Marxist will claim that the male domain of the Castle reflects male-dominated relations of production and reproduction in the Village, and that unassuagable desire has as much to do with ever new needs generated by the market as it has with a drama of infancy. But the mental does not simply reflect the material. Castle and Village so interact that when the phallic tower finally crumbles, its fall must involve both mental and material change. How far do Castle and Village appear as open to change? Though hard to reach, the Castle looks like a historical accumulation of ramshackle structures, not a seamless monolith; and its crumbling tower is perhaps held together only by its veil of ivy: remove the veil and the tower might collapse. Down in the Village, electric light, the telephone and a female schoolteacher disrupt the vaguely feudal atmosphere. Frieda and K. are a notional nuclear family from which K. excludes the Assistants who would once have lived in the extended working household. A mini-family enclosed in a school enclosed in a village under the shadow of a Castle conveys the interlocking institutions which produce the dominant discourses of bourgeois society.

Nevertheless, *The Castle* perpetuates a degree of mystification to the extent that the anachronistic mix of institutions tends to assimilate modernity to timelessness: the historically specific, petty-bourgeois relations in *The Judgment* or *The Metamorphosis* and the banks and urban slums in *The Trial* have given way to an anti-pastoral landscape where snow obscures even seasonal change. K.

introduces irritation, but reaches a semi-accommodation, whereas the end of *The Trial* is, by comparison, more subversive, involving the death not of a man, but of form of manliness, broken on its own contradictions. In its very mastery, Kafka's masterpiece, *The Castle*, is less radical. On the other hand, its anatomy of patriarchy uncovers endless contradictions: there may be accommodation, but scarcely affirmation, and a subterranean humour makes the scandal of patriarchy ludicrous. Although the humour offers no programmatic exit, it is a kind of rebellion beyond the compass of humourless K., but to measure its effectiveness would require another paper.

References

Bachofen, J. (1948) *Das Mutterrecht*, Schwabe, Basle
Beauvoir, S. de (1983) *The Second Sex*, Penguin, Harmondsworth
Bovenschen, S. (1979) *Die imaginierte Weiblichkeit: Exemplarische Untersuchungen zu kulturgeschichtlichen und literarischen Präsentationsformen des Weiblichen*, Suhrkamp, Frankfurt/Main
Fichte, J. (1971) *Werke*, vol.3, de Gruyter, Berlin
Foucault, M. (1981) *The History of Sexuality*, Penguin, Harmondsworth
Hegel, G. (1972) *Grundlinien der Philosophie des Rechts*, Ullstein, Frankfurt/Main
Hegel, G. (1973) *Phänomenologie des Geistes*, Ullstein, Frankfurt/Main
Kafka, F. (1970) *Sämtliche Erzählungen*, Fischer, Frankfurt/Main
Kafka, F. (1983) *Das Schloß*, ed. Malcolm Pasley, Fischer, Frankfurt/Main
Krafft-Ebing, R. von (1972) *Psychopathia Sexualis* (1892), translated from the 7th edition by C. Chadwick, F. Davis, Philadelphia and London
Kraus, K. (1958) *Literatur und Lüge*, DTV, Munich
Kraus, K. (1986) *Aphorismen*, Suhrkamp, Frankfurt/Main
Kristeva, J. (1986) *The Kristeva Reader*, ed. T. Moi, Blackwell, Oxford
Lacan, J. (1980) *Écrits*, Tavistock, London
Leach, E. (1970) *Lévi-Strauss*, Fontana, London
Lévi-Strauss, C. (1967) *Les Structures élémentaires de la parenté*, Mouton, Paris
Nietzsche, F. (1980) *Sämtliche Werke*, vol.4, DTV, Munich
Rich, A. (1987) 'Compulsory Heterosexuality and Lesbian Existence' in *Blood, Bread and Poetry: Selected Prose 1979–1986*, Virago, London, pp.23–75
Rousseau, J.-J. (1964) *Émile ou de l'éducation*, Garnier, Paris
Weedon, C. (1987) *Feminist Practice and Poststructuralist Theory*, Blackwell, Oxford
Weininger, O. (1980) *Geschlecht und Charakter*, Matthes and Seitz, Munich

–7–

Women Writing about Women Writing and Ingeborg Bachmann's *Malina*

ELIZABETH BOA

As a text by a woman about a woman who writes, Ingeborg Bachmann's *Malina* (1971) raises issues concerning subjectivity and gender which are much debated in feminist criticism. *Malina* is the fictional autobiography of an unnamed woman writer with a doctorate in *Germanistik*, philosophy and psychology, who shares a flat in Vienna with a male friend and *alter ego* called Malina. Her affair with Ivan, who lives in the same street, peters out miserably and she finally disappears into the wall of her room. When Ivan then telephones, Malina makes the final break, saying that he lives alone here and that no woman of that (to the reader still unknown) name ever lived at this address. The novel then closes with the words: 'It was murder.' I shall call the narrator *Ich*, the German first-person pronoun, as she herself does in the list of characters in the introductory section. This introduction is followed by three chapters entitled 'Happy with Ivan', an account of *Ich*'s affair with Ivan; 'The Third Man', a phantasmagoria about the Father who haunts *Ich*'s nightmares; and 'Of Last Things', which mixes realistic narrative and duet-like dialogues with Malina, the male double who finally displaces *Ich*.

Malina poses a challenge to the once almost exclusively male canon of traditional *Germanistik*. The right to education was a central demand in the liberal tradition of feminist politics whose success *Ich* seems initially to demonstrate. A famous writer with a doctorate and the vote, *Ich* is not confined to the domestic sphere as middle-class women once were. Her doctorate represents a triumph over the Father of her nightmares; she receives state honours; journalists seek her out for interview; and she employs a woman secretary, as eminent men do – though the secretary is another *alter ego*, as her name, Lina, a shortening of Malina, indicates. But the *Germanistik* that *Ich* studied was a male canon; the writers she cites are all men; and her doctorate and fame as a writer mark her entry into literature, which has, for millennia, been 'strictly men's business, as every woman discovers who writes the word "I"', to quote Christa Reinig (Brügmann, 1986, p.198). *Ich* needs Malina's support in this alien realm, but after the ominous closing words, the rest is silence, for Malina writing would not be a woman writing. Likewise, women's entry into the academy is not a sign of emancipation as long as what they study is an exclusively male canon.

In effect, *Malina* draws the line under a liberal feminism limited to equal rights, as I shall argue in the first three sections of this essay. Here, I examine *Ich*'s autobiographical project as a pursuit of identity which is based on the humanist conception of authentic individuality that underlies liberal politics, taking Mary Wollstonecraft (1759–97) and the German feminist Hedwig Dohm (1833–1919) as historical points of reference. I shall, however, argue that the autobiographical project fails because *Ich* remains subject to socio-sexual relations which liberal legislation has not fundamentally altered. To that extent, *Malina* confirms the radical view that women can compete equally with men only at the cost of becoming like men: Malina displaces *Ich*. It is, however, unclear whether *Ich* represents a true self overlaid by the false *persona* of Malina, or whether the novel suggests that there is no true self or essential womanhood which an individual subject might recover from social distortion. If the latter were the case, it would be because, as socialist feminists critical of both liberal individualism and radical essentialism would argue, subjectivity and sexuality change in and through changing social relations so that individual emancipation requires a social transformation going far beyond formal equal rights.

The following three sections turn to Julia Kristeva's dissertation of 1974, *Revolution in Poetic Language* (1986, pp.89–136) with its thesis of 'the feminine' in writing, the inverted commas indicating that 'the feminine' is a metaphor detached from actual women as a sex.[1] Read through Kristeva, *Malina* both confirms the critique of individualism and essentialism which I have attributed to socialist feminism, and exemplifies the tension between socialist feminism and psychoanalytic theory, which Cora Kaplan described as 'the polarization of social and psychic explanation' (1986, p.155). Whereas socialist

---

1. See Bossinade (1985) and Höller (1987, pp.239–51) who draw on the more radical theories of *écriture féminine* put forward by Luce Irigaray and Hélène Cixous.

critics focus on material oppression and read the expression of sexual and romantic longings in women's writing *negatively*, as an internalised ideology tending to lock women into a regressive femininity, critics in the psychoanalytic tradition focus on psychic repression and read the expression of female desire *positively*, as the subversive breakthrough of what patriarchy represses. I shall argue that *Ich*'s desires cannot be understood exclusively in terms of either of these interpretations. Rather, *Malina* explores the dilemma of a woman who, in seeking to escape subjection, becomes estranged from her own desires, which she experiences *both* as shameful subjection *and* as disruptive – and hence disabling and isolating. I shall throughout relate these problems of interpretation to feminism as a politics.

A Room of One's Own and the Public Sphere

Ich has that room of her own which Virginia Woolf once claimed and in which she can be, discover, or write herself. But although writing is a private activity, publication means entry into the public sphere, which invades *Ich*'s room in the form of letters from the President, journalists seeking interviews, and appeals from distressed refugees. The State, which honours *Ich*, once collaborated in the murder of millions, and the body politic of Europe, once rent by war, remains divided and is wandered by refugees who beg the famous writer for help, which womanly *Ich* cannot deny. Such material intrusions go along with psychic disturbance. The tiny private space of *Ich*'s room is an echo-chamber for a monstrous public history, and the rent body of Europe appears in *Ich*'s nightmares where the Patriarch who murdered millions and publicly burnt books, destroys the books on her shelves and reduces her to a doll's body to be enjoyed or dismembered at his whim. The Patriarch claims physical power over populations, books and bodies, together with discursive power over writing and the meanings of bodies (cf. Chris Weedon's essay below, pp.157–62). Thus, along with nightmares of the War, one of *Ich*'s earliest memories is of a boy who beckoned her with a promise, then struck her in the face; and for all her eminence, *Ich* feels constrained to inscribe on her body the signs of femininity by painting her face and donning pretty dresses for Ivan. Moreover, *Ich* experiences her emancipation as an academic and writer as the ultimate insidious violation by institutions of male power, inasmuch as Malina, the male double who shields her from the invasive femininity induced by her love for Ivan and who guards her privacy so that she can write, eventually displaces her altogether. Indeed, the connection between knowledge, writing and power is symbolised in his job: Malina is a curator in the Army Museum.

The nightmarish homology between Europe torn asunder and *Ich*'s own body implies that emancipation conceived in individualistic terms is an illusion, for the room of one's own is located in a public sphere of power politics, which poems and novels cannot of themselves transform. And when *Ich* seeks to escape feminine subjection, she succumbs to the assault of a Trinity emanating from a patriarchal culture which persists in liberal society (Bail, 1984, pp.55–6). *Ich*'s nightmares are dominated by the Father as hunter and butcher in the darkest version of the patriarchal text in which woman is an animal to be hunted and slaughtered (Bossinade, 1985, pp.89–93). The ogre of *Ich*'s nightmares assaults her eyes and mouth and eviscerates her: women are not to see, speak or desire, but to be seen, spoken and desired. Thus, while the Father dances at *Ich*'s first ball with pretty, feminine Melanie – a name suggesting the Greek word for honey and a Freudian alphabetic transformation of Malina – *Ich* must sit passive till Malina comes to save her from humiliation. Melanie, beloved of the Father, and Malina, protector from the Father, live on in *Ich*'s psyche. The Son, Ivan, promises but withholds love as the boy in *Ich*'s memory once did. To win his love, *Ich* must be a honey-sweet Melanie as in the lighter version of the patriarchal text: not an erotic initiator, but a sweetmeat to be consumed or pushed aside once the appetite is sated. Martha-like, *Ich* cooks Austrian specialities for Ivan and sits, Mary-like, at his feet, docilely losing at chess. Ivan does not like her gloomy, difficult writing and wants a story with a happy ending; but Malina, the Holy Ghost in *Ich*, revolts against such a denial of the mind and shields *Ich* from the Son as he had protected her from the Father. In so doing, however, he becomes her gaoler: the telephone, which is an intrusion into the room as a refuge, is also a lifeline out of the room as a prison, which Malina finally cuts in the closing exchange with Ivan. In sum, *Ich* must be woman either as an object of domination by the Father, or an object of pleasure for the Son, or else she must, as Malina demands, cease to be a woman. Thus, the Holy Ghost saves *Ich* from the Father and the Son but at the cost of the extinction of the woman as a subject, and hence of the autobiographical project.

Elizabeth Boa

The Difficulty of Saying 'I'

The modern genre of autobiography emerged with the rise of bourgeois individualism as male intellectuals like Rousseau or Goethe sought to throw off patriarchal and feudal chains. Whereas autobiography marks the claim to be the author of one's life, possessed of the autonomy and control reflected in the aesthetic order of narrative, *Malina* is, as a *fictional* autobiography, not a masterly narrative, but a reflection on the search for identity – i.e. for a position in time and space from which narrative would become possible. In her essay, 'The Writing I', Bachmann (1982, vol.4, pp.217–37) describes the 'self-assured, unbroken I' in memoirs of men of action like Churchill as a role which is 'vorgeschrieben' ('already written') in the public record of history. Rousseau and Goethe, if more ambiguously than Churchill, were also aware of their already written role, but most writers, Bachmann suggests, do not have a singular, Churchillian 'I' at their disposal, since they have, as readers, passed from book to book, meeting many 'I's which take possession of them. *Malina* explores the peculiar 'difficulty of saying I' (Wolf, 1971, p.164) which women experience: since women's roles have hitherto been written largely by men, how can *Ich* avoid her writing being flooded by the already written patriarchal texts?

In the same period as the rise of autobiography, Mary Wollstonecraft claimed the rights of man for women – who, she argued, were prevented from being the authors of their lives through being educated into a distorting femininity designed for a marriage market. Because society enslaved women by 'cramping their understandings and sharpening their senses' (1983, p.104), women should refuse the role of 'alluring object of desire' (p.108), 'curb the wild emotions' (p.112) and aspire 'every day to grow more and more masculine' (p.80). Thus, in refusing the status of object of desire, Wollstonecraft came close to those male ideologues who denied women's right to be desiring subjects. Rational Malina, a latter-day Wollstonecraft, shields *Ich* from reduction to an alluring object of desire, but both he and Ivan reject *Ich*'s wild emotions, and between them, the desiring subject is obliterated. Writing while the franchise campaign was developing, Hedwig Dohm was, like Wollstonecraft, critical of femininity as imagined by men and internalised by women. In an essay of 1876, Dohm surveyed collective male wisdom on women perceived either as extra-cultural enigmas bearing men's utopian dreams – 'sphinxes, Undines, *Märchen*, puzzles, mysteries'[2]

2. The water-nymph Undine is a figure from the *Märchen*, the genre collected by the

– or as sub-cultural domestic drudges (1978, p.28). Dohm anticipated the patriarchal categories of the feminine which Sylvia Bovenschen (1979) distinguished: theories of completion or of reduction whereby the feminine is defined relative to the male self-image either as that which men need to achieve completion or wholeness – Goethe's eternal feminine, for example – or as the negative necessary for the definition of positive male qualities. Conceived as the material of Nature, as opposed to man's engagement in history, woman is endlessly malleable: '*Image* of a lost, undestroyed wholeness *and* image of a future to be shaped by [man] through his understanding and work' (pp.248–9). Bovenschen is referring here to Schiller's aesthetics where 'the feminine' is a metaphor of a lost harmony to be regained through man's work of synthesis: men write 'the feminine'.

Measured against that utopian image, however, actual women, as *natural* beings who lack the preservatives of reason and morality (i.e. the qualities which raise Man above Nature), were liable to go rotten – hence the reductive theories. Thus, the feminine in writing by men is, as Dohm noted, a pot-pourri of contradictions. The female soul appears there as a chaotic mist before which man the creator utters his 'Let woman be' to call forth whatever image suits his mood. And women, subject socially and economically to men, evince the servility of the subjected, yet internalise the dreams of freedom and love. Unlike Wollstonecraft's wholesale attack on femininity, however, Dohm argued that once freed from subjection, 'woman may become a sex full of beauty and grace, strength and intelligence' (1978, p.44). Thus, Dohm sought to emancipate 'the feminine' from its status as a metaphor in male writing and to free actual women to be agents of a Schillerian synthesis of the naïve and sentimental.

The Disunities of Action, Place and Time

Ich likewise seeks to call herself forth from the chaotic mist of the female soul. The novel opens with a cast-list, a place and a time: the place is Vienna, the time 'today' – two unities, and so autobiography becomes the third unity of action. In writing 'I', *Ich* tries to assert her presence as a unified agent, and since a patrilinear surname and gendered first name are the first textual marks of

---

Grimms and adopted by the Romantics, by Bachmann in her story *Undine Goes* (vol.2, pp.253–65) and by *Ich*.

feminine subjection, her namelessness signals her rejection of the already written role of Daughter of the Father. But *Ich*'s pleasure that her initials are the same as Ivan's suggests a repressed longing to assume the Name of the Husband; and the title of *Ich*'s autobiography, which is not *her* name, strikingly signals her failure to establish a unified identity. 'Malina' seems feminine to a reader of Germanic and Latinate languages, but turns out to be a man's name, although it is sometimes a woman's name in Polish (Beicken, 1988, p.192). Thus, although the name of *Ich*'s double is less obviously masculine than such nineteenth-century pseudonyms as George Sand or Currer Bell, it marks the continuing impossibility of escaping the patriarchal text. Because *all* names derive from the male prerogative of naming, to refuse patriarchal identification is to risk evanescing into non-entity and indeed, *Ich* finally fails to assert her unity as an agent through writing 'I'.

The utopian dream of the unity of place and its historical disunity are signalled in the name of the street, the Ungargasse, where *Ich* feels so at home. 'Ungar' means Hungarian, Ivan's nationality, and Vienna was once the centre of an empire embracing now divided peoples. *Ich* and Malina both spent their childhood in the borderland of Carinthia and exchange fragments of Slovene or Wendish, languages which cross modern borders and sound like magical languages from humanity's childhood before the division of peoples produced the Babel of tongues. The dream of space without division is manifest in the *Märchen* ('fairy tale') *Ich* writes, for this is set along the Danube before the establishment of any imperial provinces, whether Roman or German. Situated at the opposite extreme from the enclosure of *Ich*'s room, this borderless landscape is a place where the woman is maximally vulnerable. Thus, out riding one day, the Princess of Kagran is abducted by Hungarian hussars from the Puszta, so losing her sovereignty. But a cloaked stranger frees her, and she rides upstream till she gets lost in a seemingly endless marshland of gurgling waters and whispering willows and reeds. Again the stranger saves her, and the Princess foretells their third meeting, more than a thousand years later, when the stranger will kiss her, but drive thorns into her heart. The whispering marshland is a psychic space without division where love can bloom like a flower: but that space threatens to engulf, the flower withers and the barb of love can kill. Thus, on her return home, the Princess falls bleeding from her horse, her heart already pierced by the first thorn. *Ich*'s autobiography continues the story a thousand years later when the saviour-murderer of the *Märchen* is implicated in the second murder, for, on exiting from her room, *Ich* loses sovereignty and is pierced by the barb of desire. But Ivan fails her, and the open space where love might have bloomed becomes a precinct of death where she is threatened with dispersal and loss of self-definition. Like the Princess, *Ich* returns home, where death finally arrives in the prison of her room as the unity achieved through separation becomes deadly, metaphorically echoing the false security of national borders which turn others into enemies. In *Märchen*, heroes save princesses, and in autobiography, *Ich* should rescue herself. But in neither genre can *Ich* write the happy ending Ivan asked for, since in neither the open space nor the closed room is union with the other or unity of the self achieved.

Ich can write 'today', the unity of time, only with dreadful effort, but is helped by Malina, whom she first saw as they stood at a bus stop, each reading a newspaper. In newspapers, 'today' means either a specific date or else a historical category of years or even decades. But it never means 'now', the urgent moment of desire, located only in the a-historical body, that time should stand still in an ecstatic union with the lover to whom *Ich* writes agonised letters pleading for a meeting 'today'. *Ich* next stumbles against Malina at a lecture on 'Art in the Age of Technology', presaging how she will lean on him to unify time and hold her identity together against the invasion of desire which disables her in the age of technology. The 'today' *Ich* writes in letters induces a-rhythmic breathing and an irregular heart-beat recorded in the jagged line drawn by an electro-cardiogram. Such body language signals a regressive femininity which puts *Ich* in thrall to the lover to whom her letters are addressed, dispersing her identity into moments which threaten to fall apart, bringing death should the heart cease to function. Thus, only suicides should say 'today' (vol.3, p.9). Malina finally orders *Ich* to kill such desire, but the narrator-*Ich* chooses instead to immure the protagonist-*Ich*, then recedes into a covert third-person mode and finally silence, so that the murder is also a suicide, as Christa Wolf suggests (1983, p.149). Yet Malina's 'today' is an age which has harnessed modern technology to the millennial violence which haunts the timeless psyche in *Ich*'s nightmares. Thus, 'today' is torn apart by the utopian dream of union with the other and the dystopian nightmare of being rent by the other.

So far, I have accused both Ivan and Malina of *Ich*'s murder and argued that her death is also a suicide. But who is the main culprit? Kaplan's socialist (1986) would see the immediate cause in *Ich*'s regressive femininity and the remote cause in oppressive social relations, for which the patriarchal ogre is an obfuscating symbol. But in the psychoanalytic tradition as modified by radical feminism,

Ich's death instantiates the ever-repeated murder of 'the feminine' resulting from the fundamental conflict between Father and Daughter, not Father and Son as Freud would have it (Höller, 1987, p.131).[3] On such a reading, the religious motifs in the text take on the force of a feminist revaluation of Christian iconography. *Ich* uses the terms 'disturbance' and 'stigmatised' (vol.3, p.9): if Ivan is the Son in a patriarchal Trinity, *Ich*'s body bears the stigmata, the signs of the true passion suffered by the woman (Bond, 1988). Because patriarchy stigmatises unregulated female desire as disruptive, *Ich*'s visions of golden-eyed women, and her panting breath and irregular pulse can be read as subversive. Just as Christ attacked the Law in the name of love, so *Ich*'s wild emotions tend to disrupt that efficient order which has produced urban alienation and the technology of war. *Ich*'s body language is also analogous to the broken rhythms of modernist poetry, which Julia Kristeva calls 'the feminine' in writing (1986, p.97) and sees as subversive. *Ich* cites Schönberg's *Pierrot lunaire*, which is a quintessentially 'feminine' work in Kristeva's sense, for its a-tonal and irregularly rhythmic *Sprechgesang* ('speech-song') elides differentiation between notes and pitch in a scandalous disruption of classical order. Wedded to his car, Ivan has never walked with *Ich* in the park where she once heard a Pierrot sing in falsetto: 'O alter Duft aus Märchenzeit' ('O ancient perfume from the Age of *Märchen*', vol.3, p.12). 'Mit überschnappender Stimme', the German for 'falsetto', suggests breakthrough from control as in the breaking voice of the male adolescent, not yet banished from the soprano of childhood into adult tenor or bass. Pierrot is masculine, but the song is sung by a woman wearing the child-like, pom-pommed costume in clownish mockery of adult male dignity, and the phrase quoted by *Ich* transports the listener from the leaden age of technology to a golden Arcadia.[4]

Kristeva and the Breakthrough of the Semiotic

For critics deploying Lacanian theory, Arcadia is a mythical trace of pre-Oedipal infancy, and Pierrot echoes the double of the mirror stage.[5] According to Lacan, patriarchy flows not from the powers of a real father, but from the symbolic order of language which sustains

---

3. See Bossinade (1985) on the helplessly complicit Mother in *Ich*'s nightmares, a role which Kristeva's already ordered *chora* inadvertently underwrites.
4. See Boa (1987), pp.61–2, and Ritter (1989) on Pierrot.
5. See my essay on Kafka (pp.112–27 above) and Richard Sheppard's essay on expressionist drama (pp.181–90 below) for a critique of Lacan's theory.

the Law of the Father established in the course of the Oedipus conflict. On discovering that the phallus is absent from the mother, the child moves from the pre-linguistic, Imaginary phase of identification with the mother's desire into the process of substitutions for the lacking phallus, out of which the chains of sliding signifiers of language are generated. The absent, and hence symbolic, phallus marks, as prime signifier, the lack both sexes experience as subjectivity develops through the recognition of Self and Other, presence and absence, subject and object. Both sexes, then, are castrated, but they follow different paths in that girls, as the second sex, identify with the Other of male desire, and boys with the paternal function as representatives of the Law of the Father.

Kristeva modifies Lacan's theory through her distinction between the patriarchal Symbolic Order and the semiotic modality in language (1986, pp.89–136), which, she argues, originates as the indeterminate articulation of the *chora* – i.e. the infantile body as a space traversed by drives and movements before the constitution of the subject. The *chora* is rhythmic, not simply chaotic, because it is already ordered by the constraints, mediated through the mother's body, of sexual difference and family structure. Nevertheless, this order is not yet the Law which will cut the bond between infantile and maternal body, thus constituting the subject in time and defining the body as a separate object in space. A crucial moment in this process is the so-called mirror stage: 'to capture the unified image in the mirror, the child must remain separate from it, his body agitated by the semiotic motility . . . which fragments him more than it unifies him in a representation' (p.100). This moment, Kristeva argues, foreshadows the instability of the subject within the Symbolic Order: the mirror-image is the precursor of the signifier which signifies (here reflects) an illusory unified subject. For, just as there is no subject in this proto-signifier, so there will be no signifying subject; and the *signified* subject (the imaged ego) is an unstable deposit within the agitated infantile body. Thereafter Kristeva follows Lacan: the discovery of castration detaches the child from the phallic mother, now perceived as lacking, so that the phallic prime signifier is not the utterance of a subject, whether deity or father, but is constituted by severance from auto-erotic and maternal enclosure.

This severance, which Kristeva calls the thetic break, produces subject and object, identity and difference – i.e. syntax. As a rupture, the break is 'the first social censorship' (p.102), but the *chora* remains active in the psyche and the thetic break is also a threshold or crossing-point of a dialectic between the semiotic and the symbolic: 'the semiotic, which also precedes [the thetic break], constantly tears it open, and this transgression brings about all the various transformations of the signifying processes that are called "creation"' (p.113). Hence, Kristeva claims, the subject is not a fixed identity, but a series of positions produced by a dialectical interplay. Should the influx of the semiotic finally eliminate the break, however, the result would be the loss of the symbolic function and psychosis induced by the deepest drive of all, the death drive: 'in "artistic" practices the semiotic – the precondition of the symbolic – is revealed as that which also destroys the symbolic' (p.103). And further down the same page:

> The subject must be firmly posited by castration so that drive attacks against the thetic will not give way to fantasy or psychosis but will instead lead to a 'second-degree thetic', i.e., a resumption of the functioning characteristic of the semiotic *chora* within the signifying device of language. This is precisely what artistic practices, and notably poetic language, demonstrate.

What does Kristeva's argument mean for literary criticism? Kristeva claims that the semiotic is evident in rhythm, syntactic distortion and fantasy. It is also evident in poetic mimesis which tends to dissolve or pluralise denotation (the positing of an object) and, especially in modernist writing, to erode meaning (the positing of the enunciating subject), so subverting the illusion of fixed identity:

> Mimesis and the poetic language inseparable from it tend to prevent the thetic from becoming theological; in other words, they prevent the imposition of the thetic from hiding the semiotic process that produces it, and they bar it from inducing the subject, reified as a transcendental ego, to function solely within the systems of science and monotheistic religion. (p.110)

Kristeva here offers a psychoanalytic gloss on alienation-effects in self-reflective literature, which, she claims, subvert the Symbolic Order, notably through the passage from one sign-system to another. This operation she calls inter-textuality or transposition, citing the novel as a signifying system which resulted from the redistribution of such sign-systems as Carnival, courtly poetry and scholastic discourse. Such intersection of sign-sytems (an idea close to Bakhtin's *heteroglossia*) means that the thetic, the 'place' of enunciation, is never single and complete, 'but always plural, shattered' (p.111).

Feminist critics have been attracted to Kristeva's theory for two reasons. First, it suggests that the Symbolic Order is not static because the semiotic, designated 'feminine' on account of its association with the maternal *chora*, can subvert patriarchal gender definitions. Second, it offers an arena of textual politics in which modernist literature is appropriated as 'feminine' irrespective of the author's gender, its ostensible content or its conscious intent. Thus, Kristeva writes of the semiotic in Mallarmé: 'Indifferent to language, enigmatic and feminine, this space underlying the written is rhythmic, unfettered, irreducible to its intelligible verbal translation; it is musical, anterior to judgement, but restrained by the single guarantee: syntax' (p.97). While Kristeva's concept of 'the feminine' has nothing to do with actual women as authors, feminist critics have valued women's writing which evinces 'feminine' and hence subversive qualities (Weigel, 1987a; 1987b).[6] Conversely, naturalistic writing which claims to document authentic female experience is held merely to sustain the patriarchal ideology of an unchanging eternal feminine and fixed individual identity (Richter-Schröder, 1986). In the above usage, 'feminine' can become virtually synonymous with any subversive antipode to a dominant culture, and since, according to the theory, patriarchy is transmitted through language, feminism becomes above all a textual politics, and linguistic subversion the prime mode of opposition.[7] At the same time, Kristeva's association of 'the feminine' with music recalls the value Romantic aesthetics attributed to music, as well as Schopenhauer's music as the purest expression of the Will and Nietzsche's Dionysiac principle. The musicalisation of literature, so Kristeva argues, marks the influx of the pre-linguistic semiotic. The link in the inter-textual chain is, of course, Freud, who revalued Will as the libidinous fuel of civilisation: in turn, Kristeva seems to recuperate psychoanalysis for feminism in calling libidinous creativity 'feminine' (cf. Richard Sheppard's remarks on the institutionalisation of binary oppositions, p.287 below).

---

6. Weigel (1983), p.110, does not, however, apply the term 'feminine' to writing by men.
7. Margret Brügmann (1986), pp.8–13, adopts for women's writing the term 'littérature mineure' used by Deleuze and Guattari (1975) to mean writing marginal to and subversive of 'grande littérature' to which it stands in binary opposition; and since Deleuze elsewhere equates such marginality with woman, 'feminine' and 'mineure' may be used interchangeably of writing which subverts a dominant culture.

Elizabeth Boa

Malina as Psychodrama?

The plot of *Malina* can be read as a Kristevan psychodrama. Constantly agitated by the semiotic, *Ich* needs Malina both as the severance which stabilises the subject and as the threshold to a position in time and space from which signification becomes possible – the three (dis)unities of my analysis. But *Ich*'s identity through separation, with gaoler Malina as the thetic break, threatens to become total isolation, and her artistic practice requires that that identity be constantly torn open by the semiotic. Thus, on Lacan's theory as modified by Kristeva, Malina's demand that *Ich* renounce her love for Ivan would doom *Ich* to silence: the movements of desire induced by lack, so Lacan argues, generate the sliding signifiers, i.e. the substitutions which Freud called displacement and which Lacan re-termed metonymy. Thus, the death of desire would mean the end of language. Kristeva replaces desire (*eros*) with love (*agape*) and metonymy with metaphor, the equivalent of Freud's condensation, claiming that 'the object of love is a metaphor for the subject' (1986, p.247), and if this holds good, then Ivan, as the beloved Other with whom *Ich* metaphorically identifies, is as much an aspect of *Ich* as Malina is: 'I have lived in Ivan and I die in Malina' (vol.3, p.315). *Ich* experiences Malina's requirement that she renounce the objects of love (Ivan and his children) as an order to kill them (vol.3, p.315), but because this would involve killing herself as well, she chooses instead a different mode of dissolution. Rather than accede to Malina's demand, *Ich* gives way to the influx of the semiotic which eliminates the break, sweeping her away from the position in time and space which Malina offers; the borderless landscape of the *Märchen* returns in fragmentary form, now empty of the beloved Other; and *Ich*, overwhelmed by *thanatos*, the deepest drive, sinks into psychosis, leaving a silent Malina, for thetic Malina cannot signify without the semiotic precondition of enunciation.

On this reading, *Malina* becomes a de-politicised psychodrama in the tragic mode, for the final causes of *Ich*'s death are not open to change: a universal death drive and a patriarchal order which 'the feminine' cannot overthrow, since patriarchy is equated with functions necessary to operate as a subject at all. 'The feminine' offers little purchase for a feminist politics, since, once lifted from its metaphorical status, it stigmatises actual women as incapable of rational intervention: if *Ich* is 'the feminine' as an actual woman, then all she can do is negotiate minor modifications of the patriarchal order or retreat behind the wall.[8] The motif of the Father, the monolith of *Ich*'s nightmares, might seem to bear out the Freudian reduction of all politics to a conflict emanating from the Oedipal triangle. But Ingeborg Bachmann is not *Ich* and the novel can be read not as an endorsement of *Ich*'s vision, but as the exploration of a mentality in thrall to an ideology which imbues psychoanalytic discourse and perpetuates the metaphoric oppositions of patriarchy by gendering syntax or logic as phallic and the irrational as 'feminine' (cf. Richard Sheppard's essay below, especially pp.287–8).

The 'Feminine' Text?

Such an allegorical reading of the *plot* of *Malina* may not, however, do justice to Kristeva, who does not equate 'the feminine' with women and who is concerned with textual politics. As a *text*, *Malina* seems eminently 'feminine' in Kristeva's sense. Not a masterful autobiography by the famous writer, Ingeborg Bachmann, it is, rather, a self-reflective experiment which uncovers its own processes of narration. The subject is not reified as a transcendental ego, and Malina, the thetic principle, is shown to be implicated in the systems of science (as curator of a museum documenting the technology of war) and monotheistic religion (as an aspect of the patriarchal Trinity). The place of enunciation is plural and shattered, producing the inter-textual variety of autobiography, *Märchen*, visionary fragments, letters, scherzo-like interviews, telephone monologues, snatches of music, and the closing third-person narration of a murder.

The musicalisation of literature which Kristeva associates with 'the feminine' pervades *Malina*.[9] Just as Thomas Mann's Leverkühn 'took back' Beethoven's Ninth Symphony, so *Ich*'s immurement 'takes back' Verdi's *Aida* in that the lovers are not united behind the wall in an operatic *Liebestod*. The opening section is like a musical overture which sets leading themes (Beicken, 1988, p.194). The three chapters have affinities with post-classical chamber music such as the autobiographical works of Janáček or Smetana, with the high-pitched wail presaging deafness in Smetana's *My Life* anticipating a death of music, like the death of writing at the end of *Malina*. And the rhythmically surging dialogues between *Ich* and Malina have markings such as *con fuoco* or *fortissimo* (vol.3, p.331). Such musical elements accompany feminine images like those Dohm found in writing by

---

8. Schuscheng (1987), p. 140, makes a comparable point on *Undine Goes*.
9. Bachmann wrote libretti for Hans Werner Henze and frequently used musical references (Klaubert, 1983, pp.123–7).

men (see above, p.133). And the watery landscape of *Ich*'s *Märchen* recalls Bachmann's story *Undine Goes* (vol.2, pp.253–63), which in turn recalls Bachofen's *hetaera*, the sexual woman who roamed swamplands before her subjection to patriarchy, or the sinuous, epicene figures of the 'feminine' *Jugendstil* which flourished in Vienna at the turn of the century as the antipode of the imperial cult of masculinity.

And so we are left with a dilemma, for the 'feminine' images in *Malina* recall the images of completion in writing by men. And although these may express what patriarchy represses, they also tend to sustain male hegemony inasmuch as they stigmatise women as irrational or banish 'the feminine' into a utopia through which men recuperate themselves in their imaginations from the trials of actuality. Kristeva differs from Schiller in stressing subversive effects rather than utopian images, but what she associates with the Freudian master-narrative can equally well be associated with a modified Marxist story, as alienation-effects uncovering sexual rather than class oppression. Thus, the variety of genres in *Malina* and the instability of the subject may signal the breakthrough of the semiotic, but equally, they may also indicate that the human essence lies not in the individual but in the changing ensemble of social relations, of which different modes of writing are the ideologically coloured deposit.

As a self-reflective text, *Malina* is anti-illusionistic in the Brechtian manner, showing forth the art-work as an artefact, not the reflection of an immutable 'reality' (cf. Steve Giles's essay below, pp.261–77). Thus, the surging operatic dialogues between *Ich* and Malina may convey the pulse of the *chora*, but they also strike an almost comic note of Mahlerian grotesquerie, suggesting a tension between the felt emotion and intellectual recognition of its social origins. Although the emotion remains nonetheless potent, it appears as an effect of an oppressive culture which melodrama – ambiguously – shows forth yet celebrates in its sharply etched assertion of sexual difference. In a nineteenth-century opera, *La Traviata*, a womanly heroine confronted her lover and his father and died a double death, at once dying of love and murdered by patriarchy to the delectation of a bourgeois audience. In the twentieth century, womanly *Ich* confronts Ivan and the Father, and, in an internalised form of melodrama, also Malina, and dies *her* double death. But the overt game with the genre of melodrama robs *Ich*'s death of sentimentality, and the sepulchral 'It was murder' brings the detective story into play, producing both a grotesque clash of genres and an intellectual puzzle: we, an audience of women, are invited not to wallow in melodrama, but to think about, if not deny, our emotions. Sigrid Weigel (1983) called such double focus 'the squinting look' of women trying to see through a self-image reflected in the distorting mirror of patriarchy, and concluded that *Malina* expresses the irreconcilable antagonism between the masculine and feminine principles today while foreshadowing a utopian synthesis between happiness with Ivan and Malina's will to survive. To this reading I would add that such gendering of principles is in itself an effect of the distorting mirror and that the mirror cannot be broken by a change of vision alone. The modes of feeling and thinking which *Ich* evinces and psychoanalytic theory reproduces are not simply false, they are the expression of social structures and relations which a purely textual politics cannot change. But socialist and liberal feminists who want to change material as well as textual practices need to recognise the subjective dilemmas which feminist politics can cause women: *Malina* suggests that there is no neat dividing-line between regression and subversion and that feminism cannot simply be set against femininity without risking the destruction of the subject.

References

Bachmann, I. (1982) *Werke*, 2nd edn, 4 vols., Piper, Munich
Bail, G. (1984) *Weibliche Identität: Ingeborg Bachmanns 'Malina'*, Heredot, Göttingen
Beicken, P. (1988) *Ingeborg Bachmann*, Beck, Munich
Boa, E. (1987) *The Sexual Circus: Wedekind's Theatre of Subversion*, Blackwell, Oxford
Bond, G. (1988) 'Sexuality and Eschatology in the Work of Ingeborg Bachmann', MA dissertation, University of East Anglia, Norwich
Bossinade, J. (1985) 'Die verratene Kreatur: Beobachtungen zu einer Motivkonstellation bei Ingeborg Bachmann' in H. Ester and G. van Gemert (eds), *Annäherungen: Studien zur deutschen Literatur und Literaturwissenschaft im zwanzigsten Jahrhundert*, Rodopi, Amsterdam
Bovenschen, S. (1979) *Die imaginierte Weiblichkeit: Exemplarische Untersuchungen zu kulturgeschichtlichen und literarischen Präsentationsformen des Weiblichen*, Suhrkamp, Frankfurt/Main
Brügmann, M. (1986) *Amazonen der Literatur: Studien zur deutschsprachigen Literatur der 70er Jahre*, Rodopi, Amsterdam
Deleuze, G. and Guattari, F. (1975) *Kafka: pour une littérature mineure*,

Éditions de Minuit, Paris

Dohm, H. (1978) 'Die Eigenschaften der Frau' in G. Brinker-Gabler (ed.), *Zur Psychologie der Frau*, Fischer, Frankfurt/Main, pp.27–44

Höller, H. (1987) *Ingeborg Bachmann: Das Werk von den frühesten Gedichten bis zum 'Todesarten-Zyklus'*, Athenäum, Frankfurt/Main

Kaplan, C. (1986) *Sea Changes: Culture and Feminism*, Verso, London

Klaubert, A. (1983) *Symbolische Strukturen bei Ingeborg Bachmann: Malina im Kontext der Kurzgeschichten*, Peter Lang, Berne, Paris, Frankfurt/Main and New York

Kristeva, J. (1986) *The Kristeva Reader*, ed. T. Moi, Blackwell, Oxford

Richter-Schröder, K. (1986) *Frauenliteratur und weibliche Identität*, Hain, Frankfurt/Main

Ritter, N. (1989), *Art as Spectacle: Images of the Entertainer since Romanticism*, University of Missouri Press, Columbia

Schuscheng, D. (1987) *Arbeit am Mythos Frau: Weiblichkeit und Autonomie in der literarischen Mythenrezeption Ingeborg Bachmanns, Christa Wolfs und Gertrud Leutneggers*, Peter Lang, Berne, Paris, Frankfurt/Main and New York

Weigel, S. (1983) 'Der schielende Blick: Thesen zur Geschichte weiblicher Schreibpraxis' in I. Stephan and S. Weigel (eds), *Die verborgene Frau: Sechs Beiträge zu einer feministischen Literaturwissenschaft*, Argument-Sonderband AS 96, Berlin, pp.83–137

Weigel, S. (1987a) *Die Stimme der Medusa*, tende, Dülmen-Hiddingsel

Weigel, S. (1987b) 'Double Focus in the Writing of Women' in M. McGowan and M. Pender (eds), *Women and Contemporary German Culture*. Contemporary German Studies: Occasional Papers No. 3, University of Strathclyde, Glasgow

Wolf, C. (1971) *Nachdenken über Christa T.*, Luchterhand, Darmstadt and Neuwied

Wolf, C. (1983) *Voraussetzungen einer Erzählung: Kassandra. Frankfurter Poetik-Vorlesungen*, Luchterhand, Darmstadt and Neuwied

Wollstonecraft (1983), *Vindication of the Rights of Woman*, Penguin, Harmondsworth

–8–

The Politics of Literature in the GDR – A Post-Structuralist Approach

CHRIS WEEDON

Introduction

In the GDR, literature plays a social and political role which differs in many ways from its role in the West. Over the last forty years, it has become an important site for challenging dominant assumptions, norms and values as they are articulated both in official party discourse and in the social practices which constitute everyday life. In the Soviet Occupied Zone and in the newly founded GDR, the Socialist Unity Party (SED) set narrow official limits to the meaning of the terms 'socialist society' and 'socialist personality' and attempted to promote specific ways of thinking and forms of individual behaviour. However, both the limitations of Marxist-Leninist theory and the gap between theory and practice provoked challenges to official definitions of socialism and what it means to be a socialist. Since then, literature has become a key site for articulating marginalised oppositional discourses which offer new meanings and forms of subjectivity that transcend the narrowly defined class subjectivity of the 1950s and early 1960s, raising broader questions of social identity and social power. In recent years, for example, literature has become an important locus for contesting issues of gender, both in its own terms and as part of a far-reaching critique of existing forms of socialism and socialist subjectivity. This paper applies a post-structuralist approach to the politics of literature in the GDR in order to throw light on how and why literature has come to play this key role. It looks at the development of the discursive field in relation to official policies and institutional structures and at some of the ways in which literature has gone beyond and redefined its official role.

Post-Structuralism is a term which describes a number of

theoretical positions. These contest the possibilities of singular meaning in language and of unitary, self-present, intentional subjectivity which functions, as in liberal humanism, as the origin and guarantee of meaning. Post-Structuralism implies approaches to language in which meaning is subject to a constant process of difference and differal and can never be finally fixed. The post-structuralist theory on which this paper draws includes Derrida's theory of *différance* and Foucault's historically specific discourse analysis. Although the main emphasis of the paper lies with Foucault, Derrida's concept of *différance* and his critique of the metaphysics of presence in which words are only signs of a real substance which is always elsewhere and in which the knowing, speaking subject guarantees meaning, together with the techniques of deconstruction, are important to the argument.[1]

In order to show social power at work and to highlight possibilities of resistance, deconstruction as a mode of textual analysis needs to be part of a theory which insists on the materiality of discourse and its location in social institutions and practices. The critique of subjectivity as presence also requires historicisation. Seen historically, subjectivity is a plurality of conflicting modes, produced institutionally and discursively, and the individual is a site for the exercising of social power through subjectivity. From this perspective, it is possible to see how social power-relations structure discursive practices in hierarchical ways, privileging certain meanings, modes of subjectivity and social interests. Foucault's historical studies offer models of such analysis, showing how the plurality of meaning, which is central to Post-Structuralism, inheres in ever-changing, historically specific discourses which constitute an inherently unstable discursive field and within which different meanings and modes of subjectivity have varying degrees of social power.[2]

Literary Theory and Politics in the GDR

In the West, there are many competing theories of literature which attempt to define what it is, how it functions and the nature of its social and political role. Criticism has, for example, attempted to

1. See the writings of Jacques Derrida, in particular, *Speech and Phenomenon* (Northwestern U.P., Evanston, 1973); *Of Grammatology* (Johns Hopkins U.P., Baltimore, 1976) and *Positions* (Athlone Press, London, 1987).
2. Particularly helpful are M. Foucault, *I, Pierre Rivière* (Penguin, Harmondsworth, 1978); *Discipline and Punish* (Penguin, Harmondsworth, 1979) and *The History of Sexuality, Vol. 1, An Introduction* (Penguin, Harmondsworth, 1981).

distinguish literature from fiction and to construct canons. It has seen in literature expressions of authorial intention and the unconscious, as well as reflections of human nature, women's nature and society. Within this plurality of approaches, some ways of reading enjoy greater power and status than others, and this tends to be linked to broader ideological and social relations. Yet in the West, the relationship between ways of reading and the suppression or marginalisation of particular social groups is usually indirect, mediated most often by discourses which privilege subjectivity as individual, non-gender and non-class-specific. These discourses can be broadly categorised as liberal humanist since they assume that the rational, conscious and autonomous individual is at the centre of language and history.

In the GDR, only one approach to fiction is officially sanctioned – a Marxist-Leninist approach according to which literature is seen as the class-based reflection of aspects of the society in which it is produced. Moreover, literature is assumed to play a serious and important social role in the formation of consciousness. The function of literature is to mediate reality and to help develop the socialist personality. Literary and cultural theories in the GDR are founded on forms of *Marxist* humanism, the roots of which go back to the 1840s. Yet neither Marx, Engels, Lenin, nor GDR theorists developed sophisticated theories of culture, ideology and subjectivity which are appropriate either to advanced capitalist societies or to socialism. Such advances as were made in Marxist theory in the 1960s and 1970s tended to be Western developments, ignored in the GDR until recently.[3] While the limitations of traditional Marxism-Leninism are now recognised officially (cf. David Jenkinson's remark on p.247), concern with theorising this area is a new development which has yet to affect cultural-political assumptions.

The development of the politics of literature in the GDR after 1949 was shaped by both the assumptions and the limitations of Marxist-humanist theory. All forms of humanist criticism, whether liberal, Marxist or feminist, share the aim of fixing the meaning of texts and have an investment in defining human nature, gender and social values in ways which may either reproduce or challenge existing social power relations. This is particularly clear in the GDR, where the state imposes narrow definitions of socialist education and the construction of socialist subjectivity; and where the

3. I am referring here to the work of the French Marxist philosopher Louis Althusser, to the rediscovery of the work of Antonio Gramsci and to recent Marxist analyses of ideology and class, for example the work of Nicos Poulantzas and Ernesto Laclau.

reception of controversial critical fiction which challenges these definitions makes the pages of the national press. The importance which the state lays on policing the meanings of fictional texts, together with the nature of the press and the other media, has given fiction a political and ideological status unequalled in the West. Party functionaries have consistently attacked texts which they consider to be critical of either party policies or the social relations and forms of socialist subjectivity to which such policies have given rise. In declaring these texts reactionary or bourgeois, critics have attempted to deny them any legitimacy in the discursive battle over the meaning of socialism and socialist subjectivity. At the same time, these attacks have created resistance among other writers and critics and political interest in fiction among a large reading public.

In the GDR, Marxism-Leninism forms an explicit and integral part of all social institutions and official discourse consists of a particular version of Marxist and Leninist political and economic philosophy which is carefully policed and reproduced by the institutions of the party, state education and publishing. (Ironically, this version is currently under challenge from developments in the Soviet Union, and the institutional and individual investments of state functionaries in resisting change and maintaining existing power relations is clear from the GDR's official reception in the party press of *glasnost* and *perestroika*.) Although, in the GDR, the truth of Marxism-Leninism is said to be guaranteed by historical-materialist science, viewed from a post-structuralist perspective, it is a particular version of Historical Materialism which is at issue. State policing of meaning through ideological apparatuses, such as education and the media, and repressive apparatuses, such as political imprisonment, can be seen as a politically powerful attempt to fix meaning and achieve the impossible.[4] From this perspective, the development of the politics of literature in the GDR over the last thirty-nine years can be read as a demonstration of the ways in which elements within the discursive field work to undermine officially sanctioned meaning.

Subjectivity

Marxism-Leninism breaks radically with liberal humanism, de-

4. The concepts of ideological and repressive state apparatuses were developed by Althusser, who was concerned to offer a theory of how ideology functions and of the relationship between ideology and the individual subject. See his 'Ideology and Ideological State Apparatuses (Notes towards an Investigation)' in *Lenin and Philosophy and Other Essays* (New Left Books, London, 1971).

centring intentional subjectivity and asserting that rational consciousness and individual experience are neither the source nor the guarantee of meaning. It argues that language and subjectivity are socially and historically produced, but that objective knowledge is possible through the application of historical-materialist science. In this process, the meaning of subjectivity is fixed as class subjectivity, and it is the function of fiction to mediate this. Recent GDR theory, particularly the work of Irene Dölling has, however, acknowledged that cultural forms and consciousness do not relate directly to the relations of production and may include elements persisting from previous modes of production.[5] Dölling argues that the formation of the socialist personality (which she calls 'individuelle Vergesellschaftung') is much more complicated than had been assumed hitherto (1986, p.5–21). Gender is, perhaps, the most important question which has forced this re-thinking and it can be argued that the problematisation of individual subjectivity and its relation to the processes of social reproduction has created a retrospective theoretical foundation for the more liberal cultural policies of recent years. Relative liberalisations in cultural policy since the 1960s have, arguably, been effected by cultural-political *practice*, particularly in the field of literature, rather than by the implementation of more sophisticated theory which reflects readings of Western Marxism. In the literary politics of recent years, women's writing in particular has been instrumental in promoting social and cultural debate and advancing new forms of socialist subjectivity.

Post-Structuralism questions the possibility of both objective knowledge and fixed subjectivity. Unlike liberal humanism or Marxism-Leninism, Post-Structuralism views meaning as a constant site of discursive and political struggle. The individual is said to be socially produced in a range of conflicting discursive practices which are historically specific and changing; neither meaning nor subjectivity is unitary or unified; temporary fixings of meaning and subjectivity are linked; discourse is said to define what it means to be a subject; and the individual is inscribed in and produced by a wide range of social discourses and practices such as the law, the welfare state, education, culture and criticism. In contrast, the state in the GDR has tried to standardise and unify the model of socialist subjectivity with which social institutions work and it attempts to

---

5. Irene Dölling's *Individuum und Kultur: Ein Beitrag zur Diskussion* was published by the Dietz-Verlag in 1986. It attempts to theorise the ideological dimension of the relationship between the individual and society and discusses the contradictory demands made on working women as a specific example of the historical development of forms of individuality.

eliminate contradictions at the level of subjectivity by insisting that the socialist personality is a fixed and recognisable entity at the centre of all forms of social practice. The highly centralised structures of the party, education, the media, the work-place and even residential areas, as well as the various mass organisations, such as the youth and women's movements and the trade unions, attempt to construct and police compatible subject positions on the basis of a narrowly defined set of values and objectives. Significantly for gender relations, however, this attempt has, for the most part, been restricted to what has traditionally been defined as the public realm, leaving domestic and inter-personal relations unaddressed.

Language, Ideology and the Role of Fiction

Unlike liberal humanism, GDR Marxism-Leninism does not assume that language is a transparent medium for the reflection of already fixed meanings. Both language and consciousness are seen as socially produced and specific to the particular society in question. Moreover, meaning is seen as plural, but the plurality of meaning is an effect of competing ideologies, and only Historical Materialism can, it is claimed, produce objective meaning. Because the GDR is said to have socialist economic relations which provide the objective conditions for socialist consciousness, the origins of social contradictions and competing ideologies are seen to lie outside of the GDR social system, produced by Western influences or by non-socialist organisations such as the churches. Feminism in its Western sense, for example, which is founded on concepts of patriarchy understood as structural power relations, is regarded as a form of bourgeois ideology.

From a classical Marxist perspective, competing ideologies represent competing class-interests. The GDR state insists, however, that within the GDR there are no conflicting class-interests: different occupational groups and strata are said to share the interests of the working class as defined by the SED. This assertion relies on linking meaning to an economistic definition of class in which class is reduced to 'objective' economic relations of production – a theory which fails to address the constitution of subjectivity at levels other than that of economic relations, and marginalises questions of gender.[6] It also assumes patriarchal norms of subjectivity and a

---

6. 'Economistic' theory of class, which had its roots in a group within the Russian Social Democratic Party known as the 'Economists' at the end of the nineteenth century, relies on a theory of history in which communism is the inevitable

patriarchal organisation of those social practices which form a largely unquestioned part of the dominant ideology.

In a society where other media, particularly the press and television, are very strictly controlled, fiction has become a privileged site for exploring critical and even dissident ideas. The refusal until recently of Marxist-Leninist discourse to recognise that meaning and subjectivity might be contradictory and unstable, and that there is always a considerable gap between official theory and actual practice, a gap occupied by other discourses and forms of subjectivity, has had important effects on the use made of fiction by both readers and writers. A range of institutions exist to secure and reproduce the dominant ideology in the field of literary politics. These include the Ministry of Culture, the Writer's Union, state control of publishing (from the titles approved to the size of print runs) and the dissemination of specific modes of reading in education and criticism. However, in spite of this, fiction has been a consistent site of challenge to dominant discourses in the GDR at least since the mid-1960s. The forms which this challenge has taken have been shaped both by state policies specific to literature and by policies with wider implications. While party functionaries, critics and the Writers' Union attempt to control meaning, it is often marginal voices, both published and unpublished, which provoke the most public interest. These find platforms in the West German media (which play an important role in publicising controversial texts and writers), in the unofficial circulation of West German editions of books, and at public readings and discussions organised inside the GDR by the Evangelical Church.

Literaturpolitik: The Development of the Discursive Field

Literary and cultural policy of the early years was based on Marxism-Leninism. Yet within Marxism-Leninism, particularly in the field of cultural policy, there were competing and, at times, conflicting discursive strands which had their origins prior to 1945. These included Marx's and Engels's writings on literature (which allocate to art and literature a special role in the formation of the individual, and privilege Realism), Lenin's writings on the central role of the Party, and the development of Soviet and Weimar

---

outcome of economic developments motivated by class struggle. Much subsequent Marxist theory has attempted to reinstate and theorise the role of politics, ideology and the individual in the historical struggle for socialism.

German socialist cultural politics up to the establishment of Socialist Realism as the official line at the 1934 Soviet Writers' Congress in Moscow.[7] The inter-war debate, however, rarely advanced beyond an opposition between two conflicting models of literature. On the one hand there was a narrow, class-based conception of fiction from which the reader was to learn from heroic, working-class communists, and on the other there was an untransformed bourgeois model, in which 'great' literature was seen as good *per se* because it embodied humanist values. This opposition extended into the post-war period and was reconstituted in early GDR cultural-political discourse as a commitment both to Socialist Realism and to a celebration of the classical German heritage (Lessing, Goethe and Schiller).[8]

The dominant cultural-political discourse of the 1950s was structured in terms of oppositions which drew upon both the political discourse of the Cold War and inter-war cultural-political debates in the Soviet Union and the West. These included oppositions between imperialism and socialism, cosmopolitanism and national consciousness, and formalism and both a national cultural tradition and a new, democratic German culture. The general nature of these concepts meant that they could be widely applied and were very effective in silencing other discourses. By linking imperialism, cosmopolitanism and formalism and reversing National Socialist articulations, the above cultural policy could claim an organic relationship between socialism, national consciousness, the national cultural tradition and new democratic German culture. Western imperialism was accused of using literature for its own ends by destroying national consciousness and cultural traditions and of replacing them with an imperialist cosmopolitanism. This accusation was not limited to literature: throughout the 1950s and early 1960s, Western popular music, long hair and jeans were seen as part of the discourse of United States imperialism. In the 1970s, however, this link was broken and such phenomena became part of a tolerated national youth culture.

7. Relevant texts by Marx, Engels and Lenin are available in K. Marx, F. Engels and V.I. Lenin, *Über Kultur, Ästhetik, Literatur* (Philipp Reclam jun., Leipzig, 1975). The Soviet Writers' Congress was attended by representatives from other Communist parties, including the KPD. Its proceedings were well publicised at the time in the magazine *International Literature* published from Moscow in several languages, including German, by the International Union of Revolutionary Writers. Speeches from the congress are currently available in M. Gorki, V. Radek, N. Bukharin, A. Zhdanov et al., *Soviet Writers' Congress 1934* (Lawrence and Wishart, London, 1977).
8. For relevant documents on cultural policy from 1946 to 1970 see Schubbe (1972).

The Politics of Literature in the GDR

After 1950, when the period of a broad, anti-fascist alliance in cultural policy finally came to an end, three possibilities were identified for literature: Formalism, Proletcult and Realism. Formalism served as a political concept signifying 'anti-humanist' and 'anti-realist' texts which were said to undermine national consciousness by failing to make 'objective reality' accessible. Proletcult, a phase of Soviet cultural politics from the immediate post-revolutionary period, was dismissed for abandoning form in the interests of content and denying the validity of the cultural tradition. But Realism became part of a discourse in which it signified particular formal and ideological criteria. The socialist-realist text was expected to depict contemporary social relations from a Marxist-Leninist perspective, using narrative techniques modelled on nineteenth-century Realism. Writers were urged to set their texts in the industrial work-place and to address the problems of the construction of socialism – which would be solved in the fiction by a hero or heroine who embodied the positive qualities ascribed to typical working-class communists.[9] The meaning of Realism, however, was not contained by its dominant discursive articulation, since other definitions were in circulation, including those of Brecht and Lukács. Indeed, it was even applied to the classical German tradition, where it was used to mark particular texts as ideologically acceptable just as the concept of Formalism marked others as unacceptable.

The effect of this policy was to police meaning closely and to reduce the scope for resistance from dissident elements within the discursive field of literature. While the theory of Socialist Realism set the agenda, particularly for prose-writing, it did not destroy the basis for the future development of alternatives, a basis produced in part by the inability of theoretical prescriptions to contain meaning. During the 1950s, resistance to the formal requirements of Socialist Realism was largely displaced into poetry and drama, and many prose writers attempted to produce a committed and relevant literature. However, it soon became clear that Marxist-Leninist literary and cultural theory was inadequate since Socialist Realism could not account adequately for the results of cultural policy (e.g. forms of dissidence and dissent and the ways in which fiction actually works). It was this radical gap between cultural theory and practice which writers sought to exploit. The transformation of the narrow definitions of literature, together with the practices of the institutions controlling its production and distribution, was to be the

---

9. For discussion of these literary forms see the proceedings of the Congress of the SED, 15–17 March 1951 (Schubbe, 1972, pp. 178–85 and Fischbeck, 1979, pp. 11–24).

main objective of cultural-political struggle in the GDR over the next thirty-nine years. Nevertheless, significant achievements were not possible until the general political climate had changed.

Since 1949, the discursive battle over what constitutes acceptable critical fiction has been influenced both by external factors and by developments within the GDR. Important external factors included the sealing of the border, the treaty between the GDR and the FRG, and international recognition of the sovereignty of the GDR, as well as recent events in Poland and the Soviet Union. After the closing of the border in August 1961, the role of the ideological state apparatuses, including literary production, was modified. Because ideology no longer bore the primary burden of convincing people that their future lay in the GDR, literature which went beyond the depiction of positive role models was officially sanctioned and space was opened up for a greater degree of social criticism within fictional texts.[10] Furthermore, under Honecker, who replaced Ulbricht at the head of the Central Committee in 1971, there was a shift in economic policy which also had important implications for the politics of literature. The direction of the economy was altered to accommodate the production of a greater range of consumer durables for home consumption in the belief that a higher material standard of living was more likely to persuade people of the benefits of socialism than the ideological campaigns of earlier years. This marked the beginnings of a recognition that the construction of socialism, and in particular the construction of the socialist personality, were more complicated than had been assumed hitherto.

While, in the 1950s, key functionaries and many lesser-known and new writers attempted to produce Socialist Realism (and, in the case of J.R. Becher, the first Chairman of the Cultural Union, even socialist folk songs),[11] the attempt to limit literature to Socialist Realism was never widely accepted. Challenged by Brecht since the 1930s – a challenge that was institutionalised in the practice of the Berlin Ensemble – Socialist Realism was questioned, too, by other writers both in their work and at the congresses of the Writers' Union. Writers, critics and, above all, ordinary readers found that socialist-realist texts failed to address the complexities of life in the

10. See Walter Ulbricht's speech to the Second Bitterfeld Conference, 24–5 April 1954 (Schubbe, 1972, pp. 956–90) An edited version is available in Fischbeck (1979), pp. 79–86.
11. The folksong had been officially defined as the authentic art of the people. In the late 1940s, J.R. Becher produced the lyrics and Hanns Eisler the music for *Neue deutsche Volkslieder* which dealt with social reconstruction and the country's debt to the Red Army. These are available on the NOVA label produced by the Deutsche Akademie der Künste, Berlin-GDR, 1971.

The Politics of Literature in the GDR

GDR and of socialist subjectivity, and so did not buy them. Even in a country where publishing is state-subsidised, economics are important. Moreover, socialist-realist texts did not have the ideological effects expected of them. The so-called 'objective' mediation of reality did not result in a more committed and productive workforce: even the attempt in 1959 to encourage new fiction about industrial and agricultural work and to overcome the gulf between intellectuals and the working class – the *Bitterfelder Weg* – had limited if, in some areas, long-lasting effects.[12]

Fiction and the Politics of Meaning

Since the early 1960s, literary politics in the GDR have focused on two key questions: meaning and subjectivity. Writers and critics have attempted to expand and transform the meanings of socialist society and socialist subjectivity, which had been narrowly defined in class terms by Socialist Realism (where attention was focused on the world of work rather than other areas of social life). In privileging class, socialist-realist texts had also perpetuated traditionally male forms of subjectivity, and it is therefore not surprising that some important attempts to break with and transform official literary policy should have combined a critique of dogmatism with an assertion of marginalised feminine qualities. This was already the case in Christa Wolf's first novel, *Der geteilte Himmel* (1963; E.T. as *Divided Heaven*, 1968) which was in part a socialist-realist text embodying the principles of the *Bitterfelder Weg*, but which broke fundamentally with Socialist Realism in its choice of heroine and the scope of its social criticism. It showed how both the division of Germany and factors internal to GDR society contained negative features which needed to be acknowledged, addressed and transformed.

12. The *Bitterfelder Weg* was a cultural-political strategy designed to overcome the gulf between writers as intellectuals and the working class, and to encourage the writing of new fiction about the concerns of industrial workers and farmers. The Mitteldeutscher Verlag, the publishing house most concerned with the production of new fiction, organised a conference in Bitterfeld in 1959. At this conference, a policy emerged which involved encouraging professional writers to spend time working with teams of industrial workers, 'Brigaden', in order to gain first-hand experience of the work-place. To complement this move and to encourage more writers from the working class, worker-writer circles were also founded in which workers discussed their own creative writing in groups led by professional writers. These circles still exist and some professional writers have maintained their personal connections with particular factories through the cultural committees of the trades unions (see Schubbe, 1972, pp. 552–64).

The reception of this novel demonstrated a pattern which would often be repeated in subsequent debates about controversial texts. Party critics attacked *Der geteilte Himmel* as negative and a-typical and, in doing so, provoked public defences by other writers and critics which played an important part in extending the limits of what the state would tolerate.[13] One result of this process was the gradual abandoning of the formal criteria of Socialist Realism. Nevertheless, the ideological principles underpinning it – that it should be written from direct social experience and from a Marxist-Leninist perspective – maintained their hegemony and were now linked to the new critical category of 'constructive criticism'. This implied a fixed opposition between texts for and against the system, an opposition which has been challenged by both writers and readers and has proved more open to the plurality of meaning than Socialist Realism.

Over the years, debates about the limits of 'constructive criticism' have been focused by a range of highly controversial fictional texts, often published in small print runs after they had appeared in the West. Important texts have included, for example, work by Christa Wolf, Stefan Heym, Ulrich Plenzdorf, Wolf Biermann, Reiner Kunze and Christoph Hein. In some cases, texts have been published only in the West and their reception has caused writers to leave the GDR or be expatriated. These texts are widely sought after and read in the GDR. Officially they have been marginalised by party critics and the Writers' Union, but they have, none the less, occupied a central position in literary debate not least because of their treatment in the West German media. The reception of controversial texts in both East and West has focused on what these texts have to say about the individual in GDR society. While much West German criticism has sought to demonstrate that the socialist system is necessarily repressive, East German readings of controversial texts attempt to produce definitive meanings which are often in conflict with one another. These readings not only demonstrate the principles of plurality and non-fixity at work, but are ripe for deconstruction. They clearly show how critics' assumptions determine the meanings produced in reading texts, and how readings rely on the construction of primary oppositions which hierarchise meanings according to whether they uphold or challenge orthodox beliefs and theories, while marginalising meanings not contained by these

13. Relevant extracts from the debate which took place in the newspaper *Freiheit* (Halle/Saale) between August and November 1963 are reproduced in Fischbeck (1979), pp. 61–76.

oppositions (see for example, the discussion of the reception of *Der fremde Freund* below). The refusal of both *Nachdenken über Christa T.* (E.T. as *The Quest for Christa T.*, 1970) (Wolf, 1968) and *Die neuen Leiden des jungen W.* (*The New Sorrows of Young W.*) (Plenzdorf, 1972), for example, to offer one fixed view of events and the relationship between individuals and social processes, in keeping with the realist tradition, demanded further thought and discussion.

This is well illustrated by the discussion in *Neue deutsche Literatur*, issue 3, 1973, of *Die neuen Leiden jungen W.* Here, Eduard Klein and Henryk Keisch questioned four young Berliners, an apprentice, a schoolgirl and two students, about their responses to the text.[14] This young audience found the text very compelling because they felt that it addressed in an engaging way real problems of young people usually excluded from public debate. This was achieved through the depiction of the charismatic central character, Edgar, who wanted to be something special and to escape 'his pre-determined path' (Fischbeck, 1979, p.100). However, the contradictions between Edgar's aspirations prior to his death – with which the young audience identified – his actual behaviour, his self-criticism from beyond the grave, and accepted social norms and values made it difficult for them to reach a clear-cut endorsement or rejection of the text. Indeed, GDR critics wishing to dismiss *Die neuen Leiden des jungen W.* normally produced readings which reduced its complexity – Friedrich Karl Kaul, Kurt Hager and Hans Koch, for example, whose criticisms are reproduced in the Fischbeck anthology (1979, pp. 97–117).

Controversial fiction has focused its critique on narrow, class-based and patriarchal modes of subjectivity. Christa Wolf's *Nachdenken über Christa T.*, for example, raised the issues of socialist subjectivity and the limits of 'constructive criticism' in a radical form in 1968. The novel has as its central character a woman who does not meet official definitions of the socialist personality, but who is presented by the narrator as embodying marginalised qualities important in the construction of socialism. These qualities, which have traditionally been associated with femininity (see Richard Sheppard's essay below, p. 287), include emotion, intuition, self-doubt, insecurity, constant questioning and sensitivity to others, and the novel suggests that there is more to socialist subjectivity than acceptance of the party line and a rational commitment to socialist ideology. Subjectivity is seen as a process formed by the past and

---

14. A range of critical responses to *Die neuen Leiden des jungen W.*, including the *Neue deutsche Literatur* discussion, are reproduced in Fischbeck (1979), pp. 97–117.

important in determining the shape of the future, and those qualities marginalised by the hegemonic discourse are important in this process. In *Nachdenken über Christa T.*, the process of self-questioning necessary for the successful construction of socialism is presented as possible only outside of the institutional structures of normal, everyday life in which social and political values rapidly become mere slogans.

Gender

Nachdenken über Christa T. shifted the political agenda by addressing the politics of the personal as an integral part of socialist construction and by drawing attention to continuities between past and present. It also raised the question of gender – which has become a major theme in recent critical fiction. The early models of socialist subjectivity under attack in *Nachdenken über Christa T.* not only made no reference to gender difference, they also marginalised traditionally feminine qualities, confining them to the domestic sphere. It can be argued that these were patriarchal models of subjectivity, based on achievements in a male-defined social world which women were expected to enter while preserving their responsibilities for the so-called 'private' sphere of family and domesticity which remained largely invisible and untransformed. The marginalisation or silencing of such issues created an absence which literature sought to fill. In Christa Wolf's later work, together with that of subsequent women writers, issues of gender have taken on a more explicitly feminist form, linking the meaning of socialism and socialist subjectivity to a critique of patriarchy.

It would seem that social critique which privileges gender relations is widely assumed in the GDR to be the province of women writers and that the state apparatus allows it to be published despite its very negative tone. Arguably, this is because it addresses areas that have been consistently marginalised by dominant discourse. Conversely, criticism of gender relations from a controversial male author, Christoph Hein, in *Der fremde Freund* (*The Alien Friend*) (1982), was not even acknowledged by GDR critics, who, in their negative reception of that work, failed to identify patriarchal relations as relevant to the text's social critique. In *Der fremde Freund*, the female narrator is instrumental in bringing out the patriarchal structure of relations between men and women, both inside and outside the family. The picture which the book paints is very negative, being one of a society in which the family defines how people relate to one another while failing to promote the things that it is supposed to – close relationships of love, respect, support and shared interests. The family is seen to create relations of exploitation for its members, including the mental and physical abuse of women, and isolation for those outside it. Extra-marital relations, too, are depicted as power relations, and the narrator survives by opting out of intimate relationships. In *Der fremde Freund*, the implicit problem in families at work and in society at large is presented as aggressive and oppressive masculinity. Unlike many of the critiques of the social construction of gender in women's writing, *Der fremde Freund* depicts negative forms of subjectivity which are fixed in relation to a masculinity which transcends the boundaries of GDR society. This is portrayed as a form of repressed violence which surfaces across a wide range of social relations, including for example, marital and extra-marital relations between women and men, relations at work, on the street, and in places of entertainment such as bars and discos.

Der fremde Freund was reviewed by six critics in the *Weimarer Beiträge* (Bernhardt et al., 1983). The issues which surfaced in their reviews are familiar from previous cultural-political debates about the meaning of controversial texts and include the questions of whether the central character, in this case the narrator, is merely one, maladjusted individual or a recognisable product of GDR society as depicted in the text; the degree to which negative social criticism is relativised by a positive socialist perspective; and the typicality and representativeness of the range of experience depicted. Rüdiger Bernhardt, for example, argued that despite her broad-ranging social experience, the narrator focused on 'trivialities, on the marginal, on the decaying' and that her individual account of social relations made claims to representativeness which were not relativised by a broader, positive, socio-historical framework (p. 1637). Gabriele Lindner attempted to make sense of the social criticism in terms of the early experience of the narrator. Bernd Leistner read *Der fremde Freund* as a longing for wholeness, and Ursula Wilke went so far as to interpret it in existentialist terms as a text in which Christoph Hein had 'finally adopted the point of view of *Angst*-ridden Camus' (p. 1655). Because none of these critics explored the theme of violence and the way in which the text links it to forms of masculinity which transcend the historical limits of GDR society and suggest a long tradition of patriarchy, they found it very difficult to make positive sense of it.

Recent Women's Writing

It can be argued that *Der fremde Freund* offers no way forward because it describes the effects of a society founded on the patriarchal nuclear family and guaranteed by male violence, while failing to deconstruct masculinity itself. For the deconstruction of gendered subjectivity, it is necessary to look to recent women's writing – which includes feminist critiques of social and family relationships and the articulation of the perspectives of marginalised groups like old people, single women and the handicapped. Such texts, for example the work of Irmtraud Morgner, Helga Königsdorf, Helga Schubert, Elfriede Brüning and Rosemarie Geppert, question the quality of life in GDR society and ask why people behave as they do. They also look to forms of social power other than class to explain social behaviour and, in moving outside of official Marxist-Leninist discourse that is dominated by a narrow conception of class, they avoid direct conflict with official ideology. They also provide a good example of how literature functions in the GDR as a site for the articulation of issues and perspectives which are not contained by official discourses but which have important implications for the future shape of socialism.[15]

Until very recently, the Marxist-Leninist approach to the question of women followed Engels in assuming that the material basis of women's emancipation lay in access to work under the socialist relations of production, equal rights legislation, education, the social provision of child-care facilities, contraception, abortion, and positive discrimination at work.[16] In making these provisions, the state assumed a pattern of work and family life based on a male norm according to which the worker has a wife to take primary responsibility for the home and children. It failed to see that femininity, masculinity and patriarchal modes of relating, both in and outside the home, are political issues requiring transformation. GDR concepts of the socialist personality do not explicitly involve differences between women and men, but neither do they deconstruct or attempt to transform traditional norms of femininity, masculinity and patriarchal power.

15. For an account of GDR women writers see Christel Hidebrandt, *Zwölf schreibende Frauen in der DDR* (no imprint, Hamburg, 1984, distributed by the Frauenbuchvertrieb, Berlin).
16. See F. Engels, *The Origin of the Family, Private Property and the State* (1884) (Lawrence and Wishart, London, 1972). For accounts of GDR policy on women see H. Shaffer, *Women in the Two Germanies* (Pergamon, New York, 1981) and I. Uhlmann (ed.), *Kleine Enzyklopädie. Die Frau* (Bibliographisches Institut, Leipzig, 1987).

It was literature which brought these issues to the fore. In 1975, a volume of *Protokolliteratur* ('Reportage'), Maxie Wander's *Guten Morgen, du Schöne* (*Good Morning, Beautiful One*), was published. This dispelled the myth that all was well in GDR family life by allowing women to express their perceptions of the sexual division of labour and dominant gender norms. The interviews published here focused on sexuality, motherhood, women's dual role and the contradictions implicit in dominant norms of femininity which still work within conventional oppositions and which offer women conflicting subject positions such as those of sexual object, romantic heroine, career woman, wife, mistress and mother. Eleven years later, in 1986, a companion volume of *Männerprotokolle*, edited by Christine Müller, was published and stands as an indictment of the failure of men to transform ingrained and oppressive patriarchal modes of relating. The interviews published here suggest that many men in the GDR still regard women as either sexual objects or sources of domestic labour whose main function in life should be to enable men to combine a successful career with a narrowly defined familial role. This *Protokolliteratur*, together with recent women's fiction, has exposed areas of social life such as sexuality and oppression within the family which were previously hidden from view. In doing this, they have used techniques of first-person narrative which, claiming an authenticity guaranteed by individual experience, have more in common with liberal humanism and Western feminism than Marxism-Leninism, and highlight the inadequacies of Marxist-Leninist theory as far as the social construction of gendered subjectivity is concerned. This writing has created a space for discussion of the politics of the personal, exposing the ways in which issues such as gender, sexuality and women's perspectives have for years been marginalised and silenced, and it is having direct effects on how gender is perceived outside of literary discourse.[17]

Recent GDR women's writing, like all other forms of literature in the GDR, cannot be read in separation either from the material contradictions of daily life or from the ideological pressures of both official and Western discourses. Material contradictions are experienced at the level of individual subjectivity – for example, for women, the contradictions which are produced by their dual role. How these contradictions are interpreted, however, will depend on the discursive positions to which individuals have access and will be a site of ideological and political struggle. The narratives of women's

---

17. See, for example, Dölling (1986), pp. 131–61, where direct reference is made to the treatment of gender in women's writing.

lives which characterise the work of younger women writers in the GDR present the effects of patriarchal relations in which women and men comply with the sexual division of labour and gender norms. Texts which do not present gender as the effect of structural power relations tend to depict it as an individual problem, requiring personal change by women or their partners. Where, however, femininity is seen as a patriarchal social construct – as, for example, in the work of Irmtraud Morgner, Helga Königsdorf, Helga Schütz and Christa Wolf – the texts imply that real change is not possible merely at the level of the individual. Thus, they put a question-mark over current social values; suggest that the worlds of work, politics and family life need to be transformed; and make gendered subjectivity a political question directly related to the future of socialism in the GDR.[18]

Conclusion

As yet, feminist voices occupy a marginal position in the hierarchy of discourses which shape the social practices constituting GDR society. But the discursive field is not static, and it is fiction which continues to be a central force for change. From a post-structuralist perspective, the key feature of the politics of literature in the GDR is, perhaps, its resilient ability to show that meaning and subjectivity are socially constructed, plural and contradictory, in spite of the huge state and institutional energy which is put into controlling both meaning and subjectivity. The question of gender well illustrates this point. Moreover, literary politics in the GDR demonstrates that the exploration of difference in literature and the impossibility of producing one final, definitive reading of fictional texts preserve a necessary and productive critical challenge to dominant meanings and values as defined by the party and the state organisations. For these reasons literature plays a key political role in the GDR.

18. In addition to the works of Christa Wolf listed in the reference section, see, for example, C. Wolf, 'Selbstversuch' in *Erzählungen* (Aufbau, Berlin and Weimar, 1985) and *Kassandra* (Aufbau, Berlin and Weimar, 1983); Irmtraud Morgner, *Leben und Abenteuer der Trobadora Beatriz nach Zeugnissen ihrer Spielfrau Laura* (Aufbau, Berlin and Weimar, 1974) and *Amanda: Ein Hexenroman* (Aufbau, Berlin and Weimar, 1983); Helga Königsdorf, *Meine ungehörigen Träume* (Aufbau, Berlin and Weimar, 1978) and *Der Laufe der Dinge*, (Aufbau, Berlin and Weimar, 1982); Helga Schubert, *Lauter Leben* (Aufbau, Berlin and Weimar, 1975) and *Blickwinkel* (Aufbau, Berlin and Weimar, 1984).

References

Bernhardt, R., Kändler, K., Leistner, B., Lindner, G., Schick, B. and Wilke, U. (1983) '"Der fremde Freund" von Christoph Hein', *Weimarer Beiträge*, 29, 9, 1635–55

Dölling, I. (1986) *Individuum und Kultur: Ein Beitrag zur Diskussion*, Dietz, Berlin-GDR

Fischbeck, H. (1979) *Literaturpolitik und Literaturkritik in der DDR*, Diesterweg, Frankfurt/Main, Berlin and Munich

Hein, C., (1982) *Der fremde Freund*, Aufbau, Berlin-GDR and Weimar

Klein, E. and Keisch, H. (1973) 'Der neue Werther: Ein Gespräch' in Fischbeck, 1979, pp. 98–106

Müller, C. (1986) *Männerprotokolle*, Der Morgen, Berlin-GDR

Plenzdorf, U. (1972) *Die neuen Leiden des jungen W.*, Hinstorff, Rostock

Schubbe, E. (ed.) (1972) *Dokumente zur Kunst-, Literatur- und Kulturpolitik der SED*, Seewald, Stuttgart

Wander, M. (1975) *Guten Morgen, du Schöne*, Der Morgen, Berlin-GDR

Wolf, C. (1963) *Der geteilte Himmel*, Mitteldeutscher Verlag, Halle/Saale

Wolf, C. (1968) *Nachdenken über Christa T.*, Mitteldeutscher Verlag, Halle/Saale

–9–

Unholy Families –
The Oedipal Psychopathology
of Four Expressionist
Ich-Dramen

RICHARD SHEPPARD

Methodological Introduction

The work of Lévi-Strauss (1970) and Propp (1968), concentrating on societies 'in which the psychological subject has not yet been constituted as such, and therefore in which later categories of the subject, such as "character", are not relevant' (Jameson, 1981, p.124), has taught literary critics (for whom, within the last two decades, such basic categories of bourgeois humanism as subjectivity, indi-

---

This article first appeared in *Orbis Litterarum*, vol.41 (1986), pp.355–83 and is reproduced here by kind permission of the editors. The term *Ich-Drama* has been translated as 'Egocentric Drama' (Ritchie, 1976, p.64) and denotes a drama 'of extreme subjectivity' in which the ego of the protagonist dominates the foreground of the stage and in which there is considerable identification between the dramatist and his protagonist. The four plays discussed here are: Reinhard Sorge, *Der Bettler* (*The Beggar*) (written late 1911/1912); first publication as a book: Berlin, 1912; first performance on 23 December 1917 in Max Reinhardt's Deutsches Theater (Berlin) with Ernst Deutsch in the title role. Georg Kaiser, *Von morgens bis mitternachts* (*From Morn to Midnight*) (written 1912); first publication as a book: Potsdam, 1916; first performance on 28 April 1917 in the Kammerspiele (Munich). Walter Hasenclever, *Der Sohn* (*The Son*) (written Autumn 1913/Winter 1914); first public reading in Kurt Hiller's literary cabaret GNU (Berlin) on *c.* 19 February 1914; first published in *Die weissen Blätter* April–June 1914; first publication as a book: Leipzig, 1914; first performance on 30 September 1916 in the Kammerspiele of the Deutsches Landestheater (Prague); first significant performance on 8 October 1916 in the Albert-Theater (Dresden) with Ernst Deutsch in the title role. Hanns Johst, *Der Einsame* (*The Lonely One*) (written 1917); first publication as a book: Munich, 1917; first performance on 2 November 1917 in the Schauspielhaus (Düsseldorf). As there are so many editions of the above plays, I will refer to *Der Bettler* and *Der Sohn* by means of the numbers of acts and scenes (e.g. IV/2) and to Johst's play, which is divided into nine 'Bilder' ('Sets'), by means of one number only (e.g. VII).

viduality and the controlling consciousness have ceased to be self-evident) four major methodological lessons.

First, they have learnt to approach texts not as consciously controlled, extrinsically directed representations of an assumed 'real world', but as unconsciously generated models of a fantasy-structure which is in part individual and in part collective. Accordingly, it has become possible to see a literary text as though it were a folk-tale which 'contains very little pertaining to everyday life' (Propp, 1968, p.106) or a myth which 'operate[s] in men's minds without their being aware of the fact . . . in accordance with a code independent of sense experience' (Lévi-Strauss, 1970, pp.12 and 19). Second, they have learnt to view that generative fantasy-structure dialectically, as the locus of interaction between a historically conditioned imagination and a historically conditioned problematic, and the literary text as the product and outworking (or, to use Propp's term, the 'morphology') of that interaction. Third, they have learnt to understand in functional terms what, from the humanist point of view, were termed the 'characters' of a literary text – to approach them not as independent if imaginary beings borrowed from the 'real world' beyond the text, but as actantial aspects of the dialectic which has conditioned the text (cf. Propp, 1968, p.96) and whose function is either to assist or to hinder its outworking (Propp's 'helpers' and 'villains'). Fourth, they have learnt to account for the events of a literary text not at one level only, in relation to its linear/diachronic story (Jameson's 'manifest text', 1981, p.46), but at several levels, in relation to the non-linear/synchronic deep structure from which the manifest text has been generated. Or, to use Propp's terminology again, the double, or even multiple morphological meaning of a single function (1968, p.69) means that one narrative event may have several deep-structural motivations: 'themes can be split up *ad infinitum*. Just when you think you have disentangled and separated them, you realize that they are knitting together again in response to the operation of unexpected affinities' (Lévi-Strauss, 1970, p.5).

Moreover, the work of the Deconstructionists has taught critics, their attention focused on the deep structures of texts, to look for gaps, rifts, contradictions and discontinuities in the manifest text which indicate that fundamental seismic disturbances are happening in the dialectical process underlying it – places from which an element is missing, junctures where a strange element intrudes for no apparent reason, situations in which an *actant* behaves unexpectedly or fails to act at all, moments at which the apparent direction of a text is altered, and events which subvert a text's ostensible message (cf. Jameson, 1981, p.56). If we accept Lévi-Strauss's contention that any text combines two 'systems', two 'articulated mechanisms', two 'levels of articulation' (1970, pp.20–1), of which the first (the referential) points outwards to the 'real' world of common experience and the second (the abstract or semiotic) points inwards/downwards to the dialectical fantasy-structure which has generated it, then the critic who wishes to get beyond the limitations of humanism and reflectionism needs to dwell less on the reassuring images and continuities of the first level and more on the puzzling structures and discontinuities of the second.

Such methodological refocusing is indispensable for the reading of those texts which are, to a greater or lesser extent, abstract systems 'adrift' (Lévi-Strauss, 1970, p.25), only loosely attached, representationally speaking, to empirical reality. And when this general approach is combined with the insistence of Freud and his revisionist follower Lacan that the human unconscious is structured logically, according to the dictates of the Oedipus complex,[1] the critic is given an extremely useful set of ideas with which to discuss German Expressionism, especially its drama, combining as it does a tendency to abstraction with an obsession with the Father that is summed up in Georg Heym's famous diary entry of 3 November 1911: 'I would have become one of the greatest poets if only I hadn't had such a swine of a father. At a time when I needed understanding care, I had to use all my strength to keep this sod at arm's length' (1960, p.171).

Nevertheless, the reception history of expressionist drama involves considerable resistance to both abstraction and Freudian readings. On the first count, the naturalistic stage-directions for *Der Sohn* (*The Son*), *Von morgens bis mitternachts* (*From Morn to Midnight*) and parts of *Der Bettler* (*The Beggar*); the precise location of *Der Einsame* (*The Lonely One*) in Detmold and Act V of *Der Bettler* in Berlin and the strange (im)precision of the location of *Von morgens bis mitternachts* in the 'small town of W' (i.e. Weimar, with its famous hotel *Zum Elefanten*) and the 'great city of B' (i.e. Berlin) meant, as Michael Patterson's work has shown (1981, pp.53, 63, 69 and 76), that early productions could remain in the naturalist mould. And it is still not impossible to read the four plays in question as though they were more or less realistic family dramas of historical interest rather than abstract dramatisations of more basic human problems.

On the second count, the resistance has been stronger and taken more subtle forms. Half a century ago, Otto Rank (1926) and Kurt

---

1. See Freud (1950), p.156 and Lacan (1977), pp. 22–5, where Lacan, referring to *Totem and Taboo*, also assumes the centrality of the Oedipus conflict.

Wais (1931) showed how prominently the father–son motif features in Western literature and how central it becomes in times of upheaval (like the years 1880–1930 in Germany) (Rank, 1926, p.182; Wais, 1931, vol. 2, p.vii);[2] and ever since then, works of secondary criticism have reiterated that insight. Nevertheless, it is a strange fact that, having made that point, writers on Expressionism shy away from its implications. For example, although Walter Sokel understands the expressionist play abstractly, as 'a dramatization of the stream-of-consciousness or rather the stream of the subconscious' (1964, p.41), he fails to foreground the Oedipal implications of plays like *Der Bettler* of whose existence he is clearly aware (p.37). Similarly, Walter Hinck (1968, p.350) and Horst Denkler (1967, pp.185–6) accord the father–son conflict a peripheral status only, seeing it as a secondary aspect of a broader social problem rather than as the central complex in which the dynamics of that problem are encoded.

More commonly, however, critics avoid the difficult and challenging implications of the Oedipal conflict by simplifying the relationship of the dramatist to the protagonist to one of identity, abstracting the central (son) figure from the actantial totality of the drama and taking over the perspective from which and the rhetoric in which he accounts for his relations with the world. Thus, even though Denkler sees that the heroes of the *Ich-Dramen* rarely, despite their rhetoric, achieve anything concrete (1967, p.191), he can, by taking over the idealistic and autistic perspective of Hasenclever's Son, assert: 'This "conflict between the generations" [and the inverted commas betray Denkler's uncertainty and defensiveness] is, however, not the main point of the play but the raw material for

2. In order to explain this literary phenomenon and, incidentally, to answer Ritchie's question (1976, p.71) as to why so weak a play as *Der Sohn* should have been such a theatrical success during this epoch, two complementary reasons may be advanced. On the one hand, the father-figure who, by his absence or presence, dominates so many expressionist texts, was clearly the literary hypostasis of the alliance, peculiar to Germany around the time of the Great War, between old, semi-feudal and new, capitalist power. On the other hand, German society during the same period was fraught with inner contradictions and clearly suffered from a deep-seated fear that this patriarchal constellation, notwithstanding its apparently monumental weight, was fragile, threatened by the sons (cf. Paul Federn, *Zur Psychologie der Revolution: Die vaterlose Gesellschaft* (Anzengruber, Vienna, 1919)). The proclamation by Nietzsche's madman of the Death of God perfectly encapsulates this paradoxical situation: the source of authority still exists and wields power over men's unconscious, but that authority, being unreal, is disappearing as its source decays (cf. Lacan, 1979, pp.27 and 59). Expressionist literature can thus, to a considerable extent, be seen as the 'rewriting or restructuring' of (i.e. imaginative response to) this 'prior historical or ideological *subtext*' (i.e. problematic) (Jameson, 1981, p.81).

concretising an exemplary process of growth and change in which a youth who was in flight from reality turns into a man who affirms that reality' (p.184). And Ritchie, privileging the prophetic fantasies of Sorge's *Beggar*, locates the 'true significance of the play' in the protagonist's missionary intention (1976, p.64). By the same token, Denkler (1967, pp.189 and 207), Ritchie (1976, p.64) and Sokel (1964, p.41) all see the secondary characters of the *Ich-Dramen* as reflections, aspects or manifestations of processes within the (central) protagonist rather than as aspects of an (uncentred) Oedipal situation in which that protagonist is involved as one of several *actants*. And this causes Ritchie, for example, to state that *Der Sohn* involves no point of view other than the Son's. Throughout the secondary literature on expresssionist *Ich-Dramen*, critics set out to restrict the Oedipal problem to a very small area within the foreground action of the plays rather than see it as the libidinal structure which governs their entire morphology – so that when Ritchie remarked that the language of *Der Sohn* was '*uncomfortably* [my italics] reminiscent of Freud's Oedipus complex again' (1976, p.74), he may have been articulating a more general critical unease.

With these considerations in mind, I hope, in this study, to achieve a more consistently abstract reading of the four plays in question, to analyse them as dramatisations of the Oedipal situation without abstracting the father–son relationship or privileging the protagonist's perspective, and, by giving more precise definition to the relationship of the four dramatists to their dramas, to show how this relationship affects the ways in which the Oedipal drama is presented and worked through. In doing this, I am not proposing to psychoanalyse the four protagonists as though they were patients on a couch (and in any case, as Ritchie points out, 'there are no characters in the proper sense' (1976, p.68) about whom we have any case-historical information). Nor am I suggesting, as Rank did, that literary texts are simply the sublimated forms of writers' suppressed Oedipal fixations (1926, pp.623–6). Nor do I wish to succumb to the classically Oedipal temptation of rewriting literary texts allegorically, as though they were conscious transcriptions of an authoritative master-code or '*Ur*-narrative' (cf. Jameson, 1981, pp.22 and 58). Rather, to adapt a formulation of the French Lacanian critic, André Bleikasten, I want to suggest that Lacan's psychoanalytical texts and the four dramatic texts can be read as 'differential versions of common concerns and, perhaps, of a common quest for knowledge, the former attempting to articulate in theoretical terms what the latter [are] trying to express through the language of [drama]' (1981, p.120). This will, I hope, finally throw

Four Expressionist Ich-Dramen

as much light on Lacan's ideas as on the plays themselves and go some way towards explaining features of the latter which have, hitherto, puzzled critics.[3]

The Oedipal Situation

According to Propp (1968, pp.92 and 102), the dynamics of all folk-tales are generated by an initial villainy or lack which the hero then seeks to redress or make good. The same can be said of the dynamics of our four *Ich-Dramen* since all begin from that state of alienation or 'primordial Discord' (Lacan, 1977, p.4) which, in Lacan's view, is the irreducible condition of mankind – the *Urbild* of the ego (1977, p. 138). According to Lacan, and contrary to the Western Idealist tradition (1979, p.221), there is no core to the human personality, no transcendental signified in which the subject is grounded and from which she/he might develop, but only a 'preontological . . . gap' (1979, p.29), a hole whose shape is determined by the gaze of the Other (1979, p.106), a 'central lack' (1979, p.265). This means that for Lacan, all movement within the subject derives from an unresolvable dialectic between the massive authority of the patriarchal Law (variously called the 'Symbolic Order' or 'the demand of the Other') which seeks to assimilate the subject by severing him/her from the source of independent *jouissance* (1977, p.319)[4] and the subject (who either learns to accept this state of castration with lucidity or else vainly struggles against it).

---

3. E.g. the fact that Hasenclever's Son has grown up away from his father in a motherless household (Rank, 1926, p.183; Ritchie, 1976, p.71); the question of whether Sorge's Beggar really does murder his parents (Hinck, 1968, p.353); the coincidental death of the Father in *Der Sohn* (see Fritz Engel's review of the Dresden Performance in the *Berliner Tageblatt* of 9 October 1916 and Emil Faktor's review of the same performance in the *Berliner Börsen-Courier* of 10 October 1919); Grabbe's cruelty to Hans and Isabella; the strangely anomalous scene between the Lady and her son in *Von morgens bis mitternachts* (Patterson, 1981, p.76).
4. As Alan Sheridan, the English translator of the *Écrits*, notes (Lacan, 1977, p.x): there is no English equivalent of *jouissance*, a word which means pleasure but also has strong connotations of sexual fulfilment ('jouir' being slang for 'to achieve orgasm'). Lacan's usage of the term is complex, but very important inasmuch as *jouissance* lies 'beyond the pleasure principle' (1977, p.x) and thus hints at a faculty in human nature which might elude the circularity of the Oedipal conflict. Consequently, *jouissance* tends to stand in opposition to Lacan's more characteristic assertion that the human subject is fundamentally fissured, nothing in itself, and merely the product of the gaze of the Other. That Lacan leaves room, despite himself, for the possibility that there may be a hierarchy of human faculties, with

In saying this, however, three major points must be remembered. First, because Lacan is speaking at the level of unconscious process rather than everyday interaction between persons, the castrating, Oedipal Father is a hidden, absent force rather than a concretely present person, whose power, accordingly, resides in his Name (the signifier) rather than his physical presence (the signified) (cf. Davis, 1981, pp.2–3). Second, according to Lacan, neurosis arises when the subject's fantasy confuses the concrete with the symbolic, the signifier with the signified, the part-object (the 'object little *a*' (1979, p.180)) with the unconscious process (1977, p.321). Accordingly, the neurotic is said to be the subject who, instead of accepting her/his situation of castration without illusion, denies it (1977, p.323) and directs his/her desire[5] towards reappropriating the part-object which stands, in her/his fantasy, for what has been removed. As Lacan succinctly put it: 'the phantasy is the support of desire; it is not the object that is the support of desire' (1979, p.185). And third, because, for Lacan, freedom from *'the discourse of the Other'* (1979, p.131) must always be an illusion; because the subject must always occupy a space which is 'the space of the Other' (1979, p.144); because Lacan cannot, with any consistency, imagine that the potentially emancipatory faculty of *jouissance* might be powerful enough to overcome the 'primordial Discord' or make good the basic

---

one more essential than the rest is also hinted at in exploratory (but unanswered) questions such as: 'But I am asking where the peace that follows the recognition of an unconscious tendency comes from, if it is not more true than that which constrains it in the conflict?' and 'What is this truth without which there is no way of discerning the face from the mask, and outside of which there appears to be no other monster than the labyrinth itself? In other words, in what way are they to be distinguished in fact, if they are all of equal reality?' (1977, pp.118 and 119). How, Lacan is asking, can neurosis be recognised as neurosis and undone unless there is something in human nature which eludes neurosis? Nevertheless, Lacan's more typical exclusion of any fundamental faculty or drive as an illusion of Western Idealist metaphysics (which, incidentally, is by no means the case) can lead Lacanian critics to be either concessive or incredulous before a 'moment of peace and unity' like the one which occurs at the end of Melville's *Pierre* (Durand, 1981, p.71). Because the Lacanian critic is so often caught in the Oedipal position of the captive son, he, like his mentor, glimpses but will not foreground the possibility of an end to a conflictual understanding of reality.

5. 'Desire' in Lacan's usage is quite distinct from *jouissance*, being the gap between need and demand and, as such, 'essentially excentric and insatiable' (Lacan, 1977, p.viii). Whereas *jouissance* approaches the status of an autonomous faculty that permits fulfilment, 'desire' is generated by the Name-of-the-Father or patriarchal Law (Lacan, 1979, p.48) which causes the castrated son to seek, unavailingly, to reappropriate the phallus which has, in his fantasy, been removed from him. Where *jouissance* is related to Freud's concept of *Bedürfnis*, 'desire' is the product of Freud's *Not* – which nothing can satisfy (Lacan, 1979, p.167).

ontological lack, the castrated subject is permanently tied to and dependent upon the power of the Other/Law that castrates him/her. The Oedipal relationship is circular (1979, p. 213), a mixture of presence and absence (1979, p.221), not mere antagonism but an ambivalent love-hate relationship as that is described by Freud in *Totem and Taboo* (1950, pp.50–1 and 143) and, 'at its crudest and most savage', it can degenerate into a sado-masochism, 'into a system of self-perpetuating violence and cruelty, based on endless cumulation of guilt and endless repetition of revenge' (Bleikasten, 1981, pp.119 and 135).

The initial situation of all the protagonists of our four *Ich-Dramen* accords closely with Lacan's ideas. However, it should be noted that the massive hold which the patriarchal Law has over the expressionist imagination (see footnote 2) means that the situation of castration from which the plays proceed does not have a neat 'structural function' whereby sexual difference is (positively) established (Coward and Ellis, 1977, pp.113–14 and 117). Rather, it is latent with a (negative) tragic potential. Thus, for example, the first words of Hasenclever's Son, expressing his (fantasy) desire to build a monument for eternity, are, on a Lacanian reading, the product of the anxiety of never-having-lived, i.e. the reflex of a sense of being castrated. Although the true nature of such feelings is hidden from Hasenclever's protagonist, they are entirely justified since the Son (whose mother, as if by an act of pre-emptive Oedipal jealousy, died in giving him birth) has been incarcerated by his father in a bourgeois prison-cell, the view through whose window is dominated by a single factory chimney (the symbol of phallic, patriarchal authority). Furthermore, the Father, who is absent to the extent that, though alive, he lives elsewhere and haunts the Son like the ghost of Hamlet's father (IV/2), has continually castrated his son by holding before him an ideal image (scholastic achievement) to which he can never satisfactorily conform. Indeed, when, in I/1, the Son describes the circumstances of his most recent scholastic failure to his tutor (in what are almost the first words of the play), the imagery is that of castration and impotence: the Son failed 'over the formula for the *truncated cone*' [my italics]. Moreover, we hear that in the examination room, the Son took hold of the piece of chalk (reappropriation of the part-object or symbolic phallus), but could not write with it even though he knew it was a question of subtracting the smaller from the larger cone (i.e. separating himself from dependency on his father). Finally, the Son explains his failure to his tutor in terms of sado-masochistic dependence ('I think there's something which pushes us towards pain. I couldn't have stood the freedom') and self-mutilation ('I bled to death on/because of myself ['an mir']').

Kaiser's Cashier (or in German, 'Kassierer', a word which is very close phonetically to 'Kastrierter', the German word for 'castrate') is in a very similar situation. He, too, is imprisoned by an absent Father (the impersonal routine of the Bank) and has lost his tongue (phallus), saying nothing for the play's first ten pages until he asks, symbolically, for a glass of water – an action that initiates his attempt at self-emancipation. He shows his dependence on the absent Father by passing on his/its sadistic violence to the Bank's customers and replicating the prison of the Bank at home (where he inverts roles by functioning as the absent patriarch whose name is invoked there to legitimise the prevailing Symbolic Order). Both the Bank Director and the Man on the Sofa – habitués of the Bank world – are round and fat like eunuchs; and, as if to stress the link between the Bank and castration, the Man on the Sofa at one point takes a bag/sac/purse ('Beutel') from the Bank Messenger, saying: 'Now you've lost your bag/sac/purse' and then deposits his own leather bag/sac/purse before the Bank Manager as an offering! Thus, when the Cashier revolts against the Father and breaks out of the Bank world, it is entirely appropriate that he should, in his fantasy, reappropriate his missing potency symbolically by stealing 'rolls of money' and breaking one of those part-objects in two before the eyes of the Lady who has suborned him.

By means of the sophistication of their imagery, Hasenclever and Kaiser indicate that they have some distance from and awareness of their protagonists' situations. Sorge and Johst, however, identify much more strongly with their protagonists, present them in the first instance in a much more unequivocally heroic light, and thus invite the audience to acquiesce in their own, fantastic accounts of themselves. Nevertheless, both Sorge's Beggar and Johst's Grabbe are, once that rhetoric is ignored, in a very similar situation to that of the Son and the Cashier. If Sorge's Beggar is to be effective in the real world, then he must accept dependence upon the Symbolic Order as that is represented in Act I by the Patron of the Arts – a displaced father-figure who lacks the violence of the classically Oedipal Father. But this the Beggar refuses to do, and although his art is presented as one of heroic revolt, he actually regresses after Act I from the public to the narrowly familial sphere in order to engage in a fantastic and much more typically Oedipal love-hate relationship with his real father (who is absent to the extent that he is insane). This regression is not surprising once it is realised that the Beggar's messianic power-fantasies, schizoid autism and latent sadism (I/6)

Four Expressionist Ich-Dramen

are, despite the revolutionary surface of his rhetoric of emancipation in Act I, structurally identical with those of his father (III/7, II/5 and II/6). Unconsciously, the Beggar allows himself to be drawn back into his father's mad world because he is trapped in (i.e. castrated by) the discourse of the Father – an attachment which he graphically expresses at the end of III/11 by kneeling before his father's corpse and pressing his head into its lap. Beneath the Beggar's egomaniac stridency, there is, as the Third Critic perceives, a fundamental lack: 'This poet lacks something in the depths of his being and that lack is judging him' (I/2b) – which explains why, to the confusion of the reader, the Beggar is given several different names during the course of the play, none of which is, therefore, his real one. The Beggar perfectly illustrates Lacan's contention that 'the neurotic has been subjected to imaginary castration from the beginning; it is castration that sustains this strong ego, so strong, one might say, that its proper name is an inconvenience for it, since the neurotic is really nameless' (1977, p.323). And this also explains why Sorge's protagonist should be called a 'Beggar' at all: he is seeking to reappropriate (to beg back) what has, in his fantasy, been taken from him by the Law of the Father. Johst's Grabbe is in a similar situation: the narcissistic and megalomaniac state of feeling that he is 'God the Father Almighty' in which we find him at the start of (I) is illusory; and as the play proceeds, Grabbe's real impotence becomes ever plainer. Grabbe's natural father is dead and he is a 'big child' (II), dependent upon the absent Father (convention, the Lacanian Symbolic Order) against whom he employs the rhetoric of revolt but whose approval he secretly desires (as is evident from the scene in the inn (VII) where he dances to the tune of the Detmold town worthies). But Grabbe's desire is doomed to frustration, and the poet is condemned by the absent Father to rejection and self-consuming despair.

Strategies of Compensation

If all protagonists are caught in the classic double bind of castration by, and yet covert dependence on, a more or less sadistic but absent Father, then the dynamics of all four plays can be understood as encoded strategies on the part of playwright and protagonist (the boundary-line between them being unclear) for dealing with this unacceptable situation. Four such strategies are distinguishable: (i) violent or symbolic revolt against the Father; (ii) displaced vengeance on the Father through fracturing the Oedipal chain (i.e.

death or rejection of a child); (iii) occupation of the mother's position *vis-à-vis* the Father; and (iv) incestuous union with a mother or mother-substitute.

Revolt against the Father

Hasenclever's Son's revolt against the Father is relatively uncomplicated. Having overcome his childish fear of going through dark tunnels (i.e. being born (I/6)) and fortified himself against his natural father by injecting himself with an overdose of messianic fantasy (II/2), he runs away, associates himself with a group of right-wing anarchists (III), is arrested, like the unfortunate Otto Groß,[6] at the behest of his sadistic father, whom he then tries to murder by means of the symbolic phallus of a pistol. But this strategy of emancipation is only superficially successful for, whatever the Son may like to imagine, it is his father who controls the play's crucial action in having him brought back home. Furthermore, the Father eludes the Son's power by dying of heart failure before he can be murdered, and dominating the stage with his corpse even after the last words of the final scene have been spoken.

Accordingly, the Son's revolt, being concentrated on the part-object of his natural father rather than the Law which locks both of them in the Lacanian double bind, brings him nothing – so that when he says: 'Your name dissolved ... you are still alive only in your commandment' (II/2), he is mistaken. The Name-of-the-Father will not dissolve because of the Son's revolt, and the Law which lies behind it is no mere phantasm – a point made symbolically by the Maid who, when the Son is about to run away (II/5), shows the extent to which he is still bound by patriarchal structures (of which she is, in part, an agent) by tying his tie ('Binde') round

6. The reference to Otto Groß (1877–1920), the first anti-Freudian Freudian, is by no means gratuitous since Groß, the son of the famous Hans Groß, Professor of Criminal Psychology at the University of Graz, was a *cause célèbre* in winter 1913/14 – i.e. at exactly the time when Hasenclever was writing *Der Sohn*. Groß, whose early work was, broadly speaking, an attack on patriarchy in the name of matriarchy, rebelled against his father by leaving the respectable academic world for the anarchist *bohème* of Munich and Berlin and propagating utopian ideas of revolution through psychic emancipation and sexual freedom which were particularly appealing to the expressionist generation. On 9 November 1913 his father had him arrested in Berlin and deported to an asylum in Austria on the authority of an affidavit, declaring him to be a dangerous psychopath, which was signed by C.G. Jung. This action resulted in a successful campaign for Groß's release in expressionist journals like *Die Aktion*, *Revolution*, *Kain* and the *Wiecker Bote* (see A. Mitzman, 'Anarchism, Expressionism and Psychoanalysis', *New German Critique*, no. 10 (Winter 1977), pp.77–104).

his neck. Indeed, far from compensating for his missing capacity for *jouissance*, the Son's revolt leaves him in a state of emotional emptiness at the end of the play (V/3). Although Hasenclever conveniently cuts the play short before we learn what happens to the Son after the Father's death, it seems likely that the prophecy made by the Father towards the end of II/2 is coming true: the patriarchal Law is tearing to ribbons the wings of the one who has revolted against its authority. The fate of the Friend reinforces the above pattern: in the name of revolt against the Father, he has become involved with a group which looks revolutionary. Nevertheless, one of its number is a prince who subscribes to the 'iron law' that sons must succeed their fathers (III/3); another, von Tuchmeyer, who has financed the group with his dead father's fortune as an act of defiance, sees his resultant disillusion and bankruptcy as an act of revenge by his dead father (III/3); and the Friend himself, having encouraged the Son's messianic fantasies, unexpectedly kills himself in a state of disillusioned exhaustion after the Son has been returned to his father. In all cases, the message is the same: revolt against the Father is fruitless and serves only to strengthen his ineluctable power.

The pattern in *Von morgens bis mitternachts* is similar, and, if anything, even more carefully worked out. The Cashier is impelled to revolt against the patriarchal authority of the Bank by being shown, in the exotic 'southernness' of the Lady and the associated painting of Adam and Eve in the Garden of Eden, an ideal mirror image of prelapsarian *jouissance* from which his life, in its banality, has been severed. Indeed, at one point in the play's First Part, he makes his yearning for that lost Eden explicit by saying, punningly: 'I'm in the picture'. But the lost Eden which he so ardently desires is illusory. Although Kaiser attributes the picture to Cranach, and although Cranach painted several similar pictures, that painter, as Patterson pointed out (1981, p.65), never created precisely such a work, and on its back is pasted a reminder of the banal reality which all such beautiful illusions conceal: a photograph of the publican who owns it. Moreover, when the Cashier symbolically reappropriates his lost phallus by stealing the rolls of money, he also takes a heap of 'Scheine', a German word which means 'illusions' as well as 'banknotes' and which, earlier in the Bank scene, was explicitly associated with money in all its forms and the beauty spot on the face of the Lady.

The Cashier's revolt, the imagery implies, is built on illusions so that when, in the play's Second Part, he acts at the Six-Day Bicycle Race as though, through the power of his phallic rolls of money, he were the detached, omnipotent Father-God, watching almost contemptuously over the six days of his Creation, the arrival of a real power-figure, the unnamed and unseen 'His Highness', can subvert without difficulty the illusory power which the Cashier has appropriated. As the play goes on, the Cashier's supply of money dwindles until, by the end, the rolls are associated with artificial props (the wooden legs on two of the subsidiary characters) and, muttering 'the wooden leg' to himself, the Cashier admits his castration and the impotence of his chosen part-object and hurls his money at the crowd in the Salvationist meeting. But this gesture of lucidity and disillusion brings him nothing either: although he finds himself standing with the Salvation Army Girl like Adam next to Eve in the fictitious Cranach painting, it is the forces of Law and Death, the ultimate Law, that have the final word. Thus, the policeman's remark on which the play ends – 'there's a short-circuit in the system' – refers both to the Cashier's own 'short-circuit' (his neurotic confusion of the signifier with the signified) and to the closed circuit of the Oedipal drama whose end is no advance over its beginning because the Law of the absent Father negates all revolt and allows the subject no real movement.

Sorge's Beggar and Johst's Grabbe use the phallic power of the dramatist's pen as the symbolic substitute for the potency they have lost and as a weapon against the power of the Father. But again, in both cases, the revolt fails because of the neurotic confusion at its core. Thus, although Grabbe claims in (I) to have redeemed the 'Menetekel'[7] through his writing, the 'shadow' child of whom he claims to be the father turns out to be the megalomaniac fantasy Napoleon of his play: far from abolishing paternal authority by his writing, he has perpetuated it. And in *Der Bettler*, the fact that the Father desires death as an act of mercy (II/6) and the confusion over the poisoned glasses in III/6–III/10 means that we are dealing with a killing which is only superficially an act of Oedipal revolt. Nothing is achieved by the Beggar's father's death and, in the dream sequences of II/7, the absent Father has the last word. Consequently, even after his father's death, the Beggar stays trapped in the same patriarchal structures which sent his father mad, and so, in IV/2, stresses the continuity between himself and his parents by declaring:

7. The word is, of course, a reference to Daniel 5:25 where a hand appears at Belshazzar's Feast to write in letters of fire on the wall the judgement: 'Mene, Mene, Tekel, Upharsin'. But, ironically, Grabbe forgets that the hand is that of the vengeful patriarch Jahweh and that 'Mene Tekel' ('Thou art weighed in the balances and art found wanting') refers as much to his own primordial lack as to the judgement which he thinks he is passing on the world.

'The circle is closed'. After that, he indulges in fantasies of patriarchal kingship at the end of V/1 which are very similar to his dead father's mad fantasies, and confirms this identity at the beginning of V/2 by appearing in his father's blue night-shirt, carrying a phallic candle. Moreover, as with Hasenclever's play, the Father's death, far from filling a gap, leaves behind an even greater psychological hunger whose implications we are prevented from seeing because Sorge, like Hasenclever, stops his drama at the very point where Johst's begins. That point is the one beyond which it would become evident that Oedipal revolt, which derives from a primordial lack and focuses on substitute part-objects, must, given the structure of the playwrights' imaginations, either end in despair (as the gap, without the restraint of the Law, expands to universal dimensions) or in the replacement of the Father by a Son-become-Father (as the Law, which has not been harmed by the destruction of its signifier, reasserts its authority over the would-be rebel).

The Breaking of the Oedipal Chain

In the sadistic world of all four *Ich-Dramen*, children die or are rejected. In *Der Sohn*, for example (I/3), we hear, for no obvious reason, of the death of a little girl which, in the Son's fantasy, is explicitly associated with his failure to kill himself and his ecstatic resolve to revolt against his father: 'From out of her little hands, the night of existence has fallen around me, like a golden rain which falls upon the seed sown by the shepherds.' Similarly, the Cashier, by running away from the Bank and his home, refuses fatherhood; Grabbe's baby dies; the child which Hans and Isabella might have produced is never conceived because of Grabbe's treachery; and Sorge's play ends with the Girl resolving to give her baby away in order to be more totally committed to the Beggar. Within the libidinal economy of the plays, each of these gestures can be seen as an attempt on the part of the dramatists to see whether it is possible to break the Oedipal chain by the elimination of a symbolic object (the children) and the refusal of fatherhood. But none of these attempts succeeds. The death of the little girl in *Der Sohn* confirms the power of a patriarchal order (in which the Female, like the Son's mother and the woman whose suicide is mentioned in II/1, must either die or play an ancillary role) and frees the Son to become a father in his turn by saving him from committing suicide. Nor is the Cashier's refusal of fatherhood of any avail. He leaves behind a rigidly structured family which is dominated by, and will, presumably, continue to be dominated by, an absent father – and before which, although consisting of women, he worships dutifully at the shrine of institutionalised patriarchal power (like Kronos, the primal Father, the Cashier even controls time so that his elder daughter can say: 'If Father is coming, it's midday'). The death and refusal of the children in the other two plays are equally futile: the playwrights may have eliminated two part-objects, but by doing so, they confirm the patriarchal pattern in that they sadistically forestall a possible Oedipal revolt by eliminating potential rebels. In other words, the lack which is basic to the Oedipal universe and felt by the playwrights as much as by their protagonists cannot be made good by the sacrifice of a child.

The Assumption of the Mother's Role

In his essay 'The Passing of the Oedipus Complex' (1924), Freud suggests that one way in which a child may seek to resolve the Oedipal situation is by playing the mother's role *vis-à-vis* the father – thus making the mother superfluous. Although this strategy is not investigated in *Von morgens bis mitternachts*, it is more or less clearly discernible in the other three plays. The first encounter between Hasenclever's Son and his father (II/2) begins with an image of castration (the Son sees an executioner in his father's eyes). But before the Son attempts to avoid his fate by active revolt, he plays, in the first part of the same scene, a stock female role, falling on his knees before his father like the heroine of a melodrama before the wicked squire, and begging him to love and not reject him. Something similar happens in *Der Einsame*. At the end of VI, Grabbe feels betrayed by his washerwoman mother, who then, within the libidinal economy of the play, has to die (see below). Consequently, in VII, Grabbe takes over his dead mother's subservient role, demeaning himself by reading from his work to the Detmold worthies (the representatives of the Law) even though he knows that they will understand nothing. And in *Der Bettler*, something akin to Oedipal competition takes place in II/5 and II/6 when the Beggar sends his mother and sister away and acts in an almost uxorious manner towards his lunatic father. But again, in all three cases, the strategy is doomed: in *Der Sohn*, the Father viciously rejects the Son's advances; in *Der Einsame*, the Detmold worthies laugh Grabbe to scorn; and in *Der Bettler*, the sadistic fantasies of the Father become, despite the Beggar's attempt to soften them, even worse in Act III. In other words, when the protagonists of the *Ich-Dramen* bow to patriarchal authority and accept their castration by playing conventionally wifely roles, that authority, far from being appeased, is confirmed and provoked to act even more sadistically.

Incestuous Union

The most obvious way in which the authors and protagonists of the *Ich-Dramen* attempt to overcome an Oedipal universe is through flight to an idealised mother (cf. Freud, 1914, p.58), mother-substitute or part-object associated with the mother – for, as Lacan points out, the object of the drive is indifferent (1979, p.168). Within an Oedipal universe, this action has three, mutually reinforcing levels of motivation and significance. At the first, it is the classic gesture of incestuous aggression against the Father. At the second, it is the gesture of the castrate who, in order to compensate for his impotence, seeks 'to be that which the mother's desire named, that is, in psychoanalytic terms, the phallus' (Hanzo, 1981, p.34; cf. Lacan, 1977, p.289). And at the third, it represents a turning away from the primal lack and sadism of the Oedipal chain towards that narcissistic state of pre-natal, uterine bliss or post-natal, oral gratification in which there are no limits to need or satisfaction (cf. Davis, 1981, pp.9–10) and in which the illusion of omnipotence is constantly fed. Consequently, the protagonists of the *Ich-Dramen* engage in relationships which are, in Freud's terminology, 'anaclitic'. They involve a 'primary narcissism', 'marked sexual over-estimation' and a 'state suggestive of a neurotic compulsion, which is thus traceable to an impoverishment of the ego in respect of libido [i.e. castration] in favour of the love-object' (Freud, 1914, pp.44 and 45).

Accordingly, when Hasenclever's Son was being examined (I/1) and held the substitute phallus in his hand, he dreamt in compensation of 'archduchesses' and 'sweetness'. The same desire is evident, when he is about to leave home, from the assertion: 'Soon I shall enjoy nectar and ambrosia in the lap [German 'Schoß' also = 'womb'] of women with whom I am in love' (III/5). Similarly, like the protagonists of the other three *Ich-Dramen*, he craves the experience of ecstasy (I/1, I/7 and II/2), that strange mixture of uterine bliss, orgasmic release and feelings of omnipotence, and, to this end, he demands that the Maid (who is an Oedipal mother-figure at the start of the play to the extent that she is an ally of the Father)[8] be his mistress, oral mother and Oedipal accomplice all in one (I/6). He is confirmed in this desire by the Friend who says: 'Your mother, too, was a woman like her [the Maid]. You will be

---

8. For an explanation of the terms 'uterine mother', 'oral mother' and 'oedipal mother', see Deleuze (1971), p.49.

her child' (I/5) and by the Maid herself, who acquiesces in this fantastic demand (II/1 and II/6) and acts, at the end of the play, like an oral mother to the now desolate Son. At the same time, however, Hasenclever continually deconstructs this mode of revolt. He shows us its infantilism in the scene with the prostitute Adrienne, who, far from agreeing to be another version of the all-giving oral mother, turns into a vengeful Oedipal mother who is linked with the demonic Carmen and acts as the accomplice of the castrating Father in accusing the Son of being not a messianic figure but just a little boy. He shows us its illusory nature in the figure of the Friend (who, having encouraged the Son's fantasies, collapses inwardly and commits suicide). He shows us its political and moral dangers in the ease with which the Son is seduced by the cynical, violent and treacherous members of the Club 'For the Maintenance of Joy' (III/1–5). And he shows us its psychic consequences in the Maid's inability to assuage the Son's sense of emptiness at the end of Act V. In the scenes in blank verse (notably I/2, I/7, II/6 and V/3 – which are reminiscent of Goethe's *Faust* and, in some places, the poetry of Stefan George), Hasenclever closely associates himself with the flight to the Mother which constitutes so much of the Son's revolt.[9] But in the prose scenes, Hasenclever very clearly dissociates himself once more – which suggests, perhaps, another reason why, within the play's libidinal economy, the Son's mother could not live, and why, at the beginning of II/1, we hear, apparently gratuitously, of a woman's suicide. The former death is not only a prophylactic action lest the Mother collude with the Son, but also a displaced revenge for her inability to save the Son from the sadism of an Oedipal universe;[10] and the latter death is a displaced judgement on the inability of anaclitic relationships to compensate for a primal lack.

The pattern is similar in *Von morgens bis mitternachts*. Having imprisoned himself in a Bank and, in his role as castrating Father,

9. There are considerable biographical parallels between Hasenclever and his Son (see Fritz Engel's review cited in note 3) and Otto Rank tells us that according to the newspaper reports, Hasenclever, who was present at the October 1916 performance of his play 'suffered a severe nervous shock and is supposed . . . to have suffered from delusions of having shot his father' (1926, p.183). Although I have, to date, found no newspaper reports to substantiate this, two unpublished MSS in the Weimar Archive, set down at the time by Hasenclever's friends for the benefit of his psychiatrist, appear to do so (see K. Kändler, 'Hasenclever-Handschriften im Goethe- und Schiller-Archive Weimar', *Weimarer Beiträge*, vol.6 (1960), pp.135–8).
10. Critics of expressionist literature have often commented on the frequency with which the father–son conflict appears there, but almost no one seems to have noted, let alone tried to explain, the aggression towards the mother which also occurs there (cf. Wais, 1931, vol.1, p.xii).

reduced his family to a situation of de-sexualised cosiness, the Cashier is suborned by a mother-figure who, in his over-heated fantasy, promises to be a 'primitive, uterine, hetaeric mother, mother of the cloaca and the swamps' (Deleuze, 1971, p.49) – indeed, the Bank Manager uses the very word 'swamp' ('Sumpf') in her connection. Like the Venus-figure at the beginning of Sacher-Masoch's *Venus im Pelz* (*Venus in Furs*) (1870), the Lady in *Von morgens bis mitternachts* is wrapped in furs 'lest she catch cold in our abstract northern climate, in the icy realm of Christianity' (Deleuze, 1971, p.124) and associated with a painting. Moreover, she is, at the start of the play, in conflict with the patriarchal Bank Manager; emanates a scent of sexual promise and suggests a legitimised (i.e. unpunished) incestuous union to the Cashier both through the fictitious Cranach painting (for Eve is Adam's wife and Adam's daughter) and her strangely erotic relationship with her son. But such redemptive promise is deceptive, and although the Cashier gets his tongue back through her, he fails to read the contrary signs: the Lady comes from Florence, the city where Severin, the hero/victim of *Venus im Pelz* endures his worst humiliations; she assists in the castration of the Bank Messenger (whose 'Beutel' (see above) is removed for looking at her); she is associated with 'make-up' and 'illusions' ('Scheine' – see above); she creates disorder wherever she goes; she is called a 'siren' by the Bank Manager and she is identified with the temptress Eve.

In short, the apparently hetaeric mother-figure (whom the Cashier explicitly links with Canaan, the Promised Land, in the family scene) is, in reality, the vengeful Oedipal mother. She becomes reconciled with the Bank Manager by the end of the play's First Part and, having held up a seductive image to the unfortunate Cashier, severs him from it by taking the painting, rejecting him and refusing his reappropriated phalloi (the 'rolls of money'). And this explains why, at the beginning of the play's Second Part, the Cashier's younger daughter should be playing the Overture to Wagner's *Tannhäuser*. It is not, as Patterson suggests, simply a question of creating an atmosphere of bourgeois cosiness (1981, p.70), but of suggesting that the Cashier has, like Wagner's knight, fallen from grace by entering the Venusberg. Unlike Tannhäuser and Severin, however, the Cashier never re-emerges from the Venusberg or the process of corrective punishment, so that the rest of Kaiser's play replicates the initial pattern of seduction and betrayal.

Having tried to achieve the ultimate in ecstasy at the Six-Day Bicycle Race, the Cashier is rendered impotent, on the point of achieving orgasm, by the ithyphallic authority of the royal patriarch.

We are told that the 'smouldering fire' in both the Cashier and the crowds is extinguished by a 'polished boot' ['Lackstiefel' – and in this context, the punning value of the first syllable of the German word is a happy coincidence] on the leg of 'His Highness'. In the dance hall (which the Cashier enters bearing a phallic 'rattan cane with a gold knob'), some of the girls wear masks to disguise their ugliness, and one even has a (phallic) wooden leg with which she shatters the Cashier's dreams of achieving uterine bliss through erotic excitement (hence the references in the same episode to Carmen and the crowing of the cock at Christ's betrayal). And in the final episode, the Salvation Army Girl, having looked as though she is going to play Gretchen to the Cashier's Faust by promising uterine ecstasy through the joy of religious conversion (the mood of the Salvationist meeting being identical with that of the Six-Day Bicycle Race), betrays him to the police. Within Kaiser's play, the flight to the Mother is of no avail so that, to adapt a famous quotation from *Faust* II, 'The Eternal Feminine drops us in it' might stand as its motto. Consequently, it is not surprising that the play's libidinal economy should require the death of the Cashier's mother. Her indirect murder at the hands of her son is a subterranean revenge for her inability to save him from, and, in some of her transformations, her readiness to collude in the castration required by, the sadistic patriarchal Law – the 'Cosmic Police Force' as the Cashier puts it in the scene in the snow-covered field.

Sorge's Beggar, too, seeks to evade the demands of the Symbolic Order by a flight to the womb. He desires dissolution in the dark blue of the night (which is equated with 'maternal softness' (II/7)), in the love of the Girl (who is described as the mystic-maternal symbol (II/7) and who, like the Maid of *Der Sohn*, exists for him merely as a source of narcissistic/uterine gratification), and in drunken ecstasy (II/8, IV/1–3, V/1). *Der Einsame* begins with Grabbe in the same state of drunken ecstasy and then goes on to investigate his disillusion when the bubble bursts and he finds himself delivered over, as ever, to the merciless Law – a process which explains the increasingly bleak settings in which the action is set, and, to an extent at least, the curtains which are opened and closed on stage throughout the play's length. Desperately seeking to evade the Law (and, incidentally, the ultimate Law of Death by asserting his immortality), Grabbe at one point seeks succour in his mother (VI). First, he declares his love for her as though she were his mistress – and Johst's stage-direction accidentally emphasises the sexual motivation by indicating that he does this 'eindringlich' ('insistently' – literally 'penetratingly'). This metaphor is then extended when Grabbe, having said that he cannot get through to his mother, adds that he would like to 'penetrate ['eindringen'] into the realm of the other', and Grabbe's incestuous desire is finally made quite explicit when he says to his mother: 'Und es wäre schön, wenn ich in deinen [accusative – the case in German denoting movement into] Schoß [= 'lap' and/or 'womb'] hineinweinen dürfte – wie ich wollte . . .! Den Strom, den ich aus dir als Milch saugte, zurückbetten könnte – als Tränen!!' ('And how beautiful it would be if I were to be allowed – as I wanted – to cry myself back into your lap [womb] . . .! To divert the stream, which I sucked from you as milk, back into you, its bed – as tears!!').

As the flight is successful in neither play, the mothers of both protagonists have to die: Grabbe's mother simply disappears, driving Grabbe to seek narcissistic relief in the 'thrice holy demon' of *Schnaps*, and the Beggar's mother dies by poisoning, though whether her death is a conscious or unconscious murder or suicide is carefully concealed by the stage business. The death of Grabbe's wife, Anna, has a similar subliminal motivation. Although she appears in (I) as a catalyst of Grabbe's ecstatic feeling of being 'God the Father Almighty', her power is not great enough to prevent the despair which is beginning to overtake her husband by the end of the scene. Moreover, her death in (II) reinforces Grabbe's sense of betrayal; functions as a punishment for that fantasy betrayal; and convinces him that the universe is governed by the sadistic Law of the absent Father – hence his reference to Christ's Passion at the scene's end. By the same token, an Oedipal motivation also underlies Grabbe's lethal betrayal of his friend Hans and his seduction of Hans's fiancée Isabella. Because he can find no relief from the sadism of the absent Father in his fantasy flight to the Mother, he pales 'before the image of a completeness closed upon itself, before the idea that the *petit a*, the separated *a* from which he is hanging [i.e. the breast], may be for another the possession that gives satisfaction, *Befriedigung*' (Lacan, 1979, p.16). Consequently, he is led to destroy the two lovers from sheer Oedipal envy.

Without providing a structural explanation, Walter Hinck noted the large number of legitimised murders in expressionist drama (1968, pp.351–2), and by now it should be clear why this is so. In that drastically Oedipal world, protagonists and creators alike are trying to overcome their sense of castration and evade the patriarchal Law. But when their various strategies fail, as fail they must (since they tend to be neurotic in the Lacanian sense that they are directed against the signifier rather than the signified), scapegoats (largely women and children) must be found. But, paradoxically, this process only reinforces the might of the Oedipal Law whose ultimate purpose is, according to Deleuze: '[the] effective end to all procreation' (1971, p.52). As Johst's Grabbe laments in the scene with his mother (VI): 'The same circle ['Ring'] over and over again'.

The Playwrights' Perspectives on their Dramas

Hasenclever, Sorge and Johst disguise the surface of their plays by putting a rhetoric of revolutionary prophecy, cosmic mission and redemption into their protagonists' mouths. Nevertheless, these high sentiments are implicitly deconstructed (as they would be in Kaiser's drama, too, if its protagonist went in for such rhetoric) by the Oedipal nature of the plays' deep structure, according to which human relationships consist in a more or less sadistic power-struggle that cannot be resolved. That it is so easy to overlook this deep structure in favour of the foreground rhetoric (cf. Ritchie, 1976, p.65) derives from the fact that three of the four playwrights, because of their close emotional identification with their protagonists, do not wish to face this fact themselves and so evolve series of manipulative strategies for masking the metaphysical implications of their plays from themselves and their readers. Such strategies, however, very rarely work convincingly, with the result that the Oedipal implications continually break through to the plays' surface to disrupt that 'unified perspective' (Ritchie, 1976, p.65) which they seem to sustain.

Of the four dramatists, Kaiser (who must have been tempted to identify with the phonetically related Kassierer (= Cashier)) seems most aware of what is at stake, least prone to mask the grim, Oedipal 'eternal recurrence of the same', and most successful at sustaining a consistently ironic distance from his protagonist. As Hinck saw, *Von morgens bis mitternachts* is the ironic presentation of disillusion with the cult of ecstasy and ego-inflation (1968, pp.348–9). Indeed, so severe is Kaiser's detachment that he could be said to be performing an ambiguous totemic sacrifice after the manner described in *Totem and Taboo*. On the one hand, he is killing a hated father/totem animal (Freud, 1950, pp.142–3) and on the other, he is sacrificing a rebellious son for his attempt to break the Oedipal chain: 'in order to keep the temptation down, the envied transgressor must be deprived of the fruit of his enterprise; and the punishment will not infrequently give those who carry it out an opportunity of committing the same outrage under cover of an act of expiation' (p.72). It is this doubly sacrificial motivation which explains the ritual quality of parts of the action and produces the inevitability of the play's tragic end (where, aptly enough, the broken ('cassé') Cashier is identified with the crucified Christ). However, unlike in the Christian myth or Freud's understanding of the totemic meal, the Cashier's sacrifice is not followed by resurrection or 'festive rejoicing' (Freud, 1950, p.140). So massively oppressive is the absent Oedipal Father who, through the 'Cosmic Police Force', has the last word in *Von morgens bis mitternachts*, that after the 'short-circuit in the [electrical] system', there is only darkness.

Being more intimately involved with their protagonists, the other three dramatists are far less willing to countenance the stark, Oedipal dynamics which motivate their plays. Johst begins by identifying closely with Grabbe, but as the play goes on, he finds that he is increasingly forced to distance himself from Grabbe, as Grabbe, on the one hand, acts in an increasingly cruel and thoughtless manner towards his friends and relatives, and, on the other hand, tends inwardly towards a state of despairing exhaustion. However, in order to mitigate the darkness of this process and turn what is, in essence, an Oedipal tragedy into a more commonplace (and reassuring) drama of misunderstood genius, Johst does two things. First, he particularises the action to a much greater extent than is the case in the other three plays, giving his protagonist and many of the other *actants* names, and setting them very specifically in realistic contexts and the (named) town of Detmold. And second, to quote Hinck, '[he] heroises the wilful arrogance of this singular human being by presenting it in monumental terms', turns Grabbe, by surrounding him on his death-bed with a halo of Beethoven's music, into a latter-day Egmont. But the ending is self-defeating, for the Beethoven is tatty and thin, being played by amateurs on a clarinet, trumpet and *Waldhorn*, and serves to draw attention to the contrast rather than the similarity between Grabbe and Goethe's hero. Accordingly, this provides another reason why, throughout *Der Einsame*, curtains on stage should be opened and closed around central *actants* at key moments: now we are allowed to see the Oedipal structures in their nakedness; now they are concealed from us.

As was remarked above, Hasenclever's relationship with his protagonist fluctuates between closeness and critical distance. Nevertheless, even in the prose scenes, when Hasenclever has gained considerable distance from his protagonist and could afford to face his drama's implications, he uses several means of mitigating its Oedipal nature. First, of course, there is the rhetoric of 'radical renewal of the world' (Hinck, 1968, p.350) through which the complex motivations of the Oedipal relationship can be reduced to a simple ethical action, and which serves as a means of concealing, as Hinck put it, 'a moral vacuum, into which even the inhuman can thrust its way' (1968, p.353). Second, Hasenclever makes use of reassuring *raisonneur* figures like the Tutor, who rationalises the Oedipal situation of the Son into temporary depression deriving from overwork and tries to persuade him that his lot is not as bad as he thinks (I/1), the Maid, who tells the Son how kind his father is professionally (II/1) and the Police Inspector, who tries to defuse the Oedipal conflict by offering a sensible reconciliation between father and son and a sensible explanation of the Son's actions. In other words, the function of such *actants* is to reduce Oedipal drama to soap opera dimensions; to be the detergents which remove Oedipal stains quickly and easily.[11] Third, Hasenclever displaces the ritual sacrifice of the Son on to the Friend, thus obviating the need for the Son's Oedipal revolt to be expiated by death (as happens in Kaiser's and Johst's plays). Fourth, by allowing the Father to drop dead in a realistic setting and for a realistic reason, Hasenclever prevents the Oedipal conflict from having to be taken to its logical conclusion: as Fritz Engel pointed out in his early review (see note 3), Hasenclever loses his nerve. And fifth, Hasenclever forecloses the action before the subjective effects on the Son can be laid as bare as they are in Kaiser's and Johst's plays. But, in view of the effect of the Dresden performance on Hasenclever (see note 9), one may doubt the efficacy of such strategies: if the Oedipal conflict is to be resolved dramatically, then it has to be faced head-on, so that one wonders whether its absence from Hasenclever's later drama and revolutionary poetry (cf. Wais, 1931, vol.2, pp.51–2) indicates resolution or mere avoidance.

Sorge's urge to avoid or mitigate the rawness of the Oedipal conflict informing *Der Bettler* is even more blatant and manifests itself in five strategies. First, if one compares Act I with Acts II–V, one sees that a large, public world, populated by variegated urban types, has been replaced by a small, familial, extra-urban one. This means in turn that the cosmically fatal consequences of Oedipal revolt, set out in Act I in the list of natural disasters (I/2a) and the latter-day version of the Icarus legend which is intoned chorically by the Airmen (I/7), can be repressed in Acts II–V. The large context

11. Interestingly enough, the critic of the *Dresdner Volkszeitung* (who witnessed the second performance of *Der Sohn*) seems to have sensed the reassuring function of these three characters since he referred, in his review of 9 October 1916, to the 'authentic resonances' which they emitted.

in which the 'Storms of Heaven' might rage as a tragic necessity has been almost totally eliminated and survives only in the displaced forms of the Father's schizophrenic fantasies and the 'subdued' noise of the city 'behind the curtain' of Act V. Second, Sorge skews the Oedipal conflict, allowing the son's one active gesture of revolt to be directed (non-fatally) against the sentimentally tolerant Patron of the Arts, who then, conveniently, disappears without exacting any revenge. Third, Sorge makes the Beggar's father mad so that his sadism and megalomania can be seen as accidental (the results of illness) rather than basic to his nature. Fourth, in order to disguise the underlying sadism of his Father-dominated world, Sorge is at pains to overlay the central Oedipal conflict and two classically Oedipal gestures (the Girl's abandonment of the child and the Beggar's killing of his parents) with a rhetoric of moral idealism and a highly moral motivation (humility and pity) – a fact which several commentators have noted without understanding its significance structurally (Wais, 1931, vol.2, p.44; Sokel, 1964, p.149; Denkler, 1967, pp.186–7; Hinck, 1968, p.353). The Youth (a transformation of the Beggar) summarises this strategy at the end of IV/3:

> Thou knowest much now.
> And above all knowledge for whose sake we endured,
> The sun can only rise, in ever greater radiance,
> And we with it, in heart as with our eyes!

– saying, in effect, that a sun-lit veil has been drawn over the cruel reality of Sorge's Oedipal world. Finally, like Hasenclever, Sorge stops his play before reality (the Law) can intervene to arrest or punish the Beggar for his parents' death and while the Beggar, after a brief, token period of ascetic remorse (V/2), is still in a state of euphoric ecstasy. But, as I have argued, the Beggar's exultant sense that the course of play has been one of 'great completion according to Goodness and the Law' (IV/2) is an idealistic construct involving the concealment of anything that might contradict it. By the end of the play, nothing has changed: the Beggar has not abolished the Law by killing his father, but has succeeded his father as executor of the Law even if, for the moment, his patriarchal fantasies of power (V/1) are being given a utopian, moral gloss. And because Sorge cannot bear to admit this fact, he naturally has recourse to the one strategy finally open to him: he stops the story short – symbolically castrates it – thereby perpetuating the very Oedipal chain whose power and brutality he has consistently tried to mitigate.

The pessimistic conclusions to which all four dramas tend –

ritual death without the possibility of rebirth, inner exhaustion, and pre-emptive castration concealed by a messianic rhetoric whose stridency is the index of its unreality – are the inevitable products of what Deleuze and Guattari called the 'oedipalised' imagination (1977, p.133).[12] Because of the weight of the Law pressing down upon their imaginations (see note 2), none of the four playwrights is capable of imagining and giving actantial expression to free libidinal energy – Deleuze and Guattari's 'desiring-production' ('production désirante') which, existing outside the Oedipal triangulation, might break it and prevent 'the entire situation from falling back on the familial complex and becoming internalized in it' (1977, p.97). Consequently, the four plays implicitly suggest, notwithstanding any revolutionary rhetoric in the foreground, that a nihilistic hopelessness is the only alternative to the dominant, patriarchal code.

Deleuze and Guattari asserted: 'Oedipus is like God; the father is like God; the problem is not resolved until we do away with *both the problem and the solution*' (1977, p.81), but our four dramatists are incapable of arriving at such a resolution imaginatively. No sooner does an 'anoedipal' drive manifest itself in the plays, than it is assimilated into the Oedipal chain of lack and dependence; rendered harmless by being allowed to exhaust itself in aggression against part-objects; or turned into a regressive flight to the Mother. Nor can Nature, that traditional refuge for the German literary imagination, be of any assistance in such an oedipalised universe. Being associated with the Female, it is either excluded from the plays altogether (*Der Sohn* and *Der Einsame*); presented as a destructive threat (see the list of natural disasters recited in I/2a of *Der Bettler*); tamed, like the Beggar's mother, into impotent domesticity (cf. the garden setting of Act III of *Der Bettler*); violated (cf. the Beggar's father's killing of the bird (III/6) and fantasies of chthonic domination (II/6)); or, as happens through the skeleton in the tree in the snow-covered field scene of *Von morgens bis mitternachts*, declared to be a realm governed by Death.

Seen from this perspective, the four plays not only illustrate, but also function as an implicit critique of Lacanian psychology inasmuch as they demonstrate the limitations of the 'ideology of lack' (Deleuze and Guattari, 1977, p.295) in which that psychology is grounded. The *Ich-Dramen* cannot envisage a fundamental drive in the human personality which, in Deleuze and Guattari's words, is a 'desire lacking nothing, a flux that overcomes barriers and codes'

---

12. For a short account of the origins of Deleuze and Guattari's book, see Schneiderman (1983), p.29.

Four Expressionist Ich-Dramen

(1977, p.131) and which, participating in the flux of Nature (pp.4–5, 54 and 293), can produce free individuals, 'irresponsible, solitary, and joyous, finally able to say and do something simple in his own name, without asking permission' (p.131). Similarly, Lacan seems to have increasingly deprived the concept of *jouissance* of any potential to act as a countervailing ontological moment in his Oedipal universe by associating it closely with the death-instinct (cf. Schneiderman, 1983, pp.53–4). Just as the *Ich-Dramen* put the (matriarchal) realm of Nature under a negative sign and implicitly set forth the ineluctability of (patriarchal) Law, so Lacan turns the Unconscious into a merely cultural phenomenon by reducing it to 'the sum of the effects of speech on a subject' (Lacan, 1979, p.126). Thus, he severs it from the wider realm of Nature (cf. Hanzo, 1981, p.36) and secretly suggests that the Symbolic Order must have the last word. Just as the *Ich-Dramen* end either with the encroachment of the *néant* or by masking that encroachment in a hollow rhetoric of renewal, so Lacan's hard shell of language continually masks the tragic implications of the fact that for him, there is, in the end, only '*aphanisis* of the subject' (1979, p.221), the indelible frustration of desire (1979, p.167; 1977, p.42) and, consequently, a universe that is ultimately vain (1977, p.317).[13] Just as, at the time, the Dadaists attacked Expressionism on the grounds that its oscillation between the poles of idealism and nihilism allied it with conservative forces,[14]

13. Schneiderman recalls a seminar at which Lacan said 'that his writing style, his enigmatic way of expressing himself, was necessitated by the fact that if he had spoken otherwise, "they" would not have let him speak' (1983, p.175). Although Schneiderman admits that Lacan was 'for the most part trapped ... within the realm of tragedy' (p.166), he, writing from the American tradition of positive thinking, tends, in his memoir, to mitigate the pessimism of Lacan's tragic vision. Thus, he offers a narrowed-down vision of the 'they' to whom Lacan refers, speculating that Lacan meant 'the dead ... the ghosts [of those who died in World War II] that continued to haunt the minds of the survivors' (p.175).
14. When Deleuze and Guattari said that 'schizoanalysis' [i.e. their understanding of man] '... sets out to explore a transcendental unconscious rather than a metaphysical one; an unconscious that is material rather than ideological; schizophrenic rather than Oedipal; non-figurative rather than imaginary; real rather than symbolic; machinic rather than structural – an unconscious, finally, that is molecular, microphysical, and micrological rather than molar or gregarious, productive rather than expressive' (1977, pp.109–10), they were, as they knew, standing in an anarchist tradition of psychoanalysis which goes back through R.D. Laing and Herbert Marcuse to Georg Groddeck (p.54) and Wilhelm Reich (p.118). But they did not realise first, that the line is older, extending back to Otto Groß (see note 6); second, that Groß was one of the major theoretical inspirations behind Berlin Dada; third, that there are extensive parallels between their ideas and those at the heart of Dada (cf. R. Sheppard, 'What is Dada?', *Orbis Litterarum*, vol.34 (1979), pp.175–207); and fourth, that there are also extensive parallels between their critique of Lacan and Dada's

so too, one may enquire about the implications, in the Lacanian view of things, of the analyst's suspension of the subject's certainties until her/his 'last mirages have been consumed' (1977, p.43). What does it mean for the neurotic subject to understand that his/her desire is governed by a castration (1977, p.323) if that castration can never be made good? Surely, unless *jouissance* is given greater status, then the end of Lacanian analysis must be the renunciation of desire in favour of conformity to the Symbolic Order, understood as the last, protective refuge from the *néant*?

The issue at stake lies at the heart of many contemporary debates in the realms of philosophy, psychology and literary criticism. We may well accept Lacan's oft-repeated assertion that the word 'person' means 'mask' and no longer be able to believe in Christian-Platonic concepts like spirit, soul and *Geist* (let alone the primacy of consciousness and the ego (cf. Handwerk, 1985, p.107)), but the Oedipalism of Lacan's psychoanalytic theory and the expressionist *Ich-Dramen* compels us to ask whether it might be possible to recover a sense of a creative principle in human nature which is strong enough to elude both the harsh polemical assaults of the former and redeem the dark, convoluted world of the latter. The question is of particular relevance for literary criticism, since if it cannot be answered positively, then literature becomes something akin to the child's repetition of 'gone/there' which Freud commented upon in *Beyond the Pleasure Principle* – an activity which does little more than render tolerable a loss that can never be made good (cf. Irwin, 1981, pp.152–3).

References

Bleikasten, A. (1981) 'Fathers in Faulkner' in Davis, pp.115–46

Coward, R. and Ellis, J. (1977) *Language and Materialism: Developments in Semiology and the Theory of the Subject*, Routledge and Kegan Paul, London

Davis, R. (1981) 'Critical Introduction to the Discourse of the Father' in *The Fictional Father: Lacanian Readings of the Text*, University of Massachussetts,

---

critique of Expressionism (cf. R. Sheppard, 'Dada and Expressionism', *PEGS*, vol.49 (1979), pp.45–83). Deleuze and Guattari's declaration that '*the unconscious is an orphan*' (p.49) and the Dadaists' transformation of the Oedipal Father of Expressionism into the anoedipal 'Dada' tend in exactly the same psychological direction.

Amherst, pp.1–26
Deleuze, G. (1971) *Sacher-Masoch, An Interpretation, together with the Entire Text of Venus in Furs*, Faber, London
Deleuze G. and Guattari, F. (1977) *Anti-Oedipus: Capitalism and Schizophrenia*, Viking, New York
Denkler, H. (1967) *Drama des Expressionismus: Programm – Spieltext – Theater*, Fink, Munich
Durand, R. (1981) '"The Captive King": The Absent Father in Melville's Text' in Davis, pp.48–72
Freud, S. (1914) 'On Narcissism: An Introduction' reprinted in *Collected Papers*, ed. J. Strachey, 5 vols., Hogarth, London, vol.4, pp.30–59
Freud, S. (1924) 'The Passing of the Oedipus Complex', reprinted in *Collected Papers*, ed. J. Strachey, 5 vols., Hogarth, London, vol.3, pp.269–76
Freud, S. (1950) *Totem and Taboo*, Hogarth, London
Handwerk, G. (1985) 'Irony as Intersubjectivity: Lacan on Psychoanalysis and Literature', *Comparative Criticism*, 7, 105–26
Hanzo, T. (1981) 'Paternity and the Subject in *Bleak House*' in Davis, pp.27–47
Heym, G. (1960) *Dichtungen und Schriften*, vol.3, Heinrich Ellermann, Hamburg
Hinck, W. (1968) 'Individuum und Gesellschaft im expressionistischen Drama' in E. Catholy and W. Hellmann (eds), *Festschrift für Klaus Ziegler*, Niemeyer, Tübingen, pp.343–59
Irwin, J. (1981) 'The Dead Father in Faulkner' in Davis, pp.147–68
Jameson, F. (1981) *The Political Unconscious: Narrative as a Socially Symbolic Act*, Cornell U.P., Ithaca and London
Lacan, J. (1977) *Écrits: A Selection*, Tavistock, London
Lacan, J. (1979) *The Four Fundamental Concepts of Psycho-Analysis*, Penguin, Harmondsworth
Lévi-Strauss, C. (1970) *The Raw and the Cooked: Introduction to a Science of Mythology*, vol. I, Jonathan Cape, London
Patterson, M. (1981) *The Revolution in German Theatre 1900–1933*, Routledge and Kegan Paul, London
Propp, V. (1968) *Morphology of the Folktale*, 2nd (revised) edn, Texas U.P., Austin and London
Rank, O. (1926) *Das Inzest-Motiv in Dichtung und Sage*, 2nd (revised) edn, Deuticke, Leipzig and Vienna
Ritchie, J. (1976) *German Expressionist Drama*, Twayne, Boston
Schneiderman, S. (1983) *Jacques Lacan: The Death of an Intellectual Hero*, Harvard U.P., Cambridge, Mass. and London
Sokel, W. (1964) *The Writer in Extremis*, McGraw-Hill, New York, Toronto and London
Wais, K. (1931) *Das Vater-Sohn Motiv in der Dichtung*, 2 vols., de Gruyter, Berlin and Leipzig

–10–

Deconstructing Classicism – Goethe's *Helena* and the Need to Rhyme

ANTHONY PHELAN

We Have Ways of Making You Talk

The largely Parisian theories which go under the general name of Post-Structuralism, and Derrida's 'Deconstruction' in particular, seem to fly in the face of a central tradition in German culture. For German language and thought have long been expert in discovering ways of articulating a sense of self. Indeed, the re-positioning of human subjectivities within a larger system or field of discourse has been a continuous and powerful gesture from Hegel to Freud; and here, the underlying claim has been that the transformations of the subject which were set in train by this re-location would also set free a power of (self-)knowledge. Conversely, the new ways of making us talk that have been developed over the last twenty years and within other national traditions, have met certain resistances and anticipations.[1] The project of semiological analysis represented by Roland Barthes's 'Introduction to the Structural Analysis of Narrative' (Barthes, 1983, pp.251–95), for instance, and the larger *théorie d'ensemble* which succeeded it were blocked both by older senses of totality and, specifically, by the German preference for C.S. Peirce's doctrine of the sign – deployed, for example, in Max Bense's development during the 1960s and 1970s of an aesthetics based on

---

This essay has benefited from my reading of Schlaffer (1981), Norris (1982 and 1987) and Bennett (1986). It will be apparent that the most important texts of Derrida underlying it are those in his *Margins of Philosophy*. There are moments e.g. 'the anamnesis of the concha resonates alone on a beach' (1982, p.xviii) and 'Rising towards the sun of presence, it [the *phōnē*] is the way of Icarus' (1973, p.104) which have clear relevance for *Faust II*, but which I have not been able to pursue in the detail they deserve.

1. There is an amusing account of these differences in Baier (1986).

Information Theory (cf. Helmut Kreuzer's essay above, p.15). The anti-humanist strain of his work can be recognised variously in the writing of other avant-garde figures (like Arno Schmidt and Helmut Heißenbüttel), as well as in such phenomena as concrete poetry and 'das neue Hörspiel' ('The New Radio-Drama') and its successors. Such groundwork in the avant-garde seemed to provide a perspective from which the pioneering work of French Structuralism looked tangential.

Something of the same pattern of resistance has also been apparent in relation to more recent developments of Parisian theory. Reception Theory, for instance, has continued to develop quite independently of the structuralist project, in spite of their common origins in the Formalism of the Prague school; while on the other hand, the importance of Gadamerian Hermeneutics for Reception Theory links it with a body of thought symmetrically, if not diametrically, opposed to Deconstruction. For Hermeneutics as a science of *reading* (of 'interpreting') can be exactly opposed to the 'grammatology' (or science of *writing*) which Derrida has presented as one definition of what is more generally known as Deconstruction.

From the German perspective, then, in spite of all the efforts to displace, to dis-locate, the Subject on the other side of the Rhine (and, for that matter, on the other side of the Atlantic), ways can still be found of 'making you talk'. None the less, if this native German tradition is not significantly invoked by the dominant themes of this volume (for that we go to names like Barthes, Althusser, Kristeva, Bakhtin or – here – to Derrida), it remains *for that very reason* critically important. There are two ways of putting this point. The first would be to trace the massive investment in the Subject and subjectivity which has characterised modern literature in Germany and which, quite clearly, constitutes the peculiar significance of the German cultural tradition at this juncture.

The second would be to point to the growing body of literature which explicitly draws attention to the anticipations of post-structuralist (Parisian) thought in the writings of the early German Romantics, the generation of the 1770s. Thus, for example, in his recent (1987) account of 'post-structuralist thought and the claims of critical theory', Peter Dews, using German theories of subjectivity as his conceptual lever, makes the important suggestion that the problematics of displaced or decentred subjectivity are already available in the very core of German Idealism and cites Fichte's *Bestimmung des Menschen* (*The Calling of Mankind*, 1800), for example, where a radical version of the old theme that 'la vida es sueño' reduces the self to a 'confused image of images' and reality to a dream without subject or reference (p.31). But we do not need to go to the philosophers to find a version of this destabilisation of the Subject among the German Romantics. Friedrich Schlegel's doctrine of irony as simultaneous self-creation and self-destruction, from the *Lyceum* fragments to the manifesto of a Romantic 'progressive universal poetry', also sketches out a diacritical practice which is not, it seems to me, necessarily grounded in any absolute settlement. Within any individual moment of such an ironic text(uality), the apparent singularity of reference is not simply cancelled by an authorial irony, it is simultaneously referred and deferred into the virtual infinity of textual interplay (see Phelan, 1984 and 1986).

In other words, German thought marks out the field for the debate involved in recent French theory. Hence, in Lacan as well as Derrida, Freud becomes the occasion for the redefinition of the Subject and its authority. Discourses of and on the Subject, the specifically *German* ways of making you talk, from Hegel to Freud, are the constant terrain of Derrida's alternative way of putting, of *displacing* the questions of philosophy. Thus, in this important sense, German culture remains – within the purview of Derridean Deconstruction – a central European subject. In what follows, I shall attempt to sketch some of the salient features of Derrida's position before examining the ways in which his attack on the metaphysics of the Subject might engage with the classical aspirations of late eighteenth-century literature, and particularly Goethe's own reflections on the recovery of antiquity in Act 3 of *Faust II* with special reference to the scene in which Faust instructs Helena in the art of rhyme.

Inside and Outside the Text

Until very recently, strict grammatical and morphological rules governed the ways in which it was permissible to talk about Derrida's project, and I shall use them to illustrate some of its features. The basic principle was very simple: *Deconstruction may not be given the epistemological status of a systematic doctrine* – which amounted to the injunction not to refer to Deconstruction*ism*. A further rule followed: it was considered improper to refer to any critic subscribing to such a projected system as a Deconstruction*ist*. Thus, Deconstruction allowed its corresponding verb only an infinitive mood, and maybe a kind of middle voice.[2] However, it is quite clearly also possible to say

---

2. This point is made by Cotterill (1988), p.228. I am greatly indebted to this article and its author.

that people 'do' deconstruction and that Derrida or de Man offer deconstructions – but on what and of what? Here at least the answer is refreshingly simple: on and of texts. *Textuality* is the realm in which deconstruction occurs, and can, under certain kinds of interrogation, be seen to occur. To speak of Deconstruction as a something without the systematics of an '-ism' or the subscriptions of '-ists' amounts to the offer to define a *praxis* or a constantly reiterated *condition* (*of* textuality, let's say) which is radically without subjects in either the grammatical or the psychological sense. If it were possible to subscribe to such a 'view', the subscriber (the ghostly '-ist' lending forbidden being to the abstraction) would need to stand outside the process of deconstruction, outside the text as agreement or contract in order to *under*-write it by *adding* her signature. Although such a *sub*scriber would be an *under*-writer insuring against a risk (whose?), it seems we can be offered no guarantees.

If a signature is added to text, the appended signs must originate *outside* the limits of the writing to which it is subjoined. But where is the limit? Is my signature on a letter a mere addition made possible by my stretching *across* the bottom margin *into* the text? Or is the signature itself an integral part of a letter or document? Thinking about signatures, and hence about the authority invested in Subjects and writing, allows us to disrupt and render ambiguous the boundaries of the textual space. This sort of radical ambiguity (sometimes called undecidability in the context of American Deconstruction) is the whole point of some of the games and strategies of Derrida's essays. His texts, *Margins of Philosophy*, close as follows: 'as a disseminating operation *separated* from presence (of Being) according to all its modifications, writing, if there is any, perhaps communicates, but does not exist, surely. Or barely, hereby, in the form of the most improbable signature' (Derrida, 1982, p.330). Whereupon there follows the written name-and-initial 'J. Derrida'.

The fact that *Margins of Philosophy* is a *translation* raises some intriguing and relevant problems. For how are we to read this initial J? Does it rhyme with – say – gay? Or are we to give it a French name and value, a dental fricative followed by the long vowel represented phonetically as /i:/ and standing in a relation to G which is the inverse of the English one (French calls 'g' gé and 'j' ji)? Because the signature is, by definition, written, these cultural differences and the uncertainty they produce remain irreducible. This translation of a name (if that is what it is) cannot be made articulate by my voice for you (as you read), but nor can it be either by your voice or, for that matter, by Derrida's – as the marginal remark parallel to this signature makes clear: '(*Remark*: the – written – text of this – oral – communication was to have been addressed to the *Association of French Speaking Societies of Philosophy* before the meeting. Such a missive therefore had to be signed. Which I did, and counterfeit here. Where? There. J.D.).' 'Writing', which disseminates meaning as it engenders it, has taken precedence over the voice which lends us the cosy sensation of 'knowing what we're talking about', and attempts to authorise a written text with a signature simply get us into an infinite regress of signed validations. As Derrida has notoriously observed in another context: 'il n'y a pas de hors-texte' ('there is no outside to the text') (Derrida, 1976, p.158). And in the same way, the decision to put our names to Deconstruction, as just one more kind of textual practice, assumes that there is a place outside textuality from which we might add a signature. Textuality is a (our) condition.

The embargo on any claim to define Deconstruction as a systematic and therefore closed whole also allows us to see some of the recurrent stratagems of Derrida's texts. In many ways they have a familiar Romantic look in a German context. First, there is the sense of play – as a textual joke, a pun maybe, a tactic or strategy to *out*-play our natural sense that we somehow stand 'outside' language and textuality. In this sense it has become common to speak not of philosophical or critical arguments, but of moves or manoeuvres. Both this sense of playing to outplay and of the irreducible reflexivity of linguistic activity can be traced in Novalis, at the beginning of *Glauben und Liebe* (*Faith and Love*), for instance, in his notion of a language of 'tropes and riddles', or in the ironic circularities of the *Monolog*. Second, *commentary* becomes a characteristic form of the deconstructive activity, an acknowledgement of the enchainment of one text by or to another. This can reach fairly amusing proportions, and the chain which began with Derrida's reading of Lacan's reading of Poe's story 'The Purloined Letter' continues to spiral away (see Muller and Richardson, 1988). Here, too, we may recall the actual practices of Schlegel and Hardenberg, writing their own notes in the margins of a reading of (say) Fichte as a displacement of his text, or permitting mutual commentary on, across, and among their own *Fragments*. In this Romantic form, writing as an inscription of meaning is always a place of incompleteness. 'Fragmentary' writing declares its pursuit of plenitude, of full intended sense, and is therefore marked by a lack or absence. It could only come to such fullness by being supplemented by the absent totality or system of which it is, by definition, a fragment. But if the fragment needs to be supplemented, then it is itself supplemental – additional to, supplementing and exceeding intentions. The Romantic fragment knows this perfectly well for it is a means of suggesting but also of destabilising an anticipated totality. And the element of what has already been called the Derridadaesque offers a means of shaking whatever seems in (its) place – i.e. the metaphysical agenda of settled hierarchies and defined powers present to themselves.

My skirmishing with the processes of Deconstruction has alluded to some of its terms of art: presence/absence, inside/outside, speech/writing, identity/difference, and to these we might add law/transgression, limit/excess. All of them indicate the 'procedure of criticism' which Derrida has enjoined on criticism with a philosophical bent – an injunction which Stephen Heath has formulated as 'go to the hierarchical opposition, go to the marginal and excluded and write from there...' (1987, p.293). This clearly glosses Derrida's own summary:

> an opposition of metaphysical concepts (for example, speech/writing, presence/absence, etc.) is never the face-to-face of two terms, but a hierarchy and an order of subordination. Deconstruction cannot limit itself or proceed immediately to a neutralization: it must, by means of a double gesture, a double science, a double writing, practice an *overturning* of the classical opposition *and* a general *displacement* of the system. (1982, p.329)

The Classical De-centred

Lurking among the terms of this account of Deconstruction there lies a revolutionary metaphor which I have echoed in my use of words like strategy, manoeuvre, skirmish. In Derrida's own definition, this imagery is confirmed: not merely the destabilisation but the general displacement of the metaphysics of presence is called for. The habits of thought which attempt to anchor meaning in a secure Subject (ultimately by chaining it to the throne of godhead (cf. Eagleton, 1983, p.131)) or a literal meaning (a 'sens propre' which knows its place) cannot be locally neutralised: only a revolutionary overturning will do. It is a very large claim, especially when a major opponent is Hegel, whose whole project was, after all, to guarantee through all the possible differentiations of History and Nature the identity of a transcendent Mind (*Geist*) which could eventually know itself as truth in absolute reflexive consciousness.

The familiar conception of this trajectory of *Geist*, like the *Phenomenology of Mind* itself, as a *Bildungsroman* of the Spirit indicates the lines of communication which are open between the metaphysics of absolute self-presence as these are enshrined in Hegel, and Goethe's

Classicism. Indeed, this Hegelian sense can be re-applied to *Wilhelm Meisters Lehrjahre* itself. Goethe's novel is both an encyclopedic summation of what was available in the novel generically (Reed, 1980, p.101), and represents the growth to moral, emotional and aesthetic self-awareness of a central and (self-)centred personality under the hierarchising and hierarchised control – or, at any rate, stage-management – of the 'Society of the Tower'. Goethe's hero, no less than Hegel's, is the secure focus of this process, and the prospect of social and personal integration is never seriously in question. Every experience is designed to clothe the hero and hence to reveal his true stature, which is adequate and appropriate to all that life brings. And at a different level, the appropriateness of experience to its Subject is paralleled by the adequacy of language to express it. The self and its experience, like the signifier and the signified, exist in a harmonious balance, quite unlike the disruption caused as much to the personality as to grammar and syntax in Goethe's 'Sturm und Drang' writing.

Wilhelm Meister is also classical, of course, both because of the 'literary status and authority' it had for the succeeding tradition of the *Bildungsroman*, and because of its historical context of 'social stability; cultural maturity; intellectual community and conformity'. The terms I have quoted from Reed's *The Classical Centre* (1980, p.15) are derived from Aulus Gellius, Sainte-Beuve, T.S. Eliot, and Sartre,[3] but *Wilhelm Meister* was written not only *with* the benefit (or at least in pursuit) of the last three conditions, it was crucially written *about* them, as an account of how a mind and personality capable of classic ambitions might be formed. It comes as something of a surprise that this sense of the 'classic' can dispense with any ambition to enter into a relationship with the ancients. For Reed believes that the requirement, for the definition of Classicism, to include elements 'drawn from "classical" antiquity' is additional to his four 'guiding concepts'. 'Are the ages', he asks, 'which imitate antiquity in these respects [form, plot, preferred subject-matter and style] necessarily also the stable, mature ages in which the great works of a national culture are created?' The answer is that 'there is no logical necessity that they should be. Yet in practice connections do exist' (1980, p.16). Indeed they do – very obviously in the drama, and in all the hexameter and pentameter forms which made 'speaking Schiller' such a jaw-wrenching art in Voß's view.[4] Clas-

---

3. There is an important discussion of the first three of these in Kermode (1983), pp.15–21.
4. Voß famously parodied the inadequacy of Weimar's classical imitations: 'In Weimar und in Jena macht man Hexameter wieder,/ Aber die Pentameter sind

sicism and those who promoted it consistently set out to rival the ancient classics, and as Nisbet has recently demonstrated (1988), a whole programme of translation and imitation was thereby initiated. By 1826, when Act 3 of *Faust II* – which he called the *Helena* – is consciously present for Goethe as a review of this general project, there can no longer be much doubt about the necessity of a relation to antiquity, but the plausibility and even possibility of such a revival is also in question.

I have elided the important distinction between a Latinate Classicism and one which emulates Greek models. T.S. Eliot, of course, identified the classic almost exclusively with Latinity, and for Kermode it is always Virgil and metropolitan civility which are decisive in each successive *renovatio*. Common to both, however, is the sense that Classicism defines a regulated writing (registered in notions of status, authority, stability and conformity) in pursuit of a sovereignty – we could call it a *national* sovereignty – which, it claims, has been properly inherited from antecedents that are validated by its very practice and canon, just as these are validated by them.

A number of senses of sovereignty and textual authority are engaged with each other in this view of Classicism as the national hegemony of a stabilised culture. What comes to fruition in *Iphigenia on Tauris* (1786) has little or nothing to do with the cultural and narrative forms represented in a work like Wieland's *Agathon* (1768) or even in his great late work *Aristippus and some of his Contemporaries* (1802). There, the 'classical' amounts to a scholarly *mise-en-scène* which remains wonderfully domestic and pastoral, even where it invokes Socrates and Plato themselves. Goethe, on the other hand, restores what Lessing had needed to deracinate in order to make the project of a German literature possible at all. Weimar Classicism confirms the successful establishment of a cultural hegemony – as of a republic of scholars ('Gelehrtenrepublik'). Notoriously, that sense of cultural sovereignty came to replace any other kind in Germany, and the rupture remained as the failure of metropolitan civility. As the *Xenien* observed in 1795: 'Germany – wherever is it? I cannot locate the country. Where its academy starts is just where its politics stops' (Goethe, 1950, p.455). But the Classicism we associate with Weimar also enters the lists *against* other national sovereignties by discovering, across a far larger range of genre and theme than any other European Classicism, the formal and linguistic means to

doch noch exzellenter.' Subsequently, of course, Heine thought something similar about Voß's prosody. See Book 1 of Heine's *Die romantische Schule* (Heine, 1971, pp.383–4).

imitate antiquity. That was possible only on the basis of a real *translatio studii* which, one might conjecture, did perhaps achieve, in the *Roman Elegies* (1788–90), the civility of a certain Latin tradition and hence a *translatio imperii*, not for the first time 'a Francis ad Germanos' (see Kermode, 1983, p.30).

Although this formal range of classical expression is, of course, retrospectively rehearsed in the Helena Act of *Faust II*, we also begin to sense an over-compensation. If, on the Tauris of *Iphigenia*, dissent and disruption are finally impossible as much for Orestes as for Thoas, it is because the serene wisdom of Neo-Classicism has *re-interpreted* the oracle. The heroes and the goddess depart to leave Thoas with the insurmountable sadness of that farewell, 'Lebt wohl', which Karl Kraus found so heart-breaking – 'as if it were the first farewell ever taken in the whole world' (Kraus, 1986, p.61). The recovery of the classical images, of Artemis and of Iphigenia herself, is achieved at the expense of rewriting Homer and Euripides. That expense entails an absolute loss, and so the same farewell echoes and re-echoes as a long goodbye – in Schiller, in Hölderlin, and even in the contrivance of a minor masterpiece like Voß's poem 'Der Rebensproß' ('The Vine Shoot') (1802) which – as Goethe complained to Eckermann in 1827 – was probably already forgotten 25 years after its composition:

> Mir trug Lyäos, mir der begeisternden
> Weinrebe Sprößling, als, dem Verstürmten gleich
>   Auf ödem Eiland, ich mit Sehnsucht
>   Wandte den Blick zur Hellenenheimat.
>
> Schamhaft erglühend, nahm ich den heiligen
> Rebschoß und hegt ihn, nahe dem Nordgestirn,
>   Abwehrend Luft und Ungeschlachtheit,
>   Unter dem Glas in erkargter Sonne. (Voß, 1983, p.289)

(Lyaos bore to me a shoot of the inspiring grape, when, like one cast upon a barren island by the storm, I turned my gaze with longing to the homeland of the Greeks. Blushing and modest, I took the sacred vine-shoot and kept it, near to the North Star, fending off the air and barbarity, beneath the glass in diminished sunlight.)

One can easily forget that Voß is talking about a greenhouse, and there is a sort of absurdity about what the poem calls a 'competition with ancient song'. Probably he is thinking of Horace's *Odes* III: 25. Yet what to us seems absurd about this belated effort of renovation is, in fact, the measure of Voß's heroism, and of the secondary nature of the classicist enterprise. He understands the condition of

Neo-Classicism to be an exile which generates the gaze of desire ('I turned my gaze with longing') for a Greek homeland which can be contemplated in this way only *because* it is lost. Both the effortfulness and the sadness are present in the very forms and cadences of German verse in classical metres which are elegiac in our loose, modern sense; and the last and fondest farewell occurs in another 'classical centre' – Act 3 of *Faust II*.

Staging *Helena*

The opening of the Helena Act accomplishes a dislocation: from the baroque and operatic extravaganza of the Aegean festival which closes the Classical Walpurgis Night, the action moves to a setting outside the palace of Menelaus in Sparta. This is necessary not only because that is where Helena happens to be, but also because it establishes the necessary conventions for Goethe's impersonation of the Greek tragedians. For such kinds of action, the scene needs to be set outside a palace in a way which provokes a number of obvious queries: Where has Helena come from? How has she got there? Where, specifically, has she arrived? All these are characteristically the questions of a Greek chorus, and hence the questions appropriate to a theatrical space, for, in an important sense, Helena stands outside Menelaus's palace *and* upon a stage.

The emergence of the forms of Greek drama at this point are in themselves a powerful disruption,[5] but Helena is dis-located too. Although she claims that she has come by sea, with Menelaus, after the fall of Troy, she is not speaking the truth. 'Faust, we know, has made two descents from the plane of human life – one to the Mothers in Act 1 and one to the Underworld in Act 2 – in his efforts to bring Helena to the stage. But if, on the other hand, she is not lying, then something very odd has happened to chronology, and Act 3 'precedes' Act 1, in a kind of parallel to the disruption of place and *persona* in Euripides' *Helen*. Goethe's Helena keeps up the

---

5. This was one of the most startling effects of David Freeman's recent *Faust* production at the Lyric Theatre, Hammersmith. The decision to put the interval after Act 3 reinforced the dramatic break between the collective celebration of the close of the previous scene and the utterly solitary arrival of Helena as a single figure stepping into the space of the stage.
6. If this seems a very literalist complaint, see Fuchs (1971), which sets out to establish Helena's person and history quite unequivocally. Staiger (1959, pp.358–60) is more judicious and recognises the equivocation of Goethe's remark – in paralipomenon 70 – that Helena appears 'as having just landed', but ignores it in the 'Nun *soll* sie ... zurückkehren' of paral.73.

pretence to the end, when, upon the fall of Euphorion, she cries: 'Persephone, . . . take now the child and me' (Goethe, 1959, p.210), as if addressing the Queen of the Underworld for the first time. It is Panthalis and the rest of the chorus who give the game away: it was 'the magic . . . With which the old Thessalian hag would bind the soul' (Goethe, 1959, p.210; ll.9962f.) which kept them in place, and this hag is identified as Mephisto in his guise as one of the Phorcyades – who seems to function as a kind of stage-manager to the whole piece (see the stage direction after l.10038; Goethe, 1959, p. 214).

The appearance of Helena outside the palace and upon this stage is determined by other forces, however. Earlier, in Part One, Faust had been 'attracted . . . to an ideal, unapproachable vison of female beauty' (Boyle, 1987, p.57) which has been identified with Helena, and is partly so identified by Faust himself in ll.6495–7 (Goethe, 1959, p.87) when he speaks of 'a pale foam-phantom of such beauty'. Faust's quest is always for Helena's full presence, and it reaches a preliminary climax when, in Act 2, we lose sight of him in the company of Manto to whom Chiron has brought him. Manto offers to smuggle Faust down into Hades for an audience with Persephone from whom, like Orpheus, he may be able to secure the release of the object of his desire – in which case we are bound to ask what he thinks *he* is doing in his encounter with Helena. Are we to think that Faust 'acts out' a meeting with her or is he deceived by Mephistopheles? Does Helena know her lines and, therefore, what to expect? Or is she no more than a puppet manipulated by Mephisto and hence no more materially present than in her ghostly and explosive 'appearance' in Act 1 of Part Two?

A recent commentator explains this paradox in Helena's stage appearance in terms of her existential insecurity, claiming that she is 'a figure revivified from Hades, uncertain as to whether she is a phantom, an eidolon, or a living individual' (Williams, 1987, p.164). But this possibility emerges only some 400 lines into the Act (ll.8834–81; Goethe, 1959, pp. 170–1), in Helena's exchange with Phorcyas. Helena's identity is not only dispersed across a wide range of literary and mythical 'texts', to which Mephisto alludes in these lines: even as absolute beauty she seems to be constituted in and by her differential relationship with Mephisto in the guise of the ultimately ugly Phorcyas. Yet, however alarming the power which Mephisto's existential opposition gives him, such an interpretation merely stabilises in allegorical form the dislocation of theatrical representation which takes place in relation to personality, identity, chronology and motivation when Helena steps on to the stage. The paradoxes which the *mises-en-abîme* of the *plot* involve can thus be smoothed away, leaving 'a simple dialectical complication of the living present as an originary and unceasing synthesis' (Derrida, 1982, p.21) – and indeed, that may sound like a satisfactory gloss on Goethe's ever-popular doctrine of polarities.

The ambiguous position of Helena, together with Faust's role in staging the classical revival of Act 3, offers a reflexive summary of the whole classical project: the bringing back of some element of antiquity from the past and its reinstatement in the present – in *presence*. Hence, the whole action of the Helena Act gives new meaning to the term representation – which is now a re-presentation, a restoration to presence.[7] Consequently, Goethe's retrospective and ironic representation of 'Classicism', as appropriating and so author(is)ing antiquity,[8] destabilises the personal identity of its central figure by insisting on her allusive character.[9] As one much praised and much blamed (1.8498), Helena seems to know this in the announcement of her arrival. But here too, her words exceed her knowledge, for the praise and blame to which she might historically refer, as it were, would be those of the Greeks or the Trojans, while *we* know that her words imply the whole tissue of myth transmitted not only by Greek literature, but also by Shakespeare, for example, in *Troilus and Cressida* – of which she can know nothing.

Helena appears on stage from the beach, having just landed on her native shore – and she announced the fact at the opening of the earliest version of the Act. The self-(con)textualisation 'much admired, and blamed as much' (1.8498) is a later addition. Line 8499 – 'Vom Strande komm' ich, wo wir erst gelandet sind' ('I ... am come/ From yonder strand where newly we have disembarked') – with which Helena arrives in the text of 1800, is accessible to a range of readings. Primarily, we take 'wir' ('we') to refer to Helena, Panthalis and the chorus of Trojan women. But it soon becomes clear that we, the (reading) audience, are also involved in this arrival: either because we, too, have 'just landed', arriving from the coast of the Aegean and the end of Act 2 so that now we are all

---

7. Schlaffer (1981, pp.101 and 109) argues a similar case on the basis of his 'monetary' analysis of allegory.
8. Williams (1987, p.95) stresses that this is only a 'phantom image, a "Schaumbild"' in comparison with Helena herself. My point would be that the phantasmic nature of this presence is always a condition of its perception.
9. This is roughly Williams's view of ll.8880–908: 'unless [Helena] is reinvigorated by assimilation into a different culture, she will be dead, a lifeless monument to a past age. Her emergence from her swoon after l.8908 marks her emergence from her historical past as the "sun" of Western culture' (1987, p.165). This final remark is amusingly ambiguous.

properly in 'classical' Greece; or because the audience has long been in Greece and Helena and her entourage have only just ('erst') landed. But at another level, the line must also mean 'I, Helena, emerge or re-emerge from those German shores where we have only recently arrived' in the sense that 'I am a product of the interest shown in Greece by the *German* literary revival of the late eighteenth century'. And beyond this reading there is one final twist inasmuch as the line could be taken to mean: 'Now, in retrospect, I [Helena, Goethe] return to antiquity and the stage, in pursuit of the authentically classical, having been released from the Hades of my shadowy existence as a figment of the German imagination.'[10]

The ambiguities of Helena's arrival derive from the 'shifters' 'wo' and 'erst' ('where', 'only just'). Neither in narrative, nor in dramatic discourse, nor in literary allusion ('Bewundert viel und viel gescholten, Helena') ('I, Helena, who have been much admired and much censured'), nor, most definitely, in self-naming as an anticipatory 'signing-in' ('Helena'), can her presence be secured. Nevertheless, in this littoral existence, the German language has found a 'way of making Helena talk', not always easily, but in a passing impersonation of the iambic trimeter of Greek tragedy.

It is a curious effect of classical metre that, as it suppresses the natural (stressed) rhythm and syntax of German speech, it makes the voice (heard or imagined) work that much harder to compensate. After the relative ease of the first two lines of Act 3, the sheer weight of classical vocabulary, of place names and theology, makes it clear that a new kind of writing is beginning, marked perhaps by the point in l.8490 where the substitution of a tribrach announces the instability of the iambic pulse still dominating ll.8498–9. Here, as elsewhere in the realm of Greek metre, the *effect* of successful appropriation is a profound sense of the distinctness of two systems of articulation. Two authorities pull apart from each other as much as they validate each other, and the duality of the two kinds of regulative (stress and quantity) seems to be stable, whatever it does to the syntax, with each crossing over from its own terrain to supplement the other.

Between Greek and German what border is crossed, what limit or margin is exceeded? Helena may have landed, but how is Faust to land her? Such a limit has been a recurrent theme of Derrida's writing, and he has constantly renamed it or rediscovered its ambiguous 'presence' in the figures of the hymen ('more honoured in

---

10. Dr Eva Fox-Gál suggested to me that this account was indebted to Empson's methods: I would be glad if this were so.

the breach than the observance', says Hamlet), the margin and the tympanum of the ear. These apparently steady border-lines elude our attention; and, as we have seen, the *status* of the figure of Helena in this representation of the Classical introduces similar uncertainties. To question this status is to ask where Helena stands, on this side of her 'Strand'. It is Greece and Germany, but above all it is the stage of *Faust*, where the resonance of verse in a 'play for reading' ('Lesedrama') indicates that it is indeed the tympanum that is the place of presence and encounter.

Wherever Helena is, Greek is not spoken there, but German policed by the voice of Classical prosody. Helena has returned to her own from those realms where she is the object of praise and blame. It is because she is admired that she has this 'place' in antiquity, but she is irrecoverably 'outside the myth of . . . a lost native country of thought' (Derrida, 1982, p.27). Helena's presence and being consist of necessary supplements; there is no essential or fundamental 'Helen of Troy' about whom a succession of stories are told: rather, Helena *is* the stories, in all their contradictory variety, and no one of them presents a single truth to which the others are accretions. Mephisto spells this out until her existence disappears: 'Ich schwinde hin' (1.8881; Goethe, 1959, p.171 gives 'I swoon, becoming to myself a wraith'). Faust must secure her presence and does so, of course (or so we are told, e.g. by Staiger, 1959, pp.376–9; May, 1972, pp.161–6), in language, in the forms of Germanic verse. In this respect, the prosodic and dramatic forms are not incidental but fundamental to the classical *renovatio*, for the balance or equivocation between two metrical schemes in 'classical verse' is supposedly resolved in two *voices* harmonised and united by rhyme.

First, Helena must be brought *within* the castle walls, and her approach to the moment of consummation is marked by a drift from the metrical regulatives of Greek towards blank verse, until she finally asks:

> Doch wünscht' ich Unterricht, warum die Rede
> Des Manns mir seltsam klang, seltsam und freundlich.
> Ein Ton scheint sich dem andern zu bequemen,
> Und hat ein Wort zum Ohre sich gesellt,
> Ein andres kommt, dem ersten liebzukosen.
>
> FAUST. Gefällt dir schon die Sprechart unsrer Völker,
> O so gewiß entzückt auch der Gesang,
> Befriedigt Ohr und Sinn im tiefsten Grunde.
> Doch ist am sichersten, wir üben's gleich;
> Die Wechselrede lockt es, ruft's hervor.

HELENA. So sage denn, wie sprech' ich auch so schön?

FAUST. Das ist gar leicht, es muß von Herzen gehn.
Und wenn die Brust von Sehnsucht überfließt,
Man sieht sich um und fragt –

HELENA. wer mitgenießt.

(This man [Lynceus], how comes it that his speech/ Chimed strangely in my ears, so strange, yet kind,/ Each tone in full accord with what came next?/ No sooner has a word well pleased the ear,/ Than comes another, as with a caress./ FAUST. If in mere speech our people charm your ear,/ O then most surely will their song enchant,/ and satisfy the hearing's inmost sense./ But best it is we practise now this art,/ Alternate speech will call it forth./ HELEN. For words so lovely, how the gift impart?/ FAUST. Soon said: it must come welling from the heart;/ And, overflows heart's bliss without alloy,/ We lift our eyes and ask –/ HELEN. Who shares the joy? (Goethe, 1959, p.189; ll.9367–80))

If this manner of speech ('Sprechart' not 'Sprache', language in general, and anyway Helena has been speaking German since her 'arrival') pleases, then song (the other privilege of the voice), Faust explains, satisfies 'the hearing's inmost sense' (Goethe speaks metonymically of the *ear* in l.9374). Hearing and sense, material utterance and conceptual inscription are satisfyingly *grounded*, and this 'deepest ground' lies with the priority of passion. Rhymed speech must come from the heart (l.9378), and the unity of the rhyme discloses the community of feeling when the 'breast overflows with desire' (ll.9378–80). Language is thus the 'beyond' in which the *over*flow of great feeling occurs; it is secondary to the passion itself and so merely supplements interior feelings which retain their priority. But, paradoxically, language is also the only measure of their intensity: if feeling did not overflow from interiority into language it would not count as intense at all. These paradoxes mark the language itself. For the apparent balance of 'ear and sense' is, of course, semantically unstable. 'Sinn', for example, covers too much: it indicates mind in general over and against the senses (sensual perception, the ear), but also reduplicates the ear with its meaning as sensual perception and, finally, indicates meaning itself in the opposition between 'sound and sense' – a conflict of meanings which suggests that the balanced relation is not as easily symmetrical as Faust would like.

At the tympanum – 'a membrane which at once divides and acts as a sounding board to transmit sound vibrations – connecting, by its transmission, the inside and the outside it separates' (Culler,

1983, p.136) – rhyme institutes a passage which appears to establish the primordial unity of sound and sense, signifier and signified, in undivided presence. As the exercise in 'Wechselrede' ('stichomythia') proceeds, Faust and Helena are conjoined in the present ('And only in the present – bliss we find'; l.9382; Goethe, 1959, p.190). In their second duologue they rhyme with themselves, and Helena intensifies the formal constraints by adding 'inner rhymes' (May, 1972, p.163) in an ecstasy of 'being present': 'Ich fühle mich so *fern* und doch so nah/ Und sage nur zu *gern*: Da bin ich! da!' ('So far away I feel, and yet so near/ And most I long to say "Here am I, here"' (ll.9411–12; Goethe, 1959, p. 191)) – where the final 'inner rhyme' is self-identical ('Da . . . da'). Helena, the figure of classical antiquity, seems thus to have transcended the dimensions of time ('die Gegenwart allein') and space ('so fern und doch so nah') to arrive without detour or deferral in undivided presence. Indeed, Faust prohibits critical reflection on this unique destiny since such presence is ethically imperative, however momentary: 'Dasein ist Pflicht, und wär's ein Augenblick' ('Being is duty, were it a moment's space' (ll.9417–18; Goethe, 1959, p.191)).

In being thus contracted to Helena, Faust appears embarrassingly close to satisfying the conditions of his initial contract with Mephisto – indeed, the key word 'Augenblick' brings Mephisto-Phorcyas in on cue. But far from demanding his rights, he simply pours scorn on Helena's and Faust's loving rhymes in a parody of their speech which demonstrates his own skill as a rhymester and, far from incidentally, drives Faust back to the iambic trimeter for his next lines. 'Buchstabiert in Liebesfibeln' ('Spell out [words] from love-primers') he tells them (l.9419). Mephisto knows very well that the unitary presence of 'sound and sense' in rhyme is far from invulnerable and insists on the letter ('Buchstabe') of their discourse, on the identity of the phoneme (which makes their rhymes – and all rhyme – possible) as the point at which the differential play of the language system is inaudibly marked. The phoneme, writes Derrida (1982, p.xviif., citing Derrida, 1973, p.104), is the 'phenomenon of the labyrinth', drawing each punctual moment of signification into 'difference'.[11] Because of this: 'the movement of signification is possible only if each so-called "present" element, each element appearing on the scene of presence, is related to something other than itself, thereby keeping within itself the mark of the past element, and already letting itself be vitiated by the mark of its relation to the future element' (Derrida, 1982, p.13). The present

---

11. See Norris (1987), p.15, for a reluctant 'definition'.

and presence of Helena, celebrated by Faust in a frame of mind which looks neither forwards nor backwards (1.9381), and realised in the discovery of rhyme, which he believes is (and she experiences as) the mark of such presence, must be similarly vitiated by the play of difference which divides every apparently unitary moment of rhyme or of secured meaning from itself. Euphorion, the child of Helena and Faust, demonstrates, however, the ultimate failure of poetry which attempts to fly up to immediacy, for his fall marks the end of Faust's – and Goethe's – attempt to make language hold absolute beauty in an unequivocal present.

Karl Kraus was surely thinking of the 'Reimerfindungsszene', considered above, when he offered his verse definition of rhyme: 'Er ist das Ufer, wo sie landen,/ Sind zwei Gedanken einverstanden.' ('It is the beach whereon they land,/ if two thoughts one another understand.') Mephisto knows, cynically, that there is no landing. That 'différance' which Derrida calls '"older" than being itself' (1982, p. 26) is his stock-in-trade (see ll.1349–58; Goethe, 1949b, p.75 at 'Part of a part am I . . .' and the subsequent lines); like 'différance', he has no name (1.1327) and he knows that Helena, the figure of the classical, remains phantasmic. The margin of the bay where she 'arrives' cannot ultimately be crossed, her exchange with Faust is written in sand. As another poet said, 'All is shore-line': 'Alles ist Ufer, ewig ruft das Meer.' Das Mehr.[12]

References

Baier, L. (1986) 'Zeichen und Wunder: Eine semiologische Modeschau', *Kursbuch*, no.84, 17–33

Barthes, R. (1975) *S/Z*, Cape, London

Barthes, R. (1983) *The Barthes Reader*, ed. S. Sontag, Collins, London

Bennett, B. (1986) *Goethe's Theory of Poetry*, Cornell U.P., Ithaca and London

12. The lines are from the end of the second part of Gottfried Benn's poem 'Gesänge' – 'everywhere is a shore, eternal calls the sea'. Phonetically 'das Meer' ('the sea') is indistinguishable from 'das Mehr' (a neologism formed from the word 'mehr' ('more'), and meaning 'surplus' or 'what is additional; hence 'the supplement'). Faust knows this call of the supplemental and excessive only too well. In Act 5, l.11570 (Goethe, 1959, p.269), the sea is to be the constant supplement and margin of Faust's life-project, as Blackall (1985), pp.6–7, makes abundantly clear.

Blackall, Eric (1985) *Faust's Last Speech* (1984 Bithell Lecture), Institute of Germanic Studies, London
Boyle, N. (1982/83) '"Du ahnungsloser Engel du!": Some Current Views of Goethe's *Faust*', *German Life and Letters*, 36, 116–47
Boyle, N. (1987) *Goethe: Faust. Part One*, Cambridge U.P.
Bressem, M. (1967) *Der metrische Aufbau des Faust II* (1931), Kraus-Reprint, Nendeln
Cotterill, R.E.H. (1988) '"Sunt aliquid manes": Personalities, Personae and Ghosts in Augustan Poetry' in A. Benjamin (ed.), *Post-Structuralist Classics*, Routledge, London, pp.227–44
Culler, J. (1983) *On Deconstruction*, Routledge, London
Derrida, J. (1973) *Speech and Phenomena*, Northwestern U.P., Evanston
Derrida, J. (1976) *Of Grammatology*, Johns Hopkins U.P., Baltimore and London
Derrida, J. (1982) *Margins of Philosophy*, Harvester Press, Brighton
Derrida, J. (1986) 'But, Beyond . . .', *Critical Inquiry*, 13, 155–70
Dews, P. (1987) *Logics of Disintegration*, Verso, London
Eagleton, T. (1983) *Literary Theory: An Introduction*, Blackwell, Oxford
Frank, M. (1983) *Was ist Neostrukturalismus?*, Suhrkamp, Frankfurt/Main
Fuchs, A. (1971) 'Helena', *Recherches germaniques*, 1, 101–8
Goethe, J.W. (1949a) *Faust*, ed. Erich Trunz, *Hamburger Ausgabe*, vol.3
Goethe, J.W. (1949b) *Faust Part One*, trans. Philip Wayne, Penguin, Harmondsworth
Goethe, J.W. (1950) *Sämtliche Werke*, 25 vols., ed. Ernst Beutler, vol.2 (*Gedichte aus dem Nachlaß*), Artemis-Gedenkausgabe, Zurich
Goethe, J.W. (1959) *Faust Part Two*, trans. Philip Wayne, Penguin, Harmondsworth
Heath, S. (1987) 'Literary theory, etc.', *Comparative Criticism*, 9, 281–326
Heine, H. (1971) *Sämtliche Schriften*, 7 vols., ed. Klaus Briegleb, vol.3, Hanser, Munich
Kermode, F. (1983) *The Classic*, 2nd edn, Harvard U.P., Cambridge, Mass. and London
Kraus, K. (1986) *Heine und die Folgen: Schriften zur Literatur*, ed. C. Wagenknecht, Reclam, Stuttgart
May, K. (1972) *Faust II. Teil in der Sprachform gedeutet*, 2nd edn, Ullstein, Frankfurt/Main
Muller, J. and Richardson, W. (1988) *The Purloined Poe*, Johns Hopkins U.P., Baltimore and London
Nisbet, H. (1988) 'Karl Ludwig von Knebel's Hexameter Translation of Lucretius', *German Life and Letters*, 41, 413–25
Norris, C. (1982) *Deconstruction: Theory and Practice*, Methuen, London
Norris, C. (1987) *Derrida*, Fontana, London
Phelan, A. (1984) '"Das Centrum das Symbol des Goldes": Analogy and Money in *Heinrich von Ofterdingen*', *German Life and Letters*, 37, 307–21
Phelan, A. (1986) 'Romantic Affinities of "Der andere Zustand" in Musil's

Der Mann ohne Eigenschaften' in H. Castein and A. Stillmark (eds), *Deutsche Romantik und das 20. Jahrhundert*, Akademischer Verlag, Stuttgart, pp.141–55

Reed, T.J. (1980) *The Classical Centre*, Croom Helm, London

Schlaffer, H. (1981) *Faust Zweiter Teil: Die Allegorie des 19. Jahrhunderts*, Metzler, Stuttgart

Staiger, E. (1959) *Goethe*, vol.3, Atlantis, Zurich

Voß, J. (1983) *Werke in einem Band*, Aufbau, Berlin and Weimar

Williams, J. (1987) *Goethe's Faust*, Allen and Unwin, London

-11-

The Poetry of August Stramm – A Suitable Case for Deconstruction

RICHARD SHEPPARD

The only Postmodernist I know of was August Stramm, a modernist who worked in a post office.

Heiner Müller

The State of Stramm Criticism

Prone though it is to mystify its logical procedures and to justify that mystification by the implicit suggestion that anything less than unintelligibility is a surreptitious concession to Western logocentrism, the critical school known as Deconstruction is teaching the literary-critic-in-the-street four important and very practical lessons which can, I suggest, be accepted without taking over Deconstruction's (anti-)ontology (cf. David Jenkinson's remarks, pp.252 below). First, to become aware of and hence relativise the assumptions and rhetoric which derive from a specific (Platonic) tradition of metaphysics; second, to abandon, as a result of that, the assumption that a writer is in control of his/her work; third, to listen for those junctures where a text, eluding such control, 'undoes' itself and reveals precisely those elements which the author had sought to repress; and fourth, to focus upon precisely those elements which have been excluded from the consensus view of a writer because they do not fit in with the (Platonically derived) canons of that consensus.

More fundamentally still, the need – powerfully evinced by the work of Fredric Jameson (1972), Gerald Graff (1979), Frank Len-

---

A longer version of this article first appeared in the *Journal of European Studies*, vol.15 (1985), pp.261–94 and is reproduced here by kind permission of the editors. I would like to acknowledge the major contribution made to Stramm criticism in general and this article in particular by Dr Jeremy Adler and Dr John White of the University of London, since it was largely through the stimulus provided by their work that this article came about.

tricchia (1980) and Edward Said (1984) – to go beyond the more extravagant critical and ontological claims made for Deconstruction has forced the literary critic to wrestle with the problems of the generative source of texts, the nature of meta-language and the relationship between texts and History. What is a text and 'what (if not naked being) does shape and inform the play of [textual] signification' (Lentricchia, 1980, p.173); how can anything be said about texts if their mimetic or referential status is denied; and how, by the same token, does History get into a literary text? The solutions to these thorny problems seem to lie in a mode of reading which understands texts neither as the products of a transcendental signified nor as the products of conscious mimetic intention, but as the products of a largely unconscious dialectic between an active faculty of apperception and a many-levelled problematic (cf. Lentricchia, 1980, p.269).[1]

Such an account has several theoretical advantages. First, it implies that texts are not the passively determined, superstructural by-products of substructural forces (be these termed *langue*, *écriture*, 'discursive formation' or 'the relations of production' (cf. Lentricchia, 1980, pp.189–95 and 333)). Second, while forgoing the notion of a transcendental faculty in human nature which always remains 'outside the structural field, subject to no conditions' (Lentricchia, 1980, p.72), it leaves room for an active human faculty of response. Third, it implies that texts, being the sites on which the dialectic between sub- and superstructures, individual and collective is played out, are interesting more for the unconscious interaction between problematic and response which are encoded within them than for their lateral referentiality to the 'real world'. Fourth, it avoids the reification which tends to set in when texts are viewed as models of static, homogeneous structures rather than the products of

1. In using the somewhat un-English term 'problematic', I am referring to Louis Althusser, *For Marx* (1965) (New Left Books, London, 1977) (cf. Jameson, 1972, pp.135–6). Here, the notion of 'problematic' is said to be characterised by its relationship 'to the real problems to which its deformed enunciation gives a false answer' (p.67), by its propensity to transcend the 'domain of the objects considered by its author, because it is not an abstraction for the thought as a totality but the concrete determinate structure of a thought and of all the thoughts possible within this thought' (p.68), and by its institutionalised propensity to suppress concepts which are not compatible with its terms. Conversely, I would wish to imply that the imaginative faculty of apperception tends, by its very nature, to grasp and grapple with the 'deformations' of any given problematic, to question the totality of its terms, to resurrect and verbalise precisely those elements which it has suppressed, and to manifest this critical/creative response in the form of texts, of which so-called 'literary' texts are usually the most dense (cf. Michael Titzmann's essay above, p.64).

dialectical process (cf. Jameson, 1972, pp.119–20). Fifth, it permits the critic, while rejecting mimetic realism, to rediscover History in the generative interaction between historically determined problematic and historically determined consciousness – to remain, as Lentricchia put it, 'inside the labyrinth of discourse' (1980, p.166). And sixth, it compels critics to concern themselves with the literary and meta-literary conditions out of which texts have been generated and thus to set texts against – in the double sense of that word – the basic *topoi* of Western metaphysics (cf. Gasché, 1979).

Such an approach – combining deconstructive eccentricity and a theoretical alternative to reflectionism – is particularly helpful in the case of that notoriously complex expressionist poet August Stramm (1874–1915). It encourages us to identify the major assumptions of and gaps in the critical consensus which has developed since Thea Pokowietz published the first major article on him in 1956, abstract the principal insights which have arisen within that consensus, pair these with alternative insights which both oppose and complement them, and see the resultant, a-symmetrical series as a microcosm of the metaphysical debate which lies at the heart of European Modernism.

To date, Stramm criticism, while by no means monolithic, has displayed seven salient characteristics which are worth describing in detail since they amount to one, predominant strategy for dealing with the aporias of Stramm's poetry. First, Stramm criticism has frequently been most at ease with individual poems[2] and has, correspondingly, been chary of giving an account of Stramm's work as a whole. Thus Hering (1971), Adler (1973/4), Piel (1978), Adler (1979), Radrizzani (1979a) and Bridgwater (1980), assuming the autonomy of the isolated text, focus on individual poems and deal with these at a linguistic level only. Accordingly, they do not see with any consistency that the ambiguities of Stramm's language and syntax are not just the (mimetic) reflections of a world in chaos, but also the phenomenology of dialectical 'deep structure' whose nature is more than literary and whose import is more than mimetic.[3] Thus, Bozzetti's excellent dissertation (1961), whose detailed account of

2. The abbreviation *Werk* plus a page number refers to August Stramm, *Das Werk*, ed. René Radrizzani (Limes, Wiesbaden, 1963). I have tried, wherever possible, to provide translations of Stramm's poetry. But as the significance of so much of Stramm's poetry derives from the way in which its signifiers function in the context of normal German paradigms rather than from any lexical meaning, it has not always been practicable to attempt a translation.
3. It is because Arnold's perspective on poetic texts is limited in just such a way that he regards it as 'wasted effort' to seek any common factors between expressionist and dadaist poetry (1966, p.55).

the morphology of Stramm's syntax 1914–15 provides a massive amount of phenomenological data for a deconstructive analysis, is unable to move away from a mimetic account of its peculiarities and draw any meta-literary conclusions about the conditions that generated it. And Bridgwater's (1980) account of some of Stramm's war poems – easily the most illuminating to date – is trapped in mimetic assumptions that cause it to be more concerned with the extent to which individual texts adequately mirror the inner experience of battle (p.33) and less concerned with the complex dialectic out of which Stramm's work as a whole was produced.

Second, like that 'cursory observer' to whom Bozzetti referred (1961, p.53), Stramm criticism has been over-impressed by Stramm's neologisms. Implicitly equating these with a linguistic radicalism and assuming, on the basis of that equation, that Stramm's use of language is somehow 'progressive', Stramm criticism has asked itself only rarely why Stramm should have needed to create neologisms at all, let alone considered the literary-historical situation of that need. Where the above question *has* been asked, the answers have often been too simple: because Stramm wanted to say something unusual, did not want to let language rigidify and was a creative personality (Bozzetti, 1961, pp.53, 75 and 76); because he wanted to avoid clichés (Arnold, 1966, p.38); because he wanted to achieve an abstraction equivalent to the planar construction of modern painting (Hering, 1971, p.100); because of his 'concern with onomatopoeic effect' (Jones, 1977, p.258); because he was trying 'to turn the mere word into a "complex of sensations"' (Bridgwater, 1979, p.36) or 'express an unparalleled experience of reality' (Bridgwater, 1980, p.32). In every case, the explanation is the product of a 'subjectivist humanism' (Lewis, 1982, p.12) which either equates literary history with a history of surface 'style', or assumes that the point of poetry is to create an original aesthetic effect which the poet controls through his conscious manipulation of words. In none of the instances cited above is it realised either that Stramm's near-obsessive use of neologisms opens up metaphysical issues, including the nature of language and the nature of the *brisure* that occurs in the history of Western literature around the time of the Great War, or that, in the end, Stramm's need to work with tortured neologisms calls into question – deconstructs – the reassuring, logocentric assumptions underpinning the aesthetics of reflectionism, the notion of a developmental history of style and, indeed, linear conceptions of History in general.

Third, encouraged by Stramm's own desire to arrive at a single, mimetic signification for any given word (which Stramm, significantly, called 'Begriffe' ('concepts') as though words were simple tools with which to 'grasp' reality – German 'greifen' = 'to grasp'),[4] Stramm criticism has been more concerned to assign simple, referential meanings to Stramm's neologisms and/or syntactically difficult passages than to envisage multiple, possibly aporetic readings of these within any given text.[5] It has also been more concerned to arrive at a single, referential interpretation of a text than to see its lack of closure and account for that in terms of the problematic from which the text was generated. Thus, Bozzetti declared 'Sonne wundet' to be an intransitive construction (1961, p.62–3), not seeing that 'wundet', precisely because it is a neologism, can also be read as an objectless transitive verb. Michelsen reduced the syntactically and semantically ambiguous 'Armen' of 'Zwist' (*Der Sturm* [hereafter *DS*], December 1914; *Werk*, p.22) to the recognisably familiar 'umarmen' (1964, p.294). Arnold said of the line 'Lichte dirnen aus den Fenstern' of 'Freudenhaus' (*DS*, June 1914; *Werk*, p.14), 'The meaning remains clear' (1966, p.38), not seeing that its first two words could be read as an adjective plus noun or as an adverb plus verb or as a noun plus verb. Bridgwater showed a similarly reductionist tendency when he wrote that 'what might at first glance appear to be infinitives are more often than not verbs in the third person plural of the present tense' (1979, p.42). Adler saw the word 'Einen' in 'Urtod' (*DS*, July 1915; *Werk*, pp.87–8) as connoting union in contrast to words which connote individuation (1979, p.9), not seeing that 'Einen', too, if read as the accusative singular of the masculine indefinite article or pronoun, could equally connote individuation. And Radrizzani, discussing 'Allmacht' (*DS*, November 1914; *Werk*, p.38), wrote (and the inverted commas suggest the inadequacy of what is asserted): 'the "correct" paraphrase [of the line 'Du siegst Gott'] is thus: in the encounter with the Thou, I triumphantly experience the divine; the triumphantly divine emerges' (1979a, p.103), even though, as I shall argue below, the line permits other, contradictory readings.

Analogously, at the level of entire poems, Adler, while perceiving

---

4. See his letters to Herwarth Walden of 22 May and 11 June 1914, in *Der Sturm: Ein Erinnerungsbuch*, ed. Nell Walden and Lothar Schreyer (Woldemar Klein, Baden-Baden, 1954), pp.75 and 76. Hereafter cited in the text as *DSeE*. Since I completed the typescript of this article, a new edition of Stramm's letters has appeared: *August Stramm, Briefe an Nell und Herwarth Walden*, ed. Michael Trabitzsch (Edition Sirene, Berlin, 1988).

5. Neumann's discussion of the multiple semantic possibilities of 'glasen' (1977, p.272), White's insight that 'there is no *single* meaning to "Berge" [in "Patrouille" (*Werk*, p.86)]' (1979, p.68), and Bridgwater's insight that 'Krieg' 'can be read in at least two ways' (1980, p.43) are rarities.

oppositions and balances (1973/4, pp.30–40) in 'Abend' (*DS*, February 1915; *Werk*, p.74) and even hinting that that poem may involve a fundamental contradiction (p.28), ultimately acquiesced in Stramm's essentialist appeal to the 'original/primal meanings' ('Urbedeutungen') of words (p.22) and was concerned to impute a positive ending (i.e. a single meaning) to the poem even though there is no particular reason why its final, syntactically isolated 'Du' should be read positively – or, indeed, in any one way at all. Piel regretted the absence from 'Urtod' (*DS*, July 1915; *Werk*, pp.87–8) of any 'fixed point of reference . . . in relation to which several words might be aligned in *one* [my italics] direction' (1978, p.576). Radrizzani's discussion of 'Allmacht' (*DS*, November 1914; *Werk*, p.38) centred on the assertion that the poem communicates the impression of an almost monumental unity (1979a). Bridgwater claimed that 'Schlachtfeld' (*DS*, January 1915; *Werk*, p.68), despite its neologisms, 'conveys an exact meaning' and is 'totally intelligible' (1980, p.38). And Adler argued for Walden's right arrangement of the poems in the *Du* collection because, so ordered, the poems suggest 'a cyclical progression, and a *definite* [my italics] development' and 'an advance which, if not exactly linear, is *unambiguous* [my italics] in its path from frustration to fulfilment' (1979/80, pp.129–30). In arguing thus, Adler forgot that the haphazard sequence in which the poems were first published in *Der Sturm* makes the significance of the individual poem more problematic precisely because of the absence of the tidily straightforward context which such a cyclical arrangement provides. Unconsciously, all such readings thematise the desire to reduce turmoil to a clear pattern which Stramm evinced when, writing to Walden on 8 April 1914 (*DSeE*, p.74), he said that his '*Du*-poems' were destined for a collection of poems to be entitled *Der Kreis* (*The Circle*): the geometric regularity implied by the title was to predispose the reader to reduce the complex, shifting possibilities of the individual poems to one, simple pattern.

Fourth, Stramm criticism has rarely asked how radically unconventional Stramm's syntax really is in any given case, preferring to impute a general a-syntacticality to his work. For example, Michelsen maintained, far too simply, that 'in Stramm's poetry, because there is no difference between classes of words, no one class of words is more important than any other' (1964, p.294) and thus failed to see that Stramm's poetry transcribes a struggle – between forces which make for syntactical anarchy and the desire to prevent that anarchy by means of conventional syntactical hierarchies. Arnold said that Marinetti taught Stramm that one could circumvent syntax (1966, p.45) and Bridgwater suggested that Fritz Mauthner did the same for him (1979, pp.33 and 45; 1980, p.30), but neither critic saw that Stramm, at another level, simultaneously resisted these lessons very strenuously indeed. Haller asserted, despite copious contrary evidence, that Stramm tends to avoid subject–object relationships (1969, p.242); Hering listed Stramm's novel linguistic techniques (1971, p.99) but failed to see how these co-exist with a linguistic conservatism; and although White was very conscious of the conservative aspects of Stramm's typography (1979, p.49), he only hinted at his scepticism *vis-à-vis* the assumption that Stramm sought to 'destroy' syntax. Only rarely, in, for example, Bozzetti's thesis (1961), where the morphology of the syntactical patterns in Stramm's poetry overall is examined in detail, or Neumann's (1977, p.283) analysis of 'Vorfrühling' (*DS*, April 1914; *Werk*, p.109) has Stramm criticism conceded that Stramm's poetry tends simultaneously towards extreme a-syntacticality *and* towards syntactical conventionality, and hence realised that many passages, and even some whole poems, can be read from these two opposing/complementary perspectives at once.

Fifth, encouraged possibly by Stramm's letters to Walden of 22 May and 11 June 1914 in which the poet implicitly lays claim to conscious and rational control over the effects produced by his poetry, Stramm criticism has tended to impute a simple, consciously controlled intention to Stramm's work. Pokowietz, discussing 'Dämmerung' and 'Wunder' ['Ich'] (*DS*, June and November 1914; *Werk*, pp. 30 and 32), stressed the consciousness of the mind behind them, the 'ego which sets itself up as absolute and *thinks* [my italics] itself godlike in its creative power' (1956, p.123). Likewise Bozzetti (1961, pp.82–3), Haller (1969, p.242), Adler (1973/4, p.21), Jones (1977, p.259), Hering (1979, p.29) and Bridgwater (1979, p.45; 1980, *passim*) based their readings of Stramm on notions of conscious intentionality. And Michelsen asserted the congruence of Stramm's poetry with the highly cerebral *Wortkunsttheorie* ('Theory of Verbal Art') propagated by Walden in *Der Sturm* (1964, p.297). Only rarely, as, for instance, in Bozzetti's assertion that Stramm's work is excessively full of images 'which express the urgency of his longing ['Drang'] for eternity, a-temporality and infinity and which, at the same time, manifest the problematic inherent in this yearning' (1961, pp.127–8) or Neumann's conclusion that Stramm's poetry is full of simultaneous contrasts 'which arise through those intangible relationships of tension within and between words' (1977, p.285) does one get any sense that Stramm's work is the statement of and simultaneous response to a many-levelled problematic and that the processes by which that dialectic has been verbalised are, to a great extent, unconscious, outside the poet's ability to control, despite his conscious, and at times almost obsessive concern to do so.

Sixth, where Stramm critics have tried to give an account of Stramm's work as a whole, they have frequently written either as though the poems were all of a piece, e.g. exemplars of Walden's Absolute Verbal Art (Pokowietz, 1956, p.125; cf. also Hering, 1950, p.51 and Neumann, 1977, p.243) or manifestations of a 'quest for the primal/original meaning of the individual word' (Hering, 1979, p.30); or as though Stramm's work fell into two neatly distinct halves – pre- and post-August 1914 (e.g. Pokowietz, 1956, p.125; Haller, 1969, pp. 245–6). It is only when one sets the implications of Bozzetti's syntactical analyses (1961) and, say, Haller's claim that Stramm's work is not a unity (1969, p.232) against Adler's claim that Stramm 'makes no hard and fast distinctions between "love poems", "war poems", and "religious" works' (1979, p.86) that one realises that Stramm's poetry as a whole defies description in terms of stylistic or thematic (dis)unity and cannot be reduced to a one-dimensional literary 'development'. Rather, Stramm's poems are the product of a more than literary problematic which, though present in his earliest *Du* poems, became more complex, more visible and more dramatically expressed in the poems written after the outbreak of war. Correspondingly, the responses to that problematic which inhere in the poems vary considerably in their nature, complexity and intensity so that it is a falsification to order them, as Stramm would clearly have liked to do himself, according to too strict or simple a pattern.

Finally, Stramm criticism has been concerned to establish the 'influence' of other writers and texts on Stramm without having a very clear notion of the meaning of that term, let alone a sophisticated understanding of Reception Theory. This means that Stramm critics have not, on the whole, begun their deliberations about Stramm's relationship with other writers from a model of the structure of Stramm's imagination. Moreover, on the materialist-mechanistic assumption that 'influence' is a cumulative process whereby new elements are continually added to the subject, they have been unable to say with any great differentiation how that structure was modified or reinforced by Stramm's encounters with the work of Holz, Marinetti, Walden, Vaihinger, Mach and the American Platonists Prentice Mulford and Ralph Waldo Trine. Thus, because critics have focused so overwhelmingly on Stramm's consciousness, they have not allowed either for the possibility that an 'influence' which was greeted *positively* by Stramm (e.g. Marinetti) may, at the unconscious level, have had a *negative* effect upon the structure of his imagination; or for the possibility that Stramm's conscious account of the relationship of an 'influence' to his poetry (e.g. Walden's Theory of Verbal Art) may be at best partial and at worst inaccurate; or for the possibility that certain 'influences' on Stramm (like Mulford and Trine – see Hering, 1959, p.64) may have acted less as agents in a cumulative process and more as final lines of defence against chaos and despair.

Given these seven features, Stramm criticism is rich in insights which are true of his poetry to an extent or at one level only, but which need re-situation by a reading that focuses less on Stramm's mimetic intentions and more on the unconscious processes at work in his imagination and language – with all their contradictory, deconstructive possibilities. Consequently, this essay will try to broaden the context in which Stramm's poetry has hitherto been understood (cf. Culler, 1983, p.12); describe the complex generative system which makes its ambiguous signifying events possible (Culler, 1983, p.111); and, by refusing to assume the 'organic unity' of that poetry (Culler, 1983, p.200) or the conscious control of the poet over his work (cf. Lewis, 1982, p.12), attempt to make explicit the 'metaphysical oppositions' (Culler, 1983, p.109) which are concealed there.

A Logocentric Imagination

Despite its surface radicalism, Stramm's poetry is, to an extent which has not always been appreciated, the product of an imagination which was informed by a highly conservative, classical set of beliefs (cf. Arnold, 1966, p.30, and White, 1979, pp.49–50), some of which Stramm held and understood consciously, others of which, however, took the form of profound and implicit presuppositions. To begin with, it is clear that Stramm consciously believed or at least *wanted* to believe in a metaphysically ordered universe (cf. Hering, 1979, p.14). It is this conviction or desire which speaks from Stramm's letter to Walden of 23 February 1915: 'I sometimes feel as if we were an undivided whole. Zero distance. Thus I sometimes experience the world as I, the whole universe! Thus I experience you! And those are moments of wonderful intoxication' (*DSeE*, p.88), and from his letter to his wife of 27 May 1915, where he speaks of 'taut threads as thick as your arm' holding the edifice of the world together (quoted in Adler and White, 1979, p.148).

The same conviction explains why Stramm's two favourite books should have been the German translations of Prentice Mulford's selected essays entitled *Der Unfug des Sterbens* (1909) and Ralph Waldo Trine's *In Tune with the Infinite* (1897) (cf. Hering, 1959, p.64), both of which assert that the world of matter is informed by and reveals regular metaphysical processes or laws, and both of which argue that man's highest task is to bring himself into a state of harmony with these. At the level of consciously held belief, Stramm clearly assented to Trine's statement: 'And in all the great universe there is but one centre – the Infinite Power that is working in and through all'[6] and doubtless identified that power with the 'world-spirit' which, he felt, had entrusted him personally with an (unspecified) mission (see his letter to Walden of 23 March 1915 (*DSeE*, p.92)). The same conviction or desire also explains why Stramm so readily accepted Walden's cyclical arrangement of the *Du* poems (Adler, 1979/80, pp.125 and 133); why Stramm reacted so positively to Salomo Friedlaender's interpretation of the War as a period of purification within a cyclical process of destruction and renewal;[7] why Stramm wanted to collect some of his early poems under the title *Der Kreis* (*The Circle*); why Stramm's longest poem, *Die Menschheit* (*DS*, July 1914; *Werk*, pp.43–55) 'sets up a myth of the eternal cycle of the creative processes at work in the world' (Bozzetti, 1961, p.121) and why a good number of his poems – especially those of earlier date – tend towards circular form (e.g. 'Tanz' and 'Vorfrühling' (*DS*, April 1914; *Werk*, pp.105–7 and 109) in which the last line echoes the first) or invoke the image of the circle/circling/circularity.

Second, Stramm also believed or wanted to believe in the reality and stability of the self and the mystical potential of the I–Thou relationship. Hence his positive reception of Friedlaender's 'Geist und Krieg' ('Spirit and War') (see note 7) in which the core of the personality, described as 'spirit, inwardness, soul, heart, sensibility', the 'absolutely individual self', the 'absolutely undivided soul' is likened to the sun at the centre of the cosmos; hence, too, his positive reception of Trine and Mulford, where the same status is assigned to the core of the personality and the same power attributed to love. The same desire or belief informs Stramm's desperately passionate declarations to his wife of 29 December 1914 (Adler and White, 1979, p.132) and carefully constructed poems like 'Heimlichkeit'

---

6. Ralph Waldo Trine, *In Tune with the Infinite* (1897) (Bell, London, 1900), p.142; translated into German by Dr Max Christlieb as *In Harmonie mit dem Unendlichen* (Engelhorn, Stuttgart, 1905).
7. See Stramm's letter to Walden of 25 August 1915 (*DSeE*, p.98) where he calls Friedlaender's essay 'Geist und Krieg' (*DS*, vol.6, no.9/10 (August 1915), p.50) 'very good and right'.

(*DS*, December 1914), 'Wunder' (*DS*, November 1914), 'Trieb' (*DS*, November 1914), 'Spiel' (*DS*, November 1914) and 'Abend' (*DS*, February 1915) (*Werk*, pp.25, 33–4, 37 and 74) which, at one level at any rate, celebrate the love-relationship as a means of access to the metaphysical powers behind the cosmos. It is probably too much to say, as Hering did (1959, p.64), that Stramm's mystical proclivities *derived* from the ideas of Trine and Mulford, but it is clear that the ideas about the nature of the human personality which these writers helped him to articulate were constant articles of his conscious *credo*, even when his wartime experience was subjecting them to radical assault.

Third, it follows from the above that Stramm's beliefs about language, notwithstanding the surface radicalism of his poetry, were intensely conservative as well. For Stramm, the *logos* of the humanly uttered word, the organising logic of the conscious mind (which, *vide* his letters to Walden of 22 May and 11 June 1914, he thought able to control signification), and the metaphysical *Logos* informing the world of objects composed a substantial unity. To use Culler's formulations, Stramm's beliefs about language were grounded in a 'metaphysics of presence' which conceives of meaning on the one hand as 'a signifying intention present to consciousness at the moment of utterance' and on the other as 'an ideal norm that subsists behind all appearance' (1983, p.109). Both assumptions are clearly present in Stramm's essay 'Deutsche Titel' ('German Titles') (first published on 15 August 1912 in the *Blätter für Post und Telegraphie*; in Adler and White, 1979, pp. 153–7). Here, Stramm attacked latinate official titles whose meaning had become 'ambivalent' ('mehrdeutig') through usage, and advocated their replacement by German neologisms with a consciously implanted and unequivocal signifying intention whose 'essence' ('Wesen') derived from '*one* core' ('*einen* Kern'). As Radrizzani suggests (1979b, p.163), behind Stramm's conscious quest for such a 'primal/original word' ('Urwort') lay the conviction that if the falsely (i.e. unconsciously) accreted layers of signification could be deliberately stripped away from words, a fundamental and original meaning would be revealed which, paradoxically, both designated one integral category of objects and yet pointed beyond itself and that category into the realm of metaphysical essences.

Stramm's almost obsessive desire to attach the right word or combination of words to an object, event or feeling (cf. Hering, 1959, pp.67–8; Bozzetti, 1961, pp.60 and 70–1; Michelsen, 1964, pp.285 and 289; Arnold, 1966, p.40; Hering, 1979, p.30; Jordan, 1979, p.124) involved the Platonic belief, present also in Trine's and

Mulford's books, that all objects are aspects of the infinite and that, accordingly, its essence may be perceived through them (cf. Bozzetti, 1961, p.72). Strangely enough, Stramm's decisive encounter with Marinetti's 'Technical Manifesto of Futurism' in Autumn 1913 seems to have left these fundamental attitudes to language intact and simply to have radicalised the means by which Stramm sought to translate them into poetic practice. Marinetti's almost chemical notion of 'Universal Dynamism' may, metaphysically speaking, have been a long way from Stramm's more Platonic views. Nevertheless, at another level, Stramm was totally predisposed to receive Marinetti's idea that language, once stripped down to its basic syntactical components, enabled the poet to penetrate further into the essence of matter (cf. Haller, 1969, p.241). And this explains, at least in part, why Stramm, after the manner prescribed by Marinetti, makes so much use of the infinitive form in his poetry (see Bozzetti, 1961, p.99). As Michelsen perceived, it is that form of the verb which is tied to no tense and in which 'the active or passive significance which is inherent in the concept of the verb in question ... is encapsulated "as such", "absolutely"' (1964, p.293).

Moreover, although in his quest for the 'primal word' Stramm was prepared to mutate and mutilate the conventional forms of words, his metaphysically grounded linguistic conservatism made him much less willing to destroy syntax than has often been assumed. Mauthner, as Bridgwater suggests, 'may have taught Stramm in theory that conventional syntax is simply a matter of codified customs, and as such unworthy of any particular respect' (1979, p.33), but in practice – and this is particularly true of Stramm's earlier poetry (cf. Neumann, 1977, p.283) – a great deal of Stramm's writing obeys normal syntactical rules. As Neumann put it: 'the syntactical relationship does not, however, disappear as a result of that – it is simply no longer foregrounded' (p.284). For example, many of Stramm's poems (like 'Mondblick', 'Erfüllung', 'Untreu', 'Siede', 'Schrapnell', 'Frostfeuer', 'Kampfflur' or 'Gefallen' – to make a random selection from all phases of Stramm's short creative life) begin with a line which is syntactically unexceptional (even if it does contain neologisms or make unusual use of words), and by so doing, they establish an intelligible context in which any subsequent, a-syntactical passages may be set. Then again, the second half of 'Siede' (*DS*, June 1914; *Werk*, p.17) looks a-syntactical at first reading, with its one-word lines, strange neologisms and unusual semantic combinations, but in fact, there is little ambiguity about the syntagmatic relationships. Michelsen maintained that 'Zwist' (*DS*, December 1914; *Werk*, p.22) contains neither a logical subject nor an object (1964, p.294), and yet a closer inspection reveals that there is at least one passage (ll.11–14) which can be read perfectly well as four subject-verb statements. 'Abendgang', too (*DS*, November 1914; *Werk*, p.40), seems a-syntactical to begin with, and yet a more careful reading shows that it actually makes conventional use of syntax and that its difficulty derives from the attempt to grasp the precise meaning of (untranslatable) neologisms like 'schmiege', 'krampfes', 'flimmt', 'schlafe', 'armt' and 'dünsten'. Admittedly, as time went on, conventional syntax in Stramm's poetry became less evident, more strained and more part of a poetic structure which permitted much syntagmatic and interpretative ambiguity. Nevertheless, even in Stramm's later poetry, it *did* persist, forming an attenuated structure of order which, in terms of Stramm's increasingly precarious belief-system, was grounded in a cosmic order and, as such, in conflict with those forces of disorder and a-syntacticality which continually threatened to destroy it.

Stramm's adherence to 'the classical notion of the sign as the representation of an object endowed with intrinsic value' (Lewis, 1982, p.10) went hand in hand with beliefs about the nature of poetry which were equally conservative. Despite the 'radical' or 'innovative' look of his poems, Stramm's letters to Walden clearly imply that Stramm took a very high view of art and thought of poetry as a means of mirroring and celebrating what is pure and enduring. Hence the elevated sentiment which forms the foreground of so many of the *Du* poems and the feeling thereby engendered that Stramm would dearly have liked to write with the cosmic ease and eloquence of, say, a Mombert. Oddly enough, Stramm's conscious and admitted 'attraction . . . to Walden's conception [of art]' (letter to his wife of 29 December 1914, in Adler and White, 1979, p.132) derived from a similar source. Walden's Theory of Verbal Art may have looked thoroughly modern in its advocacy of abstraction, but it rested on classical assumptions about art and the artist which derived, in turn, from a fundamentally logocentric set of attitudes.[8] When Stramm, writing in desperation to Walden from the Front on 27 June 1915, said that his tortured poems, once written down, were nothing more than 'a schematic form, saying nothing' (*DSeE*, p.96), he was not renouncing his deeply held views on poetry, but registering the impossibility of realising those ideals in a universe gone mad.

---

8. Cf. R. Sheppard, 'Kandinsky's Early Aesthetic Theory: Some Examples of its Influence and some Implications for the Theory and Practice of Abstract Poetry', *Journal of European Studies*, vol.5 (1975), pp.25–6.

Logocentrism Assailed

At the same time, there was an immense gap between Stramm's ideal beliefs and the implications of his experience, especially after the outbreak of war. Several passages in Stramm's letters clearly indicate that he would have been in sympathy with Trine's statement from *In Tune with the Infinite*: 'The one who is centred in the Deity is the one who not only outrides every storm, but who through the faith, and so, the conscious power that is in him, faces storm with the same calmness and serenity that he faces fair weather...' (pp.148–9; G.T., p.150 (see note 6)) and shared Trine's belief that evil and its results were illusions, arising 'through ignorance' (p.100; G.T., p.99); other passages, however, testify to the increasing subversion of those beliefs and the imaginative structure in which they were embedded by ever more violent experiences of primal chaos.

The damage done to Stramm's Platonic metaphysics by his experience of battle is very visible in his letters to his wife of 4 February and 20 May 1915, where, describing his new sense of reality, he wrote: 'And interspersed with all that, the howling of the heavy shells, like wild beasts. You just can't imagine what that's like. One is just sobbing past above my head. We scarcely dare to look up any more. Sometimes it feels as if the whole sky was one great mass of sobbing and crying and impotent howling' (Adler and White, 1979, p.135) and: 'I've never experienced anything like that, I wouldn't want to experience it again and I don't want to talk about it any more!... It wasn't world, but underworld!' (Adler and White, 1979, p.147). In similar vein, Stramm described reality in his letter to Walden of 6 October 1914 as: 'Wretched, cowardly, treacherous terror, and the very air sniggers sneeringly as well and gurgles and thunders down from the mountains... It's none of it true and all of it a lie' (*DSeE*, p.79). Writing to Walden again, on 14 December 1914, he doubted the existence of meaning, calling his experience of battle 'Horrendous!... meaningless!' and asking 'What is meaning?' (*DSeE*, p.84); and on 21 March 1915, in an equally despairing tone of voice, he wrote to his mentor: 'I no longer have a sense that there's any meaning, simply process ['Werden'] all around. For me there is only process = meaning. But meaning is death' (*DSeE*, p.92).

Ever since his exposure to Marinetti's ideas in Autumn 1913, Stramm had been developing an increasingly strong sense that reality was composed of dynamic energies rather than static objects. But whereas, in the days of peace, Stramm had viewed that dynamism in more material terms and had been able to reconcile it theoretically with a sense of inherent providential order, his experience of war opened up an ever-widening gap between those two concepts. Even though Stramm was probably attracted to Mulford's book because it encouraged him to believe that that gap could be bridged by the power of 'positive thinking', the above passages from Stramm's letters, co-existing though they do with passages where Stramm desperately asserts his faith in providence and destiny, testify to the increasing loss of belief in a metaphysically ordered universe (cf. Bozzetti, 1961, pp.134–5). Correspondingly, as Michelsen accurately put it, objects, for Stramm, increasingly lost their substantiality and threatened to turn into 'abstract and grotesque discharges of their energy' (1964, p.300); increasingly ceased to be aspects of the creative *Logos* and turned into violent, hostile, shrapnel-like fragments. As far as Stramm's poetry is concerned, this loss of belief generated a decreasing incidence of compound (i.e. synthetic) adjectives (Bozzetti, 1961, pp.58–9); an increasing use, as adjectives, of verbal or nominal roots without an ending (p.60); a diminishing use of compound verbs (p.70); an increasing use of verbs which, deprived of their normal prefix (pp.71–2), were much less transitive in character; an increased incidence of verbs beginning with 'zer-', the German prefix denoting disintegration (pp.72–3); a diminishing use of nouns denoting points in time and object-ive motion (pp.79–80) and an increased incidence of sentences composed of two units only (p.85). As time went on, Stramm, even while trying desperately to hang on to a sense of metaphysical order, made increasing use of a language which, by overemphasising or diminishing the syntactical elements which make for a sense of causal and syntagmatic connectedness, deconstructed that sense.

Second, as his faith in an ordered and ordering *Logos* was subverted, Stramm, much against his inclinations, was increasingly forced to give up his notions of the self as a stable, positive, controlling power (cf. Piel, 1978, p.576) and the mystical potential of the I–Thou relationship. Shortly after the outbreak of war, on 6 October 1914, Stramm wrote to Walden of his discovery of 'such an infinitely large amount of death in me, death and death' (*DSeE*, p.78); and as the carnage worsened, so Stramm found within himself a positive fascination with and even delight in the primal violence of battle, so that, on 20 December 1914, he could write to Walden:

> We ourselves are demons and laugh at all the others. That's how the soldier in the field feels. There's nothing greater than him, and he doesn't acknowledge anything as his superior. He kicks the earth and shoots Heaven to death. And there is horror within him and around him, he

himself is horror... Everything's a game to him. And he even casts himself like a die. That's how I see things now and know that that's how it is. (*DSeE*, p.85)

And in his letter to Walden of 12 January 1915, Stramm went so far as to admit his savage joy in destruction (*DSeE*, p.86). Similarly, in the letter to his wife of 5 June 1915, he wrote (and the syntax is ambiguous after the manner of his poetry so that the German word for 'both' ('beides') can be read with the 'I' ('Ich') as though the two preceding predicative adjectives referred to *its* qualities): 'It was all so great and terrible! both I can't say anything yet' ('Es war alles so groß und entsetzlich! beides Ich kann jetzt noch nichts sagen!) (in Adler and White, 1979, p.150). And in the letter to his wife of 18 August 1915, he described the war, in similar vein, as 'so frightful and yet so great' (in Adler and White, 1979, p.152).

As Stramm's letters progress, so their author becomes increasingly aware of the extent to which the human personality is controlled by destructive, unconscious and instinctual rather than creative, constructive and rational powers, so that on 25 February 1915 he could write to Walden: 'I am conscious of the unconscious'; on 21 March 1915: 'What I know I don't experience any more'; and on 30 June 1915: 'I simply can't say at all what I want' (*DSeE*, pp.90, 91 and 97) – and the result of this discovery is the harrowing sense of being 'torn apart' ('Zerrissenheit') which is so painfully evident in Stramm's final letters from the Front.[9] Correspondingly, Stramm's faith in the redemptive nature of love was increasingly undermined as well. Indeed, the very emphases of the following passage from Stramm's letter to his wife of 29 December 1914 indicate, sadly, that Stramm was desperately trying to preserve his belief in something which he secretly knew to be slipping away from him:

> Elle, indeed that's it; but what does that concern *us*, why should that have any effect on what's between *us*. Nothing *is to be allowed* ['*darf*'] to come *between* us, we *must* be one, especially now that we are separated by so much space! No, my dear one, that *will not be allowed* to be any different; [the thought of] that grinds me into pieces. (In Adler and White, 1979, p.132)

And once poems like 'Vorübergehen' (*DS*, June 1914), 'Traum' (*DS*,

---

9. As Jordan (1979) accurately put it, 'the predominant tone of the letters is one of despair at the powerlessness of the individual faced with a process of killing and being killed over which he can exercise no control' (p.179).

December 1914) or 'Verzweiflung' (*DS*, December 1914) (*Werk*, pp.19, 21 and 23) are detached from the reassuring pattern which Walden imposed upon them in the *Du* collection and allowed to speak for themselves, a less containable scepticism about the redemptive power of the love-relationship emerges. That scepticism grew stronger as the War progressed so that where thirteen of the thirty-one poems of the *Du* collection were resolved by ending in a personal pronoun (3 × 'Ich'; 2 × 'Mich'/'Mir'; 6 × 'Du'; 1 × 'Wir'; 1 × 'Sich'), only three of the thirty-one poems of the later *Tropfblut* collection do so (1 × 'Ich'; 2 × 'Du'). Furthermore, the majority of the *Tropfblut* poems, (where, in any case, the more pronouncedly downward, vertical thrust of the poetry throws even more weight on the final word than is the case in the *Du* poems), far from ending on any kind of triumphal note, tend towards bleakly negative words like 'death' ('Tod') (three times); 'Nothingness' ('Nichts') (three times); 'Zergehren' (an untranslatable neologism which might be roughly rendered as '[to] desire/ferment into pieces'); 'Nichtall' (an untranslatable neologism which implies the nothingness of everything in the universe) and 'grave'/'burial vault' ('Gruft'). Thus, when Stramm wrote to Walden on 14 January 1915 that his poem 'Freudenhaus' ('Brothel') (which had been published in *DS* in June 1914; *Werk*, p.14) 'is just beginning to provide the keys to many things' (*DSeE*, p.86), he may well have been implicitly considering the possibility that his earlier vision of the world as a place permeated by mystical love was giving way to a sense that the world was turning into a bordello, the seat of pestilence and death.

An entirely consistent process of erosion can be seen in Stramm's attitude to language. As early as 1911, Stramm may, as Bridgwater has argued (1979, p.11), have been attracted to the fundamental thesis of Hans Vaihinger's *Die Philosophie des Als Ob*, according to which the scientific hypothesis is a fiction and 'advanced with the consciousness that it is an inadequate, subjective and fictional manner of conception, whose coincidence with reality is, from the start, excluded'.[10] But the effect on Stramm of that circumscribed linguistic scepticism (which was, in any case, counterbalanced in Vaihinger's work by a sturdily positivistic materialism) was slight in comparison with the damage done to Stramm's linguistic confidence by his experience of modern warfare. As the War went on, Stramm increasingly lost his faith in the necessary, and, in the strict sense,

---

10. Hans Vaihinger, *Die Philosophie des Als Ob* (Reuther und Reichard, Berlin, 1911), p.606, translated into English by C.K. Ogden as *The Philosophy of 'As If'* (London, Routledge and Kegan Paul, 1965), p.268.

essential connection between language and reality, and, concomitantly, in the ability of language to pin things down. Thus, on 6 October 1914 he wrote to Walden: 'I simply can't read and think any more. Words stick in my throat for sheer terror' (*DSeE*, p.78); on 4 and 12 February 1915 he wrote to his wife of the utter impossibility of describing the chaos and violence of battle (in Adler and White, 1979, pp.135 and 136); and on 27 June he wrote to Walden of his lack of words and the complete inadequacy of those at his disposal *vis-à-vis* his experiences of trench warfare (*DSeE*, pp.96 and 97).

This erosion of linguistic faith explains a large number of the syntactical trends noted by Bozzetti (1961). As Stramm lost his sense of the necessary connection between language and reality, the number of verbs and nouns denoting a point in time diminished (pp.68–9 and 79); as Stramm increasingly lost his faith in the ability of language to mirror an a-causal reality, the distinction between transitive and intransitive verbs became blurred (p.87); as Stramm's experience of reality increasingly became one of incompleteness and disconnectedness, reflexive words (p.89) and punctuation marks (p.94) increasingly disappeared from his poetry. As a result of his experience of war, Stramm's essentialist assumptions about language were increasingly assailed by the realisation that language is relative, arbitrary and limited, so that, paradoxically, the stripping down of language which Bozzetti noted when comparing Stramm's early and late poetry (p.56); the veering between syntagmatic pattern and patternlessness (White, 1979, p.62); and, indeed, Stramm's increasingly contorted search for neologisms with which to grasp the ungraspable (cf. Bozzetti, 1961, pp.72–3) all testify to a highly conservative imagination refusing to give up and yet being forced, in the face of shatteringly contradictory experience, to give up its profoundest assumptions about language. To use modern parlance, while Stramm's experience pushed him towards the renunciation of the belief that 'a language consists of words, positive entities, which are put together to form a system', all his conditioning held him back from the acceptance of the notion that linguistic units are merely the 'effects of difference' (Culler, 1983, pp.98 and 99).[11]

11. There is a significant parallel between the implicit self-deconstruction of Stramm's poetry and the explicit self-deconstruction of that other product of the battlefields of the Great War, Wittgenstein's *Tractatus Logico-Philosophicus*, whose author compared it to a ladder which had to be thrown away after one had climbed it (Proposition 6.54). On the one hand, the *Tractatus* sets out and affirms the assumptions of a logical positivism – the material (i.e. irreducible) nature of

Concomitantly, Stramm increasingly sensed that the high, mimeticist tradition of literature to which he instinctively assented, grounded in notions of a transcendental *Logos* (cf. Lewis, 1982, p.12), was also under radical threat by dark, fluctuating and disruptive forces. Consequently, he was increasingly compelled to forego that ease of expression which betokens an imagination at one with its own assumptions, and to resort to a tortured mode of writing in which the poet seeks to grasp and stabilise those forces. To use the post-structuralist idiom, Stramm's logocentric imagination, while seeking to celebrate the 'same', simultaneously found itself forced to deal with a radically subversive 'other' (cf. Lewis, 1982, p.17). The 'difference' which that encounter involved generated several characteristics of Stramm's syntax: his tendency to avoid the definite article and thus lift his nouns out of time and space (Bozzetti, 1961, pp.91–2); his tendency to nominalise verbs of violent movement (as in ll.4–7 of 'Granaten' (*DS*, September 1915; *Werk*, p.94)) by turning them into infinitives (cf. Bozzetti, 1961, p.83 and Piel, 1978, p.575); his tendency to use grammatical forms which can be read as an infinitive or plural noun as well as a verb in the third person plural of the present tense; his tendency to transform, especially in his early poetry, present participles (with their dynamic immediacy) into less immediately dynamic adjectives ending in '-ig' (cf. Bozzetti, 1961, pp.61–3); his tendency to create composite neologisms from a noun/pronoun plus a past participle (e.g. 'duumträumt', 'ichumbraust', 'krampfzerrissen' or 'glutverbissen') which are notable, despite their verbal origin, for their heavy nominality; his tendency to invent adjectives (e.g. 'hetze', 'schmerzes', 'kreuze') which have a pronounced nominal quality; his tendency to abandon the freer rhythms of his early poetry for the trochaic regularity of the late work (Bozzetti, 1961, pp.104 and 106); his tendency to end-stop lines when the inherent force of the rhythm or the logic of the syntax would naturally enjamb them; his tendency to create a fixed pattern of expectation (as in 'Vernichtung' (*DS*, January 1915; *Werk*, p.70)) or to repeat words and phrases within a poem (Bozzetti, 1961, p.203); and his tendency to write poems with a quasi-triangular form which concentrates their emphasis on the final, stabilising

---

reality (2.027), the consonance of language and reality, both of which are said to be held together by a substantial (i.e. metaphysical) 'logical Form' (4.12 and 6.124) and the adequacy of language as a means of grasping object-ive reality (3.2 and 3.203). But on the other, it intersperses those propositions with alternatives according to which an unknowable reality exists beyond the material world (6.522) and language is a set of relative conventions (4.01), limited and ultimately inadequate (4.121, 5.6 and 7). Nowhere is this duality more evident than 4.01, where Wittgenstein simultaneously asserts the mimetic and the conventional nature of language.

word (e.g. the 'Ich' of 'Angststurm' (*DS*, September 1918; *Werk*, p.98)). Wherever one looks in Stramm's poetry, one finds Stramm's desire to celebrate enduring values being assailed by drastically antagonistic forces so that he is simultaneously compelled to resort to equally drastic, formal and linguistic measures in order to contain and stabilise them.

Consequently, it is far too one-dimensional to discuss Stramm's poetry exclusively in terms of its approximation to Walden's Theory of Verbal Art (cf. Michelsen, 1964, p.297)[12] or in terms of a simple 'transition from the objective to the abstract' (Hering, 1959, pp.70–1; cf. also Bozzetti, 1961, pp.56–67 and Haller, 1969, p.239). Although it clearly *is* true that Stramm's poetry, moving between the Impressionism of 'Mairegen' (*DS*, June 1914; *Werk*, p.110) and the abstraction of 'Urtod' (*DS*, July 1915; *Werk*, pp.87–8), does increasingly free itself from particular signifieds (hence the diminution of Impressionistic elements (Bozzetti, 1961, pp.57–9, 67, 73–9 and 91), such an account glosses over the conflictual elements which have been identified above. Additionally, any description of the morphology of Stramm's poetry must take account of the fact that Stramm's attitude to this already complex process underwent a fundamental change as well. In the months following his encounter with Marinetti, Stramm, encouraged by his contact with Walden, *Der Sturm* and the Theory of Verbal Art, clearly greeted the radical deconventionalisation of his poetic imagination (for which his reading of Vaihinger, Holz and possibly Mach had already prepared him theoretically) as a positive development. But with the passage of time and the corrosive impact of the War, Stramm seems to have realised with ever greater consciousness that that process of deconventionalisation was more than verbal, more than literary – that it threatened to destroy the very structure of his psyche and that it had, in consequence, to be resisted – hence his sense of opposition between the implications of modern abstract art and his love for his wife (see the letter to his wife of 29 December

---

12. Because of Stramm's own admitted attraction to Walden's conception of art (Adler and White, 1979, p.132), the similarities between Stramm's poetry and Walden's Theory of Verbal Art have been stressed and the profound differences overlooked. Although both Stramm and Walden wanted art to celebrate a hidden, abstract order, for Walden, that order derived from the human consciousness, whereas for Stramm, that order derived from a cosmic *Logos*. Furthermore, Walden's theory was ignorant of the primal violence which Stramm experienced in battle and which played so important a role in his poetry: Walden's Theory of Verbal Art derived from a comfortable neo-Humanism, Stramm's abstract poetry was the product of a confrontation between a Platonism and the threat of engulfment.

1914, in Adler and White, 1979, p.132); hence, too, the increasing importance for him of the work of Mulford and Trine.

The Conflictual Structure of Stramm's Poetry

With this contextual model in mind, Stramm's poetry can be read in terms of a conflict between two simultaneously present but fundamentally irreconcilable belief-systems – between the 'problématique' (see note 1) of classical idealism with which the bourgeois world on the brink of the Great War concealed its internal contradictions from itself and the shattering implications of stored-up, mechanised violence. This conflict was present embryonically in the *Du* poems of 1914 and even his doctoral dissertation, *Das Welteinheitsporto* (an investigation into the possibility of introducing unified, world-wide postal charges), published in 1910 in Halle, that most Prussian of universities.[13] But it became more and more intense as the poet's imagination threatened to rip itself apart under the impact of the War, and is, from the formal point of view, reflected in the increasingly obvious tension between the 'horizontal' and 'vertical' possibilities of Stramm's syntax (cf. White, 1979, ll.57–8).

13. Critics have smiled many a superior smile at the thought of Stramm, the wild mutilator of language, solemnly devising a system for deriving unified, world-wide postal charges. But if one approaches Stramm's doctoral dissertation without assuming a clear division between literary and non-literary texts, then striking structural affinities emerge between that dissertation and Stramm's poetry. First, Stramm the administrator, like Stramm the poet, was centrally concerned with the realisation of ontologically harmonious concepts like 'rigorous implementation of the principle of the reciprocity of services', 'correspondence' (p.5) and 'unified standards/tariffs' (p.40) – nevertheless, he was also acutely aware of disruptive elements in reality which made this desire unrealisable (pp.40–3). Second, Stramm the administrator, like Stramm the poet, wanted to be optimistic about human nature and so rested his scheme for a system of unified, world-wide postal charges on an appeal to 'ideas of brotherhood' and the 'human spirit' – nevertheless, he also knew that his ideas were utopian (p.91), impracticable because of the darker sides of human nature. Third, Stramm the administrator, like Stramm the poet, was very concerned with the transmission of units (letters/signifiers) which had been properly assessed and whose weight/signified was clearly indicated by a stamp of agreed value – nevertheless, he was aware that this, too, was impossible, and said as much in his conclusion (p.92). In his latter years, the Dadaist Tristan Tzara wrote: 'if words were nothing but signs / stamps affixed to things / what would remain of them / dust / gestures / wasted time / there would be neither joy nor sorrow / throughout this crazy world' (*Oeuvres complètes*, ed. Henri Béhar, 5 vols. (Flammarion, Paris, 1980), vol.4, p.279) and there is a clear sense in which these reflections throw light on Stramm's thinking about 'correspondence' in both senses of that intricate word.

Stramm himself referred to this conflictual process when he spoke of the contradictory and chaotic nature of reality in his letters to Walden of 22 March 1914; 6 October 1914; 14 December 1914; 12 January 1915 and 30 June 1915 (*DSeE*, pp.74, 78, 84, 86 and 97). Where, however, the letter written *before* the War, seeing the 'radical oppositions' ('scharfe Gegensätze') in an aesthetic context only, took positive pleasure in them, the wartime letters, evincing an intensifying sense that reality as a whole is contradictory, display an increasing pain in the face of this vision, until, in the last-cited letter, that contradictoriness threatens to tear Stramm apart as well. Given this, Stramm's poetry lends itself perfectly to a deconstructive reading – which, refusing to assume that a text is in possession of or transparent to itself, looks for those 'points of condensation, where a single term brings together different lines of argument or sets of values' (Culler, 1983, p.213) and seeks to demonstrate how the text subverts itself (cf. Culler, 1983, pp.22 and 86).[14]

At a metaphysical level, one can see this double movement in several of Stramm's poems, both early and late. 'Tanz' (*DS*, April 1914; *Werk*, pp.105–7) concludes with the words with which it opened, but instead of following these with a full stop or an empty space, uses the three dots which signify incompleteness. In the final line of 'Vorfrühling' (*DS*, April 1914; *Werk*, p.109), 'tummeln' is substituted for 'jagen' of the first line even though the rest of the poem's first line is repeated. Thus, in both poems, the circular form (which is closely bound up with the logocentric metaphysic of completeness) is both affirmed and subverted. And as Adler (1979, p.98) has pointed out, the very shape of 'Urtod' (*DS*, July 1915; *Werk*, pp.87–8), with its column of single words, illustrates the contradictory metaphysical implications of circular form: clear pattern and centredness on the one hand, but on the other, unlimited duration and 'Gleichwertigkeit' ('the absence of a hierarchy of values'/'the situation where everything is of equal value').

The ambiguous implications of formal shape are paralleled elsewhere by syntagmatic ambiguity. The last lines of 'Allmacht' (*DS*, November 1914; *Werk*, p.38) for example – 'Hölle Teufel/Du siegst Gott' can be read as: 'You, oh my God, are victorious'; 'You [i.e. a

---

14. Bozzetti's highly revealing stylistic analyses are limited by an inability to grasp the contradictoriness of Stramm's poetry and the ambivalent attitude of Stramm himself towards that contradictoriness. Because Bozzetti reads Stramm's poetry overall in a linear manner (i.e. simply in terms of increasing abstraction), he does not always see that his syntactical data point in two ways. Of all Stramm critics, Radrizzani (1979a, p.170) and Jordan (1979, p.124) have best grasped the contradictory nature of Stramm's imagination.

second (human) person] are victorious after the manner of a God'; 'You [i.e. a second (human) person] are victorious over God' or 'You [referring back to the Devil] are victorious over or after the manner of God'. Given Stramm's tendency, throughout the entire poem, to blur the distinction between transitive and intransitive verbs and to omit articles, there is absolutely no need, as Radrizzani does (1979a, p.100), to reduce the ending to one, metaphysically optimistic meaning. Instead, the poem includes within itself the possibility that, in the end, there may be no all-powerful God behind Creation. The same is true of *Die Menschheit* (*DS*, July 1914; *Werk*, pp.43–55) which, according to Bozzetti (1961, p.149) is about the creation of humanity *ex nihilo* and its death 'back into the state of divine oneness/omni-connectedness ['göttlichen Allzusammenhang'] which he had previously left'. In fact, the poem is metaphysically much more ambiguous: images of patterned circularity are set against a vocabulary of insistent, forward movement ('Voran Voran') which ultimately leads only to 'Tränen' ('tears'), and, as so often in Stramm's poems, the repetition of a word, far from creating a stable pattern, reduces that word to something approaching a meaningless noise. Thus, by the end of the poem, the constant repetition of 'Voran Voran' ('On On') subverts itself, creating a sense of confusion rather than direction, and the threefold repetition of 'In den Raum' ('Into space') produces just a hollow resonance. Moreover, the final line – 'Tränen kreist der Raum' – is ambivalent inasmuch as 'Tränen' can be read as one of Stramm's homemade adverbs, so that one cannot be sure, within the ambiguous context created by the previous passage, whether the line means 'space circles [i.e. encloses, patterns] tears' or 'space circles tearfully' – and this in turn means that in the end, the poem points as much to an ultimate emptiness and sorrow as it does to Bozzetti's 'göttlichen Allzusammenhang'.

'Werttod', too (*DS*, January 1915; *Werk*, p.71), can be read from two entirely contradictory points of view. If one reads it out loud, stressing its doggerel rhyme-scheme, then 'Wahnsinn' ('madness') has the final word – like Pilate, it washes its hands and remains 'ewig unverletzt' ('eternally unharmed'). But if one concentrates on the visual placing of the words on the page, then the effect of breaking the doggerel pattern by putting 'Ewig' and 'Unverletzt' on two separate lines and giving each a capital letter is to give 'Ewig' more of a nominal status, as though it were a word in its own right, unconnected with the line which preceded it. In which case, despite the death, madness and suffering of the preceding seven lines, it is the 'Ewig' ('eternal'/'infinite') which remains unharmed. A final example of this kind of metaphysical ambiguity – and there are many more – is provided by 'Krieg' (*DS*, May 1915; *Werk*, p.80) which, despite its title ('War') is full of words and images connected with birth ('Wehe', 'Kreißen', 'Bären', 'gebärt' and 'jüngt'). But what, precisely, is being born? 'Erschöpfung' ('exhaustion') of line 8 can be read as the object or the subject of 'gebärt' ('gives birth [to]') and/or the subject or object of the normally intransitive 'jüngt'. And what, precisely, is the force of 'jüngt'? Lexically, it means 'to bring forth', but given Stramm's propensity to interchange syntactical functions, it could also be read – with the adjective 'jung' ('young') in mind – as 'juvenate'. In other words, the syntax and placing of the words on the page allow us to read the ending of 'Krieg' as though 'Der Tod' ('Death'), standing monumentally on its own, had the last word or as though 'Der Tod' itself were involved in a complex process of birth and 'juvenation'. Just as, according to Adler (1973/4, p.28), 'Abend' (*DS*, February 1915; *Werk*, p.74) does and does not have a centre, so do more than a few of Stramm's other poems simultaneously affirm and deny a metaphysical centre to Creation – even though, as is clear, his work overall tended towards a cosmic pessimism as 1915 went on (cf. Bozzetti, 1961, p.112). Or, to put it epigrammatically, Stramm's neologism 'krieseln' points as much to 'kriseln' (a verb which is used to denote a crisis brewing up) as it does to 'kreisen' ('to circle').

An entirely consonant double movement can be seen in Stramm's presentation of the material world. On the one hand, as has often been pointed out, this became increasingly dynamic – especially after the outbreak of war (cf. Michelsen, 1964, p.300). And yet, on the other hand, Stramm consistently sought to stabilise this movement and preserve the object-ivity of objects. Hence the increased incidence of 'Stammadjektive' ('uninflected adjectives'/'adjectives minus the normal adjectival ending') such as 'berg' instead of 'bergend', 'gell' instead of 'gellend' etc. (Bozzetti, 1961, pp.60–1). These, while tending towards verbal (i.e. *present* participial) status, by omitting the ending '-end' ('-ing'), either become strongly nominal, or as Neumann argues, are *past* participial in their effect, producing 'the paradox of activity which is both incomplete and in the process of being completed' (1977, p.269). Hence, too, Stramm's drastically increasing use of infinitives (Bozzetti, 1961, p.99) which contrive to be verbal and nominal, dynamic and static, temporal and a-temporal all at once.

Indeed, most of Stramm's poetry can be read as a dialectic between dynamic energies and elements whose function is to object-ify or stabilise that dynamism. In 'Mondblick' (*DS*, August

1914; *Werk*, p.12) for instance, a conventional series of reflections about the moon shining through the window of the beloved is continually invaded by surreal elements which threaten to remove things from their conventional places or explode their conventional proportions, and which the poet has simultaneously to stabilise. Hence the difficulty of deciding whether the verbs in ll.3, 5, 7, 9, 10 and 11 are governed by the neologism 'Das Schläfern' or absolute, subjectless constructions; transitive or intransitive ('Bleicht' and 'Stülpt'); indicative or imperative or, in the case of 'Verfröstelt', participial. Hence, too, the impossibility of deciding whether 'Glast' of ll.17 is a noun or the third person singular of the present tense of a neologism ('glasen'). Hence, too, Stramm's insertion of the command 'Halt Halt Halt!' ('Stop Stop Stop!') at that precise point in the poem when verbal energies, despite their nominalisation into capitalised infinitives, are multiplying and accelerating. However, this command (which also threatens to deconstruct itself inasmuch as it can be read out aloud as 'Hallt Hallt Hallt!' ('Echoes Echoes Echoes!') is of some avail and, by the concluding lines of the poem, it seems as though familiar, stabilised things have returned 'in peace' to their 'old place' (cf. ll.28–9). Nevertheless, the poem ends on a paradoxical and surreal image: the (dark) night is said to 'blinzen' (imagery of light), gathers in the window as though it were a monster and thus obliterates the distinction between fore- and background.

A similar dialectic is visible in the significantly entitled 'Zwist' ('Quarrel'/'Dispute') (*DS*, December 1914; *Werk*, p.22). In ll.1–8, it is impossible to say whether the first word of each line is a plural (albeit verbal) noun which governs and stabilises the succeeding verbs, or the third person plural of a verb in the present tense (like the other verbs in the line) with an accidental capital letter which functions as just one more aspect of omnipresent motion. This pattern is resolved by the more unequivocally conventional syntax of ll.9–12, but is then broken again by the (untranslatable) syntactical and semantic ambiguity of 'Armen sträubet/ Quälen küßt/ Vergessen/ Lacht!' Likewise, Stramm's long poem *Weltwehe* (written late 1914; *DS*, April 1915; *Werk*, pp.57–64) is constructed almost completely around the syntactical ambivalence of capitalised infinitives standing as lines on their own. Sometimes, an apparently less ambiguous line emerges (such as 'Wiegen kreisen engen locken' or 'Nachten nachten' – where the absence of capital letters from all but the first word indicates, fairly clearly, the presence of verbs). But such lines are preceded and succeeded by such a welter of syntactically equivocal words that their apparent syntactical clarity is obscured and the words beginning with small letters are read as though they too were verbal nouns and not third person plurals of verbs in the present tense governed by plural nouns. Similarly, 'Schlacht' (*DS*, May 1915; *Werk*, pp.77–8) begins with a dialectic between verbs which involve motion on or around a stable point ('ringt', 'würgt', 'stehn', 'kracht', 'stockt', 'starrt' and 'blutet') and verbs where the static element is less pronounced ('Stampfet', 'Windet', 'wühlt', 'wächst'), which is resolved by the clear noun-plus-verb patterns of ll.26–34. But then, this clarity dissolves in the chaotic accumulation and interchange of the verbal nouns of ll.37–46 on which the fivefold 'Und' ('and') cannot impose any deceleration, differentiation or sequential order. Indeed, by the last three lines, that word (as we shall see below) has deconstructed itself by the very frequency with which it is used, becoming an almost meaningless grunt. Finally, 'Frage' (*DS*, September 1915; *Werk*, p.92) makes use of two lines (2 and 4) in which one is not sure whether key words are verbs, verbs governed by plural nouns without capital letters or adjectival neologisms plus nouns (e.g. 'schlanken weiten', 'schwanken brüten'); one line (19) where a word ('wellen'), depending on whether one sees or hears it, can be read as a noun ('waves') or a verb ('[to] surge'/'well'); and a verbal pattern ('Und/ Gehen Gehen') which, again, deconstructs itself into near meaninglessness through frequent repetition. In all these cases, then, energetic elements battle bewilderingly with stable elements for predominance.

A similar double movement characterises Stramm's presentation of the self, especially in the *Du* poems. Indeed, one may say that the very emphasis which Stramm gives to the personal pronouns in thirteen of the *Du* and three of the *Tropfblut* poems by isolating them in the final, stressed position, capitalising them, and following them, in thirteen out of the sixteen instances, with an exclamation mark, generates as much a sense of unnatural precariousness as of unself-conscious ontological security: the very weight which these pronouns have to carry tends to deconstruct what they apparently signify.[15] Moreover, that ambiguity is often compounded by the ambiguity of the syntactical context. For example, although the first eight and last five lines of 'Liebeskampf' (*DS*, August 1914; *Werk*, pp.9–10) affirm, if read conventionally, the distinctness of the 'Ich' and the 'Du' and the reality and separateness of both, a second,

---

15. Bridgwater (1980, p.51) approached this insight when he pointed out that the German first-person pronoun is used only *once* in the war poems – in 'Angststurm' (*DS*, September 1918; *Werk*, p.98) – and that it 'receives immense emphasis' by being capitalised.

slightly more eccentric reading subverts all that. That is to say, if the 'Nicht' of l.3 is read in conjunction with the second 'fliehst' of l.2, the 'Du' becomes an elusive subject which is caught between two movements and defined by neither. If the 'nicht' of l.4 is read with the 'Ich' of l.5, it is the 'non-ego' which becomes the subject of 'Will' of l.6. If 'nicht' is read as a Strammian neologism – as though it were the third person singular of the present tense of a verb like the 'Icht!' of 'Sehnen' (*DS*, December 1914; *Werk*, p.27) – with 'Suchen' of l.4 as its subject and 'Ich' of l.5 as its object, then the ego, by virtue of its questing, becomes subject to 'nihilation' or 'noth-ing'. The same is true of the last five lines of the poem if the three 'Nichts' there are read in a similar way; and the poem's final 'Ich' – which looks stable and firm enough if read in isolation – is threatened drastically if taken with the preceding 'Nicht'. Indeed, one might say that the 'Liebeskampf' ('Love[rs'] struggle') of the poem is less between the 'I' and the 'Thou' and more between those two persons and the powers which threaten to reduce them merely to 'Wellen auf den gleichen Strom' ('Waves onto the same stream/current/river').

It is the same with 'Trieb' (*DS*, November 1914; *Werk*, p.34), where the 'Ich's' and the 'Du's' of ll.6, 10 and 14–16 can be read as independent points of order and stability amid a chaos of nominalised infinitives or as the drastically threatened objects of a complex of variously combinable plural nouns and verbs. In this poem, the carefully constructed order noted by Hering (1979, p.17) co-exists with and is, to an extent, deconstructed by radical disorder. 'Angriff' (*DS*, July 1915; *Werk*, p.83) can be read, as its title suggests, as the description of an attack – but the poem as a whole suggests the sexual act. If, on the latter reading, the poem's title is set aside, its import is harmless enough, but when the title is taken into account, then the violent associations thereby generated deconstruct Stramm's earlier picture of the world held together and mysteriously transformed by the miracle of mystically conceived Eros (such as one finds in 'Wankelmut' (*DS*, June 1914), 'Blüte' (*DS*, June 1914) or 'Wunder' (*DS*, November 1914) (*Werk*, pp.15, 29 and 32)). Similarly, if 'Angststurm' (*DS*, September 1918; *Werk*, p.98) is read 'straight', the 'Ich' appears to be the last point of stability amid total and violent disorder. But, inevitably, l.2, when read aloud, turns into 'Ich un dIch un dIch un dIch' so that the distinction between persons is blurred, 'un-' turns into the prefix of monstrosity (as in 'Unding' ('monster'), 'Unflat' ('filth') etc.) which undoes the personhood of the second person pronoun, making it the monstrous counterpart of the 'Ich', and the uncentred composite pronoun 'Ich un dIch' becomes associated with the surrounding terror. Concomitantly, the final 'Ich' can be seen to be as much the product of as the counterweight to all the violence which has preceded it – with the result that the poem does two things at once: it affirms personhood while showing it to be illusory, the fictitious product of impersonal processes. In view of the slight phonetic difference between 'wir' ('we') and 'wirr' ('confused') (cf. 'Wankelmut' = 'vacillation'), one may say that personhood, fusion and confusion are very close to one another in Stramm's poetry.

Given the above, it inevitably follows that Stramm's attitude to language is riven with contradiction as well. His letters to Walden of 22 May and 11 June 1914 (*DSeE*, pp.75 and 76) in which he discusses 'Untreu' and 'Freudenhaus' (*DS*, June 1914; *Werk*, pp.16 and 14) clearly indicate, with their vocabulary of intentionality and conceptuality and their precise statements about the implications which certain phonemic combinations had for him, that Stramm thought of himself as being in control of his texts. And yet, it is equally clear that Stramm's poems often work in ways which undermine this classically logocentric assumption. For instance, one of the strangest things to happen is that 'und' ('and'), his most frequently used word (212 times), ceases, because of that very frequency (together with its often isolated situation on the page and the sheer weight that Stramm puts upon it), to be a conjunction of connectedness, subordinate to the words it appears to link, and becomes a force in its own right, governing verbs as though it were itself a noun. Thus, in 'Liebeskampf' (*DS*, August 1914; *Werk*, pp.9–10), the 'Und' of ll.10, 12, 14, 16 and 17 tends to function as the subject of 'reißt', 'ebbt', 'schrumpft' and 'keucht'. In 'Erhört' (*DS*, December 1914; *Werk*, p.20), the 'Und' of ll.2, 5, 8, 11, 14 and 17 tends to function as the subject of 'Wirft', 'Schüttelt', 'Wirrt', 'Schluchzt', 'Reißt' and 'Wirbelt'. And in 'Schlacht' (*DS*, May 1915; *Werk*, pp.77–8), the 'Und' of ll.2, 5, 8 and 11 can, by virtue of its isolated position, be read either as the object of 'ringt', 'würgt', 'stehn' and 'kracht' or as the subject of 'stampfet', 'windet wühlt und stemmt' and 'schellet'. Indeed, by the end of 'Liebeskampf' and 'Frage' (*DS*, September 1915; *Werk*, p.92), 'Und' has become little more than a guttural grunt, devoid of signification, and in all the cases cited above, that word which normally denotes connectedness has become involved either as subject or object of a violent process of disintegration, distortion and destruction.[16]

16. This point is reinforced by comparing the way 'und' functions in Stramm's poetry with the way it functions in the superficially similar poetry of Lothar Schreyer, another *Sturm*-poet. As Jones (1977, p.261) pointed out, although both poets 'use "und" in anaphora with nouns and verbs, Schreyer rarely repeats it in

In other words, despite Stramm's clear desire to 'grasp' ('be-greifen') reality with his words/concepts ('Begriffe'), his language continually tends to break free from that reality, take on an independent and anarchic life of its own, and work against its conventional patterns of signification. This process is particularly visible where Stramm's use of neologisms is concerned. Stramm was forced to invent an *increasing* number of verbs (Bozzetti, 1961, p.73) because he wanted to pin down, conceptualise, 'be-greifen' an increasingly chaotic reality which eluded conventional verbs. But precisely because these verbs *are* neologisms and have no clearly established signification, they inevitably elude Stramm's conscious intention. The reader's imagination has much freer play with 'krumen' than with 'krümeln', or with 'schläfern' than with 'einschläfern', and there is no guarantee that his or her understanding of these words will match Stramm's. As Neumann asked (1977, p.272), what *is* the reader to make of a neologism like the one-word line 'Glast' in 'Verzweifelt' (*DS*, December 1914; *Werk*, p.23)? Does it derive from a verb, 'glasen', and mean 'mit Glas versehen', 'wie Glas tun', 'glasig, gläsern machen', 'zu Glas machen', 'in Glas ein/aufgehen'? Or is it the noun 'Glast' ('gleam' or 'glow')? Or indeed, does it mean any combination of some or even all of these possibilities simultaneously? And as White rightly perceived: 'there is no *single* meaning to "Berge" [in 'Patrouille']; the word does not belong unequivocally to one grammatical category – even if there is a possibility that its various meanings could be hierarchically systematised' (1979, p.68).

Throughout Stramm's poetry, the assumption that there is a necessary connection between language and nameable – i.e. humanly orderable – reality is continually subverted and language continually takes off in dynamic, barely comprehensible strings of infinitives(?)/gerunds(?)/third person plural verbs(?) (cf. Neumann, 1977, p.267) – as in 'Spiel' ll.4–5 (*DS*, November 1914), 'Dämmerung' l.14 (*DS*, June 1914), 'Zagen' ll.4–7 (*DS*, September 1915) or 'Angststurm' ll.3–5 (*DS*, September 1918) (*Werk*, pp.37, 30, 95 and 98). In all four cases, the lines in question free themselves chaotically from any controllable naming process or syntagmatic pattern and seem, as often as not, to be constructed by accidental phonetic

---

one sentence, as in Stramm's "Signal" . . . [and] tends to incorporate it in longer sentences which prevent it functioning as an onomatopoeic and rhythmic element in the poem as a whole'. Although 'und' occurs in Schreyer's poetry fifty-two times more than it does in Stramm's, it is never permitted to break free from the bonds of conventional signification – as so frequently happens in Stramm's poetry.

association rather than logical process. And when, in 'Urtod' (*DS*, July 1915; *Werk*, pp.87–8), Stramm tries to stabilise such a process by containing it within the repetition of 'Raum/Zeit/Raum' ('Space/Time/Space') – two of Kant's three *a priori* categories of the transcendental ego – he fails to the extent that those words, again through excessive repetition, lose their significatory force and become, by the end of the poem, hollow incantatory sounds. Consequently, there is a sense in which Stramm's early poem 'Untreu' ('Faithless') thematises his incipient sense of the faithlessness of language, and 'Urtod' ('Death of Deaths'/'Primal Death') of one year later the all but total collapse – the '*Ur*-death' – of those transcendental (logocentric) categories in which his faith in language had been grounded.

Stramm, the pedantically conscientious postal official, would-be poet of high sentiment, dutiful husband and nobly courageous captain must have been particularly moved and encouraged by the following statement from the German translation of Trine's *In Tune with the Infinite*: 'Are you a writer? Then remember that the one great precept underlying all successful literary work is, *Look into thine own heart and write. Be true. Be fearless. Be loyal to the promptings of your own soul*' (p.163). Ironically, however, it is precisely because there was more in Stramm's poetic imagination – his 'heart' – than either he (or Walden) could consciously 'see', that he is more than a late Romantic epigone, more than an imitator of Holz or Marinetti, and more than a slavish practitioner of Walden's Theory of Verbal Art. To cite Culler once more: 'The value and force of a text may depend to a considerable extent on the way it deconstructs the philosophy that subtends it' (1983, p.98); and Stramm's poetry, encapsulating several dilemmas that are fundamental to the problematics of European Modernism, illustrates this assertion to perfection. Unlike many latter-day theoreticians, however, Stramm experienced those dilemmas[17] without the protection of well-endowed Ivy League

---

17. When the theoretical dust has settled, Structuralism and Post-Structuralism may well be seen as belated responses by the academic world to a problematic whose nature was first defined by people largely working outside the academic establishment during the so-called modernist period (1890–1930). Structuralism, with its appeal to 'deep structures' embedded either in human nature (Chomsky, Todorov and Lévi-Strauss – cf. Lentricchia, 1980, pp.105, 115–16, 125–8 and 164) or History (the early Foucault – cf. Lentricchia, 1980, pp.200–1), can be seen as the inheritance of those Modernists who, having undergone a 'Death of God' experience, sought a reliable *Ersatz*-absolute (cf. Jameson, 1972, pp.109–10). Post-Structuralism, with its rejection of the idea of self (Lacan), refusal of all metaphors of depth (the later Barthes) and polemic against logocentric conceptions of History in whatever guise (Derrida), can be seen as

walls (cf. Lewis, 1982, p.4), as acutely painful problems which involved his whole personality, not just his abstracting intellect. And it is for this reason that his strange, challenging poetry will continue to intrigue long after so much of the autistic inflation which masquerades as 'theory' has been consigned to the waste-paper baskets of intellectual history.

References

Adler, J. (1973/4) 'An Appreciation of *Geschehen, Rudimentär, Sancta Susanna* and "Abend"', *PEGS*, 46, 1–40

Adler, J. (1979) '"Urtod", An Interpretation' in Adler and White, pp.84–98

Adler, J. (1979/80) 'The Arrangement of the Poems in Stramm's *Du/Liebesgedichte*', *GLL*, 33, 124–34

Adler, J. and White, J. (eds) (1979) *August Stramm*, Erich Schmidt, Berlin

Arnold, A. (1966) 'Zur Linguistik des Expressionismus: Von Marinetti zu August Stramm' in *Die Literatur des Expressionismus*, Kohlhammer, Stuttgart, Berlin, Cologne and Mainz, pp. 16–56

Bozzetti, E. (1961) 'Untersuchungen zu Lyrik und Drama August Stramms', unpublished Ph.D. dissertation, Cologne

Bridgwater, P. (1979) 'The Sources of Stramm's Originality' in Adler and White, pp.31–46

Bridgwater, P. (1980) 'The War Poetry of August Stramm', *NGS*, 8, 29–53

Culler, J. (1983) *On Deconstruction: Theory and Criticism after Deconstruction*, Routledge and Kegan Paul, London

Gasché, R. (1979) 'Deconstruction as Criticism', *Glyph*, 6, 175–215

Graff, G. (1979) *Literature against Itself: Literary Ideas in Modern Society*, Chicago U.P.

Haller, R. (1969) 'August Stramm' in W. Rothe (ed.), *Expressionismus als Literatur*, Francke, Berne and Munich, pp.232–50

Hering, C. (1950) 'Gestaltungsprinzipien im lyrisch-dramatischen Werk August Stramms', unpublished Ph.D. dissertation, Bonn

---

the inheritance of those Modernists who, having undergone the same experience, also renounced the quest for any *Ersatz*-absolute and chose to see human psychology and History in terms of lacks, cultural relativity and the play of fictions (cf. Terry Eagleton, 'Capitalism, Modernism and Postmodernism', *New Left Review*, no.152, 1985, pp. 60–73, and John Burt Foster Jr., *Heirs to Dionysos*, Princeton U.P., 1981, pp.420–1).

Hering, C. (1959) 'Die Überwindung des gegenständlichen Symbolismus in den Gedichten August Stramms', *Monatshefte*, 51, 63–74

Hering, C. (1971) 'August Stramm – Untreu' in H. Denkler (ed.), *Gedichte der 'Menschheitsdämmerung'*, Fink, Munich, pp.97–105

Hering C. (1979) 'Die Botschaft des Schweigens' in Adler and White, pp.14–30

Jameson, F. (1972) *The Prison-House of Language: A Critical Account of Structuralism and Formalism*, Princeton U.P.

Jones, M. (1977) 'The Cult of August Stramm in Der Sturm', *Seminar*, 13, 257–69

Jordan, L. (1979) 'Familie und Krieg: Zu August Stramms Briefen an seine Frau' in Adler and White, pp. 116–27

Lentricchia, F. (1980) *After the New Criticism*, Chicago U.P.

Lewis, P. (1982) 'The Post-Structuralist Condition', *Diacritics*, 12, 2–24

Michelsen, P. (1964) 'Zur Sprachform des Frühexpressionismus bei August Stramm', *Euphorion*, 58, 276–302

Neumann, B. (1977) *Die kleinste poetische Einheit*, Böhlau, Cologne and Vienna, pp.138–287

Piel, E. (1978) 'Das Ich und sein Verhängnis – Zu August Stramms Sprachexperimenten', *Neophilologus*, 62, 568–83

Pokowietz, T. (1956) 'August Stramm' in H. Friedmann and O. Mann (eds), *Expressionismus: Gestalten einer literarischen Bewegung*, Wolfgang Rothe, Heidelberg, pp.116–28

Radrizzani, R. (1979a) '"Allmacht". Ein Liebesgedicht' in Adler and White, pp.99–115

Radrizzani, R. (1979b) 'Vom Fremdwort zum Urwort' in Adler and White, pp.158–64

Radrizzani, R. (1979c) 'Sprache und Gesellschaft' in Adler and White, pp.165–71

Said, E. (1984) *The World, the Text, and the Critic*, Faber, London

White, J. (1979) 'Aspects of Typography and Layout in August Stramm's Poetry' in Adler and White, pp.47–68

/# –12–

The Potential and Limits of a Marxist Methodology for *Germanistik*

DAVID JENKINSON

Introduction

In this paper, I wish to offer some personal views concerning ways in which, as teachers and writers in the field of German literary studies, Marxists might address some of the problems facing literary scholarship, and make use of some of the insights and approaches developed by Marxist writers. I do not intend to imply any evaluation of what has or has not already been achieved since that would be a formidable undertaking quite beyond the scope of this paper.

A recent survey of the achievements of Marxism in various areas of inquiry during the hundred years following Marx's death (McLellan, 1983) contains sections on culture, history, sociology, and philosophy, but not on literature. Although Roger Garaudy believed that 'the conception of aesthetics is the touchstone of the interpretation of Marxism' (Arvon, 1973, p.2) and Georg Lukács chose literary theory as a field within which he could write about the whole range of problems facing Marxism in this century, the view is still often encountered that Marxism has nothing significant to say about literature or, indeed, about any of the arts. This view may be heard from Marxists as well as non-Marxists. The late Raymond Williams (1977, pp.1–5) probably spoke for many when he described how, for several decades of his working life, his interest in Marxism (one hesitates in Williams's case to write simply 'Marxism') and his literary scholarship ran, as it were, along parallel tracks, with little contact or interaction. For many, Marxism is still a simplistic materialistic reductionism that treats works of art essentially as the product of social and historical factors, with no more sophisticated interpretative tools at its disposal than a primitive reflection theory. Our task, formulated in the most general terms, is to work towards removing this prejudice.

In doing so, I wish to address seven fundamental questions. First, can a Marxist theory of literature give a precise account of the relationship between socio-economic base and cultural superstructure[1] in the case of literary texts and thereby define the epistemological status of such texts? Second, the closely related question: should Marxists continue to oppose the notion of the autonomy or 'privileged' status of at least some literary texts? Third, how should Marxist criticism approach the task of evaluating and interpreting literary texts? Fourth, what should our attitude be towards the challenge of Structuralism and Deconstruction? Fifth, should Marxist criticism address the still unsolved problem of the nature of literary language? Sixth, what considerations should guide our work as teachers and critics – in particular, how should we regard the existing canon of German literature? And finally, can Marxism uphold, in literary scholarship, that claim to 'scientificity' which many see as the essence of the Marxist enterprise?

Literary Theory

Anyone who is on the mailing lists of our academic publishers is reminded almost weekly that literary theory continues to be a growth industry. Since the 1970s, following the structuralist revolution, theory has established itself as central rather than peripheral to literary study, though *Germanistik* in Great Britain appears to have come less completely under its dominance than either English and French studies in this country or German *Germanistik*. But here too

---

1. The widespread impression that Marx regarded the superstructure as wholly dependent on the economic base gains its strongest support from the following, polemically overstated passage from the *Manifesto of the Communist Party* (1847), in which Marx was rejecting a wholly Idealistic account of cultural life: 'Does it require deep intuition to comprehend that man's ideas, views and conceptions, in one word, man's consciousness, changes with every change in the conditions of his material existence, in his social relations and in his social life? What else does the history of ideas prove, than that intellectual production changes its character in proportion as material production is changed?' (Marx and Engels, 1968, p.54). But Marx was equally emphatic in his rejection of a one-way deterministic materialism and insistence on the dialectical relationship of base and superstructure, as can be seen in the following passage from the third of the *Theses on Feuerbach* (1845): 'The materialist doctrine that men are products of circumstances and upbringing, and that, therefore, changed men are products of other circumstances and changed upbringing, forgets that it is men that change circumstances ... The coincidence of the changing of circumstances and of human activity can be conceived and rationally understood only as *revolutionary practice*' (Marx and Engels, 1968, p.28).

the notion has taken root that any critical practice which does not take at least some account of theory is irredeemably naïve. As a result, Marxists, like others, have devoted much of their energy to the attempt to answer the question: What *is* literature? The underlying general question of the nature of the base–superstructure relationship is, of course, of the most intense philosophical interest. But I would suggest that we ought also to be trying to comprehend that relationship empirically, through close attention to individual texts and authors, taking as we do so the opportunity to give our students some inkling of the centrality and complexity of that relationship and thereby combating both simplistic Idealism and vulgar-Marxist, one-way materialistic determinism. All serious discussion of Marxism nowadays takes the dialectical relationship of base and superstructure for granted – often, indeed, to the point of overlooking or underestimating the very real and massive existence of class-determined attitudes that serve to perpetuate social structures without in the least helping to modify them dialectically. None the less, the popular misapprehension of a one-sidedly deterministic materialism is still so widespread among the general public that the perceived contradiction between Marx's own bourgeois origins and life style and his anti-bourgeois convictions can be complacently put forward as a refutation of his entire thinking.

Any attempt to ascertain precisely what Marx himself thought about literature in its relationship to the material base is doubtless doomed to failure, given the multiplicity and inconsistency of his statements on the subject. Nevertheless, there is considerable point in being regularly reminded not only of Marx's wide and deep knowledge of literature (Prawer, 1976), but also of his life-long insistence that it could not and must not be reduced to a by-product of economic factors. To stress this, be it said at once, is in no way to lend support to the notion that the arts constitute a realm of their own, wholly independent of the material base – the notion underlying the grotesque extreme of Kenneth Clark's (1969) apparent conviction that 'civilisation' is to be found almost exclusively in the history of art. The sterile Idealism of that conviction will, of course, only be encouraged by revulsion from a one-sided emphasis on the material concomitants of all cultural activity. Instead, we need to restore to its original centrality Marx's insight that artistic creation is a form of production in its own right, following its own laws within a given social context (Gallas, 1971, p. 175).

Terry Eagleton has succinctly formulated the problem of the epistemological status of art thus: 'Is art reflection, refraction, creation, transformation, reproduction, production?' (1977, pp.87–8).

But that formulation seems to imply that, somewhere, there is one final answer to the question, whereas the truth may well be that the relationship of art to reality is one of an infinite variety of unquantifiable permutations, allowing of no general formula, but inviting careful description of individual manifestations. To accept this would perhaps make it easier for Marxists also to accept that the notion of a fully 'scientific' study of literature, the 'euphoric dream' of the early Barthes (Thody, 1977, p.107), is dead, however insistently it may resist burial, without having to fear that this must entail a relapse into that institutionalised prejudice of which the legacy of F.R. Leavis is, to Marxists at least, the most notorious lasting reminder.

The Status of Literary Texts

A recurrent target for most of the proponents of recent literary theory has been the supposed 'myth' of the privileged status of literature, together with the role of individual creativity and the centrality of the individual author. But after very thorough attempts to demolish these notions by, for instance, Barthes, Lacan and Eagleton, we seem to be finding that they refuse to go away. So perhaps it is time for Marxism, as a theoretical orientation which still allows literature the central humanistic function of illuminating the world and extending human consciousness, to take the lead in reaffirming, not a Nietzschean/Arnoldian notion of literature as a surrogate religion, but at least the difference between general creativity and *significant* creativity.

To perceive literature as one cultural practice among many; to acknowledge that all literary expression must make use of a pre-existing system of signs; to recognise that every writer is, in part, a child of his or her time (or even the 'ensemble of his or her social relationships') – none of these admissions necessarily means that we have to abandon any distinction between what is perceived as significantly creative and what is merely part of that vastly increased general creativity that characterises our culture. By this I mean, of course, the superabundance of words and visual images with which, in the mass media, design and entertainment, we are surrounded throughout our daily lives. To single out certain literary texts, certain paintings and certain musical compositions as constituting a 'high art' different in kind from the products of the entertainment industry has come to reek of self-validating arbitrariness and elitism, and it is difficult to rebut this accusation theoretically. But the fact

A Marxist Methodology for Germanistik

that we will always be faced with numerous problematic borderline cases, and the fact that we cannot, for the moment at least, validate the above distinction scientifically, need not deter us from holding fast to it. The qualitative distinctions which in practice we cannot do without are still widely accepted as intuitively persuasive. The high arts have, after all, not been engulfed by popular culture; more has not meant worse as far as public interest in our cultural heritage is concerned; and we should not align ourselves, in the name of the rejection of 'bourgeois elitism', with the desire to devalue a heritage which is far too precious to be left to the bourgeoisie.

To imagine that one must prove one's Marxist credentials by affecting to despise anything that the bourgeoisie admires is one of the most benighted forms of vulgar Marxism, and one of the greatest satisfactions of a recent visit to the German Department of the Humboldt University in East Berlin was the discovery that this realisation is now (at last) firmly established there. And if this provokes the gibe that we are back with Leavisite subjectivity in left-wing clothing, we may answer that we are actually back with Karl Marx, who, throughout his life-long interest in literature, acknowledged the reality of individual creativity by granting it a large degree of independence from the material base. This fact is, of course, widely perceived as a problem: Marx, it has often been said (e.g. Williams, 1977, p.52), did not provide even the starting-point for a materialist theory of literature because he viewed it entirely from within the existing Idealist paradigm.

Interpretation and Evaluation

To insist on the reality of significant creativity involves us in the activity of evaluation, an activity which has, in our time, become increasingly marginalised as literary study has attempted to become more and more of an objective science. We need to hold fast to the conviction that although many things are true, some truths are more important than others, whilst remaining aware that, as Anna Seghers reminded Georg Lukács, we cannot always be certain which truths these are – i.e. what, in the terminology of Socialist Realism, is or is not 'typical' (Seghers, 1970, p.178). But evaluation cannot be a matter of awarding points to a writer on the basis of the degree of his alignment with the working class or the amount of Marxist thought which he has managed to incorporate in his or her work. Doubtless, any Marxist aesthetic must put content rather than form at its centre, and some notion of referentiality is essential. But this should not lead us to follow Lukács in automatically favouring traditional realism over any kind of modernism (though we may well agree with Lukács in rating Thomas Mann – to say nothing of Heinrich Mann, see below – higher than Kafka).

Even less should we adopt that puritanical hostility to anything that smacks of 'decadence' with which Marxism is still widely identified and which achieved its crowning absurdity in Lukács's pronouncement that Mann's *Doktor Faustus* was the 'fullest artistic and intellectual confirmation of the decree of the Central Committee of the Communist Party of the Soviet Union on modern music' (Lukács, 1972, p.22). The most useful corrective here is Herbert Marcuse's claim (deeply indebted to the aesthetics of Theodor Adorno) that all artistic creativity is inherently subversive (Marcuse, 1977, *passim*). Marcuse's work is not, of course, anti-Marxist, as his English translator, with his misrendering of Marcuse's title, would have us believe. Nevertheless it is a powerful attack on the kind of Marxist criticism which timidly dissociates itself from any art that goes beyond the conventions of realism. Lukács's task is still ours: to make the bourgeois heritage fruitful for our cause within a society that is increasingly indifferent to that cause – but we need to define that heritage more comprehensively.

Interpretation and evaluation are influential activities that must be practised responsibly. All literary criticism, like all literature, is an intervention: far from standing apart from the existing universe of discourse, it adds to and hence modifies that universe. This realisation, allied with the potential unleashed by Deconstruction, can tempt Marxists into abandoning any attempt at impartial interpretation of texts and turning literary studies into a battleground on which we arbitrarily politicise every text that will further our enterprise, even where this entails systematic misconstruction. Such wholesale politicisation is the programme urged by Bennett (1979, pp.167–75), exuberantly girding up his loins to do battle with a conservative academic establishment. It is a tempting programme. Faced, for example, with that misconstruction of Brecht's plays which systematically strips them of their socialist meanings (I think, as one example among many, of the recent production of *Mother Courage* at London's Barbican Theatre), one can easily be goaded into responding in kind, by reading socialist meanings into texts where no such meaning was intended. But I can scarcely imagine any programme more certain to discredit both literature and Marxism in the eyes of both our students and the general public.[2]

2. It so happened that I took time off from putting the final touches to this paper to

A Marxist Methodology for Germanistik

Whatever the temptations, we must resist the wholesale carnivalisation of literature into a joyous free-for-all. At the other extreme we have to prevent literary study from degenerating into an abstruse, socially marginalised meta-discipline. On no account must Marxist literary scholarship become, as so much structuralist writing has become, a way of leading the reader away from actual texts into rarefied, self-validating theorising. On the contrary, we need actively to save literary study from those of its practitioners who, inspired principally, it would seem, by Lacan and Derrida, are busy digging their and our graves by turning that study into a wasteland of unintelligible mock-discourse.

We must continue to assert the social relevance of literature, the fact that a relationship exists between literary works and the social reality within which they are produced. But we must also accept that that relationship is not one of simple homology (see Jörg Schönert's article, pp.75–6 above). On no account must we over-react to the denial of all referentiality to literary texts by reverting to any form of naïve reflectionism which reduces, as so much Marxist criticism has done, the intricacy and subtlety of works of art to simple mirror images of the real world (cf. Steve Giles's essay below, pp.261–77). At its worst, such criticism becomes what Eagleton has rightly castigated as 'feebly empiricist "sociology of literature", mechanistically coupling empirical literary facts with empirical sociological ones' (1977, p.90) – i.e. a procedure which 'offers lazy minds a handy prefabricated system of interpretation' (Arvon, 1973, p.113) and which loses sight almost entirely of a work's aesthetic qualities. Who has not at some time heard or read accounts of, say, the novels of Heinrich Böll to which these strictures apply? Yet the relatively simple case of Böll is sufficient to demonstrate the extent to which a writer is the product of a specific time, place and social class and to which he or she has been shaped by prevailing notions of the function of literature. But the same case also demonstrates how far a writer's *oeuvre* is shaped by his or her

---

watch on television Janet Suzman's celebrated production of *Othello* with South African actors. In a brief introduction by Ms Suzman, the play was given a political interpretation by imputing to Iago a racialist motivation that is not to be found in Shakespeare's text. (To Ms Suzman's credit she did not cut from her superb production those passages which rendered her interpretation unsustainable, in which Iago expounds his actual motives of thwarted ambition and sexual jealousy.) This misrepresentation was undertaken in an unquestionably good cause: to increase awareness of the inhumanity of South African racialism; and the response of South African audiences, of which we were given glimpses, appeared to justify it. Yet it must also, for many viewers, have helped discredit the whole concept of the politicisation of literature.

conception of the writer's task, by the available techniques of the genre in which he or she is working, and by his or her own unique, creative imagination. Böll's work also illustrates as well as any how fictional characters and situations simultaneously reproduce, reflect, refract and transform material from the social-historical world in combination with material springing directly from the individual imagination, and how, at the same time, they give voice to those existential absolutes of human experience which are independent of social factors.

Eagleton, influenced here by Macherey, has attempted to replace reflectionism by the notion of ideology, i.e. the basic cultural assumptions which have been 'inscribed', often heavily disguised, in a text, and which it is the critic's task to make explicit, thereby 'explaining' (not 'interpreting') the text (cf. Michael Titzmann's concept of an 'integrative literary history', pp.58–70 above). But in practice, this easily becomes, as E.P. Thompson has demonstrated at some length (1978, pp.193–398), an arid pedantry that is scarcely more illuminating or persuasive than the most naïve reflectionism. More fruitful notions are those, derived from Bakhtin's writings, of 'organised signification' and the 'dialogical' relationship – by which I mean both the dialectical relationship between literature and society and the inter-textual relationships within the universe of literature whose formal resources develop independently of ideology – for the view that this independence is never complete, see the essays above by Titzmann (pp.58–70) and Schönert (pp.71–94). These notions enable us to hold together the separateness of literature from reality and its illuminating relationship to that reality, and also the uniqueness of each individual work of art and its interrelationships with other works. The same comprehensiveness can be found in Lucien Goldmann's (1964) model of a genetic approach to literature. Although this approach takes social factors into account, it avoids any simplistic, materialistic monocausalism by treating the superstructure as to a large degree autonomous, and it investigates both those relationships which evolve *within* the superstructure and those dialectical relationships which evolve *between* superstructure and base.

A currently popular off-shoot of the recent concern with the sociology of literature (see Jörg Schönert's essay above, pp.78–81) is reader-response theory, seductively interesting but of little real value for the understanding of literary texts (see Margot Zutshi's essay above, pp.95–111). The task of criticism is to refine the reader's response, not merely to record it – which is in any case possible only to a very limited extent. The well-known finding that many young GDR readers of Plenzdorf's *Die neuen Leiden des jungen W.* took Edgar Wibeau as a role model is of course of considerable interest, even if it hardly comes as a surprise (see Chris Weedon's essay above, p.157), but it should not deflect us from an investigation of Plenzdorf's much more subtle, distanced presentation of his character. Similarly, while the news that some youthful members of the audience at the première of Christoph Hein's *Die wahre Geschichte des Ah Qu* in East Berlin (1984) stood up and cheered at the line 'Es lebe die Anarchie!' ('Long live anarchy!') tells us something about a particular segment of East German youth, it tells us nothing about Hein's ambiguous and problematic evaluation of that particular utterance within its dramatic context – and it is this latter which is our proper concern.

Structuralism and Deconstruction

The opposite extreme to wholesale materialist reductionism is formed by the structuralist-deconstructionist premises that 'all we have is the words on the page' and that old-style interpretation of texts is an impossibility. The air is nowadays thick with manifestly absurd pronouncements to the effect that literary texts refer to nothing beyond themselves. Similarly, much recent discussion, centring particularly on the work of Bakhtin, Barthes, Foucault, Lacan and Derrida, has addressed the questions of whether the concepts of an 'author' and his 'intention' are at all relevant to the consideration of literary texts and whether, indeed, there is any such thing as an 'author' (Foucault, 1979; cf. Fish, 1980, pp.303–55). In this extreme view, all texts are purely 'inter-textual', i.e. generated by other texts, so that, as Osip Brik appears to have been convinced, *Eugene Onegin* would have been written even if Pushkin had never existed, just as surely as America would have been discovered if Columbus had not lived (Jefferson, 1982, p.124)! A rudimentary understanding of dialectics is enough to demolish this latter absurdity – can it possibly have been meant seriously? – and to bring the relationship, to use T.S. Eliot's terms, between tradition and the individual talent into proper focus. One can then proceed to an investigation of the specifics of that dialectical relationship in any particular case. For the rest, we must energetically demonstrate that we have very much more than the words on the page – fortunately, since words, marks made by printer's ink on paper, mean nothing until they are contextualised and interpreted. It is impossible to view them purely 'as they are', free from any culturally determined presuppositions about their meaning; they do not solve problems, they create them.

Nor must we lose our nerve in the face of massive contemporary scepticism about the referential function of language. That scepticism, which Deconstruction has elevated to one of its supreme principles, has had so formidably sobering an effect on some critics that they appear to be uncertain about whether the study of literature as we know it can continue at all (Feilpern, 1985, p.217). But to recognise that language is a fluid, context-dependent medium which is beset by existential uncertainties and relates to the real world only obliquely and at one remove, via culturally constructed images, need not force us to conclude that language is a 'prison-house' (Jameson, 1972), or drive us to the hysterically defensive overreaction of Derrida's 'il n'y a pas de hors-texte' (1976, p.158).

This latter position is no doubt unassailable on its own terms, but it is useless to anyone who wishes the study of literature to be more than a mandarin academic diversion. Of course words can mean more than one thing; of course we say that we 'know' a thing when we cannot in fact give a precise, watertight account of it; and all use of language is doubtless a 'ride across Lake Constance' (Peter Handke).[3] But we are not obliged to be paralysed by these realisations: even if we cannot remove all uncertainties and ambiguities from linguistic texts, we can at least, by careful contextualisation, remove as many as possible. Let us concede what are, since Wittgenstein, two philosophical commonplaces: that all use of language is ultimately ludic, and that 'meaning' is ultimately a matter of expedient, not to say conspiratorial consensus. Let us further concede that, as Leibniz was the first to prove, any finite set of observations can be accommodated within an infinite number of theories, so that any text is capable of an infinite number of 'interpretations'. We may not be able, in strict terms, to disprove the notion that Gregor Samsa's father is the real hero of *Die Verwandlung*, or the Army Chaplain of *Mother Courage*, or that Shui Ta is 'right' in *Der gute Mensch von Sezuan*, or that in any drama some or all of the characters, for all or part of the time, are insane, or pretending to be insane, or dissimulating for the benefit of an invisible observer, or that they do or do not mean what they say, and so on. But let us also assert the utter pointlessness and worse of allowing literary study to

3. The reference is to the ballad by Gustav Schwab 'Der Reiter und der Bodensee' (1828/9), which tells of a horseman who unwittingly crossed Lake Constance when it was frozen, and died of shock on realising what he had done. Peter Handke's play *Der Ritt über den Bodensee* (1971) alludes to this ballad as a metaphor for the false sense of security with which people use everyday language.

degenerate into a random scanning of such peripheral possibilities.

Reviewing Roman Jakobson's long-awaited, posthumously published *Language and Literature*, a literary critic of *The Financial Times* felt able to proclaim with satisfaction: 'There are no structuralists now' (Watson, 1988). One awaits with some impatience a similar obituary to at least those forms of Deconstruction which offer not just a method of unpacking complex texts that has its uses in some cases, but elevate that method to the status of a crypto-ontology. Marxists should certainly see it as part of their task to hasten the demise of that disastrous aberration since it will, after all, not necessarily die a natural death. On the contrary, there are signs that, institutionalised and routinised (though admittedly never predictable), it is fair set to find work for whole generations of scholars in rendering our entire literary heritage either trivial or unintelligible. But we will be able to counter the mysterious appeal of Deconstruction only by providing a better, more evidently rewarding form of literary study. For the rest, let us take de Man, Derrida and the like at their word and see them not as massively intimidating individual presences but as manifestations of a particular cultural malaise (cf. Richard Sheppard's remarks below, pp.288–9). While they deconstruct us, let us historicise them (see Jameson, 1984, for an indication of the form such historicisation might take), and get on with the real job of addressing the problem of literary referentiality in our own way. Meanwhile it is cheering to see that believers – not just Marxist ones – in the illuminating power of 'realism', however problematic that concept has become, are striking back (Graff, 1979; Said, 1984; Stern, 1986; Tallis, 1988).

We must try to help interpretation re-emerge, enriched by its bruising encounters with those structuralist and post-structuralist poetics which would condemn all interpretation as naïve and arbitrary, and made more cautious and self-critical, but not thereby helplessly intimidated to the point where we hand literature over to those who insist that it doesn't 'mean' anything. Furthermore, the revulsion from Deconstruction may be expected to encourage a revival of other approaches as well. There are, for example, alarming signs that the Leavisites are on the move again, with their militant elitism which seeks to elevate myopic anti-urban and anti-modernist prejudices, via a particular literary canon, into first principles for the evaluation not only of literature but of culture and society in their entirety. Witness the success of Simon Gray's play *The Common Pursuit*, which has prompted one influential critic to speculate that the time might be ripe, ten years after Leavis's death, for the emergence of his successor (Hayman, 1988). This too will need to be energetically combated, but Marxists must not make the same mistake of allowing their own convictions to generate a one-sided alternative canon watched over by a self-regarding priesthood.

Literary Language

The question of a work's 'literariness', declared by Jakobson to be the sole legitimate object of literary scholarship (cf. Jefferson, 1982, p.21), cannot enjoy that status for a Marxist. But neither can it be avoided altogether. It is time for Marxists to go beyond Althusser, Eagleton and Macherey and to confront, even if they cannot solve, the problem posed by the special nature of aesthetic experience, that problem of which Marx recorded his puzzled awareness when he reflected on his response to Greek art (cf. Jameson in Arvon, 1973, p.xvi). This means that we must address the exceedingly difficult question of what constitutes 'literary' language, rather than sidestep it either by means of dismissive references to 'commodity-fetishism' or 'the text-as-object', or by reducing it to a question of ideology or social practice, or by narrowing down our critical interest to such texts – like the novel and drama of Social Realism – as appear to 'reflect' the real world in a relatively straightforward way (cf. Michael Titzmann's discussion of this question on pp.58–70 above).

For the time being, I would suggest, the question of what constitutes literary language is another question which can be answered only empirically and ostensively, by a close descriptive account of specific texts. It is of course perfectly possible for such accounts to draw on all the insights that Formalism and Structuralism have provided into the way literary language operates, not at the expense of a social-historical contextualisation but as a necessary complement to it. In the absence of a precisely formulated theory, the best thing for any scholar to do is make careful and precise observations – knowing, of course, that no observation can be entirely free of prior theoretical assumptions, but consoling himself with the awareness that even the most theory-dependent observations may, in their turn, help to generate new and better theories. As Lord Beveridge put it fifty years ago, speaking of the young science of Economics and using an illustration from the history of Astronomy:

> As a theorist [Tycho Brahe] believed to his last day in the year 1601 that the planets went round the sun and that the sun and the stars went round the earth as the fixed centre of the universe. As an observer he made with

infinite patience and integrity thousands of records of the stars and planets; upon these records Kepler, in due course, based his laws and brought the truth to light. If we will take Tycho Brahe for our example, we may find encouragement also. It matters little how wrong we are with our existing theories, if we are honest and careful with our observations. (Lipsey, 1983, p.xii)

Wider Considerations and the Canon of German Literature

The more general tasks facing Marxist literary criticism and teaching are very obvious. We must keep alive, in dark times, a socialist critique of capitalist market-place barbarism, and be thankful that we have Brecht's masterpieces, and more, to help us. We may expect in the years ahead an increasing number of students who have been taught at school that history is more centrally about events in the lives of various royal families than about anything to do with social or economic change. We must offer them, through the study of historical fiction and drama, an alternative conception of history, and thus of those political and economic factors in their own lives which find little or no place in their school curriculum. They may well also have been taught that, as Kenneth Baker, then Education Secretary, was recently able to inform Russian schoolchildren, Tennyson's 'Charge of the Light Brigade' is 'great poetry'. We must try to persuade them otherwise, with the help of the legacy of German anti-war literature from Heym and Stramm to Böll and Grass. We must also challenge any teaching of eighteenth-century classical literature that omits a critique of its liberal, individualist assumptions and down-grading of collective values, in particular of the central, Schillerian notion of ethical education via aesthetic experience (the novels of Arnold Zweig are of great value here). But we must not, in so doing, align ourselves with those who, by their profoundly anti-humanist antics, lend support to those political forces which are already hostile to the whole notion of education and scholarship in the arts. This is no to time to help create a crisis in our subject by rhetorically proclaiming the existence of one. On the contrary, our task is to rebut the incessantly repeated charges of ivory-tower elitism, to demonstrate the social relevance of literary studies, and to insist, with Habermas, on the continuing project of the Enlightenment in which literature has a central role to play in the raising of human consciousness.

A whole host of works await fundamental reassessment. Macherey's (1966) strategy, taken over also by Eagleton (1976), of interrogating literary texts for their gaps and silences is particularly applicable to German literature, so much of which purports to be socio-critical while actually rooted in fundamentally conservative assumptions. A few examples. In place of the supposed 'objectivity' to which Naturalist drama laid claim, we need to foreground the deep conservatism of Gerhart Hauptmann's early work, especially that of *Die Weber*. Thomas Mann's *Mario und der Zauberer* needs to be seen as a severely flawed allegory of the appeal of Fascism because of its almost total bracketing-out of political and economic factors, rather than as the brilliantly prophetic masterpiece as which it is generally presented. We need to demonstrate by close analysis that Heinrich Mann's *Der Untertan* is of far greater value than *The Magic Mountain* to anyone seriously interested in arriving at a closer understanding of Wilhelmine Germany, and superior to *Doktor Faustus* in its illumination of the roots of Fascism. We do not need to see, with Brecht, every conversation about trees as almost a crime because it includes a silence about so many atrocities. But we should certainly challenge, as Eagleton has done with *Middlemarch* (1976, pp.118–23), the standing of *Buddenbrooks* as a masterpiece of realistic fiction, by pointing out all those aspects of nineteenth-century Germany that it omits: industrialisation, the rise of the labour movement, changes in the position of women, and a lot more besides.

It is often objected that to level such criticisms is to claim an illusory, absolute, final knowledge of history as a yardstick by which works of fiction can be arrogantly measured. Although in Macherey's own case this criticism appears justified, no such arrogance is necessarily entailed. All we are doing by foregrounding the gaps in texts is making value-judgements to set against other value-judgements. Our appeal is not to some supposed monopoly of historical understanding, but merely to a general consensus regarding what is historically important (cf. Michael Titzmann's remarks on 'historical knowledge' above, pp.62–4). Such reassessments – and readers will doubtless be able to provide many more examples – are not a matter of applying a sophisticated new methodology, but simply of asserting the importance of political and historical perspectives as essential elements in the interpretation and evaluation of these works.

The German literary canon needs to be revised. The very idea of a literary canon has, of course, often been rejected by Marxists as a particularly obvious manifestation of Marx's insight that at any given time and place the ruling ideas are the ideas of the ruling class. But without some degree of consensus as to what we ought to be studying, we would have no subject, and in practice we should aim for modifications of the existing canon. This must not be a matter of seeking to promote minor writers beyond their real worth on the basis of their progressive political alignments. Rather, it is a matter of claiming due status for major writers who have been persistently down-graded because of such alignment; of helping, for example, to establish Heinrich Mann, Anna Seghers and Arnold Zweig as writers of the first rank. It also involves rescuing from the deformations of anti-Marxist scholarship those major writers whose status is not in dispute, but whose political allegiances are systematically suppressed. The outstanding example from the nineteenth century is the Marxist *avant la lettre*, Büchner; and in the twentieth century it is Brecht, of whose major masterpieces a full socialist interpretation has yet to be provided for the British public.

The study of GDR literature is, of course, an obvious wide and varied field for Marxist scholars. I wish here to single out only one topic which seems to me to be in urgent need of reassessment: the theory and practice of Socialist Realism, which in the first place needs to be properly contextualised and historicised (it being now more of a historical than a contemporary phenomenon). It then needs to be rescued from the almost universal and indiscriminate disdain with which it has been dismissed by Western Marxists as a product of philistine dogmatism. Marxists should not feel that they need to prove their intellectual and aesthetic sophistication by such disdain, but should, on the contrary, be defending the concept. This is best done not by extending the notion of realism, as Garaudy did (Baxandall, 1972, p.253), to include whatever we happen to approve of (in Garaudy's case Kafka, St John Perse and Picasso), but by stressing both the value *per se* of a committed art which attempts to grapple with the great social themes of our age, and the importance of the theory for those writers, from Brecht and Anna Seghers onwards, who have used it as a means of clarifying their own creative intentions. These include writers who have produced, quite recently, valuable work entirely within the conventions of the theory, e.g. Hermann Kant's *Der Aufenthalt* (1977) and Dieter Noll's *Kippenberg* (1979).

The Claim to Scientificity

Marxism tends to be listed among the 'dogmatic' schools of literary theory, and a major part of our effort must be invested in the attempt to free Marxism from that reputation, first by insisting, in our critical practice, that it is a set of tools, not dogmas, and second, by accepting the historical and rhetorical nature of Marxist (as of any other) discourse. Our approach will gain a hearing not by virtue of the 'provability' of its basic assumptions, but by virtue of its practical fruits. We will persuade others to accept our view of the world as 'intelligent', i.e. as not merely serving our own vested interests, only if we can offer 'intelligent' criticism in Kermode's sense (1982).

Marxist literary scholars must also accept that they are in competition with other theoretical and critical approaches and, moreover, that various forms of Marxism, especially 'humanist' and 'structuralist' Marxism, are in competition with one another. Indeed, we will benefit by stressing the wide variety of Marxist approaches in our subject. We must accept that good science, as Kuhn and Feyerabend have taught us, is not the product of any particular theory or methodology, but simply what good scientists do (Jenkinson, 1982, pp.22–4). We must pursue our craft in good faith, not hiding behind theoretical insights into the ultimate ambiguity of all linguistic utterances in order to impose *parti pris* readings of our own. We must not claim a chimerical 'scientificity' (that this 'euphoric dream' has not entirely evaporated is demonstrated by Michael Titzmann's essay in this volume). Let us remember that, as Gödel showed, not even Mathematics is an entirely self-validating discourse; but let us not be demoralised by that fact. Bertrand Russell may have commented, on reading Gödel's celebrated proof, that 'arithmetic totters', but he, along with the rest of us, continued to do arithmetic with some confidence as to its practical efficacy. And if we cannot have 'scientificity', let us avoid the pretence of it, such as Eagleton's proliferation of abbreviations (GMP, LMP, AI, AuI and the rest), which has prompted at least one critic to suspect (or affect to suspect) Eagleton of parody (of Althusser) or self-parody (Feilpern, 1985, p.56). Nor must we claim any privileged access to historical understanding, but simply continue to assert the importance of striving for as full a historical understanding as possible of the phenomena with which we are concerned. We must, in short, attempt to contribute to an inter-subjective consensus in the hope that that consensus will increasingly come to include the Marxist vision.

We must also accept that not all literature, either wittingly or unwittingly, illuminates history and society, and that there are other human needs which it meets. Indeed, we must argue forcefully that to postpone indefinitely those other needs on the grounds that there are more important tasks for literature, is one of several disastrous extensions of the blinkered materialism of 'Food is the first thing. Morals follow on',[4] in which vulgar Marxism joins hands with petty-bourgeois philistinism. Men can no more afford to defer the satisfaction of aesthetic needs than they can afford, in the West, to defer concern for the poor, the old and the sick until the affluent declare themselves satiated, or, in the East, to defer basic human and civil rights until a socialist economy has been fully established (cf. Chris Weedon's essay above, pp.158–62). As Jefferson and Robey acknowledge (1982, p.13), commitment to Marxism, as to any other 'theory', is a matter not just of epistemology, but of ethics, and although we cannot prove that ours is the best way forward for humanity, we may hope that it will nevertheless one day be accepted as such, and work in our way towards that end. As Goldmann saw (Birchall, 1977, p.105), since there is no prospect of radical change for the time being, the best thing that Marxists can do in pursuit of that end is to keep their vision alive while competing with bourgeois scholarship on its own ground. More is at stake than scholarship.

References

Arvon, H. (1973) *Marxist Aesthetics*, Cornell U.P., Ithaca and London

Baxandall, L. (ed.) (1972) *Radical Perspectives in the Arts*, Penguin, Harmondsworth

Bennett, T. (1979) *Formalism and Marxism*, Methuen, London

Birchall, I.H. (1977) 'Marxism and Literature' in J. Routh and J. Wolff (eds), *The Sociology of Literature: Theoretical Approaches*, University of Keele, pp.92–108

Clark, K. (1969) *Civilisation: A Personal View*, BBC Books, London

Derrida, J. (1976) *Of Grammatology*, Johns Hopkins U.P., Baltimore

Eagleton, T. (1976) *Criticism and Ideology: A Study in Marxist Literary Theory*, New Left Books, London

Eagleton, T. (1977) 'Marxist Literary Criticism' in J. Routh and J. Wolff (eds), *The Sociology of Literature: Theoretical Approaches*, University of Keele, pp.85–91

Feilpern, H. (1985) *Beyond Deconstruction: The Uses and Abuses of Literary Theory*, Clarendon Press, Oxford

Fish, S. (1980) *Is There a Text in This Class?*, Harvard U.P., Cambridge, Mass. and London

---

4. Macheath's dictum from Brecht's *The Threepenny Opera* (cf. Steve Giles's essay below, pp. 261–77).

Foucault, M. (1979) 'What is an Author?' in J.V. Harari (ed.), *Textual Strategies*, Methuen, London, pp.141–60

Gallas, H. (1971) *Marxistische Literaturtheorie*, Luchterhand, Neuwied and Berlin

Goldmann, L. (1964) *Pour une sociologie du roman*, Gallimard, Paris

Graff, G. (1979) *Literature against Itself: Literary Texts in Modern Society*, Chicago U.P.

Hayman, R. (1988) 'Will the next F.R. Leavis please stand up?', *Independent*, 17 May 1988

Jameson, F. (1972) *The Prison-House of Language*, Princeton U.P.

Jameson, F. (1984) 'Postmodernism, or The Cultural Logic of Late Capitalism', *New Left Review*, no.146, pp.53–92

Jefferson, A. (1982) 'Russian Formalism' in A. Jefferson and D. Robey (eds), *Modern Literary Theory: A Comparative Introduction*, Batsford, London, pp.16–37

Jefferson, A. and Robey, D. (1982) 'Introduction' in *Modern Literary Theory: A Comparative Introduction*, Batsford, London, pp.1–15

Jenkinson, D. (1982) 'Towards a "Scientific" Study of GDR Literature: Some Reflections on a New Approach', *GDR Monitor*, 8, 15–26

Kermode, F. (1982) 'Intelligent Theory', *London Review of Books*, 7, 20 October 1982

Lipsey, R.G. (1983) *An Introduction to Positive Economics*, Weidenfeld and Nicolson, London

Lukács, G. (1972) *Studies in European Realism*, Merlin, London

Macherey, P. (1966) *Pour une théorie de la production littéraire*, François Maspero, Paris

McLellan, D. (ed.) (1983) *Marx: The First Hundred Years*, Fontana, London

Marcuse, H. (1977) *Die Permanenz der Kunst: Wider eine bestimmte marxistische Ästhetik*, Hanser, Munich (E.T. as *The Aesthetic Dimension: Towards a Critique of Marxist Aesthetics*, Macmillan, London, 1979)

Marx, K. and Engels, F. (1968) *Selected Works in One Volume*, Lawrence and Wishart, London

Prawer, S.S. (1976) *Karl Marx and World Literature*, Oxford U.P.

Said, E. (1984) *The World, The Text, and The Critic*, Faber, London

Seghers, A. (1970) *Über Kunstwerk und Wirklichkeit: I. Die Tendenz in der reinen Kunst*, Akademie-Verlag, Berlin-GDR

Stern, J.P. (1986) 'In Praise of Erich Auerbach's *Mimesis*', *London German Studies*, III, 194–211

Tallis, R. (1988) *In Defence of Realism*, Arnold, London

Thody, P. (1977) *Roland Barthes: A Conservative Estimate*, Macmillan, London

Thompson, E.P. (1978) *The Poverty of Theory*, Merlin, London

Watson, G. (1988) 'Old Concepts in Any Language', *Financial Times*, 25 June 1988

Williams, R. (1977) *Marxism and Literature*, Oxford U.P.

−13−

From Althusser to Brecht – Formalism, Materialism, and *The Threepenny Opera*

STEVE GILES

I'm not exactly asking for an opera.
          Macheath, *The Threepenny Opera*

This isn't an opera. It's *Realpolitik*.
          Balicke, *Drums in the Night*

Introduction

In the course of the 1970s, radical sociology, philosophy and cultural studies in Britain came to be dominated by the work of Louis Althusser. Indeed, for many left-wing intellectuals, his ideas became a part of everyday life and were considered to be synonymous with Marxist theory as such (Benton, 1984, p.228; Lovell, 1983, p.4). This was due above all to his rejection of the simplistic philosophical basis of the orthodox Marxism of the Second International[1] and his critique of economism and technological reductionism in Marxist sociology. The originality of Althusser's position lay in the fact that his rethinking of Marxism was grounded not in the neo-Hegelian, humanist reading of Marx sanctified by the Paris Manuscripts of 1844, but in French Structuralism and the conventionalist philosophy of science of Gaston Bachelard (Benton, 1984, pp.1–31; Jay, 1985, pp. 385–42). Althusser was particularly influential through his reformulation of Marxist theory of ideology, and his insistence on

---

This paper was completed while I was an Alexander von Humboldt-Stiftung Fellow at the Freie Universität, Berlin, and I would like to acknowledge the help of the Alexander von Humboldt-Stiftung. I also wish to thank Cathy Raymond for her helpful comments and I am particularly indebted to Stephen Hinton for his invaluable advice, expertise and encouragement.
1. The philosophical presuppositions of classical Marxism are outlined in Arato (1973/4).

the relative autonomy and transformative potential of superstructures played a crucial role in the appropriation of his work by radical cultural critics hostile to the tired clichés of Socialist Realism and reflection theory (Lovell, 1983, pp.79–87; Bennett, 1979, pp.95–110 and 127–42).

Althusser's aesthetic theory is contained in three essays produced in 1962 and 1966: 'The "Piccolo Teatro": Bertolazzi and Brecht. Notes on a Materialist Theatre' (1982a), 'A Letter on Art in Reply to André Daspre' (1984a), and 'Cremonini, Painter of the Abstract' (1971). In these essays, Althusser engages with the traditional problems of Marxist criticism in the context of his main concern from 1960 to 1965, the rewriting of Marxist philosophy and social theory, so that he is particularly interested in the relationships between art and ideology, art and the subject, and art and knowledge. These preoccupations will be reflected in my own discussion of Althusser and Brecht, which will be in three parts. In the first, I shall present the main contentions in Althusser's essays on art; in the second, I shall attempt an Althusserian reading of *The Threepenny Opera* (Brecht, 1979); and in the final part, I shall assess the applicability and viability of Althusserian aesthetic theory.

Rewriting Marxist Criticism

The central categories in Althusser's account of the relationship between art and ideology are perceptibility and distance. In his 1966 essays, he repeatedly points out that 'authentic' art, as opposed to 'works of an average or mediocre level' (1984a, p.174), has the capacity to stimulate our perceptual awareness of the ideology from which it emerges. This capacity derives from a process of internal distanciation which is, presumably, modelled on Brecht's conception of 'alienation' or *Verfremdung*.[2] By disrupting our relationship to ideology, authentic art challenges our entire mode of being in the world because, for Althusser, ideology is not simply a cognitive or theoretical category, but 'slides into all human activity' and is 'identical with the "lived" experience of human existence itself' (1984a, p.175). In describing ideology in this way, Althusser implicitly draws on his 1963 essay 'Marxism and Humanism' (1982b). Here, ideology is characterised as an *unconscious* system of represen-

---

2. The standard French translation of the Brechtian term 'Verfremdung' is 'distantiation' or 'distancement'. See Althusser (1962) and Barthes (1964), pp.48–52, 84–9. Brecht's reception in France in the 1950s is dealt with in exemplary fashion in Hüfner (1968).

tations which performs a *necessary* function in the social totality. *Unconscious*, because its representations structure human consciousness and behaviour so fundamentally that we are unaware of the ideological constitution of the realities which we take for granted in our inner and outer worlds, and *necessary*, because, in constituting individuals as social subjects, it is essential to the process of social reproduction and cannot therefore be overcome or dispensed with in any social formation.

The latter points are elucidated in Althusser's most substantial discussion of ideology, the 1969 essay 'Ideology and Ideological State Apparatuses' (1984b). Here, the subject is said to be *constituted* by ideology in the sense that personal and social identity are structured by the system of collective representations at work in a particular social formation. Consequently, *social reproduction* is secured by virtue of the role ideology plays, first, in ensuring that subjects assent to the legitimacy of the social formation and their position or status within it, and second, in equipping them with the skills and attitudes necessary for the successful performance of their social roles. At the same time, in capitalist society at least, the subject's conception of personal and social reality is said to be problematic inasmuch as ideology represents to us not the system of real economic and political conditions that govern our existence, but our imaginary relationship to those conditions. Thus, by subscribing to the humanist myth that we spontaneously generate our actions and beliefs, we fail to grasp that, as subjects, we are in fact structured by networks of societal relations over which we exert no conscious or voluntary control.

Given Althusser's theory of the Subject, it is not surprising that he should reject what he terms the humanist account of artistic production, according to which the work of art is a direct expression of the artist's creative powers. In his discussion of Cremonini's paintings, Althusser commends the fact that they explicitly repudiate the categories of humanism by presenting the human face, which is otherwise taken to be the soul and site of subjectivity, in a deformed and anonymous manner. As a result, he claims, the percipient is prevented from identifying with Cremonini's images so that the circuit of ideological recognition and confirmation is broken. This appears to be the closest art can come to attaining cognitive status. As Althusser observes: 'We cannot "recognize" ourselves (ideologically) in his pictures. And it is because we cannot "recognize" ourselves in them that we can *know* ourselves in them, in the specific form provided by art, here, by painting' (1971, p.218).

It might seem at this point that art is being vested with a cognitive capacity far superior to that of simply making ideology perceptible. Nevertheless, Althusser's formulation is consistent with his general account of the relationship between art and science. According to Althusser, the crucial distinction between art and science consists not in the fact that they deal with different domains of reality, but in the way in which they present the same object – namely the system of complex mechanisms and relations which constitutes lived experience but is not immediately visible to us. While science develops concepts which make it possible to identify and explain social reality in logical and propositional terms, art is restricted to perceptual mediation of the real. It is as if 'art makes us "see" "conclusions without premises", whereas knowledge makes us penetrate into the mechanism which produces the "conclusions" out of the "premisses"' (1984a, p.176). If, however, art works at the level of perception and societal relations are essentially non-visible, how can art possibly give access to reality? Althusser concedes that it would be absurd to suggest that an artist could somehow 'paint' the conflict between forces and relations of production. Nevertheless, his discussion of Cremonini's work suggests that the disposition of formal relations within a painting can denote real relations negatively, either by inverting or dislocating supposedly 'normal' connections, or, as in the case of Cremonini's faces, by refusing the humanist pact of identification and implying the existence of structural relations which, because they are intrinsically non-visible, can only be depicted as an absence.

While Althusser's 1966 essays are particularly concerned to explicate the ways in which authentic art may disrupt ideology, his commentary on Brecht makes it clear that he is under no illusions about the ideological susceptibility of art-forms in general. Indeed, he suggests that, with the notable exception of Shakespeare and Molière, classical theatre simply reproduced the dominant ideology of the epoch. It uncritically transmitted 'the "familiar", "well-known", transparent myths in which a society or an age can recognize itself (but not know itself)' (1982a, p.144),[3] and sustained this process of recognition by inviting the audience to identify with the consciousness of the central figure. Brecht, on the other hand, wished 'to produce a critique of the spontaneous ideology in which

3. Althusser's discussion here appears to be heavily indebted to Barthes (1957) – on which Barthes was working when he wrote his review essays on Brecht in the mid-1950s. There are numerous parallels between the account of Brecht in Barthes (1964) and the discussion of ideology and myth in Barthes (1957), pp.203–47. The most convincing attempt to present a structuralist reading of Brecht is Heath (1974).

men live' (1982a, p.144), and thus radicalised the spectator's consciousness by shattering the mirror of self-recognition provided by classical theatre. Brecht refused to make the central figure's illusory self-consciousness the centre of the dramatic universe and distanced the spectator from the protagonist in order to generate an active and critical relationship between spectator and performance which was the precondition for the spectator's completion of the play in real life. Although Althusser concedes that the theatrical devices associated with *Verfremdung* played a crucial role in developing this new relationship, he also emphasises that theatrical distance is grounded in the distance at the heart of the play itself. In Althusser's view, the overriding feature of Brecht's 'great' plays is their a-symmetrical structure: they are 'works marked by an internal dissociation, an unresolved alterity' (1982a, p.142). Indeed, it is this latent formal property which constitutes their critique of the illusions of consciousness and elucidation of its real conditions, rather than any explicit political statements included in the text – in the songs, for example. Because consciousness can gain access to the real only by discovering 'what *is other than itself*' (1982a, p.143), a truly materialist theatre can only generate critique thanks to the dynamics of an internal structure which enables the spectator to discern the abstract relationship between the ideological consciousness of the figures in the play and the real conditions of their existence. By the same token, Althusser claims that an authentically materialist criticism must attend not to manifest or surface features of action and characterisation, but to the deep and hidden meaning which these indirectly imply.

Re-reading *The Threepenny Opera*

In order to facilitate an Althusserian reading of *The Threepenny Opera*, I shall structure my analysis in terms of the following scheme, which summarises the key propositions of Althusser's aesthetic theory:

(1) Authentic art and criticism are anti-humanist. They reject the expressive theory of artistic production together with the identificatory model of artistic reception, and presuppose a materialist theory of the Subject.
(2) The essence of the work of art consists not in the author's intentions or in the surface features of the text, but in its latent structure. It is this latent structure which an adequate reading must expose.

(3) The latent structure of an authentic work of art is characterised by formal dissociation and disjuncture. This internal distanciation enables authentic art to make ideology perceptible, so as to disrupt the spontaneous understanding of everyday life.

(4) Authentic art permits the recipient to discern the real relationship between ideological consciousness and its real conditions, thereby paving the way for the dissipation of the illusions of consciousness in real life.

Bertolt Brecht's Theoretical Anti-Humanism

The theoretical writings which Brecht produced in relation to *The Threepenny Opera* make it quite clear that his position was rigorously anti-humanist. In his 1931 comments on *The Threepenny Opera*, Brecht noted that the emergence of epic forms in drama is bound up with the development of materialist philosophy, and he even claimed that only epic forms of representation are adequate to the Marxist theory of the Subject, according to which the human essence consists in 'the ensemble of all societal relations' (Unseld, 1978, p.100).[4] In *The Threepenny Lawsuit*,[5] Brecht presents two main arguments in support of these contentions. First, he suggests that the representational techniques of illusionism can no longer adequately reproduce reality because social reality can no longer be directly perceived or experienced in its totality by an individual subject. All that is immediately visible to us in capitalist society is the reification of human relationships, since social reality as such has become functional and abstract (Unseld, 1978, p.135). Second, this fundamental shift in the nature of social reality involves the disintegration of the individualistic conception of the Subject – which Brecht exemplifies with reference to the nineteenth-century novel. By dissolving everything into processes and concentrating on the individual's external behaviour, capitalism destroyed the introspective psychology of the bourgeois novel together with the notion that man is the measure of all things. Accordingly, both capitalism and behaviourism, its ideological counterpart, should be seen as in-

---

4. Willett translates this phrase as 'the sum of all social circumstances' (Brecht, 1978, p.46) and entirely misses the point that Brecht is quoting Marx's Sixth Thesis on Feuerbach.
5. Bertolt Brecht, 'Der Dreigroschenprozess: Ein soziologisches Experiment' in Unseld (1978), pp.117–76. Stephen Hinton informs me that contemporary criticism tends to refer to the legal controversy surrounding this text as Brecht's *Beule* [pronounced 'boiler'] suit.

herently progressive phenomena, and modern art must take full account of their revolutionary impact on social relations and the theory of the Subject (Unseld, 1978, p.143; Brecht, 1978, p.50).

The Threepenny Lawsuit also contains important discussions of artistic production and reception. Brecht utterly rejects expressive theory, though his argument focuses on capitalist economic realities rather than invoking a materialist conception of the subject. According to Brecht, the work of art is radically separated from its producer as soon as it is marketed and takes on the form of a commodity. Once it has been subjected to market forces, its structural integrity is shattered: instead of organically embodying the personality of its creator, it resembles a motor car in that it is divisible into a set of composite parts which are related merely mechanically (Unseld, 1978, pp.150–4). Capitalism undermines the propositions of bourgeois aesthetics so fundamentally that, as Brecht concedes, when speaking of the commodified cultural forms of capitalism, it may be necessary to abandon the category of art altogether since art can no longer be conceived of as sacred, eternal and disinterested (Unseld, 1978, pp.169–70). Progressive cultural forms, on the other hand, must, according to Brecht, be anti-expressive and scientific, providing the recipient with detailed information about human conduct that can be applied in everyday life. Instead of motivating action in terms of the individual's character or inner life, progressive art concentrates on the typical external behaviour of figures performing specific functions, and this means in turn that it is necessarily anti-empathetic. Progressive art aims not to establish a bond of identification between recipient and work or recipient and author, but seeks to enable the recipient to derive causal relationships inductively from the behavioural attitudes presented in the work (Unseld, 1978, pp.131–2; Brecht, 1978, p.48). As far as the theatre is concerned, Brecht concludes, the spectator must be given the opportunity to compare the various modes of behaviour displayed by the actors in order to adopt a critical perspective on the political and economic relationships that underpin observable social reality. Only then will he or she be able to see that human beings are both conditioned by specific societal relationships and capable of changing them (Brecht, 1978, p.86).

Towards a Materialist Hermeneutic

The above demonstration of Brecht's anti-humanism draws on material directly or indirectly associated with *The Threepenny Opera* and so might appear to contradict the basic premises of Althusserian theory. To the extent that this material attempts to produce scientific knowledge of art and society, the objection can be refuted, but different considerations apply to Brecht's specific discussions of *The Threepenny Opera*. Since Althusserian theory rejects reference to the author's intentions as a means of grasping the essence of a particular work, any acquaintance with Brecht's commentaries, including the detailed 'Notes' of 1931, would appear to be superfluous to a materialist reading of *The Threepenny Opera*.[6] However, the problematic status of the text makes such an interpretative strategy highly questionable. Although *The Threepenny Opera* was first performed and published in 1928, the 'standard' text, which forms the basis for virtually all critical analysis of the work, derives from the revised version published in Volume 3 of the *Versuche* in 1931,[7] which also contained Brecht's 'Notes to *The Threepenny Opera*'. It has been argued that the alterations to the 1928 text and the 'Notes' are complementary parts of a strategy intended to make the work seem more explicitly Marxist in order to counter 'the deep-rooted moral ambivalence' of the earlier version (Speirs, 1977, p.29). Nevertheless, it is difficult to see how even the most rigorously Althusserian reading of *The Threepenny Opera* could ignore Brecht's interventions here, if only to argue that the greater explicitness of the later version is politically and aesthetically suspect. Epic theatre is, however, characterised precisely by a tendency to explicitness which is intended to link it with other institutions of intellectual activity, and is best exemplified in its use of songs and titles.

The songs in *The Threepenny Opera* usually play a crucial part in its interpretation, not least because they deal overtly with the ideological implications of the action. This applies most obviously to the three 'Threepenny Finales', which deliberate on the material constraints informing human behaviour, and to the 'Ballad of Sexual Slavery', which is located literally at the work's centre. It is also true, though more indirectly, of those interpolated songs which do not play any evident role in characterisation or in furthering the action, the classic example being Polly's 'Pirate Jenny' song, which is sung by Jenny in the film version and which Ernst Bloch, somewhat ingeniously, interpreted as an apocalyptic anthem of revolution (Unseld, 1978, pp.290–4). Given Althusser's insistence that an adequate reading of a work of art must expose its *latent* structure, a strict Althusserian reading of *The Threepenny Opera* would have to

6. See Brecht (1979), pp.89–98; Brecht (1978), pp.43–7, 84–90 and Hecht (1985), pp.9–16, 62–4.
7. See Speirs (1977) and Hennenberg (1985). For a comprehensive account of the differences between the two main versions of the work see Giles (1989).

refuse any consideration of this material. At the same time, the formal dissociation and disjuncture required of authentic art is exemplified in the musical and theatrical settings of the songs, whose presentation plays a crucial role in establishing the separation and multiplicity of discursive levels specific to epic theatre. This is achieved partly through lighting changes and the projection of song titles, and partly by virtue of the visible change in the actor's theatrical function when singing. The aim of such techniques is to encourage the spectator to engage in complex seeing, thereby preventing his or her incorporation into a unilinear theatrical process designed to maximise empathetic identification with the central figure(s). In the case of the songs, this shift towards discursive plurality is reinforced by the fact that the singer may sing against the melody – or even not sing at all – and by the dissociation of melody and rhythm typical of Weill's music.[8]

Distance, Perceptibility and Ideology

In his brief comments on didacticism and entertainment in the type of theatre associated with Piscator and *The Threepenny Opera* (Hecht, 1985, p.64), Brecht argues that such productions were characterised by disruption and dissociation rather than organic unity, and this appears to be borne out by the above discussion of song. There, attention was directed to issues of performance rather than text, yet in his analysis of Giorgio Strehler's production of *El Nost Milan*, Althusser insists that a play's latent structure is essentially a textual property, logically independent of the intentions of writer and director (1982a, p.141).[9] Althusser's own detailed account of one particular realisation of *El Nost Milan*, however, renders his sharp distinction between text and performance problematic, and although I shall demonstrate that the text of *The Threepenny Opera* is indeed characterised by internal disjunction and dissociation, it is important to remember that the degree to which a play makes ideology perceptible depends in practice on the nature of its theatrical realisation. This crucial point must be borne in mind throughout the following discussion of the structural and self-conscious aspects

8. See Brecht (1978), pp.84–6; Theodor W. Adorno, 'Zur Frankfurter Aufführung der *Dreigroschenoper*' and 'Zur Musik der Dreigroschenoper' in Unseld (1978), pp.271–7; Ernst Bloch, 'Zur Dreigroschenoper' in Unseld (1978), pp.287–9. For further discussion see Hinton (1990).
9. Giorgio Strehler pioneered epic theatre in Italy in the 1950s, and his first public production of a Brecht play was *The Threepenny Opera* on 10 February 1956. Willett reprints extracts from a conversation between Brecht and Strehler about this production in Brecht (1979), pp.100–5.

of *The Threepenny Opera* and that work's presentation of the relationship between self and role.

In structural terms, *The Threepenny Opera* is a classic piece of epic composition. It constantly undermines the evolutionary dynamic of dramatic writing in that there is no causal or organic link between one scene and the next, and linear flow within scenes is disrupted because they are organised in terms of montage. Moreover, the spectator's awareness of the text's epic structure is reinforced by its defamiliarisation of traditional dramatic devices. *The Threepenny Opera* consists of three acts, each of which has three scenes, and culminates in a 'Threepenny Finale' – but this symmetry is broken by the addition of a Prologue and an Interlude played in front of the curtain. Similarly, the text self-consciously plays with the temporal conventions associated with the neo-classical unities,[10] and these self-reflexive tendencies also underlie Peachum's concession to the audience that the ending has been changed so that, in the opera at least, we will see justice tempered by mercy. *The Threepenny Opera*'s most provocative piece of *Verfremdung* is, however, Polly's thematisation of epic theatre as a demonstration or replay when she introduces the 'Pirate Jenny' song, and this interpolation of epic theatre within epic theatre is particularly important in drawing the spectator's attention to the link between the text's defamiliarisation of dramatic discourse and its presentation of role play.

The opening scene of *The Threepenny Opera*, with its sardonic presentation of the rhetoric of woe, is built around the notion that acting involves a distanced display of behavioural attitudes. As a result, we are invited from the beginning to consider the relationship between figures in the work and their roles. Are they no more than the passive products of the roles they play; do they suffer from role conflict; do they actively play their roles with distance? In Polly's case, these questions are particularly difficult to resolve, presumably in order to frustrate any attempts at identification on the part of the spectator. While, on some occasions, she appears to be a rather adolescent and incorrigible romantic, on others, she comes across as a hard-boiled business-woman, lurching from role to role and even breaking down if the conflict between them becomes too acute. At the same time, we are made aware from the 'Pirate Jenny' song onwards of an element of duplicity and deceit in her behaviour which compels us to ask ourselves constantly whether or not she is

---

10. Cf. Scene 9, which is full of references to chronological time that cannot possibly be accurate, so that the implied identity of stage time and chronological time is shattered.

playing a particular role with distance. Role distance is also crucial in the presentation of Macheath. He appears to be able to compartmentalise his roles when they threaten to come into conflict, and this leads to the abrupt discontinuities in his behaviour instanced in his shifting attitudes first towards Polly and then towards his men in Scene 4. Nevertheless, even Macheath is not entirely in control of his behaviour, and this is because he is a character in transition. Although he aspires to exchange the status of criminal for that of banker, his incomplete adoption of bourgeois role attributes is signalled by the discrepancies in and between his verbal and physical behaviour in the wedding scene, ironically counterpointed by Mathias's repetitions of his high-falutin diction.

The Threepenny Opera's foregrounding of the link between role and discourse, graphically exemplified in Polly's ability to find the *mot juste* when she takes on the leadership of the gang, is fundamental to its unmasking of ideology. The text is characterised by frequent collisions between discursive levels, notably in the course of Polly's and Jenny's altercation after the 'Jealousy Duet'. Although, in this latter case, the text focuses on the figures' skill in manipulating discourse, it also exposes the inseparability of language and ideology and their saturation of inter-personal behaviour. This applies particularly to its demystification of the rhetoric of romantic love, which is inaugurated by Mrs Peachum's attack on the 'Can't-you-feel-my-heartbeat' text (subsequently taken up in the love duet at the end of Scene 2), and reaches a harrowing climax in Brown's fond farewell to Macheath in Scene 9. Indeed, The Threepenny Opera's defamiliarisation of discourse informs not just its presentation of love, but its investigation of all 'natural' human sentiments from friendship to filiality. The tone is set in the opening scene, where Peachum laments the threadbare nature of texts which are intended to provoke pity and generosity but which have become debilitated through over-use. The juxtaposition of the registers of sentiment and economics, both here and in Polly's comparison of the moon of love to a worn-down penny at the end of Scene 4, clearly implies the linguistic constitution of supposedly basic human emotions, and also invites us to consider whether a more fundamental level of self or social relations underpins the now opaque discourse of everyday belief.

Consciousness and its Other: Contemplation or Intervention?

The Threepenny Opera's concern with the relationship between representation and reality is metaphorically signified through the disjunction of the visible and the actual in the Prologue. The 'Ballad of

Mac the Knife' stresses the non-visibility of Macheath's criminality and links Macheath to his felonies by negation. In Althusserian terms, the 'Ballad' could be seen as figuring the relationship of consciousness to what is other than itself; and given that *The Threepenny Opera*'s demystification of sentiment concentrates on sexual and economic transactions, we must now consider to what extent the text embodies a materialist account of self and society.

The exploitative nature of the capitalist economy is grotesquely demonstrated through the nature of Peachum's business, as his employees exchange a proportion of their labour power for begging licences. Although Peachum's firm is a pre-industrial enterprise and the text does not address itself specifically to commodity production, it does emphasise the commercialisation of all inter-personal relationships under capitalism, especially bourgeois marriage and prostitution. At the same time, it is precisely in the sphere of sexual relationships that the apparent primacy of the economic is obscured. The 'Ballad of Sexual Slavery' implies that Macheath's behaviour is determined by his sexual appetites, and despite Brecht's claim to the contrary (Brecht, 1979, pp.92–3), Macheath's virtual satyriasis is amply confirmed by the variety and frequency of his sexual encounters. Just as Peachum's relationship to his employees denotes the economic organisation of capitalism, so Macheath's relationships to women and his implicitly homo-erotic friendship with Brown indicate its sexual organisation. *The Threepenny Opera* demonstrates that, in bourgeois society, all forms of sexuality are defined in relation to the norm of masculinity. Thus, the sexual identity of women in particular, whether as wives, lovers or prostitutes, is presented as deriving from dependency on men, even though the precise nature of this dependency is mediated in socio-economic terms.

The text's detailed attention to human sexuality is complemented by its recognition of other biologically based material needs, most starkly in the 'Second Finale': 'Food is the first thing. Morals follow on' (Brecht, 1979, p.55). At first sight, these words appear to give credence to the view that Brecht's position in *The Threepenny Opera* is ultimately no different from Freud's in *Civilisation and its Discontents*, emphasising the primacy of biological needs and human viciousness and implying that the conditions condemned in the 'First Finale' are natural and unchangeable rather than historical and political. However, this would be to overlook the fact that the immediate context of 'Food is the first thing' refers to the differential socio-economic distribution of the means to satisfy basic human requirements, and there is a strong case for arguing that the text's overall presentation of social relationships is consistent with Brecht's thesis that the physicality of human beings must be construed in terms of the socio-economic processes in which it is set (Brecht, 1978, p.46). While this involves a crucial modification of Brecht's more orthodox Marxist contention that the human essence is no more than an ensemble of societal relationships, it also means that *The Threepenny Opera*'s approach to material needs involves a descriptive and explanatory model which avoids the pitfalls of both economic and biological reductionism.

The absurd *deus ex machina* which rounds off *The Threepenny Opera* and emphasises the absence of mercy and justice for all in the non-operatic world of capitalism, is put into perspective by Peachum's reminder that the King's messengers appear only infrequently and that the down-trodden will kick back. *The Threepenny Opera*'s materialist account of the ideological and social relations of capitalism thus seems to be complemented by a confident assurance of revolutionary praxis. Nevertheless, the models of resistance encountered in the work are problematic. Typically, whether in Macheath's 'Forgiveness' ballad in Scene 9, the 'Pirate Jenny' song, or the First Finale, 'kicking back' simply involves recourse to physical violence generated by resentment or frustration of material needs, and it may well be that this is why Brecht stated in 1945 that, in the absence of a revolutionary movement, the work's message was pure anarchism (Hecht, 1985, p.16). There is certainly no attempt to present a revolutionary movement within *The Threepenny Opera*, but the work's failure to engage with the problem of generating collective political action ultimately derives from its analysis of capitalism. While *The Threepenny Opera* provides a compelling account of ideology and commodification, from a Marxist point of view it is far less adequate in its consideration of social class and can be subjected to the criticisms which Brecht levelled at Alfred Döblin's novel *Berlin Alexanderplatz* in 1929 (Sternberg, 1963, p.17). While the lower orders of capitalist society are presented exclusively as members of the *Lumpenproletariat*, state power is embodied in the pathetic figure of Brown. Consequently, there is no real sense of class conflict in the work, nor of its grounding in the conflict between the forces and relations of production. Although the final stanza of the 'Third Finale' ironically invites us to embark on a deconstruction of legal and religious superstructures, it seems to be oblivious of the fact that, for Marx, the distorted conceptions of ideology can only be overcome *practically*, by changing the contradictory societal relations that generate ideology.[11] As Brecht was to observe in his comments

---

11. Cf. Larrain (1983), pp.6–45.

on *Mahagonny*: 'Real innovations attack the base' (Brecht, 1963, p.126).[12]

Conclusion

The above attempt to produce an Althusserian reading of *The Threepenny Opera* suggests that, in certain respects, Althusser's position is entirely vindicated. Brecht and Althusser share a commitment to aesthetic and sociological anti-humanism, and *The Threepenny Opera* turns out to be a classic example of the authentic work of art, making ideology perceptible through processes of internal distantiation. At the same time, however, the deployment of Althusserian theory has raised awkward questions concerning the latent structure of the work of art, the ways in which art can represent real relations, and – at least as far as *The Threepenny Opera* is concerned – the link between critique and *praxis*. These problems are not incidental by-products of the application of a complex and coherent theory to a recalcitrant text, but intrinsic to Althusser's project, which is fraught with difficulties both because of the Formalist presuppositions of his aesthetic theory and because of ambiguities in his theory of ideology.[13]

Althusser's specification of 'great' or 'authentic' art is based on assumptions typical of early Russian Formalism. Just as, for Viktor Shklovsky, art de-automatises habitualised perceptions by laying bare its own devices, so too, for Althusser, it disrupts the common-sense understanding of everyday life by virtue of internal distantiation. From a materialist point of view, this approach is highly contentious in that it arbitrarily identifies art as such with one contingent set of aesthetic practices instead of historicising the concept of art and accounting for the formal features of aesthetic texts in terms of their economic, political and ideological settings. Furthermore, it is also not clear whether the defamiliarisation said to characterise 'great' art is a property inherent in the text or one generated by the context of its reception, and in Althusser's case, this ambiguity may well be related to the fact that he did not significantly address the institutional dimension of ideology until 1969. Althusser's account of the relationship between art and ideo-

---

12. Willett's translation 'Real innovations attack the roots' (Brecht, 1978, p.41) again obscures Brecht's Marxism.
13. Althusser's relationship to Russian Formalism is discussed in Bennett (1979), pp.122 and 127–31. For a devastating critique of Althusser's theory of ideology see Lovell (1983), pp.29–46.

logy is rendered even more problematic by his refusal to grant 'scientific' status even to 'authentic' art, and once again, his position is implicitly Formalist. The Formalist conception of art and critical methodology drives a sharp wedge between poetic and practical language in order to distinguish aesthetic discourse from the pragmatic assertions of science. Similarly, Althusser argues that whereas art works with perceptions, only the theoretically articulated concepts of science can specify the real correctly. This distinction underlies Althusser's use of metaphors of presence and absence, visibility and non-visibility when characterising art's relationship to the real: because real relations are essentially abstract and so not immediately visible to us, art can only represent them by negation, as an absence. However, even if it is possible, for example, to infer a position of anti-humanism from Cremonini's depictions of faces, it is difficult to see how his paintings might lead the spectator to grasp the specific, substantive theses of structural Marxism rather than those of any other anti-humanist position. Like Adorno, Althusser assumes that the latent structure of a text can somehow articulate processes at work beneath the surface of society, but in both cases we are left in the dark as to how particular formal strategies can function as bearers of determinate political content.[14]

In his commentaries on Brecht's work in the 1950s, Roland Barthes argued that Brechtian theatre neither depicts nor explicitly demands revolutionary action and is, instead, a theatre of consciousness. If this is so, then, from a Marxian point of view, the critique presented in Brecht's plays is intrinsically idealist. I have already argued that *The Threepenny Opera* operates at this level, but the ambiguities which permeate Althusser's theory of ideology also subvert art's role in disrupting the spontaneous understanding of everyday life. If ideology is, on the one hand, a functional prerequisite of any social formation, like the central value-system in the sociological theory of Talcott Parsons, then it must, ultimately, be ineradicable. But if ideology is construed, on the other hand, as a distorted form of consciousness perpetuating the myths of humanism, then it is difficult to see how an individual apprised of the real relations that constitute him or her as a Subject could coherently engage in revolutionary *praxis* in order to alter the relations in question. Either way, art's role in making ideology perceptible would be politically superfluous, and the project of epic theatre redundant.

14. Cf. Bürger (1979), pp.79–92.

References

Althusser, L. (1962) 'Le "Piccolo", Bertolazzi et Brecht', *Esprit*, 30, 312, 957-95

Althusser, L. (1971) 'Cremonini, Painter of the Abstract' in *Lenin and Philosophy and Other Essays*, Verso, London, pp.209-20

Althusser, L. (1982a) 'The "Piccolo Teatro": Bertolazzi and Brecht. Notes on a Materialist Theatre' in *For Marx*, Verso, London, pp.129-51

Althusser, L. (1982b) 'Marxism and Humanism' in *For Marx*, Verso, London, pp.219-41

Althusser, L. (1984a) 'A Letter on Art in Reply to André Daspre' in *Essays on Ideology*, Verso, London, pp.173-9

Althusser, L. (1984b) 'Ideology and Ideological State Apparatuses' in *Essays on Ideology*, Verso, London, pp.1-57

Arato, A. (1973/4) 'The Second International: A Re-examination', *Telos*, 18, 2-52

Barthes, R. (1957) *Mythologies*, Éditions du Seuil, Paris

Barthes, R. (1964) *Essais critiques*, Éditions du Seuil, Paris

Bennett, T. (1979) *Formalism and Marxism*, Methuen, London

Benton, T. (1984) *The Rise and Fall of Structural Marxism: Althusser and his Influence*, Macmillan, London

Brecht, B. (1963) *Schriften zum Theater 2*, Suhrkamp, Frankfurt/Main

Brecht, B. (1978) *Brecht on Theatre: The Development of an Aesthetic*, trans. and ed. J. Willett, Methuen, London

Brecht, B. (1979) *The Threepenny Opera: Collected Plays*, vol.2 (ii), trans. and ed. R. Manheim and J. Willett, Methuen, London

Bürger, P. (1979) *Vermittlung - Rezeption - Funktion: Ästhetische Theorie und Methodologie der Literaturwissenschaft*, Suhrkamp, Frankfurt/Main

Giles, S. (1989) 'Rewriting Brecht: *Die Dreigroschenoper* 1928-1931', *Literaturwissenschafliches, Jahrbuch*, 30, 249-79

Heath, S. (1974) 'Lessons from Brecht', *Screen*, 15, 2, 103-28

Hecht, W. (ed.) (1985) *Brechts Dreigroschenoper*, Suhrkamp, Frankfurt/Main

Hennenberg, F. (1985) 'Weill, Brecht und *Die Dreigroschenoper*: Neue Materialien zur Entstehung und Uraufführung', *Österreichische Musik-Zeitschrift*, 40, 6, 281-91

Hinton, S. (ed.) (1990) *Weill/Brecht 'The Threepenny Opera'*, Cambridge Opera Handbooks, Cambridge U.P., forthcoming

Hüfner, A. (1968) *Brecht in Frankreich 1930-1963: Verbreitung, Aufnahme, Wirkung*, Metzler, Stuttgart

Jay, M. (1985) *Marxism and Totality*, California U.P., Berkeley

Larrain, J. (1983) *Marxism and Ideology*, Macmillan, London

Lovell, T. (1983) *Pictures of Reality: Aesthetics, Politics and Pleasure*, British Film Institute, London

Speirs, R. (1977) 'A Note on the First Published Version of *Die Dreigroschenoper* and its Relation to the Standard Text', *FMLS*, 13, 1, 25-32

Sternberg, F. (1963) *Der Dichter und die Ratio: Erinnerungen an Bertolt Brecht*, Sachse and Pohl, Göttingen

Unseld, S. (ed.) (1978) *Bertolt Brechts Dreigroschenbuch*, Suhrkamp, Frankfurt/Main

–14–

Upstairs–Downstairs –
Some Reflections on
German Literature in the Light
of Bakhtin's Theory of Carnival

RICHARD SHEPPARD

Carnival as Opposition

According to Foucault, one can write history in terms of anything – sexuality, punishment or the treatment of the insane. But here, I want to consider the history of German literature in terms of Carnival, the Fool and Folly. Once decoded, these *topoi*, I suggest, not only take us into a conflict which is of fundamental cultural importance, they also involve a decisive move away from the hermetic study of literary texts and towards a much more wide-ranging approach to which one might give the name of cultural semiotics. As my starting-point, I shall use Mikhail Bakhtin's seminal work on Carnival, *Rabelais and his World* (1968) – a text which, precisely because it reaffirms values and attitudes which Western humanist culture in general and the canon of German literature since Gottsched in particular has largely tabooed, repressed or diabolised, is relatively unused by scholars of German literature.[1]

Bakhtin argues that during the Middle Ages and the Renaissance, 'a boundless world of humorous forms and manifestations opposed the serious tone of medieval ecclesiastical and feudal culture' (p.4). This alternative culture found its most concrete and sustained

---

1. According to the extensive bibliography included in *Le Bulletin Bakhtine/The Bakhtin Newsletter*, no.1 (1983), published by the Queen's University (Kingston, Ontario), only two secondary works dealing with German literature on the basis of Bakhtin's theory of Carnival appeared 1969–83: Kern (1980) and Eagleton (1981), pp.143–72. Both works are of Anglo-Saxon provenance and one is comparative in scope; neither Helmut Kreuzer's nor Hans Hahn's essay above makes any mention of Bakhtin; and to my knowledge, there still exists no complete German translation of Bakhtin's book on Rabelais.

expression in the festivities, spectacles and rituals connected with the season of Carnival, that classic example of cultural *bricolage* which extended from mid-November to the start of Lent (p.8) and which seems to have involved memories of various pre-Christian festivals like those marking the end of autumn, the start of winter, the winter solstice and the New Year, the Roman *Saturnalia, Matronalia, Lupercalia* and *Parentalia*, and even the ancient Greek festivals of Dionysos and *Anthesterion* (Davis, 1975, pp.101–2; Kerényi, 1976, pp.290–6; Burke, 1978, p.21; Orloff, 1980, pp.16–37). For all its compellingness, Bakhtin's account is somewhat sweeping. So it is probably prudent to add that during the Early Middle Ages, Carnival, except in very remote rural areas, was probably losing much of its original cultic character; and that by the High Middle Ages, its anthropological function at the level of local communities had become regulatory and conservative (Davis, 1975, pp.104–9) and its broader social function that of a safety-valve which was, accordingly, tolerated by many ecclesiastical authorities (Burke, 1978, pp.201–3; Orloff, 1980, p.35).[2]

During Carnival, normal sexual roles were switched (Davis, 1975, pp.136–8), everyday laws and conventions suspended, established hierarchies overturned and official rituals parodied and travestied (Bakhtin, 1968, p.14; Burke, 1978, p.192). In short, the normal world was turned upside-down (Burke, 1978, pp.188–9; Orloff, 1980, p.32). Bakhtin summarised thus: 'carnival celebrated temporary liberation from the prevailing truth and from the established order, it marked the suspension of all hierarchical rank, privileges, norms, and prohibitions. Carnival was the true feast of time, the feast of becoming, change, and renewal. It was hostile to all that was immortalized and completed' (p.10). For Bakhtin, the essence of Carnival was laughter: not the detached mockery of the satirist who 'places himself above the object of his mockery' (p.12), but that 'festive laughter' whose perpetrators know themselves to be part of the endless process of copulation, birth and death which connects human life with Creation as a whole. Carnival laughter, Bakhtin implied, affirmed that the *human* comes from and will return to the *humus*, the soil, and that its earthy *humour* reminds man – who, in

---

2. Burke quotes a defence of the Feast of Fools by French clerics of 12 March 1444 that was couched in the following terms: 'We do these things in jest and not in earnest, as the ancient custom is, so that once a year the foolishness innate in us can come out and evaporate. Don't wine skins and barrels burst very often if the air-hole (*spiraculum*) is not opened from time to time? We too are old barrels . . .' (1978, p.202). See also K. Thomas, 'Work and Leisure in a Pre-Industrial Society', *Past and Present*, vol.29 (December 1964), pp.53–4.

Western culture, stresses the gap between himself and Nature – of his more basic side. Accordingly, the grotesque human forms, abusive language, and imagery of food, defecation, pregnancy, wanton sexuality, dismemberment and disintegration which marked Carnival rituals (Bakhtin, 1968, p.319; Burke, 1978, p.186) degraded humanity in the positive sense in which waste organic matter has to be bio-degraded before it can become a source of renewed fertility. Thus, Bakhtin concluded, the practices and imagery of Carnival made people forcibly aware of 'the reproductive lower stratum, the zone in which conception and a new birth takes place ... the fruitful earth and the womb' (p.21). It renewed their consciousness of their 'link with life and with the cosmos' (p.23); put them in touch with the vital powers of transformation and rebirth; reminded them of those indispensable sides of human nature which, in conventional topographies of the body, are deemed inferior; and freed them 'from the oppression of such gloomy categories as "eternal," "immovable," "absolute," "unchangeable"' by exposing them 'to the gay and free laughing aspect of the world, with its unfinished and open character, with the joy of change and renewal' (p.83).

From Bakhtin's oppositional conception of Carnival, it is not far to the hypothesis, implicit in his contrast between carnivalesque folly and 'the monolith of the Christian cult and ideology' (p.75), that the High Middle Ages in Europe, far from being that all-embracing unity projected theologically by Aquinas in his two *Summae*[3] and so beloved of the German Romantics, actually involved the more or less (un)easy symbiosis of two estimations of human nature (cf. Orloff, 1980, p.35; Johannsmeier, 1984, p.115). In the dominant position, a 'high' or 'official' Christian value-system which, while conceding that Nature had a (largely passive) place in the divine scheme (Merchant, 1982, pp.10–13), set humanity above Nature and derived its spiritual essence from a (patriarchal) God who existed above and apart from the world of matter. And in the subordinate position, a still powerful 'low' or 'unofficial' complex of folk or pagan value-systems which saw humanity as essentially rooted in (matriarchal) Nature (cf. Kern, 1980, pp.54 and 119).[4]

---

3. The *Summa contra Gentiles* (1261/2) and the *Summa Theologiae* (1265–73) in which, according to Gilson, Aquinas tried to show that there is 'no shadow of antinomy between God's perfection and that of created being', E. Gilson, *The Christian Philosophy of St Thomas Aquinas* (Gollancz, London, 1957), p.181.
4. Johannsmeier, citing Karl Reiser's *Sagen, Gebräuche und Sprichwörter des Allgäus* (2 vols., Josef Kösel, Kempten, 1898), comments that in the folk-lore of the Alpine regions, which, like their Carnival customs, persisted in an unreformed state well

R. Southern (1953), speaking of this symbiosis in terms of a 'union of learning and high spirituality with popular form and impulses' (p.244), indicated that it had been established by the middle of the twelfth century. By this time, 'high', Christian civilization had established itself throughout Western Europe (pp.15–16); scholars were beginning to 'feel comfortable about their command of the achievement of the past' (p.195); Christian writers were giving 'new standards of conduct to secular rulers and [teaching] them, or at least the clerks in their service, the dignity of just authority' (p.94); a uniform Canon Law, based on Roman Law, was growing up (p.95); a more elaborate set of governmental laws was being formulated (p.101) and 'it was becoming common for an act of religious dedication to be added to the secular ceremonies' (p.110). Merchant reinforced the above dating when she wrote that the twelfth-century Christian Cathedral School of Chartres, using Plato's *Timaeus*, 'personified Natura as a goddess and limited the power attributed to her in pagan philosophies by emphasizing her subservience to God' (1982, p.10). And Lehmann's work on learned Latin parodies of religious forms points to the same conclusion: the symbiosis of a subordinate, 'low', 'weltfreudige Lebensauffassung' ('conception of life which rejoiced in the world') and a dominant, 'high' culture, the authority of whose forms and values was tacitly admitted through the very fact of parody, produced, around the twelfth century, an abundance of parodistic literature which then continued throughout the rest of the Middle Ages (1963, pp.19–24).[5]

From Symbiosis to Repression

Such a state of symbiosis was also a state of fissure inasmuch as it involved a struggle for hegemony between the two value-systems concerned.[6] Huizinga's *The Waning of the Middle Ages* and Burke's study suggest that until about the middle of the fourteenth century, 'official' or 'high' culture conducted that struggle by means of a dual

---

into the nineteenth century (Orloff, 1980, pp.46 and 55), the Wild Woman occurs in various forms more frequently than the Wild Man (1984, p.91; cf. Davis, 1975, pp.80–2 and 134–5).
5. Cf. also Johannsmeier's remarks on the differences between the Celtic/Breton original of *Ivain* and Chrétien de Troyes's 'high', twelfth-century version (1984, pp.86–7).
6. The Freudian psychoanalyst Otto Rank saw exactly the same conflict within ancient Greek culture and described it in terms of the '*artistic*' development from the chthonic-animalistic principle to the spiritual-creative', *Art and Artist* (Alfred Knopf, New York, 1932), p.156; see also p.147.

strategy: active repression where possible on the one hand and more or less imperfect assimilation on the other, with pilgrimages, the orders of chivalry and the cult of the saints being the points where the second aspect was most visible (Huizinga, 1965, pp.83–90; see also Southern, 1953, p.242; Burke, 1978, pp.180–1; Orloff, 1980, pp.29–31). Thus, the strictures of the Synod of Utrecht (1293) and the complaint of the Synod of Worms (1316) (Reuling, 1890, p.1) indicate that it was not uncommon for clerical writers to incorporate profane theatrical plays or masked spectacles into Christian services (cf. Johannsmeier, 1984, p.257). And Reuling's account of the popularity of those scenes in medieval religious plays which involved comic devils (1890, pp.11 and 17–18) suggests that although, at one level, such scenes existed to demonstrate the power of God, at another, they indulged in 'low', earthy humour as an end in itself because they had been imperfectly assimilated into the 'high', Christian form. In other words, it seems that the strategy of assimilation was only superficially successful, especially in rural areas. To quote Johannsmeier:

> The rural population was only superficially christianised. Using the garb of Christian festivals or the names of local saints, the common people continued to observe their heathen and magical customs. Indeed, many a monk or parish priest was driven to desperation by the sheer number and persistent vitality of the fertility goddesses, demons, witches and magically endowed objects which populated the everyday world of the peasants. (1984, pp.13–14)

During the twelfth and thirteenth centuries, Europe saw the drastic shrinking of forests, the increased use of waste land for arable farming and, concomitantly, the growth of towns (Mundy, 1973, pp.119–40; Merchant, 1982, pp.46–7). The growing population of those towns, especially the lower orders, took over the residues of ancient, 'low' forms from rural festivities and collaged them together for their own use, particularly charivari (Davis, 1975, pp.109–19; Johannsmeier, 1984, pp.50–1 and 63). But although those residues were, by now, far removed from their shamanistic and totemistic origins and adapted for new, socio-political and anthropological purposes, they still seem to have involved the consciousness that man was rooted in a world which 'still continued to thrive chaotically beyond the constraining walls of the town' and which, 'even in the late Middle Ages, still comprised the greater part of the countryside: wild, unpredictable, uncharted Nature' (Johannsmeier, 1984, pp.65–6). And to that extent, following Ginzburg (1983), Johannsmeier concludes that the carnivalesque festivities of even the late medieval towns involved 'an element of that mythical consciousness which had been buried during the process of Christian socialisation and which can live in the knowledge of the interpenetration of good and evil, life and death precisely because it feels rooted in the cyclical, cosmic processes of Nature' (1984, p.61; cf. p.152).

Where, however, such incomplete and ambivalent assimilation of carnivalesque festivities was unacceptable to the hierarchy, then, if we are to believe C.G. Jung and his school, the representatives of 'high' culture had to resort to repression, with the forms of superseded, older cultures being theologically diabolised – put under a negative sign and consigned, significantly, to the *subterranean* regions of Hell.[7] Thus, quoting a vision of the pagan Wild Hunt which is recorded in the twelfth-century *Historia Ecclesiastica* by the Norman historian Ordericus Vitalis and which a priest from Saint-Aubin de Bonneval, one Gualchelme, claimed to have had on 1 January 1091 (i.e. the Feast of Fools), Johannsmeier shows how, in the christianised, clerical imagination, the pagan folk-lore is 'distorted, re-interpreted' (1984, p.52), turned into a version of the Christian Hell (p.55).

In summary then, during the High Middle Ages, the relationship between 'high' and 'low' culture was extremely complex: 'high' culture took over and/or attempted to repress 'low' forms; representatives of 'high' culture (like students and lesser clergy)[8] who had not been completely assimilated into that culture, together with 'low', popular culture in general, parodied and travestied 'high' forms (especially during the Carnival season). Consequently, 'high' and 'low' cultures interpenetrated with one another and 'the result has to be read as a palimpsest' (Burke, 1978, p.191; cf. Orloff, 1980, p.32; Johannsmeier, 1984, p.51).

As the Middle Ages waned, however, that complex, palimpsest-like relationship which could, even in the late Middle Ages, still generate the 'almost inconceivable mixture of devotion and debauchery' described by Huizinga (1965, p.175ff.), gradually turned into one of 'open conflict' (Burke, 1978, p.219). Thus, Davis suggests that saturnalian elements were being 'slowly banished from the cathedrals' in France by the late fifteenth century (1975, p.98). Similarly, Boczkowska's article (1971), based overwhelmingly on texts and pictures from the fifteenth and sixteenth centuries produced

---

7. C.G. Jung, 'The Role of the Unconscious' in *The Collected Works* (20 vols., Routledge and Kegan Paul, London, 1953ff.), vol.10, pp.12–13; Orloff (1980), p.33; A. Stevens, *Archetype: A Natural History of the Self* (Routledge and Kegan Paul, London, 1982), p.167.
8. C.G. Jung, 'On the Psychology of the Trickster-Figure', *Works*, vol.9/1, pp.256–7.

by representatives of 'high' culture, implicitly shows how fools and their related symbols (such as the moon, the fools' boat full of revellers, and the phlegmatic temperament – deemed particularly prone to the carnivalesque sins of gluttony and drunkenness) were systematically put under a negative sign and presented, from the 'high' point of view, as images of the 'material sublunar existence of man, subject to the laws of nature and the drift towards death' (p.61).

In the sixteenth century, this process of repression and diabolisation accelerated markedly. The organic cosmos of the Middle Ages and the Renaissance began to be transformed into a mechanistic universe (Merchant, 1982, *passim*). And both Catholic and Protestant reformers sought, albeit with differing degrees of rigour (Davis, 1975, pp.120–1; Burke, 1978, p.215),[9] to undo the immediacy of the 'I–thou relationship' between human beings and Nature (Merchant, 1982, p.28), to separate the sacred from the profane in a much sharper way than had been done in the Middle Ages (Burke, 1978, pp.211–12; cf. Huizinga, 1965, pp.147–57) and to purge both 'official' religious practices and secular society of those elements which derived from the 'unofficial' value-system.[10] Theologically, this involved driving a wedge between the realms of Nature and Grace[11] and putting Nature under a negative sign. That is to say, God was removed from the immediacy of the natural world to a realm either far beyond Creation (Merchant, 1982, pp.193 and 214) or deep within the human soul – a double shift which was later to be perfectly encapsulated in the Conclusion of *The Critique of Practical Reason* (1788) when Kant said that two things filled the mind with 'awe and wonderment': 'the starry heavens above me and the moral law within me'. Correspondingly, Nature was increasingly desacralised: either declared a dead, inert, neutral territory for human exploitation (Merchant, 1982, p.293) or equated with the diabolic principle *per se*, a process from which ultimately derive the

---

9. The process of repression seems to have been carried through less systematically in Southern, Catholic Europe, even in the sixteenth century. Reuling, for example, cites an edict of the Holy Roman Emperor Ferdinand I which forbade, *inter alia*, 'Schalksnarren' ('knavish fools'), but adds that it was probably not enforced very strictly (1890, pp.53–4).
10. See, for example, P. Stubbes, *The Anatomy of Abuses* (1583), especially Chapters 11–22.
11. The history of the Doctrine of Transubstantiation is a crucial aspect of this process. Once God has been divorced from Nature, the Mass ceases to be the symbolic re-enactment of his redemptive activity there and becomes a magical act through which God is called down into the world of matter at a limited number of specific points by a privileged priesthood.

idea of the value-free nature of 'objective' science and applied technology, the typically Western urge to control rather than co-exist with Nature,[12] and, conversely, the classically German notion of 'Innerlichkeit' ('inwardness').[13] Thus, in the High Middle Ages, at least five major Western mystics – St Francis of Assisi (1182–1226), Mechthild of Magdeburg (1212–99), Heinrich Suso (*c.* 1295–1365), Richard Rolle of Hampole (*c.* 1300–49) and the Franciscan convert Jacopone da Todi in his final stage (Nigg, 1956, pp.84–6 and 94) – found no difficulty in seeing God in Nature. In contrast, the theological reappraisal of Nature which took place in the sixteenth century explains why Jakob Boehme's first mystical work, *Aurora* (1610), in which the creative power of God is presented as at work within the forces of Nature, was deemed heretical by the Protestant authorities of his native Görlitz, and why, over the last 400 years, nature-mysticism has been increasingly displaced from the centre of Western orthodoxy into the work of such outsider figures as William Blake, Richard Jeffries and Walt Whitman, or such peripheral movements as Theosophy and Anthroposophy (cf. Underhill, 1911, pp.190–5; 234–5).

If, as a result of the Reformation, Counter-Reformation and the rise of mechanistic science, Nature and the natural were stripped of their epiphanic potential and declared to be in need of Grace, or, in secular terms, of formation and control, then Carnival, with its fools and wild men who represented 'Nature, or in Freudian terms, the Id' (Burke, 1978, p.190), had little hope of surivival, especially since the work of the Reformers increasingly found support among the laity (Burke, 1978, p.240). In the Middle Ages, attempts to repress carnivalesque practices had been 'essentially sporadic efforts by individuals' (Burke, 1978, p.218). For example, Pope Innocent III had, at the end of the twelfth century, condemned the carnivalesque rite of the Feast of Asses (6 January) – and the theological faculty of the University of Paris was still doing so 300 years later (Johannsmeier, 1984, p.32). After 1550, however, especially in Protestant lands, the thrust to abolish manifestations of 'low' culture was a highly prominent aspect of a sustained and total strategy. Precisely

---

12. See Merchant, 1982, *passim* and F. Capra, *The Turning Point* (Flamingo, London, 1983), pp.22–30 and 46.
13. This aspect of the overall shift is very evident in the German and English translations of *Luke* 17:21 where the Greek 'ἐντὸς ὑμῶν' (which means both 'in you' and 'among you' and rendered in the Vulgate as 'intra vos') becomes 'within you' in the Authorised Version and 'inwendig in euch' in Luther's version. In both cases, the Kingdom of Heaven is narrowed down from a power which is active both within the human soul and the outer world to one which is purely internal.

because Carnival and such related festivals in Northern Europe as May Day, St John's Eve and St Bartholomew's Day (Burke, 1978, pp.195 and 199)[14] were times when the distinction between the sacred and the profane was especially blurred, when the order of the 'official' value-system ceded its dominance to the disorder of 'unofficial' forms and practices, and when 'a remarkable number' of those aspects of popular culture, both religious and secular, to which the Reformers most objected as unchristian could be found in combination (Burke, 1978, p.208), such festivals and their associated practices bore the particular brunt of the Reformers' onslaught.

The work of Norbert Elias and Max Weber elaborates the psychology which that onslaught involved. When, during the sixteenth and seventeenth centuries, the Reformers, especially the Protestants, attacked 'pagan practices' in general and Carnival in particular, they were implicitly making five, interrelated statements about human nature. First, they were asserting that if Nature was no longer a realm in which God was actively and presently at work but a 'disorderly and chaotic realm to be subdued and controlled' (Merchant, 1982, p.127), then man, too, had to defend himself against the 'natural' drives and affections within himself by means of an ethic of civilised restraint (Elias, 1978, pp.120–1, 187 and 214) involving 'decency, diligence, gravity, modesty, orderliness, prudence, reason, self-control, sobriety and thrift' (Burke, 1978, p.219). Second, they were registering a new confidence in the divinely grounded human *Logos* (Merchant, 1982, p.214) and, conversely, because of their sense that that *Logos* was distinct from and higher than the world of matter, an intensified sense of shame towards the body and those of its functions from which so much carnivalesque imagery derived (Elias, 1978, pp.164 and 180). Third, they were affirming the autonomous identity of 'the "self" divided by an invisible wall from what happens "outside"' (Elias, 1978, p.257) – i.e. the atomised ego grounded in a transcendent God – and therefore denying the claim, implicit in the carnivalesque experience, that man is truly human only when part of the collective in which Nature is freely at work (cf. Bakhtin, 1968, pp.23–4). Fourth, they were fusing an older, monastic asceticism with the new

---

14. See H. Morley, *Memoirs of Bartholomew Fair* (Chapman and Hall, London, 1859). In connection with the dating of the establishment of the symbiotic relationship between 'high' and 'low' culture as the middle of the twelfth century, it is interesting that St Bartholomew's Fair, that English version of Carnival, should date back to the reign of Henry I (1100–1135) and should have taken place around an Augustinian priory in the Smithfield area of London which was founded in March 1123 in honour of the Apostle Bartholomew by one Raherus (or Rahere) (d.1143) who had formerly been the King's jester.

authority of the Cartesian *cogito* and, conversely, rejecting values which are central to Carnival: 'a traditional ethic which is harder to define because it was less articulate, but which involved more stress on the values of generosity and spontaneity and a greater tolerance of disorder' (Burke, 1978, p.219), or, in Weber's words, 'the spontaneous enjoyment of life, and all it had to offer' (1968, p.166). Fifth, they were repudiating all forms of sensual gratification – the 'idolatry of the flesh' (Weber, 1968, p.169) – and an institution which involved profligate waste of time and resources[15] on behalf of an ethic which saw 'acquisition as the ultimate purpose of [human] life' (Weber, 1968, p.53) and work 'as the highest form which the moral activity of the individual could assume' in a fallen world (p.80).

Over the last 400 years, a secularised version of the Reformers' reappraisal of human nature has become synthesised with a mechanistic view of Nature and the economic principles of commercial capitalism (Merchant, 1982, *passim*) to produce the reality principle which now prevails in the West. And once the ontological implications of this process are grasped, the significance of a whole series of interconnected binary oppositions becomes apparent which, despite their conventional nature, we in the West regard as normative: culture/Nature, high/low, heaven/earth, head/heart, reason/emotion, will/impulse, spirit/matter, day/night, spiritual/animal, right/left (cf. Davis, 1975, p.130). Nietzsche subsumed these and related pairs under the master pair Apollo/Dionysos,[16] and when it is remembered that in the ancient world, the cult of Dionysos, the god of the irrational, was particularly associated with women (Kerényi, 1976, p.130), and that the hegemony of 'high', Christian culture in the Middle Ages involved, by virtue of its monastic origins, either the idealisation of woman in the person of the Virgin or the downgrading of woman in the person of Eve (Southern, 1953, p.106), then it is not hard to see how the above list is complemented by such further binary pairs as male/female, patriarchy/matriarchy, sun/moon etc. Thus, Bakhtin's concept of Carnival as the tolerated/repressed Other runs parallel with contemporary, feminist critiques of patriarchal-Apollonian culture like that implicit in the work of the anthropologist Natalie Zemon Davis (1975, pp.124–51) or that proposed by the historian of science, Carolyn Merchant – whose book *The Death of Nature*, without mentioning Carnival once, starts from the entirely carnivalesque proposition that 'to write history from a

---

15. Johannsmeier estimates that in the High Middle Ages, Carnival and related festivals took up at least a quarter of the year (1984, p.143).
16. For the inter-connection in medieval culture of several of the elements which constitute one set of these poles, see Boczkowska, 1971.

feminist perspective is to turn it upside down' (1982, p.xvi).[17]

In other words, the Reformers' suppression of Carnival, together with the desacralisation or diabolisation of Nature which it implied, was a major milestone on the road towards that rationalisation, disciplining and standardisation of human nature which is, as Weber put it, the 'condition of any valuable work in the modern world' (1968, p.180). Moreover, the same ontological shift tends necessarily, given the other poles of the binary oppositions with which Nature is conventionally associated, towards the impoverishment and pollution of the environment, the eradication of non-wealth-creating species of wild life, the mechanisation of the human body, the industrialisation of enjoyment which produces the accidental, but entirely appropriate Puritan pun inherent in the notion of a 'leisure complex', the abuse or anthropomorphisation of the animal, the 'civilisation', obliteration or commercialisation of so-called 'primitive peoples' ('Naturvölker') and the fear of the Female which, according to Davis, resulted in a deepening subjection of women from the sixteenth to the eighteenth centuries (1975, pp.125–8).

The final artistic results of the above process are, notwithstanding the Romantic attempt to reverse it, such varied texts as Kafka's novels, expressionist poems, dramas and paintings, most of Bergmann's later films, Frisch's later novels, and the plays of Herbert Achternbusch.[18] All such texts involve a covert, 'high' theology, a hidden patriarchal God (hypostatised in Lacan's concept of the castrating Law) from whom people are either completely cut off (because the way, as in expressionist works, is barred by elemental powers – latter-day versions of the angel with the flaming sword) or to whom people are allowed limited access at a restricted number of privileged points – as in Kafka's parable 'Vor dem Gesetz' ('Before the Law') – by a male priesthood. Conversely, in such texts, matriarchal Nature is either absent; or a silent landscape in which spring and summer, if the exist at all, are, as in Kafka's *The Castle*, talked about in cellars and said to last 'not much more than two days'; or a bleak landscape over which, as in Kaiser's *Von morgens bis mitternachts* (*From Morn to Midnight*) Death presides (cf. my essay

17. In this connection, it may be significant that a large proportion of the major secondary texts used in the preparation of this article – not to mention Enid Welsford's *The Fool* (1935) and Barbara Swain's *Fools and Folly* (1932), both seminal works for the subject as a whole – were written by women.
18. W. Sebald, 'Die Kunst der Verwandlung: Herbert Achternbuschs theatralische Mission' in *A Radical Stage: Theatre in Germany in the 1970s and 1980s* (Berg, Oxford, 1988), pp.174–85.

above, pp.164–91); or a demonic principle, like the gas in Kaiser's *Gas* trilogy, which brings about apocalypse.

In the field of literary theory, the same process ultimately issues in several aporias. It generates the totalitarian patriarchal Law of Lacanian psychology and Walter Benjamin's 'decentred revolutionary subject, the *Unmensch* of the future', who, being without that natural, somatic vitality which continually deconstructs and reconstructs Bakhtin's carnivalesque subject, is continually exposed to the melancholia which haunts Benjamin's work (Eagleton, 1981, p.150). Likewise, Derrida, from his deconstructive perspective, sees that the hegemony of the 'high', logocentric value-system involves putting 'low' categories like the body and all that is associated with it under a negative, excremental sign (1978, p.197). Nevertheless, he, like Nietzsche to whom his work is so indebted, is himself so much the victim of that hegemonic tradition that he can ask whether there *is* another way of looking at man (p.41) and largely restricts 'low' alternatives to the non-linear world of dream (pp.217–18 and 225) and to the 'festival' constituted by Artaud's theatre of cruelty (pp.232–50, especially 244–5). Derrida may, in an untypically lucid passage, advocate 'Nietzschean *affirmation*, that is, the joyous affirmation of the play of the world and of the innocence of becoming, the affirmation of a world of signs without fault, without truth, and without origin' (p.292) and affirm the lack of reference to the centre 'rather than bemoan the absence of the centre' (p.297). Nevertheless, having deconstructed Rousseau's revisionist metaphysic of Nature, his own sense of Nature as a positive power in which humans have their vital roots is so minimal that his attempt to formulate an alternative to 'high' ontology is, inevitably, couched in terms of negatives, lacks and absence, and seems, like that 'high' ontology itself in Derrida's estimation, to stand under the equation 'God is Death' (p.246).

The Fool in an Age of Transition

Given this, the history of the figure of the Fool, especially in his capacity as the carnivalesque Lord of Misrule, is of great significance. As far as the medieval period is concerned, something of this significance can be inferred from what we know about the illustrations in psalters accompanying the opening lines of Psalms 14 and 53: 'The Fool has said in his heart, there is no God' (Gifford, 1974). Where, in the two earliest known illustrations (from the ninth-century Utrecht and Stuttgart Psalters), the Fool appears as 'an evil prince superintending rapine and slaughter' (p.338) and 'a sinister dark-faced crooked and oriental figure with a Phrygian cap' (p.338), after the twelfth century, he is not often depicted as 'the evil prince of confusion' (p.341). And by the fourteenth century, many examples of Psalm 14 depict him as 'a jester with tiny-headed fool-stick, a fool-capped man disputing with a king and holding a bladder-stick, or a very sophisticated fool dangling his bladder-stick arrogantly before the King' (p.337). Indeed, by the fifteenth century, he often appears in that institutionalised uniform in which he was to become so familiar to us in German texts from the sixteenth and seventeenth centuries − 'as a fully-fledged court jester, with ass-eared head-dress, bells, bi-coloured or multi-coloured tunic and fool-stick' who is 'often disputing with a king' (p.336). The findings of Sandra Billington (1984) dovetail with Gifford's. Where, in the High Middle Ages, the fool behaviour endemic in 'low' folk customs was either 'largely suffered in silence as it couldn't be prevented' (p.3) or assimilated to the 'high' value-system as the innocent, Pauline folly of the natural fool (p.17), the end of the fourteenth century 'saw a watershed in ecclesiastical definitions of the Fool' (p.4). Where, before 1350, both ecclesiastical and popular customs involved 'this curious indulgence of returning to the natural [i.e. naked] state', by 1380, 'the decorated Fool was predominant' (p.5; cf. p.50).

The fact that the Fool became, over time, more 'funny' and less of a menace (Gifford, 1974, p.339); his institutionalisation around the end of the fourteenth century as a recognisable, uniformed jester who could even dispute with the king in court; and the gradual stylisation, at about the same time, of the terms on which he was admitted to a sacred text of 'high' culture all point to one conclusion. That 'low' culture which had been such a threat in the early Middle Ages when Christian culture was establishing its dominance and with which 'high' culture had established a palimpsest-like relationship by the end of the twelfth century, was, by the beginning of the fifteenth century, when that earlier, ambiguous relationship was starting to break down, ripe for active repression.

During the following three-and-a-half centuries, the period when the Western *Logos* was increasingly abstracting itself from the rest of the personality, and Western 'high' culture, increasingly located in courts and towns, was, with the help of the rising middle class, driving a wedge between itself and a Nature that was increasingly subject to the hand of man (Merchant, 1982, pp.46−7 and 143), the aristocratic and ecclesiastical representatives of that culture at first continued to keep jesters. By doing this, they were indicating that they were not averse to being reminded of a 'more primitive' developmental phase (Billington, 1984, p.12) provided that the reminder consisted in a residual, institutionalised sign, who wore motley to remind his masters of his ambivalent cultural position, and bells to warn them of his latent threat (cf. pp.39 and 47). But once the socio-cultural process of abstraction and elevation had been completed and the aristocracy and upper middle classes had totally withdrawn from 'low' culture, even that sign became unacceptable. Consequently, the court jester disappeared – as a uniformed figure from the English Court after Charles I, from the more backward Russian Court in the eighteenth century after Peter the Great, and from more peripheral, rural aristocratic households in Britain during the first half of the eighteenth century (Doran, 1858, pp.223 and 234; Burke, 1978, p.278).

At lower societal levels, the same general process of repression and peripheralisation had three major effects upon the position and activity of the Fool. First, having been deprived after the Reformation of any, even residually ritual function, the Fool of folk-culture could, until the turn of the twentieth century, find refuge only in such ephemeral and marginalised contexts as fair-grounds, Harlequinades, pantomimes or troupes of strolling players, or isolated practices like the Hoxey Hood Game (Billington, 1984, *passim*). Second, following the example of the French theologian Guilelmus Peraldus in the mid-thirteenth century (p.20), the Fool, as in such works of 'high' culture as *Piers Plowman* (*c.* 1380), *Mankind* (1460), Sebastian Brant's *Narren-Schyff* (*Ship of Fools*) (1494),[19] the English morality plays of the later sixteenth century, Stephen Butman's *A Christall Glasse* (1569) and the works of the seventeenth-century Zittau dramatist Christian Weise, became increasingly transformed into the Devil, Sin or Vice (Reuling, 1890, p.169; Billington, 1984, *passim*). And third, where, on the extra-social, travelling stage of the wandering English players in German-speaking lands, the Fool managed to retain a great deal of his 'low', carnivalesque character (Reuling, 1890, pp.67–80), as soon as he became displaced into the printed texts of 'high', bourgeois, German literature, he not only tended to lose much of his earthy, comic force and become more verbal (pp.53 and 114–28), he was also transformed into a mouthpiece for 'moral opinions' (p.82).[20]

19. A work which, between 1494 and 1500, went through twenty-six editions in four languages, thus becoming the first printed European best-seller (Virmond, 1981, p.78).
20. Kern noted the same phenomenon from a more European perspective: 'Amoral and carnivalesque tales known to the Middle Ages and the Renaissance become, under the reign of Protestantism on the one hand, and the Counter-Reformation

Thus, in such works as Brant's *Narren-Schyff* (1494), Pamphilius Gengenbach's *Die Gauchmatt* (1516) and Thomas Murner's *Die Narrenbeschweerung* (*The Conjuration of Fools*) (1518), palimpsest-like ambiguity gives way to conflictual simplicity. In the Protestant Gengenbach's play, the Fool begins by complaining that he has been driven from the centre of court society and forced to become a door-keeper. But, instead of using his new, marginalised position to clown and subvert, he adopts the role of a 'high', moral spokesman, warning people particularly, as you might expect, about commerce with Venus (cf. Reuling, 1890, pp.33–4). Likewise, the Catholics Brant and Murner (who expressed his indebtedness to Brant in lines 22–3 of his Prologue) also appropriated the Fool and Folly into the 'high' value-system, putting both under the negative sign of 'sin' and defining that category very strictly. For both, the Fool is anyone who sets any store by the things of the natural, material world and the Wise Man he who contemplates his weakness and mortality. Indeed, it is significant that Murner should locate the source of all Folly/sin in the fact that all people derive from the 'acker' ('field' or 'plough-land') of a woman's body (4, lines 99–104) and that Brant, whose book is rooted in the medieval tradition linking Folly with water, the moon, sin and death (Boczkowska, 1971, p.66), should have added a final piece to the second edition of the *Narren-Schyff* (1497) in which he specifically attacked Carnival – as though it were the master-image under which all other follies/sins could be subsumed. Finally, it is significant, in this connection, to recall that Brant's friend Johann Geiler von Kaysersberg (a Strasbourg Catholic priest who, in 1498, preached 110 sermons based on the *Narren-Schyff* which appeared in book-form in 1510 as *Navicula, sive specula fatuorum* (*The Ship or Mirror of Fools*)) was, between 1496 and 1509, involved in a controversy about the ancient figure of the *Roraffe*, a monkey-like carving attached to the organ pipes of Strasbourg Cathedral (Schneegans, 1851, pp.25–31 and 45–52). It seems that the action of the bellows caused, to the distraction of the congregation, this figure to gesticulate and his mouth to open and close. But, additionally, during the Whitsuntide High Mass (pp.31 and 36–41), a layman or priest would hide behind a carving higher up on the organ in order to accompany the *Roraffe*'s antics with irreverent songs and carnivalesque mockery as though to remind the congregation of its 'low' origins at precisely that point in the Christian year when human spirituality is most particularly affirmed. Von

---

on the other, *novelas ejemplares*, exemplary tales – and even used as sermons by preachers' (1980, p.43).

Kaysersberg, already known for his attacks on festive licence, saw the *Roraffe* as the protagonist of what is false, wicked, ancient and pagan, and his paper to the City Council of 1501 certainly contributed to the *Roraffe*'s removal some time in the early sixteenth century. Where Kaysersberg chose repression as the means of dealing with an archetypal representative of 'low' culture, Gengenbach, Brant and Murner turned him against the value-system in which he had his roots.

At the same time, however, because the period 1350–1700 was one of transition, the palimpsest-like relationship between 'low' and 'high' culture is still clearly visible in a range of important printed texts. In the first part of the Catholic Erasmus's *In Praise of Folly*,[21] for instance, Dame Folly praises natural, carnivalesque folly as a good, associating it with the underworld, childishness, Pan and Bacchus; contrasting it with Athene (the goddess born from the *head* of a *male* deity); and declaring it to be both the power behind Creation and procreation and the force which makes people human. And in the second part, from the same perspective, Dame Folly, like a *Büttenredner* ('mock preacher') at Fasching, stands normality on its head by castigating the rich, learned and powerful as the real fools. But in the final part, Erasmus shifts his speaker's perspective from 'low' to 'high' and, by making Folly a spiritual rather than an earthy quality, assimilates it into Christian theology by declaring Christ's death on the Cross to be redemptive folly. This third section, far from rescinding the first two, co-exists with it in a state of palimpsest-like ambiguity, making *In Praise of Folly* very untypical of Erasmus's works.[22] The same kind of palimpsest-like relationship between 'high' and 'low' is also visible in the work of the Protestant Hans Sachs. Sachs could write a *Schwank* (short, humorous or satirical poem) like *Ein gesprech mit der Faßnacht von ihrer aygenschafft (A Conversation with Carnival concerning its Nature)* (1540) (Sachs, 1870–1908, vol.5, pp.295–9) in which Carnival, personified as an eyeless, earless beast who lives, significantly, near a river, is castigated for creating profligacy, sexual wantonness, disease and waste. But he also wrote *Schwänke* in which he clearly derives great amusement from the 'low', faecal, carnivalesque tricks which Eulenspiegel,

---

21. Virmond tells us that *In Praise of Folly* went through thirty-one editions in its first ten years (1981, p.78).
22. As a representative of 'high', humanist culture, Erasmus normally displayed revulsion towards the carnivalesque. See, for instance, his *Supputatio Errorum in Censuris Beddae* in Desiderii Erasmi Roterodami, *Opera Omnia*, ed. J. LeClerc, 10 vols. (Gerstenberg, Hildesheim, 1962), vol.9, cols.516–17; also Nigg, 1956, pp.138–9 and 144–9.

that classic trickster figure and 'embodiment of a historically regressive position *vis-à-vis* the ascendant bourgeois culture' (Virmond, 1981, p.59), plays on representatives of 'high' culture, particularly Catholic priests. Similarly, although Sachs's *Das narrn bad* (*The Fools' Bath*) (1530) (vol.5, pp.305–9) is an attack on those fools who offend against the secularising 'high' values involved in the work ethic and the communal life of commercial towns, his remedy for such follies is typically 'low' and carnivalesque: the miscreants should be bathed in excrement! Conversely, although the speaker in *Klag der wilden holtzleut uber die ungetrewen welt* (*Lament of the Wild Men of the Woods on the Faithlessness of the World*) (1530) (vol.3, pp.561–4) is a woodwose, a 'low' figure closely associated with Carnival misrule (see Driesen, 1904; Bernheimer, 1952; Burke, 1978, p.190), that speaker, paradoxically, preaches 'high', Christian values as the remedy for the follies of the modern world. And although Sachs's play *Die Stuticia mit irem hofgesind* (*Folly and her Courtiers*) (1552) (vol.7, pp.17–40) at one level castigates various forms of extremism and immorality as folly, his *Stulticia*, like Erasmus's Dame Folly, begins by admitting that she drives away sadness, care and anxiety, is the source of joy and the daughter of the god of riches and the goddess of youth. Indeed, she even has her court jester, Jeckle, drive away the figure of Fasting because of his lean and hungry look. Finally, in *Hiob* (1558), by the Zurich writer Jakob Ruof, the 'low', libidinous, carnivalesque activities of the fool Calliopus co-exist with the 'high' seriousness of the biblical story of Job; and in the plays of Hans Sachs's successor in Nuremberg, Jakob Ayrer, various transformations of the Fool interpenetrate with and satirise 'high', classical subject-matter (Reuling, 1890, pp.37–8 and 83–113).

The same palimpsest-like ambiguity is still visible a century later in two major German novels: Grimmelshausen's *Simplicissimus* (1669) and Johann Beer's *Das Narrenspital* (*The Fools' Hospital*) (1681). Where, at one level, Grimmelshausen's narrator clearly enjoys the carnivalesque escapades of his 'lower', younger self – who, as Gutzwiller pointed out, is a multiplicity of fool-figures (1959, *passim*) – at another, in his capacity as a 'high', regenerate, moral narrator, he feels duty-bound to censure those escapades (see Rohrbach, 1959; Schmidt, 1960; Sheppard, 1972). Where, from his 'high' point of view, Grimmelshausen's narrator is sometimes impelled to see war-torn Europe as 'one huge battlefield on which God is at war with the Devil', from his 'low' point of view, the same narrator simultaneously sees the world as 'the ever-changing backdrop against which the protean Baldanders can perform his clownish tricks' (Gutzwiller, 1959, p.34) – i.e. as one huge, carnivalesque frolic from which God has withdrawn. Indeed, from this perspective, even the slaughter of the Battle of Wittstock (Book 2, Chapter 27) is presented not realistically, but as a carnivalesque set-piece on the theme of the world-turned-upside-down (Gilbert, 1964/5). Similarly, in Chapters 3–11 of *Das Narrenspital*, Beer's narrator enjoys the gross, two-man Carnival that is continuously celebrated by his unregenerate younger self and his master, the irreligious, decadent, feudal lord Herr Lorenz. But in Chapters 15–22 the same narrator, using secular rather than religious criteria, shifts to a 'high' perspective and satirises the fools who are incarcerated in the lunatic asylum, all of whose behaviour, like that of Herr Lorenz, is marked by various kinds of extremism. Nevertheless, in both novels we notice a clear move away from the palimpsest-like ambiguity of the preceding century. At the end of Book 5 of *Simplicissimus* – and of Book 6, its first *Continuatio* – Grimmelshausen's narrator rejects the 'low' world of kaleidoscopic, carnivalesque folly for the 'high' asceticism of hermitage. And Beer's account of the carnal excesses of the first half of the *Narrenspital* is marked by a distaste that is absent from *Simplicissimus*. Herr Lorenz is likened to a devil; the public openness of true Carnival has become introverted and privatised, transferred to the inside of Herr Lorenz's decaying castle; and the unrestrained, fleshly gusto and liberating carnival laughter of *Simplicissimus* have degenerated into near-pornographic smut and shameful sniggers. Consequently, it is no surprise when, at the end of the novel, Beer's narrator tries to civilise his master by encouraging him to marry; repudiates their former excesses as sinful; and, by becoming an organist, withdraws into a secular hermitage away from the follies of the world – to which, unlike Simplicissimus in the various *Continuationes* and sequels, he never returns.[23]

The Fool and Carnival in German Literature of the Classical Period

As Kern's remarks on the reception of Molière clearly imply (1980, pp.52–9 and 81–2), the second half of the seventeenth century saw a second decisive shift in the relationship between 'high' and 'low'

23. In England, the same misgivings about the 'low' world are evident at the same time in Samuel Butler's description of the Clown in his *Characters* (1665). Although the memory of the Clown's cultic origins is still residually present, Butler disdains him because, in his present, decadent form, his folly is unsightly, vulgar and bestial – devoid of whatever regenerative power it might, originally, have possessed.

value-systems – a juncture that was marked by the publication in 1687 of Newton's *Principia Mathematica*, described by Merchant as 'the most powerful synthesis of the new mechanical philosophy' (1982, p.276). In literary terms, this shift is particularly evident from the transformation undergone by one, central image-cluster. Since the confrontation between the servant Rubin and his master, the merchant, in medieval Carnival plays (Reuling, 1890, pp.12–13 and 19), European culture had thematised the fissure between 'high' and 'low' culture in a series of pairings between fat men and thin men, funny men and straight men, servants and masters. Where, in all such pairings, the thin man (or master) represented the lenten values associated with the 'high' value-system, the fat man (or servant), anchored in the world of matter, stood for those 'low', carnivalesque virtues which continually, by accident or design, subvert the serious, disembodied intellect by reminding it of its earthy origins. Just as the classic Carnival mask mocks 'high' culture by growing a 'low' phallus in the middle of that part of the body where the intellect, in Western topography, is conventionally located, so European literature knows a whole series of carnivalesque inversions which arise when the 'low' servant/fat man achieves overt or covert dominion over the 'high' master/thin man who has made the mistake of despising him or subjecting him to too rigid control. Now where, as late as the sixteenth century, such pairings as Sancho Panza–Don Quijote, Sir Toby Belch–Malvolio or Falstaff–Prince Hal were still clear, symbolic conflicts between representatives of 'high' culture and a 'low' culture that was still thriving (see Kern, 1980, pp.182–8; Bristol, 1985, pp.202–6; Hall, 1985), after the Reformers had done their work, the fat or funny man, like *Lui* in Diderot's *Le Neveu de Rameau* (written *c.* 1770) or Lamme Goedzak in the Belgian Charles de Coster's novel *Tyl Ulenspiegel* (1867), either becomes a character who has lost his cultural roots and representative status, or splits from his master and turns into the picaresque hero whose home is nowhere.[24] In other words, by about the end of the seventeenth century, when the hegemony of 'high' culture has been assured, the conflict between 'high' and 'low' culture, to the extent that it gets into literary texts that have been written for a middle-class reading public, tends to lose its original, ontological implications and become aestheticised

---

24. In our own age, such comic pairings have been largely relegated to such peripheral cultural forms as the music hall, seaside culture, children's comics, cartoons, pantomine and the popular cinema, producing, for example, Jewell and Warris, Dan Dare and Digby, Laurel and Hardy, The Cisco Kid and Sancho, Little and Large and the fat wives and tiny husbands of the comic postcard.

into merely comic interplay.

Correspondingly, by about the end of the 1730s, the obtrusive and vulgar clown Hanswurst (who had made his first literary appearance in Brant's *Narren-Schyff*) had been domesticated, as far as 'high' literature in Germany was concerned, into the tamer, italianate Harlequin, himself a humanised version of an earlier, demonic figure (cf. Reuling, 1890, pp.172–3; Richter, 1981, pp.197 and 200–1). And when, in October 1737, Karoline Neuber, concerned to make theatre respectable (cf. Billington, 1984, pp.73–4 and 88), pushed Gottsched's reservations about the Fool to an extreme and formally banned even Harlequin from her stage in Leipzig's Groß-Bosischer Garten (Wustmann, 1872, pp.149–50), the shift was complete as far as 'high' German literature was concerned. In 1746, Georg Friedrich Meier could still, in his *Untersuchung einiger Ursachen des verdorbenen Geschmacks der Deutschen* (*An Investigation into Some Causes of the Corruption of Taste among the Germans*) claim that Harlequin, 'that cracker of bad jokes, still rules in the theatre' (p.26) and that most Germans preferred 'clownish antics and Harlequin's jokes' to Molière's *Le Misanthrope* (p.7). But after the mid-eighteenth century, when, as Burke put it, 'clergy, nobility and bourgeoisie alike were coming to internalize the ethos of self-control and order' (1978, p.272), and the canon of classical German literature was being established as the cultural expression of those classes, the Fool and the carnivalesque disappeared almost entirely for a century and a half from the foreground of 'high' German literature (Wustmann, 1872, p.153), especially in the Protestant North.[25] And when they did appear, even in an attenuated, disguised or vestigial form, they were nearly always put under a negative sign.

Consequently, Johann Christian Kröger's plea for the reinstatement of Harlequin in the foreword to his two-volume translation of Marivaux (1747), Justus Möser's defence of the 'comic figure' in his *Harlekin oder Vertheidigung des Groteske-Komischen* (*Harlequin, or in Defence of the Comic-Grotesque*) (1761)[26] and Lessing's brief, but nostalgic reference in the seventeeth *Literaturbrief* (16 February 1759) and more extensive defence in the eighteenth essay of his *Hamburgische Dramaturgie* (30 June 1767) were rearguard actions. Moreover, they were relatively tame ones. Möser explicitly dissociated himself from the more primitive 'Hans Wurst' (1968, pp.28 and 31) and called

---

25. Reuling points out that the clown figure persisted in 'low', dialect plays, melodramas and Stranitzky's popular Viennese theatre long after he had been banished from 'high', North German literature (1890, pp.180–1).
26. In which, significantly, he referred to attacks on the Fool as 'this suppression of good Nature' (Möser, 1968, p.19).

the Feast of Fools (with reference to precisely that defence of 1444 cited in note 2) a 'revolting custom' (p.36). And Lessing explicitly supported Möser's tract, restricting his own defence to the plea that Harlequin be allowed to appear in his proper, role-specific costume once more.[27] Conversely, Schiller's statement that 'sensual enjoyment is the one kind of enjoyment that is to be excluded from high [schön] art' (1791, p.135) and distinction between 'low' 'raw natural feelings' and 'higher reason' ('Vernunft'), the moral dignity of human nature which was to be developed by the contemplation of works of art (1792, p.149), were clear pointers to the weight of the negative sign which had been placed over Nature in general and any vestiges of the 'low' value-system in particular. Indeed, Schopenhauer gave even more extensive expression to that value-judgement when he saw the metaphysical Will informing the whole of material Creation in negative terms, presenting it as something 'low' which was to be escaped from by the contemplation of 'high', Platonic ideas. Indeed, 'high' German literature of the classical era severed itself so decisively from what is 'low', became, as Gustav Freytag put it, so much 'the almost miraculous creation of a soul without a body',[28] that the fate of decapitation which either threatens or overtakes so many of its major characters can be seen as a very accurate, albeit unconscious thematisation of the danger inherent in that situation.

The literary results of the shift involved in the establishment of a classical German literature are manifold. Harlequin, the central figure of the 'value-free comic world of the *Commedia dell'Arte*', all but disappeared from the moralistic world of the bourgeois German comedy between 1737 and *c.* 1790, appearing only in such surreptitious, attenuated and sanitised forms as the comic servant (Steinmetz, 1965, pp.5 and 7).[29] In Lessing's *Emilia Galotti* (1772), it is Emilia's carnivalesque experience of 'the House of the Grimaldis . . . the house of pleasure' (V/7) which reveals the power of her 'low' side to her and causes her to seek death at the hands of her Father. In *Egmont* (1788), we hear that Egmont's servants wore 'caps with bells on them, fools' headgear', that the Dutch militia are a 'merry bunch', a carnivalesque Fred Karno's Army who stand no chance

---

27. A point which is made at length by Steinmetz (1965).
28. Quoted in W. Bruford, *Germany in the Eighteenth Century* (Cambridge U.P., 1965), p.292.
29. Steinmetz identifies *Die verkehrte Welt* (*The World-Turned-Upside-Down*) (1725) by the Dresden court poet Johann Ulrich von König as the one eighteenth-century German work which manages to assimilate Harlequin to the service of moral-didactic instruction (1965, p.11).

against the machine-like discipline of Alba's Spanish troops, and that the doomed Egmont refuses to change his natural, carnivalesque way of life even when mortal danger threatens (Goethe, 1948–60, vol.4, pp.400, 416 and 423). Goethe's account of the Roman Carnival which he experienced in Spring 1788 (1948–60, vol.11, pp.484–515) is marked by distance, detachment and an intellectual rather than a visceral enjoyment – as though he were chary of becoming too deeply involved in such a bewildering, topsy-turvy and even violent festival. Similarly, in *Faust I* (completed 1806), the 'Schalk' ('rogue', 'knave', 'trickster') Mephistopheles may, in true carnivalesque manner, bring about Faust's rejuvenation, but he is, though not the Devil himself, an associate of that gentleman; the carnivalesque orgy of 'Walpurgisnacht' (1 May) (which Goethe wrote at the same time as his account of the Roman Carnival (cf. 1948–60, vol.11, pp.667–9 and vol.14, p.454) is obviously diabolic; and it is clearly Faust's association with such carnivalesque-diabolic powers that causes the deaths of Valentin and Gretchen. In Schiller's *Maria Stuart* (1801), Maria's immorality is, in the very first scene, attributed to the fact that she was brought up in the festival atmosphere of a foreign court. Wallenstein's murder in the third play of Schiller's trilogy takes place at the end of the Carnival season, after a Shrove Tuesday feast, and is closely linked with his faith in pre-Christian divinities. In Kleist's *Der Findling* (*The Foundling*) (1811), the destructive passion and profligacy of the irredeemably wicked Nicolo is explicitly associated with Carnival. In Grillparzer's *König Ottokar* (1825), Zawisch, the 'mocking fool',[30] not only prevents reconciliation between Ottokar and Rudolf, thus prolonging the civil war and indirectly causing Ottokar's death, he also steals Ottokar's wife Kunigunde.

The evocation of the reign of Carnival which concludes Büchner's *Leonce und Lena* (1836) is a hopeless gesture of disbelief rather than a statement of faith in the regenerative potential of the re-enactment of the Golden Age of Saturn – and in *Dantons Tod* (*Danton's Death*) (1835), that very divinity is remembered not for presiding over a Golden Age, but for having devoured his children, just as the Revolution is now doing (I/5). In Gotthelf's *Die schwarze Spinne* (*The Black Spider*) (1842), evil in the shape of the black spider is released for the second time as the result of a pagan, carnivalesque orgy on Christmas Eve. In Stifter's *Die Narrenburg* (*The Fools' Castle*) (1843),

---

30. The reference is to Grillparzer's diary entry of 16 September 1827 where such a figure is connected with murder and heartless inability to feel remorse (F. Grillparzer, *Sämtliche Werke*, ed. A. Sauer, 42 vols. (Anton Schroll, Vienna, 1909–41), Section II, vol.8, entry 1615, p.290).

contemporary common sense in the person of the scientist Heinrich, invades, domesticates and modernises the castle, a walled-off island of antique folly, exoticism and passion, and civilises the two fairy-tale beings who live there. In Moerike's *Mozart auf der Reise nach Prag* (*Mozart on his Journey to Prague*) (1855), Mozart is seen to be burning himself out as much by his addiction to carnivalesque festivity as by his artistic genius. In Keller's *Novelle, Der Narr auf Manegg* (*The Fool on Manegg*) (1878), the fool-figure, Buz Falätscher, is associated with wild Nature and dies through his folly on the last day of Carnival. Parsifal, the 'pure fool' of Wagner's last opera (1882) who fails to understand the eucharistic celebration of Act I, is gradually redeemed from his 'low' folly and turned into the Germanic hero who, bearing a phallic spear before him as a sign of the power of patriarchy, re-establishes 'high' Christian values in Act III. He thereby cures Amfortas from a female affliction – menorrhoea – and ensures that Kundry, the ambivalent semi-animal of Act I and the seductress of Act II, discovers her proper, 'low' place as a dumb servant. In Fontane's *Unterm Birnbaum* (*Under the Pear-Tree*) (1885), the inn, far from being a place of carnivalesque festivity, is associated with greed, murder and duplicity; and in *Irrungen, Wirrungen* (*Differences and Confusions*) (1888) the illicit weekend at Hankels Wharf, a kind of abbreviated Carnival which takes place outside normal conventions and in which the lovers had invested so much pleasurable anticipation and hope, turns out, in the end, to be a total disappointment. As such, it marks the beginning of the end of Lena's and Botho's relationship and forms the prelude to heart-ache, separation and, for Botho, an empty marriage. In Hauptmann's *Novelle, Fasching* (*Carnival*) (1887), Kielblock and his wife fall through the ice and perish precisely because they are so addicted to the carnivalesque festivities of winter that they neglect and even refuse work, and waste their earnings irresponsibly. And in Detlev von Liliencron's short story *Der Narr* (*The Fool*) (1888),[31] the now minimalised figure of a dancing, tumbling fool in full costume on a lampshade is, with his 'repulsive face' (p.54), associated with battle, exhaustion and the vision of a mass grave.

Conversely, when a carnivalesque experience or figure does appear in a work of 'high' German literature during the period 1730–1890, it normally does so in such marginalised, diminished, 'non-serious' forms as juvenilia, puppet plays, or children's plays, e.g. Hanswurst in Tieck's *Hanswurst als Emigrant* (*Hanswurst Emi-*

---

31. To be found most easily in G. Schulz (ed.), *Prosa des Naturalismus* (Reclam, Stuttgart, 1980), pp.50–5.

grates) (1795) and *Der gestiefelte Kater* (*Puss in Boots*) (1797), and Hanswurst in Goethe's *Das Jahrmarktsfest zu Plundersweilen* (*The Fair at Plundersweilen*) (written 1773) and *Hans Wursts Hochzeit* (*Hans Wurst's Wedding*) (1775).[32]

Indeed, the only 'high' German texts known to me from the classical period in question which make positive use of Carnival and the Fool are Keller's *Kleider machen Leute* (*Clothes make the Man*) (1874); E.T.A. Hoffmann's *Prinzessin Brambilla* (1821) and Tieck's *Die verkehrte Welt* (*The World Turned Upside-Down*) (1798).[33] However, in the former work, Carnival has been so successfully assimilated to the bourgeois order, become so divorced from its roots, that a highly organised carnival-dance is used not to disrupt or invert normality, but to re-establish it by unmasking Strapinski as an impostor. In Hoffmann's self-styled 'Capriccio', the Roman Carnival, the descriptions of which owe much to Goethe's article mentioned above, is a jokey, magical-fantastic rather than a cathartic, dionysiac-chthonic event. Thus, although it acts as the context in which the initially callow and vain young lovers are enabled, with the help of the magus Celionati, to mature and find themselves, it does not, except in a very playful form, involve those more fundamental, 'low' reminders of copulation, birth and death which Goethe, very guardedly, perceived 'amid the nonsense' on the Roman streets (1948–60, vol.11, pp.515). And Tieck's brilliantly witty play, based on Christian Weise's play of the same name (1683), derives from a highly developed sense that in the modern world, Carnival has been virtually confined to the theatre and there civilised into a pageant of auto-destructing illusions for the literary sophisticate to enjoy intellectually. Thus, within Tieck's inverted world, Grünhelm, initially a member of the bourgeois audience, has to come on stage if he wants to play the fool; Pierrot is so tired of playing the fool that he wants to become a member of the audience; and Harlequin has become an admiral. But the central figure, the clown Skaramuz, far from playing his traditional, dionysiac role, has usurped the kingdom and role of none other than Apollo and become an advocate of reason and order! Indeed, he announces his intention of making Mount

32. Significantly, neither of the two Goethe plays is included in the canonical *Hamburger Ausgabe* but they can be found in M. Morris (ed.), *Der junge Goethe*, 6 vols. (Insel, Leipzig, 1909–12), vol.3, pp.142–56; vol.5, pp.199–212; and vol.6, pp.273–4 and 469–75.

33. When I had all but completed this article, my attention was drawn to the chapter entitled 'Carnival and Costume' in B. Fairley, *Heinrich Heine* (Oxford U.P., 1954), pp.87–111. When this article becomes a book, the positive use of the carnivalesque by Heine, in his own day an outsider to German society, will require detailed attention.

Parnassus into a wealth-creating institution by building a brewery and a bakery there, turning the Castalian Spring into a health farm, and charging the Muses an economic rent for their accommodation! Although the world of Tieck's play may be an inversion of older theatrical traditions, it is also a complex and very accurate specular image of what was happening to the Fool and his realm during the classical age of German Literature. Like Hoffmann, Tieck indulges the carnivalesque only after it has been intellectualised, turned into a private, literary event, and hedged around with multiple ironies.

The 'narrowing down' (Bakhtin, 1968, p.276) to which the carnivalesque is subject during the Classical period can be observed in other areas. During the nineteenth century, those Carnival festivities which had survived the Reformers and the Enlightenment, were, as far as possible, sanitised – purged of their violence and excesses, especially in major centres like Cologne, Mainz and Munich (Orloff, 1980, pp.45–51, 57, 62 and 67). Similarly, the anti-authoritarian, proletarian descendant of Dionysos, Mr Punch, was forced, during the same period, out of the public arena of city streets and either transformed into the (miniaturised) hero of a bowdlerised children's party entertainment, or literally (littorally?) peripheralised by being relegated to the sea-shore, or diabolised by being turned into a being like Quilp in Dickens's *The Old Curiosity Shop* (1840–1) (with whom he is explicitly associated),[34] or rendered more socially acceptable by being turned into tamer figures like Graf Pocci's Kasperl (Keimer, 1981, pp.203–4; Leach, 1985, *passim*). Then again, by the mid-nineteenth century, Tyl Ulenspiegel in Charles de Coster's novel had become so 'high', untricksterlike and unscatalogical that the author had to supplement him with Lamme Goedzak (whose huge belly and insatiable appetite make him a classically carnivalesque, albeit rootless figure). And Harlequin had ceased to be 'the king of an army of dead men's souls who simultaneously terrified and amused the carnival crowd', the 'descendant of an ancient god, half human and half supernatural being who is able to control the elements' (Orloff, 1980, p.41) and become the tearful Pierrot (china effigies of whom have enjoyed renewed popularity in trendy gift-shops over the past few years) (cf. Koebner, 1981, p.194).

Thus, when, in 1897, Rostand's Cyrano (who, with his displaced phallus/nose, seems like a last, braggadocio remnant of Carnival in the straight theatre) first died pathetically on stage and the audience

---

34. It is interesting to note that the original illustration to the novel depicting Quilp's death shows him lying in a bed of reeds with a huge, ithyphallic post appearing to protrude from his groin as though implicitly to denote the indestructible potency of the powers embodied by Mr Punch/Quilp.

went wild with delight, it was as though 'high' culture were celebrating its final, decisive victory over what was 'low' and unacceptable. As Wustmann, echoing Lessing, sensed, Hanswurst and Harlequin had become offensive to bourgeois culture because, far from being characters in the individualistic sense, they were masks, types (1872, pp.160–1), insolent reminders of the illusory nature of the individualised bourgeois ego and its claim to exercise control, and, conversely, pointers to the raw power of primitive, pre-individualised roots of the human personality. Accordingly, when the bourgeois imagination systematically repressed, diabolised, sanitised, peripheralised or miniaturised the Fool and his kingdom, declaring, as in Jakob Wassermann's novel *Kaspar Hauser* (1908), that there was no room for him in the 'real' world, its intuition was entirely accurate. Where Folly appears, the bourgeois ego is made aware of its fragility and, like the foot from the sky which stops the music at the beginning of *Monty Python's Flying Circus* before it can become too ebullient, feels compelled to stamp it out.

Revival and Repression

In his fifteenth lecture on dramatic art and literature (1808) A.W. Schlegel had written, prophetically, of the irrepressible nature of Hanswurst, saying that no sooner is he buried than he pops up again in an unexpected guise (1817, vol.3, p.384). Or, to put it more concretely: when, by the time of Mayhew's account of the puppet play in the 1840s (Leach, 1985, pp.74–5), Mr Punch had become assimilated to 'high' culture and turned into a rationally mathematical being who aped the scientific quantification of dead matter by counting corpses, Joey the Clown had necessarily to emerge in order to mock, torment and supersede him. Correspondingly, just when, in the late nineteenth century, it seemed that the Fool, Folly and the carnivalesque had been driven out of the foreground of German literature once and for all, they re-emerged, albeit in unfamiliar guises, to mock the literary culture which had so systematically repressed them.

Indeed, Nietzsche's whole *oeuvre*, especially his *Genealogy of Morals* (1887) is, with its questionable formulations, multiple contradictions, unresolved muddles and slippery argumentation, simultaneously the product of the hegemony of 'high' (Apollonian) culture and an attempt to overthrow that culture in the name of 'low' (Dionysian) values. Hence his mockery of the 'ascetic ideal' (1972, vol.3, p.305) with its attendant, self-inflicted neuroses and suffering;

attack on Western hubris *vis-à-vis* Nature (p.300); polemic against Wagner's *Parsifal* (pp.287–8); inversion of Schopenhauer (pp.290–3); celebration of the Will to Power as the 'instinct of freedom' (i.e. the vital principle in all things) (p.274); rejection of the 'diabolisation of Nature' (p.278); affirmation of the animal (p.280) and explicit preference for the concept of 'Folly' over that of 'sin' (p.281). Nietzsche's philosophising, whose light or shadow was to fall across European culture for the next half-century, was, of course, an aspect of that cultural crisis which is labelled Modernism and which, involving what Nietzsche's madman called the Death of God (i.e. the radical loss of faith by bourgeois artists and intellectuals in the fundamental canons of Western humanism in general and in nineteenth-century Idealism in particular), was closely bound up with the supplantation of an older way of life by the mass industrial city. As in Hofmannsthal's *Ein Brief* (*Chandos Letter*) (1902), the text which encapsulates most concisely the modernist experience of crisis, the collapse of a 'high', logocentric order allowed more primitive powers to re-emerge. Or, as Kandinsky put it 'The old, forgotten graveyard is beginning to quake. Old, forgotten graves are opening, and forgotten spirits are arising out of them' (1970, p.40).

Within such a context of crisis, the re-emergence of the Fool, Folly and the carnivalesque could be handled in one of three ways. Writers could either continue to diabolise them, identifying them as subversive powers which were hastening the overthrow of a (fundamentally good) old order. Or they could be presented as necessary, even comic correctives for an order which had become too rigid. Or they could be viewed as images of a complex of values which could enable individuals to find their way within a chaotic reality from which all objective, fixed points had disappeared.

Christian Buddenbrook belongs in the first category, for Mann not only depicts him as a clown with a bald head, thinning red hair around the temples, small, round, sunken eyes, a large nose and baggy trousers (VIII/1) and associates him with the Circus, he also continually links him in *Buddenbrooks* (1901) with the forces which are destroying the world of the old-established commercial bourgeoisie. Similarly, in *The Magic Mountain* (1924), it is Hans Castorp's experience with Clavdia at Fasching which is crucial in undermining his bourgeois existence as an engineer, for it causes him to stay in the Berghof, facilitates the development of his latent fascination with disease and death, brings him into the orbit of the comically Dionysiac, but self-destructive Peeperkorn, and, finally, precipitates him into the War – which Mann, significantly, describes in the last sentence of the novel as 'this world carnival ['Weltfest'] of death'.

And in Wedekind's Lulu plays, Lulu, the Earth Spirit, although a carnivalesque character who is linked with the circus and wages a one-woman war on the bloated representatives of bourgeois culture, is ultimately connected with disease, and, in the best tradition of the 'high' German canon, murdered.

As far as the second possibility is concerned, it is the Munich Carnival which confronts Tonio Kröger with his true nature and causes him to return northwards, to his proper habitat. Similarly, it is the 'low', carnivalesque street-musicians in Mann's *Death in Venice* (1911) who, in association with the other Dionysiac characters, help restore some degree of balance in von Aschenbach's excessively Apollonian personality – a figure whom Mann presents as the representative of Western bourgeois society as a whole. Similarly, we learn that Galater in Kafka's *The Castle* (1926) had sent K. the two clownish Assistants in order to cheer him up a little, to put him in touch, through their childlike antics and folly, with the lost, spontaneous sides of his over-cerebral nature. And in Hesse's *Steppenwolf* (1927), it is Hermine, a magical being explicitly associated with music, dancing, carnivalesque events and sexual generosity, who brings back the vital element into Harry Haller's dried-up routine of a life.

In the third category, one immediately thinks of Chaplin, Keaton and Lloyd, those typically modernist heroes of the typically modernist medium, all little men who, through their carnivalesque clowning, manage to keep their balance in a crazy, modern world. Not to mention Hašek's Švejk (1921–3), an archetypal fool-figure of whom one can never be sure whether he is extremely clever or extremely stupid. Švejk practises the carnivalesque virtues of eating and drinking; is good with animals; associates with Mařek (a type of intellectual court jester) and Baloun (a type of primitive fool whose very name links him with Carnival); loves topsy-turvy situations (like the Fools' Masses celebrated by the drunken Chaplain); creates mayhem by taking military orders so seriously that their intention is inverted; refuses to be locked up for any length of time; feels at home in the lunatic asylum and comes into his subversive own in interstitial situations (like the incident on the train when his period of official arrest comes to an end). Indeed, Švejk's progress to the Front can be seen as one long Carnival procession at the end of which he evades battle by the carnivalesque device of changing his clothes, so ensuring captivity by his own side. Because the world at war is a lunatic Carnival which nevertheless pretends to rationality, both Švejk and his creator sense that the only way to deal with it is to accept its folly and surpass it.

But perhaps the 'high' German modernist text which best exemplifies this third category is Mann's *Felix Krull* (written 1910–12 and 1951–3; published 1954) – a work about which the author had serious misgivings (Lehnert, 1964), presumably because, when writing it, he found himself espousing Dionysiac values about which he normally had considerable reservations. Krull is the scion of a family which is explicitly associated with Carnival, albeit in its sanitised, Rhineland form, and like those carnivalesque characters who reverse their normal sexual roles, he is androgynous. He is also a classic trickster figure who deals in deception and illusion (Beddow, 1980), particularly attracted to the circus, a residual pagan survival, and closely associated with various figures from pre-Christian mythology, notably Hermes (Nelson, 1971). But, more importantly for this essay, Krull develops from small-time con-artist and parasite to a being who becomes more and more conscious that ultimately, his protean nature, bi-sexuality, love of illusion and refusal to be trapped by rigid roles and institutions derive from having his roots in a material Creation which is itself one huge, carnivalesque pageant. If Schopenhauer had put the Carnival of Creation under a negative sign, then Professor Kuckuck's lyrical lecture (III/5), the crucial event in Krull's expansion of consciousness (Beddow, 1980, pp.88–9), inverts this evaluation, presenting the Cosmos as a 'festival' ('Fest') and locating its value in its very transience. Where, in *Buddenbrooks*, Schopenhauer had offered the tired Thomas Buddenbrooks a way out of the illusions and changeability of the world, in *Krull*, Kuckuck's carnivalesque inversion of Schopenhauer grounds Felix more securely in that world.

The same spirit of Schopenhauer without tears informs Dada, that troupe of metaphysical clowns who, precisely because they had set themselves against classical humanist assumptions, deliberately tried to displace Carnival from literary texts into more public sites again, and consciously attempted to re-inject the repressed, 'low' ontology into the mainstream of Western culture (Sheppard, 1979). Consequently, they were all but consigned to oblivion by canonical literary science for fifty years, until the upheavals of the 1960s, the neo-Dada of artists like Jean Tinguely (Poley, 1981, pp.221–2) and the advent of Post-Modernism made people aware of Dada's diverse progeny. It is no accident the most Dada events took place during the Carnival season, and Hanne Bergius has shown in detail (1981) how Dada, acting as the embodiment of the 'collective shadow' in the Jungian sense (p.214), used imagery and forms derived from such 'low' sources as the world of the madman, the child, the *variété* and the *Tingeltangel* (music hall or cabaret) – those marginalised proletarian enclaves where, as Wustmann noted in 1872, transformations of the Fool were still to be found (p.159). Moreover, precisely because the Dadaists, like Kuckuck, were intent upon confronting 'high', humanist culture with an alternative ontology which re-situated man within the flux of Nature and overturned the Western notion that Nature is an evil force to be subjugated, they were drawn to the vitalist philosophy of Henri Bergson[35] and made considerable use of Eastern and Western mystical texts which presented God as being at work in the vital processes of Nature.[36] Consequently, despite the residue of patriarchal terminology implicit in the movement's name, Dada might be described as the latter-day celebration of the ever-changing moon-goddess who presides over the *Lunapark*, as the attempt to remind those representatives of 'high', humanist culture who had brought about the First World War of the power of the 'low' *Magna Mama* who perpetually gives birth to the liberating nonsense of Carnival.[37] Hence the importance in Dada poetry of such magical, creative figures as Arp's Kaspar and Schwitters's Anna Blume (Sheppard, 1983), and the incidence, in its visual work, of images of transvestitism and bi-sexuality, the best-known of which is probably Marcel Duchamp's female *persona* Rrose Selavy (= 'arroser – c'est la vie').

Writing in the late 1970s, Edith Kern took an optimistic view of the re-emergence of the carnivalesque in twentieth-century literature after centuries of repression (1980, pp.85–116). From the lenten perspective of the mid-1980s, however, the picture looks somewhat different. First, with the end of the high modernist period and the transformation of the carnivalesque enthusiasm of Dada into a cultural hang-over (of which Max Beckmann's masterpiece, *Carnival* (1920), is a timely visual transcription),[38] the picture darkens significantly. In Ödön von Horváth's play *Kasimir und Karoline*

35. See Hugo Ball's comment of 9 September 1917 in *Die Flucht aus der Zeit*, 2nd (revised) edn (Josef Stocker, Lucerne, 1946), p.187; cf. Merchant (1982), p.263.
36. See R. Sheppard, 'Dada and Mysticism: Influences and Affinities' in S. Foster and R. Kuenzli (eds), *Dada Spectrum: The Dialectics of Revolt* (Coda, Madison, 1979), pp.91–113, and J. Hancock, 'Arp's Chance Collages' in S. Foster (ed.), *Dada/Dimensions* (UMI, Ann Arbor, 1985), pp.48–82. Nigg (1956, p.74) also implicitly suggests why, on 12 May 1917, Alberto Spaini should have read from the works of Jacopone da Todi at the Fourth *Dada-Soirée* in Zurich.
37. In this context it is extremely interesting to note the closeness between the 'matriarchal aesthetic' proposed by Heide Göttner-Abendroth ('Nine Principles of a Matriarchal Aesthetic' in Gisela Ecker (ed.), *Feminist Aesthetics* (The Women's Press, London, 1985), pp.81–94) and the anti-aesthetic of Dada described, for instance, in Sheppard (1979).
38. Now in the Tate Gallery. For a detailed analysis of this picture see S. O'Brien Twohig, *Beckmann: Carnival* (Tate Gallery, London, 1984).

(1932), the Munich October Festival takes place not under the sign of Luna, but under that of the Zeppelin, the symbol of 'high', phallic, technological power; and it involves not joyous regeneration, but sordid squabbling, furtive sexual titillation and, in the end, violence. Similarly, while Brecht made extensive use of the *topos* of Carnival, he had an equally ambiguous relationship with the whole subject. Although, in one sense, Brecht clearly enjoyed the larger-than-life, carnivalesque vitality of Baal (1922), he became increasingly critical of him as the play went on. Although, at one level, Brecht's Mother Courage (written 1939) can be seen as the presiding, bi-sexual divinity of a diminishing Carnival procession which is making its way through a world-turned-upside-down, Courage has harnessed her cart to one of the Four Horsemen of the Apocalypse. As a result, Carnival turns into a Dance of Death, and while Courage is admired for her sheer existential defiance, she is simultaneously censured for her moral and social irresponsibility. Although *Schweyk in the Second World War* (written 1943) was based on the carnivalesque hero of Hašek's novel, Brecht had to de-carnivalise Schweyk to make him credible as a proletarian hero and moral-political mouthpiece. Although Azdak in *The Caucasian Chalk Circle* (written 1943–5) is a kind of Lord of Misrule who temporarily re-establishes the reign of Saturn in a play that is 'centred on carnival motifs and a carnival "hero"' (Hall, 1985, p.139; cf. Eagleton, 1981, pp.170–1), he is also an extremely nasty piece of work, a mirror-image of the exploitative society which Brecht opposes, and entirely without the simple honesty of his forebear, Sancho Panza. Finally, the hedonistic Galileo (written 1938–9) is clearly a carnivalesque character. He is associated, in Scene 8, with Priapus, the obscene, pre-Christian god of fertility, and his scientific discoveries turn the world upside-down by destroying the distinction between above and below and overthrowing the literal authority of the Bible. Nevertheless, Scene 10 (which is set on Shrove Tuesday 1632 and identifies Galileo with the Lord of Misrule) is not without criticism of the social disorder which Galileo's discoveries have triggered off; and Scene 14 suggests that Galileo's hedonism has caused him to make light of weighty issues and thus betray science and human progress. While Brecht is drawn to the carnivalesque ethos because of its subversive potential, he is critical of it when, deprived of a well-defined location, it overflows its proper boundaries, becomes a way of life and prevents a serious confrontation with moral and political issues. As Eagleton sees (1981, p.171), Brecht may, in contrast to the conventional view, recognise the affinities between the 'funny' clown and the 'serious' revolutionary (cf. Pfister, 1987, pp.27–8). But he also invites us to ponder their differences, and he would, I think, have sympathised with the question which Mann posed in mid-1916 in connection with his cessation of work on *Krull*: 'Is it permissible, at a time when human society is in a situation of crisis, to play with serious matters and transform them into individual hilarity?' (cited in Lehnert, 1964, pp.272).

After 1945, the picture becomes darker still inasmuch as post-war German writers have, on the whole, been concerned to show even more unequivocally how little room there is for either the genuine Fool or the oppositional licence of Carnival in the highly structured world of consumer capitalism. As Günter Grass said in a speech delivered at Princeton in 1966 on the question of the writer in society: 'There are no personal advisers, there are no court jesters any more' (1980, pp.64–5). Thus, in Eva Demski's novel *Karneval* (1981), the (Mainz) Carnival has become a 'horrible masquerade' consisting of 'borrowed, worn-out, watered-down forms' (1984, p.55), a totally commercialised media event which is controlled by 'men dressed in black who looked as if they were masters of the art of making money' (p.88) and which leads to attempted murder and the nervous breakdown of the girl who is forced to play the role of Carnival Princess. In Tankred Dorst's play *Toller* (1968), the Munich Soviet of 1919, led by clownish *literati*, is presented as a carnivalesque event – an aspect particularly emphasised by Patrice Chéreau's Milan production of November 1970. As such, it is doomed from the start and results in savage repression by the forces of law and order. Grass's Oskar Matzerath in *The Tin Drum* (1959), a classic fool-figure (cf. Kern, 1980, pp.92–5) who can disrupt a Nazi Party rally with his drum – the instrument typical both of the sixteenth-century Pickelhäring (Reuling, 1890, p.70) and of Richard Huelsenbeck's activity in the Dada Cabaret Voltaire – and who is endowed with a priapan sexuality, has to grow up and become normal as soon as peace breaks out. In Peter Handke's play *Kaspar* (1967), the innocent, natural fool Kaspar (Hauser) is systematically socialised by the 'Einsager' (roughly 'indoctrinators'), the transmitters of conventional, ideologically saturated language such as radio announcers, speaking clocks, answering machines, football commentators, narrators of cartoon films, interviewers, keep-fit teachers, policemen, etc. Significantly, Kaspar's first sentence is 'I would like to be the kind of person that someone else has once been', and this urge to conform is so strong that he readily learns the language of 'order' from the 'indoctrinators', even though this language enervates him, causes him pain, deprives him of his unselfconsciousness, splits him, by the end of the play, into six, conditions him into reciting the clichés of freedom and autonomy like a mac'ine and, in the end, leads him to accept the *minutiae* of petty bourgeois behaviour. Kaspar's last words, recalling those of the betrayed Othello (IV/1), are 'goats and monkeys' – desperate, residual memories of a lost natural state or a final, clownish insult hurled at his tormentors.

In Patrick Süskind's *Das Parfum* (1985; E.T. 1986 as *Perfume*), Grenouille (who, like Kaspar Hauser, is a natural fool in that he lives without any human contact in a cave for seven years) is, in fact, the complete antithesis of his ancestor, being the embodiment of natural evil rather than natural goodness. Although Grenouille might be seen to have some connection with Carnival through his mastery of the art of perfumery and concomitant ability to liberate people from everyday banality, Süskind stresses the anti-carnivalesque, technologised nature of that art. He describes at length how it involves the violation of Nature and the reduction of living flowers and animals to sucked-out cadavers, and then reinforces that picture by having Grenouille murder twenty-five virgins in order to produce the consummate distillate. Indeed, when, towards the end of the novel, Grenouille avoids his own execution by provoking a carnivalesque orgy by means of that distillate, it brings about not catharsis, but a monumental collective hangover, shame, vile smells and the execution of an innocent man. Nevertheless, in the very last chapter, Grenouille's art proves to be self-destructive. It brings about his own death in that his ultimate distillate provokes the scum of Paris to kill and devour him in a stinking graveyard. And in Thomas Bernhard's *Wittgensteins Neffe* (*Wittgenstein's Nephew*) (1982), the central fool-figure, Paul Wittgenstein, the nephew of the philosopher and a literary descendant of Diderot's *Lui*, is so alienated from his ancient roots that he cannot stand the countryside, and so mortally sick with cancer that he is quite unable to bring any carnivalesque gaiety into the urban, bourgeois world in which he ekes out an existence as the last of the tolerated clowns.

In a world where the work ethic is firmly established as the norm and the means of transmitting the ideology which underpins and reinforces it are so pervasive that all the world turns into a constructed electronic stage (cf. Handke's preface to *Kaspar*), childhood is increasingly abolished, the imagination colonised, leisure industrialised, eggs are transformed from a fertility symbol into a hidden threat, conformity becomes *de rigueur*, and sexuality is reduced as far as possible to an anxiety-fraught fantasy activity with the particular help of the secularised visions of Hell and Damnation contained in the AIDS posters. Because, in such a world, the lenten values of slimness and leanness come into their own once more, the Fool must either be forced or conditioned into normality (Grass and Handke), destroyed (Bernhard), or, like the Clown who fronts for McDonald's hamburgers, made an agent of the process whereby we make mincemeat of the natural (Süskind). Similarly, Carnival has either to be put down by force (Dorst) or, as with Red Nose Day, appropriated by the organised fun ethic of consumer capitalism and transformed from a wanton, but therapeutic event into one which is regulated and commercial. It is in such a context that the work of Heinrich Böll acquires particular significance since Böll, who was intimately familiar with the Rhineland Carnivals, uses the *topoi* of Carnival and the Fool in strikingly complex ways.

Die verlorene Ehre der Katharina Blum (1974; E.T. as *The Lost Honour of Katharina Blum*, 1975), for example, takes place against a two-fold background of Carnival. On the one hand, there is the institutionalised Carnival in Cologne, and on the other, the world-turned-upside-down of the [*Bild-*]*Zeitung*. Like our own tabloids, the [*Bild-*] *Zeitung* is a carnivalesque collage or *bricolage* which deals in events (misleadingly called 'news') where normality is inverted; promotes the fun ethic; and provides fantasy material about media personalities. But in contrast to the authorities in the High Middle Ages, such papers have privatised Carnival and allow their appropriated version to be enacted solely in the fantasy of their readers. Indeed, they use that version much as the Catholic Church of the Counter-Reformation used the appropriated Carnival processions of *its* epoch: as a morality which both reinforces the prevailing reality principle and associates that principle with a certain kind of political message (cf. Moser, 1982). Consequently, the homogenised, latter-day fertility goddesses of the tabloids appear in their full glory not in public, on the front page, but surreptitiously, on page 3, surrounded by articles which frequently warn against precisely those carnivalesque excesses in which the fertility goddesses apparently tempt their beholders to indulge. In Böll's novel, Katharina, a very wilted flower at the outset, is affected by both forms of Carnival. The first, as though in fulfilment of its ancient function, initially brings her to life emotionally and sexually by introducing her to Schönner, only then, however, to bring about her arrest. Indeed, the deceptive, treacherous nature of the institutionalised modern Carnival is indicated by the extent to which it has been infiltrated by police disguised as sheikhs (a striking image of contemporary commercial power and its attendant fantasies), with one officer going so far as to perform his official, phone-tapping functions while sitting on that very throne from which, according to Bakhtin, so much carnivalesque imagery flows. And the second form of Carnival martyrs

Katharina, like that other St Catherine, on the wheels of its own presses, turning her into yet another fantasy-figure who both feeds and acts as a moral warning to the petty bourgeois imaginations of the [Bild-]Zeitung's readers.[39]

Analogously, in *Ansichten eines Clowns* (1963; E.T. as *The Clown*, 1965), Carnival and the role of the clown have become so appropriated and packaged by modern society that Hans Schnier refuses to train properly to become one, preferring to perform untrained in such peripheralised contexts as village halls and sports clubs. Indeed, Schnier has so little space in which to perform that he is confined almost exclusively to a practice mat within hotel rooms, and has retained so little of the ancient, subversive vitality of Carnival that he is presented as a cripple who is reduced to making insulting phone-calls to marginal signifiers of the established order – monks and priests. Conversely, in *Gruppenbild mit Dame* (1971; E.T. as *Group Portrait with Lady*, 1973), the true power of the carnivalesque is visible not in the institution of Carnival – which never features – but in the Revolt of the Dustmen, largely foreign workers, a vestigial image of the latent power of what is despised and rejected, an example of the exaltation of the humble and weak over the mighty.

The treatment of Carnival in post-war West German literature goes hand in hand with what Merchant (1982) called 'The Death of Nature'. Acid rain, moribund forests, dying seals, massive pollution, Chernobyl – all find their literary counterparts in the disappearance of Nature as a regenerative power from the modern German novel. In *Gruppenbild mit Dame*, for example, that power is confined to an eccentrically blossoming rose-tree in a nunnery garden, and in *Katharina Blum*, the whole situation is symbolised by the indefinite incarceration of Katharina, the younger, but related sister of Dada's Anna Blume ('Blume' = 'flower'). Perhaps, then, Carnival and the Fool will reappear in German literature as powerful forces for the good only when the ecological damage that we are inflicting on the environment and the psychological damage that we are inflicting on ourselves forces us to recognise that, in the true tradition of the 'world-turned-upside-down', our confident, technological rationality comes very near at times to megalomaniac folly and that the apparent folly of so-called primitive cultures may contain a deal of concealed wisdom. Perhaps, too, like Chamisso's Peter Schlemihl (1813), the real fool who sold his literal shadow to the Devil, we need to recover our metaphorical shadow as that is manifested in the

---

39. For a real-life version of Böll's fictional narrative, see 'Anatomy of a Sex Romp', *New Statesman and Society*, vol.2, no.38 (24 February 1989), pp.33–6.

natural folly of Carnival if we are not to end up as similarly lonely, rootless tourists on a poisoned planet. The carnivalesque ethic may, as Brecht and Mann clearly saw, have its limitations, but it involves a respect for Nature and the totality of the human personality that we are in danger of losing, and whose reinstatement, together with the closely related problem of the re-definition of gender roles and relations, may well form the most important task facing German writers over the next half century.

References

Bakhtin, M. (1968) *Rabelais and his World*, MIT, Boston
Beddow, M (1980) 'Fiction and Meaning in Thomas Mann's *Felix Krull*', *JES*, 10, 77–92
Bergius, H. (1981) 'Dada als Buffonade und Totenmesse zugleich' in S. Poley (ed.), *Unter der Maske des Narren*, Hatje, Stuttgart, pp.208–20
Bernheimer, R. (1952) *Wild Men in the Middle Ages*, Harvard U.P., Cambridge, Mass.
Billington, S. (1984) *A Social History of the Fool*, Harvester, Brighton
Boczkowska, A. (1971) 'The Lunar Symbolism of the Ship of Fools by Hieronymus Bosch', *Quarterly for Art History*, 86, 47–69
Bristol, M. (1985) *Carnival and Theater: Plebeian Culture and the Structure of Authority in Renaissance England*, Methuen, New York and London
Burke, P. (1978) *Popular Culture in Early Modern Europe*, Temple Smith, New York and London
Davis, N. (1975) *Society and Culture in Early Modern France*, Duckworth, London
Demski, E. (1984) *Karneval*, Ullstein, Frankfurt/Main, Berlin and Vienna
Derrida, J. (1978) *Writing and Difference*, Routledge and Kegan Paul, London
Doran, Dr J. (1858) *The History of Court Fools*, Richard Bentley, London
Driesen, O. (1904) *Der Ursprung des Harlekins*, Duncker, Berlin
Eagleton, T. (1981) 'Carnival and Comedy: Bakhtin and Brecht' in *Walter Benjamin or Towards a Revolutionary Criticism*, New Left Books, London, pp.143–72
Elias, N. (1978) *The Civilizing Process*, vol.1, Blackwell, Oxford
Gifford, D. (1974) 'Iconographical Notes towards a Definition of the Medieval Fool', *Journal of the Warburg Institute*, 37, 336–42
Gilbert, M. (1964/5) 'Simplex and the Battle of Wittstock', *GLL*, 18, 264–9
Ginzburg, C. (1983) 'Charivari, Jugendbünde und Wilde Jagd: Über die

Gegenwart der Toten' in *Spurensicherungen: Über verborgene Geschichte, Kunst und soziales Gedächtnis*, Wagenbach, Berlin, pp.47–60

Goethe, J. (1948–60) *Werke, Hamburger Ausgabe*, 14 vols., Christian Wegner, Hamburg

Grass, G. (1980) 'Vom mangelnden Selbstbewusstsein der schreibenden Hofnarren unter Berücksichtigung nicht vorhandener Höfe' in *Aufsätze zur Literatur*, Luchterhand, Darmstadt and Neuwied, pp.59–66

Gutzwiller, P. (1959) *Der Narr bei Grimmelshausen*, Francke, Berne

Hall, J. (1985) 'Falstaff, Sancho Panza and Azdak: Carnival and History', *Comparative Criticism*, 7, 127–45

Huizinga, J. (1965) *The Waning of the Middle Ages*, Peregrine Books, Harmondsworth

Johannsmeier, R. (1984) *Spielmann, Schalk und Scharlatan: Die Welt als Karneval*, Rowohlt, Reinbek b. Hamburg

Kandinsky, W. (1970) *Über das Geistige in der Kunst*, 9th edn, Benteli, Berne

Keimer, J. (1981) 'Nicht Mensch – nicht Gott – nicht Teufel' in Poley, pp.202–7

Kerényi, K. (1976) *Dionysos: Archetypal Image of Independent Life*, Princeton U.P.

Kern, E. (1980) *The Absolute Comic*, Columbia U.P., New York

Koebner, T. (1981) 'Der Narr auf der Bühne' in Poley, pp.191–4

Leach, R.(1985) *The Punch and Judy Show: History, Tradition and Meaning*, Batsford, London

Lehmann, P. (1963) *Die Parodie im Mittelalter*, 2nd (revised) edn, Hiersemann, Stuttgart

Lehnert, H. (1964) 'Anmerkungen zur Entstehungsgeschichte von Thomas Manns "Bekenntnisse des Hochstaplers Felix Krull", "Der Zauberberg" und "Betrachtungen eines Unpolitischen"', *DVjs*, 38, 267–72

Merchant, C. (1982) *The Death of Nature*, Wildwood House, London

Möser, J. (1968) *Harlekin: Texte und Materialien mit einem Nachwort*, ed. H. Boethius, Gehlen, Bad Homburg, Berlin and Zurich

Moser, D.-R. (1982) 'Of Devils and Witches, Princes, Fools and Sinners', *German Research: Reports of the DFG*, no.2, 13–16

Mundy, J. (1973) *Europe in the High Middle Ages 1150–1309*, Longman, Harlow

Nelson, D. (1971) *Portrait of the Artist as Hermes*, North Carolina U.P., Chapel Hill

Nietzsche, F. (1972) *Werke*, 5 vols., Ullstein, Frankfurt/Main

Nigg, W. (1956) *Der christliche Narr*, Artemis, Zurich and Stuttgart

Orloff, A. (1980) *Karneval: Mythos und Kult*, Perlinger, Wörgl

Pfister, M. (1987) 'Comic Subversion: A Bakhtinian View of the Comic in Shakespeare', *Jahrbuch der deutschen Shakespeare-Gesellschaft (West)*, 27–43

Poley, S. (1981) 'Interview mit Jean Tinguely' in *Unter der Maske des Narren*, Hatje, Stuttgart, pp.221–7

Reuling, C. (1890) *Die komische Figur in den wichtigsten deutschen Dramen bis*

Ende des XVII. Jahrhunderts, Göschen, Stuttgart
Richter, K. (1981) 'Die Verwandlungen des Harlekins' in Poley, pp.195–201
Rohrbach, G. (1959) *Figur und Charakter: Strukturuntersuchungen an Grimmelshausens Simplicissimus*, Bouvier, Bonn
Sachs, H. (1870–1908) *Werke*, ed. A. von Keller, 26 vols., Literarischer Verein in Stuttgart, Tübingen
Schiller, F. (1791) 'Über den Grund des Vergnügens an tragischen Gegenständen' in *Schillers Werke, Nationalausgabe*, 42 vols., Böhlaus Nachfolger, Weimar, vol.20, pp.133–47
Schiller, F. (1792) 'Über die tragische Kunst', *Werke*, vol.20, pp.148–70
Schlegel, A. (1817) *Vorlesungen ueber dramatische Kunst und Litteratur*, 2nd edn, 3 vols., Mohr, Heidelberg
Schmidt, L. (1960) 'Das Ich in "Simplicissimus"', *Wirkendes Wort*, 10, 215–20
Schneegans, L. (1851) *Das Pfingstfest und der Roraffe im Münster zu Straßburg*, J.P. Rißler, Mülhausen
Sheppard, R. (1972) 'The Narrative Structure of Grimmelshausen's *Simplicissimus*', *FMLS*, 8, 15–26
Sheppard, R. (1979) 'What is Dada?', *Orbis Litterarum*, 34, 175–207
Sheppard, R. (1983) 'Tricksters, Carnival and the Magical Figures of Dada Poetry', *FMLS*, 19, 116–25
Southern, R. (1953) *The Making of the Middle Ages*, Hutchinson, London
Steinmetz, H. (1965) *Der Harlekin: Seine Rolle in der deutschen Komödientheorie und -dichtung des 18. Jahrhunderts*, Wolters, Groningen
Underhill, E. (1911) *Mysticism*, Faber, London
Virmond, W. (1981) *Eulenspiegel und seine Interpreten*, Arbeitsstelle für Hermen-Bote und Eulenspiegelforschung, West Berlin
Weber, M. (1968) *The Protestant Ethic and the Spirit of Capitalism*, 9th edn, Allen and Unwin, London
Wustmann, G. (1872) 'Die Verbannung des Harlekin durch die Neuberin', *Schriften des Vereins für die Geschichte Leipzigs*, 2, 149–63

Notes on Contributors

Dr Elizabeth Boa is Senior Lecturer in German, Nottingham University. Her main research interests are feminist criticism, women's writing and Kafka. Her major publications are *Critical Strategies: The German Novel in the Twentieth Century* (with J.H. Reid) (1972) and *The Sexual Circus: Wedekind's Theatre of Subversion* (1987).

Dr Steve Giles is Lecturer in German, Nottingham University. His main research interests are modern critical theory, political theatre and the literature of the Weimar Republic. His major publication is *The Problem of Action in Modern European Drama* (1981).

Dr Hans-Joachim Hahn is Principal Lecturer in charge of German, Oxford Polytechnic. His main research interests are German Romanticism, the crisis of identity in German literature and the position of the intellectual in Germany.

Dr David Jenkinson is Principal Lecturer in German, Goldsmiths' College, University of London. His main research interests are Brecht and the literature of the GDR. He is currently preparing a book entitled *Brecht's Major Plays: The Socialist Vision*.

Professor Helmut Kreuzer is Professor of German at the University of Siegen, West Germany. He is the editor of several series of literary and scholarly books and of the periodical *LiLi*. His numerous publications include a book on Bohemianism (1968), two books on Hebbel, *Mathematik und Dichtung* (4th edn, 1971), *Die zwei Kulturen* (2nd edn, 1988), *Fernsehsendungen und ihre Formen* (with Karl Prümm) (1979), *Sachwörterbuch des Fernsehens* (1982) and *Magazine audiovisuell* (with Heidemarie Schumacher) (1988).

Dr Anthony Phelan is Lecturer in German Studies, University of Warwick. His main research interest is Heine and modernity. His major publication is a collection of essays entitled *The Weimar Dilemma: Intellectuals in the Weimar Republic* (1985).

Professor Jörg Schönert is Professor of German at the University of Hamburg. His main research interests are literary theory, the methodology of literary history and the relationships between literature and other areas of social experience. His major publications are *Roman und Satire im 18. Jahrhundert* (1969), *Carl Sternheims Dramen* (1975) and *Literatur und Kriminalität* (1983).

Dr Richard Sheppard is Lecturer in German, University of Oxford and a Fellow at Magdalen College. Before that he was Professor of European Literature at the University of East Anglia – where the conference took place in 1988 out of which this volume of essays grew. His main research interests are European Modernism, Literature and Politics in the Weimar Republic and the function of Carnival and the Fool in German literature from the Middle Ages to the present day. His major publications fall mainly in the area of European Modernism (1890–1930).

Professor Michael Titzmann is Professor of German at the University of Passau, West Germany. His main research interests are the semiotics of literature, literary theory (with particular reference to the methodological problems involved in writing histories of literature) and the social and intellectual history of German literature from the sixteenth century to the present day. His major publications are *Strukturale Textanalyse* (2nd edn, 1989), *Modelle des literarischen Strukturwandels* (1990) and *Probleme von Bild-Text-Beziehungen* (1990).

Dr Chris Weedon is Lecturer in German, University of Wales, Cardiff. Her main research interests are German cinema, critical theory, feminist criticism and the literature of the GDR. Her major publications are *Feminist Practice and Poststructuralist Theory* (1987) and *Die Frau in der DDR* (1988).

Dr Margot Zutshi is Lecturer in German, Royal Holloway and Bedford New College, University of London. Her main research interests are literary theory, twentieth-century German literature and the literature and institutions of the two Germanies. Her major publication is *Literary Theory in Germany: A Study of Genre and Evaluation Theories 1945–1965* (1981).

Index

Abbs, Peter, 3
Achternbusch, Herbert, 25, 288
Adler, Jeremy, 211–18 *passim*, 232
Adorno, Theodor, 36–42 *passim*, 46, 50, 72, 75, 248, 275
Alembert, Jean le Rond d', 26
Allemann, Beda, 16n10
Allende, Isabel, 22
Alt, Franz, 27
Althusser, Louis, 5, 148n4, 193, 212n1, 254, 258, 261–77
Amacher, Richard E., 4
Anders, Günther, 26, 37
Andres, Stefan, 11
Anouilh, Jean, 11
Aquinas, St Thomas, 280
Aristotle, 66
Arnim, Achim von, 47
Arnold, Armin, 213–16
Arnold, Matthew, 1, 5, 41, 246
Arp, Hans, 307
Artaud, Antonin, 289
Auerbach, Erich, 13
Ayrer, Jakob, 294

Baader, Franz von, 47
Bachelard, Gaston, 261
Bachmann, Ingeborg, 9, 128–44
Bachofen, Johann Jacob, 115
Baker, Kenneth, 255
Bakhtin, Mikhail, 138, 193, 250f., 278–315
Ball, Hugo, 2
Barthes, Roland, 52, 192f., 240n17, 246, 251, 264n3
Baudelaire, Charles, 49
Baudrillard, Jean, 22, 26, 29
Beauvoir, Simone de, 115
Becher, Johannes R., 154
Beckmann, Max, 307
Beer, Johann, 294f.
Beethoven, Ludwig van, 141, 185
Beig, Anna, 22
Bell, Currer, 134

Benjamin, Walter, 36–40, 42, 45, 47, 72, 289
Benn, Gottfried, 14f., 208n12
Bennett, Tony, 248
Bense, Max, 11n3, 15, 192f.
Bergengruen, Werner, 11f.
Berger, Peter, 85
Bergius, Hanne, 306
Bergmann, Ingmar, 288
Bergson, Henri, 307
Bernhard, Thomas, 310f.
Bernhardt, Rüdiger, 159
Beveridge, William Henry, Lord, 254
Biermann, Wolf, 10, 156
Billington, Sandra, 290f.
Bitterfelder Weg, 154f.
Bizet, Georges, 182
Blackall, Eric, 208n12
Blake, William, 285
Bleikasten, André, 168
Bloch, Ernst, 30
Blöcker, Günter, 35f., 40
Blumenberg, Hans, 25, 46
Boczkowska, A., 283f., 292
Böckmann, Paul, 13
Böhlich, Walter, 39
Boehme, Jakob, 285
Böll, Heinrich, 249f., 255, 311f.
Bohnen, Klaus, 21
Bohrer, Karl Heinz, 43–9 *passim*
Bourdieu, Pierre, 75, 85f.
Bovenschen, Sylvia, 51, 133
Bozzetti, Elmer, 213–39 *passim*
Brahe, Tycho, 254f.
Brant, Sebastian, 291ff., 297
Brecht, Bertolt, 18, 25, 27, 38, 142, 153f., 248, 252–8 *passim*, 261–77, 308, 313
Brentano, Clemens, 10, 47
Bridgwater, Patrick, 213–17, 222, 227, 236n15
Brik, Osip, 251
Broch, Hermann, 15
Brüning, Elfriede, 160

–318–

Index

Büchner, Georg, 13, 27, 257, 299
Bürger, Peter, 17n13, 45ff., 82ff.
Burger, Heinz Otto, 35
Burgess, Anthony, 3
Burke, Peter, 279–94 *passim*
Butler, Samuel, 295n23
Butman, Stephen, 291

Camus, Albert, 159
Capra, Fritjof, 31n49
Cassirer, Ernst, 47
Caudwell, Christopher, 50
Celan, Paul, 9
Cervantes, Miguel de, 296, 308
Chamisso, Adalbert von, 312
Chaplin, Charles, 305
Chéreau, Patrice, 309
Chomsky, Noam, 240n17
Churchill, Winston, 132
Cixous, Hélène, 52
Clark, Kenneth, 245
Classicism, 192–210
Constructivism, 80
Conze, Werner, 72
Coster, Charles de, 296, 302
Cranach, Lucas, 175f.
Cremonini, Cesare, 262ff., 275
Croce, Benedetto, 35
Culler, Jonathan, 206f., 219, 221, 228, 232, 240
Curtius, Ernst Robert, 13, 35f.

Dada, 2, 27f., 189, 231n13, 306f., 312
Dare, Colonel Dan, 296n24
Davis, Natalie Z., 279–88 *passim*
Deconstruction, 4, 165f., 192–242, 244f., 252f.
Deleuze, Gilles, 139n7, 179n8, 181, 184, 188ff.
Delius, Friedrich Christian, 22
Demski, Eva, 309
Denkler, Horst, 167f.
Derrida, Jacques, 2, 22, 52, 146, 192–7, 203, 207f., 240n17, 249–53, 289
Deutsch, Ernst, 164n.
Dews, Peter, 193
Dickens, Charles, 302
Diderot, Denis, 296, 310
Dilthey Wilhelm, 35
Döblin, Alfred, 15, 273
Dölling, Irene, 149, 161n17
Dohm, Hedwig, 129, 132f., 141f.
Dorst, Tankred, 10, 309, 311

Drews, Jörg, 20
Duchamp, Marcel, 307
Durruti, Buenaventura, 10

Eagleton, Terry, 28n., 40, 44, 197, 245f., 249f., 254ff., 258, 289, 308ff.
Ecker, Gisela, 51f.
Eckermann, Johann Peter, 200
Eco, Umberto, 26
Ecology Movement, 51, 53
Eisler, Hanns, 154n11
Elias, Norbert, 286f.
Eliot, George, 256
Eliot, Thomas Stearns, 2, 198f., 251
Empson, William, 42n1, 204n10
Ende, Michael, 46
Engel, Fritz, 169n3, 186
Engels, Friedrich, 147, 151, 160
Enzensberger, Christian, 43, 49f.
Enzensberger, Hans Magnus, 10, 37–40
Erasmus, Desiderius of Rotterdam, 293f.
Eulenspiegel, Tyll, 293f., 296, 302
Euripides, 200f.
Existentialism, 11, 36
Expressionism, 164–91, 288

Faktor, Emil, 169n3
Fassbinder, Rainer W., 21
Faulstich, Werner, 79
Feminism, 18, 50–3, 113–44, 150, 160–2, 287f., 307n37
Feuerbach, Ludwig, 126
Feydeau, Erneste, 100
Feyerabend, Paul K., 19, 258
Fichte, Johann Gottlieb, 113ff., 193, 196
Fish, Stanley, 251
Flaubert, Gustave, 99f., 109
Fontane, Theodor, 300
Formalism, Russian, 2, 16f., 97–100, 103f., 254, 274f.
Foucault, Michel, 22, 41, 48, 52, 62, 77, 87, 114, 119, 146, 240n17, 251, 278
Francis of Assisi, St, 285
Frank, Manfred, 47
Frankfurt School, 22, 36, 41f., 45, 49f., 53
Freeman, David, 201n.5
Freud, Sigmund, 115, 123ff., 139ff., 166ff., 170n5, 171, 174n6, 178f., 184f., 190, 192, 194, 272

Index

Freytag, Gustav, 103, 298
Friedlaender, Salomo, 220
Friedrich, Hugo, 11f.
Frühwald, Wolfgang, 18
Fügen, Hans Norbert, 38, 75f., 79

Gadamer, Hans-Georg, 16, 193
Gaiser, Gottlieb, 81f.
Garaudy, Roger, 243, 257
Geerken, Hartmut, 20
Gellius, Aulus, 198
Gengenbach, Pamphilius, 292
George, Stefan, 180
Geppert, Rosemarie, 160
Gifford, Douglas John, 289f.
Ginzburg, Carlo, 282
Gödel, Kurt, 258
Goering, Hermann, 1
Goes, Albrecht, 11
Goethe, Johann Wolfgang von, 20, 35, 66f., 76, 97, 104–10, 132f., 152, 180, 182, 185, 192–210, 298f., 301
Goetz, Rainald, 26
Goldmann, Lucien, 38, 42, 250, 259
Goldsmith, Oliver, 106
Gomringer, Eugen, 12
Gotthelf, Jeremias, 299
Gottsched, Johann Christoph, 278, 297
Graevenitz, Gerhart von, 47f.
Graff, Gerald, 211
Gramsci, Antonio, 83, 147n3
Grass, Günter, 28, 255, 309, 311
Gray, Simon, 253
Green, Julien, 11n3
Grillparzer, Franz von, 12, 299
Grimm, Jacob, 47
Grimmelshausen, Johann Jacob Christoffel von, 294f.
Groddeck, Georg, 189n14
Groeben, Norbert, 16, 74n4
Groß, Hans, 174n6
Groß, Otto, 174, 189n14
Gruppe 61, 9
Guardini, Romano, 22, 28f.
Guattari, Félix, 139n7, 188ff.
Gumbrecht, Hans Ulrich, 79
Gutzwiller, Paul, 294

Habermas, Jürgen, 21, 28f., 43ff., 71f., 87, 255
Hagelstange, Rudolf, 12
Hager, Kurt, 157
Haller, Rudolf, 217ff.
Hamburger, Käte, 15

Hamm, Peter, 40
Hamsun, Knut, 10
Handke, Peter, 29n45, 252, 309ff.
Hanswurst, 297, 303
Harlequin, 297f., 301ff.
Hašek, Jaroslav, 305, 308
Hasenclever, Walter, 164–91
Haug, Wolfgang Fritz, 40f.
Hauptmann, Gerhart, 256, 300
Hauser, Kaspar, 303, 309f.
Haushofer, Albrecht, 12
Heath, Stephen, 197, 264n3
Hegel, Georg Wilhelm Friedrich and Hegelianism, 48, 53, 113, 192–4, 197f., 261
Heidegger, Martin, 12, 25, 36, 42
Hein, Christoph, 156–60, 251
Heine, Heinrich, 46, 199n4, 301n33
Heißenbüttel, Helmut, 12, 193
Henze, Hans Werner, 141
Hering, Christoph, 213f., 217, 221, 237
Hermand, Jost, 17
Hesse, Hermann, 305
Heydebrand, Renate von, 88
Heym, Georg, 15, 166, 255
Heym, Stefan, 156
Hiller, Kurt, 164n.
Hinck, Walter, 167, 183f., 186
Hinton, Stephen, 261n., 266n5
Historikerstreit, 21
Hölderlin, Friedrich, 200
Höllerer, Walter, 12
Hoffmann, Ernst Theodor Amadeus, 301f.
Hofmannsthal, Hugo von, 3, 12, 15, 304
Hohendahl, Peter-Uwe, 49, 83f.
Hohoff, Curt, 40
Holbach, Paul Heinrich d', 26
Holthusen, Hans Egon, 12, 36, 40
Holz, Arno, 28, 218, 230, 240
Homer, 106, 200
Honecker, Erich, 154
Horace, 200
Horkheimer, Max, 36, 72
Horváth, Ödön von, 307f.
Huelsenbeck, Richard, 309
Huizinga, Johan, 281ff.
Humboldt, Wilhelm von, 5
Husserl, Edmund, 42
Huyssen, Andreas, 25

Ich-Dramen, 164–91
Ingarden, Roman, 42

Index

Innocent III, Pope, 285
Irigaray, Luce, 52
Iser, Wolfgang, 16, 41, 46, 78, 96

Jäger, Georg, 104–10
Jäger, Hans-Wolf, 16n10
Jakobson, Roman, 16, 253f.
Jameson, Fredric, 2ff., 28n40, 164–8, 211, 213, 252f.
Janáček, Leoš, 141
Jaspers, Karl, 22
Jauss, Hans Robert, 16, 37f., 41ff., 78, 95–111
Jefferson, Ann, 259
Jeffries, Richard, 285
Jens, Walter, 40
Jewell, Jimmy, 296n24
Johannsmeier, Rolf, 280–5
Johst, Hanns, 164–91
Jones, Malcolm S., 214, 217, 238n16
Jordan, Lothar, 226n9
Jünger, Ernst, 29
Jugendstil, 142
Jung, Carl Gustav, 174n6, 283, 306

Kafka, Franz, 12, 15, 49, 112–27, 252, 257, 288, 305
Kaiser, Georg, 164–91, 288f.
Kandinsky, Wassily, 1, 304
Kant, Hermann, 257
Kant, Immanuel, 49, 240, 284
Kaplan, Cora, 129, 135f.
Karno, Fred, 298
Kaul, Friedrich Karl, 157
Kayser, Wolfgang, 13f., 35f.
Kaysersberg, Johann Geiler von, 292f.
Keaton, Buster, 305
Keisch, Henryk, 157
Keller, Gottfried, 300f.
Kermode, Frank, 199, 258
Kern, Edith, 295, 307
Kierkegaard, Søren, 49
Kirchhoff, Bodo, 26
Kirsch, Sarah, 27
Kittler, Friedrich, 23
Klein, Eduard, 157
Klein, Johannes, 43
Kleist, Heinrich von, 13, 299
Klopstock, Friedrich Gottlieb, 106
Klotz, Volker, 15
Koch, Hans, 157
Kocka, Jürgen, 72
König, Johann Ulrich von, 298n29
Königsdorf, Helga, 160, 162

Koselleck, Reinhart, 72
Kotzebue, August von, 10
Krafft-Ebing, Richard von, 114
Kramer, Hilton, 29
Krapp, Helmut, 13
Kraus, Karl, 115, 200, 208
Kristeva, Julia, 52, 129, 136–42, 193
Kröger, Johann Christian, 297
Kroetz, Franz-Xaver, 25
Kuczynski, Jürgen, 77
Kudszus, Winfried, 23n24
Kuhn, Thomas Samuel, 258
Kunert, Günter, 27
Kunze, Reiner, 156

Lacan, Jacques, 2, 22, 26, 52, 87, 113, 122–7, 136f., 140, 166–71, 174, 179, 183, 188ff., 194–6, 246, 249, 251, 288
Laclau, Ernesto, 147n3
Lämmert, Eberhard, 15, 39, 41
Laing, Ronald D., 189n14
Lange, Victor, 4
Langgässer, Elisabeth, 11
Latimer, Dan, 28n40
Leavis, Frank Raymond, 246f., 253
Le Fort, Gertrud von, 11
Lehmann, Paul, 281
Leibniz, Gottfried Wilhelm, 252
Leistner, Bernd, 159
Lenin, Vladimir Ilyich, 147f., 151
Lentricchia, Frank, 211ff., 240n17
Lessing, Gotthold Ephraim, 152, 199, 297f., 303
Lévi-Strauss, Claude 113, 121ff., 126, 164ff., 240n17
Liliencron, Detlev von, 300
Lindner, Gabriele, 159
Lipp, Wolfgang, 86
Lloyd, Harold, 305
Lodge, David, 1
Löwenthal, Leo, 38
Lohner, Edgar, 15
Lohner, Marlene, 15
Luckmann, Thomas, 85f.
Luhmann, Niklas, 76f., 79f., 89–91
Lukács, Georg, 18, 36, 38, 43n2, 45, 75, 153, 243, 247f.
Lyotard, Jean-François, 22

Mach, Ernst, 218, 230
Macherey, Pierre, 250, 254ff.
Mahler, Gustav, 142
Mallarmé, Stéphane, 28, 139

–321–

Index

Man, Paul de, 195, 253
Mann, Heinrich, 248, 255, 257
Mann, Thomas, 12, 15, 97, 102ff., 108, 141, 248, 255, 304ff., 309, 313
Marcuse, Herbert, 37, 49, 189n14, 248
Marinetti, Filippo Tomaso, 216, 218, 222, 224, 230, 240
Marivaux, Pierre Carlet de Chamblain de, 297
Marquard, Odo, 29
Martens, Wolfgang, 13
Martini, Fritz, 14f.
Marx, Karl and Marxism, 22, 38, 40ff., 49–52, 72, 86f., 97, 113, 126, 145–63, 243–60, 261f.
Maturana, Humberto, 80
Mauthner, Fritz, 216, 222
Mayhew, Henry, 303
Mechthild of Magdeburg, 285
Meier, Georg Friedrich, 297
Melville, Herman, 170n5
Merchant, Carolyn, 280–312 passim
Meyer, Ulrich, 83
Michel, Karl Markus, 30
Michelsen, Peter, 215ff., 222, 225, 234
Modernism, 2, 14f., 24f., 28–32, 43–6, 91, 240, 304
Moerike, Eduard, 300
Möser, Justus, 297f.
Mohr, Hans-Ulrich, 84
Molière, 264, 295, 297
Mombert, Alfred, 223
Monty Python, 303
Morgner, Irmtraud, 160, 162
Morshäuser, Bodo, 26
Mülher, Robert, 13
Müller, Christine, 161
Müller, Heiner, 25, 211
Mukařovský, Jan, 16, 105
Mulford, Prentice, 218–22, 225, 231
Munich Group for Research into the Social History of Literature, 18, 79, 88
Murner, Thomas, 292f.
Muschg, Walter, 15n8
Musil, Robert, 28, 49

Neuber, Karoline, 297
Neumann, Bernd, 215n5, 217, 222, 234, 239
New Criticism, 1, 42n1, 96
New Subjectivity, 18, 22, 25
Newton, Isaac, 296
Nietzsche, Friedrich, 2, 4, 14, 25, 27, 115, 119, 139, 167n., 246, 287, 289, 303f.
Nisbet, Hugh Barr, 199
Noll, Dieter, 257
Novalis, 47, 196

Oberhausen Film Festival, 9
Ort, Claus-Michael, 87f.
Ossian, 106

Parsons, Talcott, 79, 86, 88, 275
Patterson, Michael, 166, 175, 181
Pehlke, Michael, 40
Peirce, Charles Sanders, 192
Peraldus, Guilelmus, 291
Perse, St John, 257
Picasso, Pablo, 257
Piel, Edgar, 213, 216
Piscator, Erwin, 269
Plato and Platonism, 199, 211, 221f., 224, 281, 298
Plenzdorf, Ulrich, 156f., 251
Pocci, Franz Graf von, 302
Poe, Edgar Allan, 196
Pokowietz, Thea, 213, 217
Pongs, Hermann, 14, 15n8
Pop Art, 37
Popper, Karl, 22, 71
Post-Modernism, 2f., 21f., 24–32, 44–50, 53, 91, 306
Post-Structuralism, 22ff., 91, 145–63, 192–210, 253
Poulantzas, Nicos, 147n3
Pound, Ezra, 2
Proletcult, 153
Propp, Vladimir, 164f., 169
Punch and Judy, 302f.

Raabe, Wilhelm, 12
Radrizzani, René, 213, 215f., 221, 233
Ramm, Klaus, 20
Rank, Otto, 166ff., 180n9
Realism, 65, 253
  see also Socialist Realism
Reception Theory, 16, 34, 41ff., 78, 80, 95–111, 193, 218, 250f.
Reed, Terence James, 198
Reich, Wilhelm, 189n14
Reinhardt, Max, 164
Reinig, Christa, 129
Reitz, Edgar, 22
Reuling, Christoph, 282–97 passim
Richards, Ivor Armstrong, 42n1
Riha, Karl, 20

Index

Rilke, Rainer Maria, 12, 15, 49
Rinser, Luise, 11
Ritchie, James M., 164n., 167n2, 168, 184
Robey, David, 259
Rolle, Richard of Hampole, 285
Romanticism, 46ff., 113–14, 132n2, 193f., 196, 280, 288f.
Rostand, Edmond, 302f.
Rousseau, Jean-Jacques, 26, 113, 132, 289
Ruof, Jakob, 294
Russell, Bertrand, 258
Rutschky, Michael, 29n45, 31n49
Rychner, Max, 35f.

Sacher-Masoch, Leopold von, 181
Sachs, Hans, 293f.
Sade, Donatien-Alphonse-François, Marquis de, 119
Said, Edward, 212
Sainte-Beuve, Charles Augustin, 198
Sand, George, 134
Sartre, Jean-Paul, 11, 198
Schäfer, Hans Dieter, 20
Scheler, Max, 85
Schelling, Friedrich Wilhelm, 47
Schiller, Friedrich, 95n1, 133, 142, 152, 198, 200, 255, 298f.
Schlegel, August Wilhelm, 303
Schlegel, Friedrich, 47, 194, 196
Schmidt, Arno, 193
Schmidt, Siegfried J., 16, 73f., 77, 79ff.
Schneider, Michael, 40
Schneider, Peter, 10, 30, 40
Schneider, Reinhold, 11f.
Schneiderman, Stuart, 189n13
Schönberg, Arnold, 136
Schopenhauer, Arthur, 139, 298, 304, 306
Schreyer, Lothar, 238n16
Schröder, Rudolf Alexander, 11
Schubert, Helga, 160
Schücking, Levin L., 38, 41
Schütz, Alfred, 85
Schütz, Helga, 162
Schwab, Gustav, 252n3
Schwitters, Kurt, 307, 312
Sedlmayer, Hans, 14, 15n8
Seghers, Anna, 247, 257
Sengle, Friedrich, 17f.
Shakespeare, William, 203, 249n2, 264, 296, 310
Sheridan, Alan, 169n4

Shklovsky, Viktor, 274
Sieburg, Friedrich, 35f.
Siegen Group, 80
Silbermann, Alphons, 79
Smetana, Bedřich, 141
Sneed, Joseph, 71
Socialist Realism, 151–6, 247, 257, 262
Socrates, 199
Sokel, Walter, 167f.
Sorge, Reinhard, 164–91
Southern, Richard William, 281
Spaïni, Alberto, 307n36
Staiger, Emil, 13f., 35ff., 201n6
Stanzel, Franz, 15
Stefan, Verena, 10, 53
Stegmüller, Wolfgang, 71
Stifter, Adalbert, 12, 299f.
Stramm, August, 2, 211–42, 255
Stranitzky, Joseph Anton, 297n25
Strauss, Botho, 29n45
Strehler, Giorgio, 269
Struck, Karin, 10, 53
Structuralism, 16f., 24, 41, 48, 58–69, 81, 121, 126, 193, 240n17, 244, 253f., 261
Süskind, Patrick, 26, 310f.
Surrealism, 2, 11
Suso, Heinrich, 285
Suzman, Janet, 249n2
Swain, Barbara, 288n17
Symbolism, 1, 11
Systems Theory, 22, 76, 79, 81, 87f., 91

Tel quel, 4
Tennyson, Alfred Lord, 253
Theweleit, Klaus, 19
Thompson, Edward Palmer, 250
Tieck, Ludwig, 300ff.
Tinguely, Jean, 306
Todi, Jacopone da, 285, 307n36
Todorov, Tzvetan, 240n17
Tolkien, John Ronald Reuel, 46
Toynbee, Arnold, 32
Trakl, Georg 12
Transubstantiation, Doctrine of, 284n11
Trine, Ralph Waldo, 218–22, 224, 231, 240
Tzara, Tristan, 231n13

Ulbricht, Walter, 154
University novels, 1, 19

Vaget, Hans Rudolf, 102ff., 109

Index

Vaihinger, Hans, 218, 227, 230
Verdi, Giuseppi, 141f.
Viëtor, Karl, 13
Virgil, 199
Vitalis, Ordericus, 283
Voltaire, 26
Voß, Johann Heinrich, 198ff.
Voßkamp, Wilhelm, 76, 79, 82

Wagner, Richard, 181, 300, 304
Wais, Kurt, 166f.,
Walden Herwarth, 215–40 *passim*
Wallraff, Günter, 22, 27
Wander, Maxie, 161
Warren, Austin, 15
Warriss, Ben, 296n24
Wassermann, Jakob, 303
Weber, Franz-Josef, 20
Weber, Max, 45, 286ff., 310
Wedekind, Frank, 115, 305
Wehler, Hans-Ulrich, 72
Weigel, Sigrid, 51f., 143
Weill, Kurt, 269
Weimann, Robert, 43n2
Weininger, Otto, 115

Weinrich, Harald, 21
Weise, Christian, 291
Wellek, René, 15, 42n1
Welsford, Enid, 288n17
White, John J., 211, 215n5, 217, 228, 231, 239
Whitman, Walt, 285
Wiechert, Ernst, 11n3
Wieland, Christoph Martin, 199
Wiener, Norbert, 15
Wiese, Benno von, 12ff.
Wild, Rainer, 83
Wilke, Ursula, 159
Willett, John, 266n4, 274n12
Williams, Raymond, 243
Wilson, Robert, 25
Wimschneider, Anna, 22
Wittgenstein, Ludwig, 228n11, 310
Wolf, Christa, 27, 53, 155–8, 162
Wollstonecraft, Mary, 129, 132f.
Woolf, Virginia, 130
Wunberg, Gotthart, 48
Wustmann, Gustav, 303, 307

Zweig, Arnold, 255, 257